NOTORIOUS

The Life of

INGRID BERGMAN

Also by Donald Spoto

Jacqueline Bouvier Kennedy Onassis: A Life

The Hidden Jesus: A New Life

Diana—The Last Year

Rebel: The Life and Legend of James Dean

The Decline and Fall of the House of Windsor

A Passion for Life: The Biography of Elizabeth Taylor

Marilyn Monroe: The Biography

Blue Angel: The Life of Marlene Dietrich

Laurence Olivier: A Life

Madcap: The Life of Preston Sturges

Lenya: A Life

Falling in Love Again: Marlene Dietrich (A Photoessay)

The Kindness of Strangers: The Life of Tennessee Williams

The Dark Side of Genius: The Life of Alfred Hitchcock

Stanley Kramer, Film Maker

Camerado: Hollywood and the American Man

The Art of Alfred Hitchcock

NOTORIOUS

The Life of
INGRID BERGMAN

Donald Spoto

DA CAPO PRESS

Designed by Alma Hochhauser Orenstein
Photo inserts designed by Barbara DuPree Knowles, BDK Books, Inc.

Cataloging-in-Publication data for this book is available from the Library of Congress.

First Da Capo Press edition 2001
Reprinted by arrangement with the author.
ISBN 0-306-81030-1

Published by Da Capo Press
A Member of the Perseus Books Group
http://www.dacapopress.com

Da Capo Press books are available at special discounts for bulk purchases in the U.S. by corporations, institutions, and other organizations. For more information, please contact the Special Markets Department at the Perseus Books Group, 11 Cambridge Center, Cambridge, MA 02142, or call (617) 252-5298.

2   3   4   5   6   7   8   9   10——04   03   02   01

with loving gratitude to

Teresa Wright
Tippi Hedren
Robert Anderson

All that's less cannot impart
Such blessedness upon thine art
As steadfast friends.

notorious:

from the Latin *notus* (known):
famous or celebrated;
secondarily, known for something not generally approved
—The Oxford English Dictionary

Contents

Photo sections follow pages 172 and 300.

Acknowledgments

MY FIRST ACKNOWLEDGMENT IS TO INGRID BERGMAN, WHOM I knew during the last seven years of her life. Although we had met briefly before the spring of 1975, it was then that she agreed to a series of taped interviews when I was preparing the manuscript of my first book, *The Art of Alfred Hitchcock*. As it happened, our conversations were not limited to her work with Hitchcock; she was, I thought, astonishingly forthcoming on a wide variety of other matters—as she was during our subsequent meetings in other cities, on various social and professional occasions.

But I had no thought of writing a biography of her. More than a decade after her death, my tapes of our conversations were squirreled away and my notes duly filed—forever, I thought. But the more I spoke to those who knew and worked with her, the clearer it became that there was a remarkable life story to be told. And so I set to work.

Ingrid Bergman's first husband, Petter A. Lindstrom, M.D., welcomed me to his home and granted an extended interview. Subsequently, he allowed me unrestricted access and the privilege of citing more than two thousand pages of letters, private papers and documents that illuminated as never before the contours of Bergman's early life and the dozen years of their marriage. I am very grateful for this extraordinary cooperation.

Pia Lindstrom, the daughter of Ingrid and Petter, is a much

admired media journalist and arts critic. We first met when my book *The Dark Side of Genius: The Life of Alfred Hitchcock* was published in 1983; I was her guest on a New York television show. Then and later, she impressed me with her keen insights about the time when, not yet a teenager, she was at the center of a worldwide media frenzy. Pia Lindstrom's assistance as I prepared this biography of her mother is everywhere evident, and I thank her for her perception and her confidence.

I never had the opportunity to meet Ingrid's second husband, Roberto Rossellini, who died in 1977. But Lars Schmidt, her third husband, was most forthcoming from the first stages of my work. He welcomed me to Dannholmen, the island home he shared with Ingrid; to Choisel, their residence in the French countryside; and to his offices in Paris. I must also thank Yanne Noorup, who now shares his life, for her warmth and hospitality.

VERY EARLY IN MY RESEARCH, I WAS GIVEN IMPORTANT ASSISTANCE BY W. H. Dietrich. He is better known simply by his surname, and is so cited in this book: Dietrich has thus signed canvases that have made him a highly respected artist whose work has duly won him worldwide respect. Like Ingrid, he emigrated from Sweden to Hollywood, and during several conversations he shared important details of that time, of his friendship with Ingrid and Petter Lindstrom, of Sweden in the 1930s and of Hollywood in the 1940s (when he was an artist at Paramount). He also allowed me to read and draw on his magnificent memoirs, one of his current works in progress. Dietrich and his wife, Patty, welcomed me on several occasions to their home in the California desert, and I am grateful for all they have contributed, by word and affection, to my life and my work. Of another member of that family, Greg Dietrich, more later.

Åke Sandler, son of Sweden's former prime minister, is a historian, professor and writer who also knew the Lindstroms well. From the first weeks of my work, he provided crucial materials and answered difficult questions completely and candidly. He and his wife, Jane, never ceased to support and encourage this project.

Obviously, a mountain of important material existed only in Swedish—until I was fortunate to be introduced to the ideal translator, Gunvor Dollis. She not only found the right words to render a difficult language into comprehensible English, she also found the right tone for the special cadences of poetry, drama, reviews, letters and essays. With warmth, alacrity, wit and a keen sense of time and place, she provided me with inestimable literary support.

For any modern biography, interviews are of course extremely important. The following people gave gladly and generously of their time, detailing the fine points of their various relationships with Ingrid. This book would be much the poorer without the contributions of:

Larry Adler, Robert Anderson, Pierre Barillet, Kate Barrett, Laurinda Barrett, the late Katharine (Kay) Brown, Gene Corman, the Baron Göran von Essen, Sir John Gielgud, O.M., Guy Green, Signe Hasso, Arthur Hill, Dame Wendy Hiller, the late Sir Alfred Hitchcock, Griffith James, Margaret Johnstone, Ted Kotcheff, Arthur Laurents, Roger Lobb, Tanya Lopert, Sidney Lumet, Lasse Lundberg, Elliot Martin, Gregory Peck, Jenia Reissar, the late Ann Todd, Paavo Turtiainen, Stephen Weiss, Teresa Wright.

For various other assistances necessary to fill in important elements in Ingrid Bergman's life, I must acknowledge the kind help of Graham Waring, M.D., Rick Carl, Roland Oberlin, Gene Feldman and Suzette Winter.

At THE DEPARTMENT OF CULTURAL AFFAIRS OF THE SWEDISH INFORMATION Service, New York City, important introductions to colleagues in Sweden came from Elisabeth Halvarsson-Stapen.

My work in Stockholm would not have been possible without the gracious and generous help of many.

At Svensk Filmindustri (the Swedish Film Institute), I worked with the help of Margareta Nordström, Head of Documentation; Ann-Kristin Westerberg, Head of the Copyright Department; Elisabet Helge, Head of the Stills Department; Maria Stenmark, Librarian; and Catharina Stackelberg, in the Production Department.

In the Stockholm City Archives, Göran Blomberg provided important documentation and smoothed the way so that I could access civic and family records.

In the Swedish National Archives, Stockholm, similar assistance was provided by Toni Fridh.

School syllabi, grade records and genealogies of Sweden are housed with meticulous care in the Royal National Library, Stockholm. The staff there located for me many precious documents and made copies available on short notice.

Ingrid Bergman attended the Royal Dramatic Theater School, Stockholm, which has kept detailed archives and fascinating historic material that enabled me to research and understand not only her time there but the amazing history of this venerable institution. At the school, I was welcomed and aided by Eva Hagman, Dag Kronlund, Britt-Marie Lindvall and Bengt Persson.

For the particular purpose of assisting me, the actress, teacher and writer Ingrid Luterkort came to meet me at the Royal Dramatic Theater School. She studied there in Ingrid's time, and so our conversation, her memories and the materials she shared were invaluable in documenting this time.

Uno Myggan Ericson made vital papers available to me and was always ready to answer important questions and to set me in the right direction.

At the office of the International Magazine Service (IMS Bildbyrå), Stockholm, Helena Westerberg enabled me to locate important rare photographs.

Eva-Maria Thornlund, sales manager at Dagens Nyheter/Presstext, Stockholm, provided immediate access to the comprehensive files of Swedish newspaper clippings documenting Ingrid Bergman's life and career.

For their articulate and detailed guided tour of Stockholm, during which they made particular reference to the city during the time of Ingrid Bergman and her family, I am grateful to Stefan and Birgitta Nilson. They also replied with alacrity from afar when I required certain documents later, during my writing.

A highlight of my time in Stockholm was meeting a much loved member of the Swedish royal family, HRH the Princess Lilian. She also knew Ingrid and shared her impressions with me. I greatly admire Princess Lilian's good humor, her compassion and her gallantry.

SEVERAL OF MY PREVIOUS BOOKS ACKNOWLEDGE THE GENEROUS ASSIStance provided by my friend Laurence Evans, the highly respected "dean" of London's theatrical agents and a mine of invaluable knowledge of film and theater history. He represented Ingrid Bergman in the United Kingdom and Europe, and so once again I availed myself of his offer to help. Through Laurence Evans, I had access to important materials and was able to locate and interview several of the most important people cited in this book. His wife, Mary, also a good friend to Ingrid, was equally helpful and encouraging. Jointly, their memories much enriched my understanding, as their friendship does my life.

The staff in the public records divisions at Somerset House and St. Catharine's House, London, assisted me when I needed to find records of wills, marriages and other legal documents relative to Ingrid Bergman's life in Great Britain.

At the British Film Institute, London, David Sharp guided me to important sections of the library's holdings—items I might otherwise have missed. Similarly, at the British Theatre Museum, Covent Garden, rich materials on Ingrid Bergman's stage appearances were made available by Jonathan Gray.

And at Warner Chappell Plays, Michael Callahan was very helpful when I required a copy of N. C. Hunter's *Waters of the Moon*.

INGRID BERGMAN WAS BROUGHT FROM SWEDEN TO AMERICA UNDER contract to the legendary producer David O. Selznick, who (as is well known) kept virtually every piece of paper relating to his many productions. The vast Selznick archives—literally thousands of cartons—are housed in the capacious and carefully maintained Humanities Research Center of the University of Texas at Austin. There, I was welcomed by Charles Bell, who enabled me to pore through box after box of material. Many hitherto unpublished documents surfaced and were made available to me through the generosity of the staff and because of the kind permission of Daniel M. Selznick, who has always been such a friendly supporter of me and my work.

Stacey Behlmer, Sam Gill, Linda Mehr and the entire staff at the Margaret Herrick Library of the Academy of Motion Pictures Arts and Sciences, Beverly Hills, were ready with their usual friendly and prompt assistance.

At the library of the American Film Institute, Los Angeles,

Gladys Irvis and Alan Braun, also not for the first time, devoted time and attention to my needs during my period of study there. Thanks to them, considerable new material came to light in the papers of Charles K. Feldman, Ingrid Bergman's agent for several years.

I am grateful, too, to the staffs of the New York Public Libraries, at both Forty-second Street and in the Performing Arts division at Lincoln Center.

MARY CORLISS, DIRECTOR OF THE FILM STILLS ARCHIVES AT THE Museum of Modern Art, New York, is well known to all who write and study film history and film aesthetics. For over twenty years, Mary has been a constant guide for me through the thickets of photographic research.

Also in the matter of photographic research, I must thank Allen Reuben at Culver Pictures, New York; he found rare images of Ingrid Bergman at work and in family life.

Mary Engel, who directs the photographic repository of her late aunt, the photographer Ruth Orkin, kindly granted permission for the photo of Robert Capa.

FOR THE FIFTH TIME, I AM FORTUNATE TO BE PUBLISHED BY A COMPANY of very good and savvy people at HarperCollins Publishers, New York and London.

To have the editorial guidance, enthusiasm and constant support of Gladys Justin Carr, vice president and associate publisher, would be any writer's dream. With ever accurate perception and good humor, she is always ready with the right direction and the proper counsel. Thanks also to Cynthia Barrett for her many editorial insights. And Gladys's first-rate team—Elissa Altman and Deirdre O'Brien—provide me with more daily, cheerful help than I can say. In the London offices of HarperCollins, things are amiably and expertly supervised by my English editor, Richard Johnson, who made important contributions to this book.

Several years ago, my French agent, Mary Kling, introduced me to the Paris company Presses de la Cité, where Renaud Bombard has been a prudent and discerning publisher and a constant friend. To him and to Sophie Thiébaut, director of publicity, my heartfelt gratitude for presenting my work to the French public.

As for my primary agent: any browser through my work of the last nineteen years knows I have the pleasantest task in trying to find new ways and words to honor Elaine Markson. But what to do? Not even ransacking a thesaurus and stringing together superlatives would be sufficient to express my gratitude for so dedicated a representative. Suffice to say that everything in my career owes to her constancy, her sound counsel, her sagacious judgment—just as my life owes so much to her loving loyalty as one of my cherished friends.

In the offices of Elaine Markson Literary Agency, I am the recipient of the amiable assistance of Geri Thoma, Sally Wofford-Girand, Sara DeNobrega, Elizabeth Sheinkman, Kai Ping Lin and Tasha Blaine. I salute them all for their many kindnesses to me and their help in managing my various interests.

IN THE FOURTH YEAR OF OUR WORKING PARTNERSHIP AND THE TENTH of our friendship, I am glad to express my gratitude to my research director and assistant, Greg Dietrich.

It is no exaggeration to say that *Notorious: The Life of Ingrid Bergman* simply would not exist without his astute collaboration, for he is a man of quick intelligence and lively humor, good judgment and creative thinking. To detail each and every aspect of his contributions would in itself comprise a book, so I must summarize. Greg facilitated introductions to key supporting players in the life and career of Ingrid Bergman. He prepared with estimable thoroughness our many research travels and shared the burden of every stage of our work in America, England and Europe. He read plays and scripts, watched films, gathered obscure documents and condensed a towering array of historic and cultural material.

ON THE DEDICATION PAGE OF THIS BOOK ARE THREE FAMOUS NAMES. IT is a great pleasure for me to elaborate on this trio of notable people. I met each of them in 1974, and each has immeasurably enriched my life with friendship deep and true.

I first met Teresa Wright when I interviewed her for *The Art of Alfred Hitchcock*, for she is the leading lady in one of his masterworks, *Shadow of a Doubt*. Everyone familiar with Hollywood, Broadway and television can name favorites among Teresa's many (and much honored) achievements—an impressive career that spans more than fifty years and continues to gather fresh laurels even as this is written. As a friend, she is more precious than gold.

Tippi Hedren is also a major name in the Hitchcock canon; I met her when she granted me interviews to discuss *The Birds* and *Marnie*, and soon we were confidants and good friends. She is a brave, kind and generous lady—one need think only of her tireless work at her beloved Shambala Preserve, on behalf of animals and animal rights. Tippi and I have shared very much in the last twenty-three years, and I look forward to the future.

Robert Anderson is one of America's premier writers. Among his many important contributions to the literature of the stage and screen, I have my personal favorites (*I Never Sang for My Father* and *The Nun's Story*, for example), but it is not easy to select from his long and prestigious catalog. I admired his work for years and never imagined that we would meet; much less could I have anticipated that he would offer me the strong arm of his friendship. Pertinent to the present book, I am grateful to add that it was Bob who introduced me to Ingrid Bergman. He is also a major presence in her story, and I am ever thankful for his abiding confidence.

Providence is revealed by the presence of unmerited largess in our lives: and so here I am, basking in the love and devotion of these extraordinarily dear people. As their constancy and these pages of acknowledgments attest, my life is very blessed indeed.

D.S.
Beverly Hills, California
Christmas 1996

Chapter One

1915–1929

An only child is never twelve.

ENID BAGNOLD,
The Chalk Garden

I T HAD BEEN A BRIGHT, CLOUDLESS DAY IN STOCKHOLM, AND BECAUSE
it was summertime, the sun shone brilliantly through the evening,
casting long, shimmering rays over Nybroviken, an inlet of the Baltic
Sea. The facades of the nineteenth-century apartment houses
fronting the harbor glistened in the angular light. Atop one of them,
Number 3 Strandvägen, just as a nearby church bell struck quarter
past eleven on Sunday evening, August 29, 1915, a midwife hurried
into the sitting room, where an anxious man stared through the
sixth-floor windows over the calm bay. Mother and child were quite
well, the midwife said, and there was no need for concern; she then
promptly returned to her duty. Half an hour later, the husband was
allowed to see his wife and their baby girl. Forty-four-year-old Justus Samuel Bergman and his wife, thirty-year-old Frieda Adler
Bergman, at once decided to name the child Ingrid, in honor of
Sweden's two-year-old royal princess.

Along the quay below, steamers ferried families home to Stock-

holm from day trips at sea, the Swedes mingling easily with their
Danish, Norwegian and Finnish neighbors; the Great War, then rag-
ing in the rest of Europe, prevented the normal influx of German
tourists. In the nearby parks around the Royal Opera House and the
Royal Dramatic Theater, young ladies were treated by their escorts
to a glass of summer wine or a cup of hot chocolate, and neighbors
stopped to exchange news. Elegant cafe orchestras and unpretentious street musicians played waltzes and popular rural folk songs.
All along tree-lined Strandvägen—a boulevard of fine shops and
stately apartment houses—could be heard the polite terms of formal address, the rustle of silk dresses and the click of leather boots.
Strollers browsed in art galleries and chic stores by day and patron-
ized fancy tearooms and grills in the evenings. It was the height of
the summer holiday, and all of Stockholm, the capital city of
400,000 in a land of 5.5 million, seemed at leisure.

A generally festive mood made the country a notable exception
in Europe that season, for Sweden had retained its staunch political
neutrality—but not its commercial impartiality—while the war
continued. Germany traded coal for Sweden's steel, pulp and ball
bearings, an enterprise that so outraged the Allies that their block-
ades eventually caused severe food shortages for the Swedish poor;
this inequity, among other factors, later contributed to the firm
establishment of a socialist government.

Despite the maneuvering of politicians who were variously
inclined toward the warring nations, the unpretentious, disciplined
tone of everyday life was set by King Gustav V, a powerless but
much beloved figurehead and the father of little Princess Ingrid. He
and his family regularly attended the opera and theater, which had
offered continuous seasonal performances in one venue or another
since 1788. Sweden has a venerable tradition of state-supported
culture, of traveling theater, concerts and exhibitions in villages as
well as in Stockholm and Göteborg, and because freedom of the
press has been guaranteed since 1766, controversy and artistic
experimentation were never impeded by censorship.

Most controversial among dramas staged during World War I
were those of the country's great playwright, August Strindberg,
who had died in 1912. His work conjoined stark portraits of inner
suffering with deft treatments of social issues, and both the extreme

naturalism and provocative symbolism of his work fascinated increasing numbers of urban audiences. At the same time, the prolific novelist Selma Lagerlöf (the first woman to win the Nobel Prize for Literature, in 1909) appealed to a broader range of society with the moral dilemmas in her lyrical romances.

But the most popular form of entertainment was provided by the thriving Swedish film business.

Until recently, Denmark had led Europe in the volume of movie production (an invention less than two decades old) and in the importing of musicians to accompany the silent flickers in improvised screening halls. Camera technologies advanced swiftly and expertly in Copenhagen laboratories, combining with the keen imagination of directors like Viggo Larsen and Benjamin Christensen, and the talents of actors like Asta Nielsen, who was as much a fashion trendsetter as a tragic heroine. These talents produced a series of successful melodramas and in fact launched the European star system. Then, in 1912, Swedish businessman Charles Magnusson recruited three partners and established in Stockholm a venture that produced an astonishing variety of accomplished, highly literate art films that were also gripping entertainments.

Within four years, Sweden had taken the lead in international moviemaking, both in quantity and distinction, and, without competition from stricken production companies in countries at war, Swedish films were exported with great financial and critical success—all to the credit of Magnusson, whose genius was to recognize that quality in others. He invited the Russian-Finnish theater director Mauritz Stiller, the Swedish actor-manager Victor Sjöström and the cameraman Julius Jaenzon to join him in a virtual takeover of Svenska Bio, an undistinguished company that was about to achieve international distinction.

Sjöström and Stiller each made thirty feature films between 1912 and 1916—entertainments remarkable for plain human emotions, yet suffused with the Swedish awe of nature. And because movie acting was not ridiculed by Swedish stage actors (as it was for generations in England, for example), gifted dramatic artists like Gösta Ekman, Karin Molander and Lars Hanson appeared in as many movies as plays. When Magnusson decided to expand his production company to include a chain of movie theaters, he started (on December 30, 1915) by opening the Röda Kvarn (Red Mill), a venue still doing brisk business more than eighty years later. Within a year, every neighborhood in Stockholm had several similar halls, and perhaps for the first time rereleases of pictures from preceding years were booked to overflow crowds.

Sjöström's direction and script for *Ingeborg Holm* in 1913, for example, had been praised all over Europe for its affectingly realistic story of a poor widow whose children are taken away from her and who is subsequently committed to a madhouse. The great Hilda Borgström acted the title role with a remarkable restraint that evoked deeper reactions from audiences than did the broad histrionics prevalent in, for example, the American flickers of the time. Sjöström's strong moral concern—more for redemption and forgiveness than for political or social diatribe—was further evident in his screen version of Ibsen's poem *Terje Vigen* (1917) in which he also played the title role of a man brutalized by war; and in *The Phantom Carriage* (1921), in which a hooded, scythe-bearing Death shows a dying cad the consequences of his actions and so enables him to seek forgiveness.

The content and style of Mauritz Stiller's work was quite different but equally successful during this golden age of Swedish cinema. Although he wrote, directed and (like Sjöström) often took parts in a series of elegant social satires such as *When the Mother-in-Law Reigns*, *Love and Journalism* and *Thomas Graal's First Child* (all made between 1914 and 1918), Stiller developed as well a talent for epics based on novels by Selma Lagerlöf. Julius Jaenzon, director of photography for the Stiller and Sjöström films, was as skilled at lighting the contours of a sensitive human face as he was at rendering a wild sea or a dangerous avalanche. It is no exaggeration to assert that Sjöström and Stiller were primary among a handful of early filmmakers who brought an affecting, recognizable humanity to their stories; jointly, they disprove the widespread misrepresentation of the Swedish cinema as a succession of uniformly dark and gloomy tales, steeped in Nordic Lutheran guilt.

In 1915, therefore, movies were an extremely popular and, astonishingly often, aesthetically robust medium of culture in bustling Stockholm. And it was no surprise that their success was accompanied by a wild profusion of both still and motion picture cameras for the masses—a business much stimulated by the release of Jaenzon's own home movies, with scenes of his wife and family at play by the seashore and in their garden. Long before the arrival of the Brownie and the Polaroid, people who could afford it were saving money for a home movie camera.

IN THIS REGARD, INGRID BERGMAN'S FATHER WAS A LUCKY MAN. BORN in May 1871 in the Kronoberg province of southern Sweden, Justus Bergman was the son of Johan Petter Bergman, a respected organist, music scholar and teacher who instilled in his fourteen children a lifelong passion for music. The thirteenth child, Justus wanted to become an artist. He left home at fifteen, worked as a shop assistant and rose early each morning to sit at an easel. Justus managed to meet the painter Anders Zorn, who offered him free lessons on condition that the boy would support himself. But by late 1889, Justus was penniless and emigrated to Chicago, where his mother's sister and several of his siblings now lived, and where he soon found work as the decorator for a group of new hotels. By this time, he was a tall, handsome young man with a gentle expression and clear blue eyes, a somewhat untidy but nonetheless attractive individual who longed to be an artist or an opera singer and still hoped, somehow, to achieve those goals.

After ten years, Justus returned to Stockholm and started a business as an art dealer. This barely provided sustenance, and so he began to think of himself as an entrepreneur for artists. Some good advice then came from Justus's cousin, the noted voice teacher Karl Nygren. From October 1903 to March 1906, after taking private painting and singing lessons, Justus was offered the chance by Nygren to lead a choir on singing tours in America, where he visited Swedish-American communities in Minnesota, Wisconsin, Illinois and Maine. From these adventures he returned flush with excitement but not cash, and occasionally he had to rely on the hospitality of his brother and sister-in-law, Otto and Hulda Bergman (who already had several children in their crowded Stockholm flat), or of his spinster sister, the devout and frail Ellen Bergman, who suffered from a congenital heart defect.

Justus might well have continued to be a struggling aesthete, but by late 1906, when he was thirty-five, he was eager to marry a

plump, pretty twenty-two-year-old German girl named Frieda
Adler. He had first met her six years earlier, when she was on holiday with her parents from their home in Kiel, not far from Hamburg, Germany. Frieda had been born there in September 1884,
and at sixteen had made her first journey to Sweden, where,
strolling with her parents one afternoon in a park, she saw a sketch
artist named Justus Bergman. He was at once charmed by her gentleness, her almost mesmerically dark and alluring eyes and her
articulate common sense. Romance bloomed with the lilacs that
spring of 1900. Justus already knew German, and he taught Frieda
elementary Swedish. But her parents were adamant. Their daughter
would not be permitted to marry a penniless artiste manqué: she
must marry well, like her two older sisters, Elsa and Luna. And so,
after his choir tours, Justus landed a job with an appliance manufacturer, put his zeal toward earning a respectable salary, and so
impressed the Adlers with his assiduity that when he traveled to Kiel
a fourth time in spring 1907 and begged to marry Frieda, her parents relented. A seven-year courtship, they admitted, did not beto-
ken a passing fancy, and, after all, Justus now presented an impressive savings account.

Years later, reading the letters they had exchanged during their
long engagement, Ingrid had the impression that her parents were a
study in contrasts. Her mother, she said, was "typically German,
extremely practical, systematic and orderly. But Father had all the
bohemian traits of an artist. It was he who had finally made all the
compromises his marriage demanded. He became a businessman
against his real nature," and this renunciation, she felt sure, led him
to "many regrets about the things he didn't do." A woman who
worked for Justus later called him, more prosaically, "a dreamer."

The newlyweds returned to Stockholm, where Justus was soon
employed in a shop that sold supplies to artists and photographers.
He did not, however, abandon his creative interests, nor the benign
pretense that he was really an artist. He was, according to one
reporter, "a well-known figure on Stockholm streets, a neat and
humorous fellow, easy to spot in a crowd because of the large artist's
hat he wore." Several times, Frieda posed patiently for him, and he
routinely accompanied himself on the piano as he crooned Swedish
and German ballads.

Frieda bore a stillborn child in 1908, and four years later their premature infant lived only a week. But she was a disciplined soul, accustomed to suppressing her emotions, and she seemed as sensibly pragmatic as her husband was lyrically romantic. While Justus was heartsick for weeks, his wife allowed herself neither self-pity nor prolonged mourning. Ever dutiful, she fulfilled the tasks for which her mother had trained her: Frieda kept house meticulously, she managed the household accounts and, a first-rate cook, she prepared rich and hearty German meals for herself and Justus. While he retained a weight proper for his six-foot-two-inch frame, she grew more portly, and so her occasional bouts of a bad stomach—what seemed to be simple dyspepsia from culinary overindulgence—had to be followed by several days of a more spartan regime.

By the time Ingrid was born, Justus Bergman was successful enough to have opened his own business on Strandvägen—a camera shop, since that device was all the rage in cinema-loving Stockholm. Somewhat more expensive motion picture cameras, also now available to the amateur, were on the market as well, and Justus (who took home one new machine after another) fervently accumulated albums crammed with photos and tins containing hundreds of feet of film of his wife, brothers and sisters, as well as documents of life along the harbor. Even more elaborate moviemaking equipment soon became available to the Bergmans, when Papa became managing director of Konstindustri, a manufacturer of technical paraphernalia for artists, photographers and recording companies. "We were not rich, but we lived comfortably," Ingrid said years later, adding that her father could afford to indulge his hobbies as well as his tastes: a season of opera tickets for himself and his wife was no harder on the budget than the latest camera.

Forever after, Ingrid kept framed photographs of herself and her family; years later, she also found fourteen minutes of the home movies, the only bits to survive the decay to which early, fragile film stock was so susceptible. In the collection, no one is more represented than the child Ingrid, who was dressed in a variety of costumes even as an infant, while her father's cameras clicked and whirred. Even in infancy, she was, thanks to her father, perhaps the most photographed child in all Sweden. On her first birthday, she was filmed, standing quite at ease before Papa's camera, smiling and waving her hands gleefully at the attention. At Christmas 1917, when Ingrid was two, Justus photographed her and Frieda on the steps of the Royal Dramatic Theater, which was very near their apartment building.

Early in the new year 1918, the cheerful routine of the Bergman household was rudely interrupted. Feverish and nauseated, Frieda was confined to bed for several days. At first, no one thought she was suffering from anything more serious than another attack of "sour stomach," the usual diagnosis of a condition that had become virtually chronic, especially after the rich menus of a holiday season. But by the twelfth of January, she was in unremitting agony, and to spare the child the sight, Ingrid was sent to stay with Uncle Otto, Aunt Hulda and their children.

Frieda's condition worsened with each hour. Her face became jaundiced, she was vomiting violently and suffering such severe upper abdominal pain that a physician, diagnosing advanced gall-bladder disease, urged her to enter a clinic at once. But as plans were being made for Frieda's transfer, she suddenly slipped into coma. On Thursday, January 18, her breathing became shallow and irregular, and after a ferocious struggle through the next day, Frieda Bergman died on Friday at ten o'clock in the evening, without regaining consciousness. She was thirty-three years old.

"I don't remember my mother at all," Ingrid often said. "My father filmed me sitting on her lap when I was one, and then again when I was two—and at three he photographed me putting flowers on her grave." That brief, odd cemetery scene, which has survived on film, may have been Justus Bergman's way of using his hobby to blunt his grief, which for several months had plunged him into severe depression. But his pastime had an odd corollary, for as she grew up, Ingrid was surrounded by photographs of her mother, who remained a monochrome image—a woman present, in other words, by her absence. By the time she was ready for school, Ingrid thus realized how different she was from other children: someone was missing—someone who in the normal scheme of things should have been there. And the more her relatives tried to supply the missing ingredient of maternal love, the more obvious was the absence.

*   *   *

Papa's cinematography continued that summer of 1918. On her third birthday, a tiny violin was put in Ingrid's hands, and without prompting she mimicked a virtuoso, but her gaze was straight at the camera, not on the instrument. At her fourth birthday party, Ingrid—a lively child with honey blond hair and alert blue eyes—snatched Grandmother Adler's spectacles and cloche hat and did a fiercely funny imitation of a German dowager. On summer days, Ingrid was photographed tossing breadcrumbs to birds and munching candy at Berzelius Park, a short walk from Strandvägen. On the rare bright winter afternoon, Justus filmed her outside, adorably tucked into a bulky suit, smiling beneath a pretty woolen cap. And so a star was born and raised.

"As I grew older, he encouraged me to dress up and improvise little skits," Ingrid recalled of her father, who sometimes joined her in front of the camera, a player as well as a director. But a child, Justus's family said, needed someone to compensate the loss of her mother. And so there arrived at the apartment, in the late spring of 1918, his sister Ellen. A short, stout maiden lady of forty-nine, she had spent her life attending sick or inconvenienced relatives and working for charitable causes in the Lutheran parishes; but that year, heart problems had forced her to curtail some of her more strenuous church duties. Generous and self-sacrificing, she devoted herself to her brother and niece, sewing, cooking and cleaning for them.

To no one's surprise, Ingrid called Aunt Ellen her mama, which caused the lady some embarrassment at a religious gathering that knew Miss Bergman only as an unmarried lady. The other discomfiture for Aunt Ellen was caused by the antics of Justus and Ingrid when they did their little pantomimes for his cameras. To amuse herself and anyone who would listen, Ingrid invented during her childhood a list of amusing characters and imaginary playmates—a saint, a witch, a villain, a parent, a child, a donkey or a turtle. For Ellen Bergman, these capers had the whiff of playacting, and acting was the work of godless souls: a good life, for Ellen, meant a serious life, not one of impersonation and fakery.

Much of the summer of 1918—and for at least part of every summer for the next eighteen years—Ingrid spent with her Adler grandparents in Germany. Justus delivered Ingrid to Hamburg or Kiel, visited a day or two, then kissed his daughter and waved farewell to his in-laws as he headed for Paris or London or Copenhagen. Her father's intentions were certainly for the welfare of his daughter, whom he wished surrounded by an extended family, but with each succeeding summer Ingrid felt more abandoned and forlorn when she arrived at her grandparents' home. Whereas her father was informal and fun-loving, the Adler household was a temple of Teutonic order and propriety. Ingrid was unhappy with the strict discipline, the constraints on her childish behavior and the strangeness of the regime as compared with life at Strandvägen.

The intervals with her mother's sisters, Elsa and Luna, were pleasanter. Both had married prosperously, but Luna's life was blighted by the loss of her husband, who had recently died at the front during the war. Elsa—whom Ingrid took to calling Aunt Mutti ("Aunt-Mommy")—was the maverick in the Adler clan. Her husband was a French entrepreneur who, when he heard about the rich soil and cheap labor of the Caribbean islands, at once smelled sacks of coffee and tons of money. By the time Ingrid was spending girlhood summer holidays in Germany, Mutti's husband was an absentee spouse, supervising his plantations in Haiti and Jamaica and enjoying the blandishments of exotic women. Elsa, meantime, lived in high luxury behind her walled estate outside Hamburg, attended by a small platoon of servants whom she directed like a drill sergeant. No one in the family was surprised when that marriage ended definitively after Elsa learned that the elder of her two boys, who had gone out to work with his father in Haiti one summer, died of typhoid fever.

Mutti Adler thus became, for almost twenty years in Ingrid's life, a part-time, second surrogate mother after Aunt Ellen. She taught Ingrid to speak good German, she encouraged her to read, memorize and recite short dramatic German poems and to sing German lieder, the better to please her father when he came to take her back home at summer's end. The return, of course, also meant the readjustment to calmer, less colorful pastimes with Ellen when Justus pitched himself more and more into work and social life. In her earliest years, then, Ingrid Bergman was given a series of mixed signals: for part of the year, she enjoyed privilege and playacting

with her German aunt—but these were disparaged by her Swedish
aunt when she returned to Strandvägen.

In the middle of it all was her father, whose life changed dramatically just before Ingrid was seven. To lighten Ellen's housekeeping chores, Justus engaged a vivacious girl named Greta Danielsson
to work several days each week. Within a month, she was in the
apartment every day; very soon after that, Greta was in the apartment every night, and sharing Justus's bed as well as board. That
summer of 1922, he was fifty-one and she was eighteen.

Ingrid—now introduced to a third, much younger mother-
figure—had a comfortable home, nice clothes and plenty to eat.
But apart from her father, she knew only a tangle of uncertain,
widely discrepant relationships. Ellen was attentive, caring, humorless and austere as a cloistered nun; Mutti tapped out the rhythms
of verse and rang for another cup of cocoa and a second slice of
butter cake; Greta sat at supper and held Justus's hand and giggled
without any apparent reason.

Aunt Ellen, livid with shame for her brother and his concubine,
promptly moved back to her tiny apartment three blocks away. But
she returned every Sunday morning to snatch Ingrid from a warm
bed and idleness and to march her off to worship at the parish
church (named for Hedvig Eleonora, the eighteenth-century queen
consort of King Charles X Gustaf). There, a darkly terrifying painting of Christ on the cross loomed over the altar, and another, of him
handed over to death by Pilate, hung under the organ gallery.

In the pulpit each Sunday stood the Reverend Erik Bergman,
who was unrelated to Ingrid's family. In July 1918, the priest's wife,
Karin, had given birth to a boy they named Ernst Ingmar, who was
also shown the wonders of movies at an early age, and who grew up
with dramatic impressions of parish life. Pastor Bergman's sermons,
much to Aunt Ellen's satisfaction, stressed (as Ingmar testified)
"concrete factors in relationships between children and parents and
God"—by which he meant honor, decency, obedience and a strict
moral code that stressed sin and guilt, contrition and repentance.

For a brief time in her childhood, especially after she was con-
firmed by Pastor Bergman and mostly in the company of Aunt
Ellen, this arcane language had the predictable effect of instilling in
Ingrid a sense of religious awe. But her father was dispassionate

about such things, and there was thus no reinforcement at home. With Papa and Greta, on the contrary, everything seemed geared toward enjoyment, leisure activities were planned according to caprice, and nothing was strict at all; there was, in other words, not much reference to stern Lutheran values. To Aunt Ellen's predictable dismay, Greta went so far with Ingrid as to take her to the movies, which seemed to women like Ellen Bergman a direct route to introducing the child to the brothel.

In 1922, for example, Greta and Ingrid sat twice through Victor Sjöström's new picture, *Love's Crucible*, a silent film set in the Middle Ages, about a woman accused of murdering her husband. She is burned at the stake during a trial by fire, hears heavenly voices and ecstatically beholds her dead husband coming to take her to paradise.

The orchestra at the movie theater sent waves of rhapsodic music over Greta and Ingrid as they sat wide-eyed before the magical effects of the tinted images, the double exposure of filmstrips conveying simultaneously the devouring flames and the lady's ecstatic gaze. The story and script certainly seemed a variant of one of the most popular themes of the year: the trial and death of Joan of Arc, who had recently been canonized and whose new status as a saint symbolized pious national purpose at the end of the war. Images of St. Joan, as well as plays, films, sermons, books and pamphlets about her, proliferated throughout Europe in the 1920s. The veneration reached its zenith in 1929, with Carl Dreyer's haunting masterwork, *The Passion of Joan of Arc*. The nineteen-year-old peasant girl who died in 1431 was set before every Christian girl as a model of faith, courage and perseverance.

"From the time I was a little girl, she has always been my greatest heroine," said Ingrid, who soon added Joan of Arc to her little repertory of characters. "I put her in a special place in my heart, and instead of saving butterflies or stamps, my hobby was to look for things about Joan of Arc, and to collect books and medals and statues of her." It is easy to understand the attraction. The accounts of Joan's early life emphasized her loneliness, her conviction about an inner calling, then the assurance confronting others despite her bashfulness. "She became the character I liked to play most. She, too, was a timid child, but with great dignity and courage." The beginning of a lifelong devotion coincided with Ingrid's brief term of attendance, with her aunt, at the local church. Her veneration of Joan endured, but the churchgoing did not.

As it happened, Ingrid's affection for the saint was reinforced from her first days at school. On September 1, 1922 (three days after her seventh birthday), she began to attend first grade classes at the Lyceum for Girls, located at 13 Kommendörsgatan, a pleasant fifteen-minute walk from home. That day, Ingrid met Ebba Högberg, the homeroom teacher, who explained to her and the nineteen other girls the school's tradition and the schedule of lessons for each day. The Lyceum, which welcomed girls from first grade through college preparatory, enrolled 385 pupils that academic year, of whom 238 were in the elementary school.

"The Lyceum's main mission," according to its catalog that year, "is not only enriching students with theoretical courses, but also forming their character. Perhaps this is what the school's founder, Dr. Gustaf Sjöberg, had in mind when he named the school after the Greek educational institution, which set as its goal the acquiring of sound minds and bodies, as well as bringing to young people the teachings of the great moral philosophers, with their healthy outlook on life." To that end, the first graders submitted to an intense regimen of subjects. There were daily recitations in Christian history, Swedish language, German (at which Ingrid excelled), the history of their country up to 1389 and the geography of Scandinavia (at which she did not), arithmetic, handwriting, drawing, singing, sewing and physical education.

The Lyceum, a five-story neoclassical structure with dozens of small warrens for classrooms, certainly conveyed the no-nonsense attitude of its founders and custodians. The girls sat on hard, inhospitable benches, their work illuminated by parsimonious light from bulbs suspended in somewhat sickly yellow cones. In this atmosphere—so different from Aunt Mutti's beautiful estate in Germany and the cozy familiarity of her father's apartment—Ingrid attended school from autumn 1922 through the spring term 1933. In successive years of grade school, her syllabus was eventually amplified to include biology, chemistry, French and cooking; of all her subjects, her least admirable achievement was in the last. With the knitting needle she became an expert, but no matter how simple the menu assigned to the students, the art of the kitchen was completely beyond her. French and German she passed well, but science bored her and occasionally she failed at it. Otherwise, Ingrid Bergman's elementary school record shows that she passed her courses; to avoid unhealthy competition, Lyceum students were not assigned letter grades, nor were they awarded prizes.

But as she progressed through elementary school, she was not a happy child. "I remember so well how, when school finished, I used to stand outside and watch the mothers come for their children. It seemed to me that they were very beautiful mothers, all perfumed and smartly dressed in their fancy hats. I would just stand there and watch them go off together. Then I would go home by myself."

IN 1924, JUST BEFORE HER NINTH BIRTHDAY, JUSTUS GAVE UP THE FLAT on Strandvägen and moved to a larger residence on the Ulrikagatan, a pleasant street very near a park. Ingrid now took a streetcar to the Lyceum, and one afternoon after her return from school, her father had what he thought was wonderful news. He had landed the assignment of leading a mixed choir of amateur singers—The Swedes, they would aptly be called—on a tour of three American cities.

For his daughter this was a catastrophe: she feared that her father would not return, that a journey across the sea would end in disaster, that she would be abandoned by him. As for Greta, it was impossible for her to accompany Justus, since widowed gentlemen with young mistresses could certainly not represent Sweden abroad. And so when he departed, early in 1925, Ingrid was more truly alone than she had ever been. Two weeks later, Greta took a job across town, saying, as she departed, that perhaps she would become an actress in the movies. Ingrid spent the time of her father's absence with Uncle Otto and Aunt Hulda and their five children, Bill, Bengt, Bo, Britt and (with sudden disregard for the established alliteration) Margit; these cousins ranged in age from eight to twenty-one.

Competing with this quintet for the adults' attention, Ingrid augmented her repertory of characters and dramatized some verses of Swedish poetry she had learned at school. Once, for example, she dressed in an old lady's shawl and a soiled apron and, with a broom and pail in her hands, came into a room filled with her relatives. She then recited a poem by Fröding, and to the surprise of her audience she was transformed into a mysterious servant, lost in reverie over a handsome soldier who may or may not have been in her past.

The boys teased Ingrid mercilessly: "How can you be an actress when you're so clumsy?" they asked, pointing out that, although but nine years old, Ingrid was already rather tall and tended to a certain awkwardness. "As an actress, I'm not myself," she replied with a certain illogical logic that defied contradiction. "I didn't choose acting," she reflected years later, referring to these early appearances. "It chose me."

As her performances continued during her father's absence, Uncle Otto overcame his stupefaction with frank disapproval. "My uncle, instead of laughing at me, used to get angry, because he was fanatically religious and believed the theater was the work of the devil." But Otto regarded most work as diabolical. "He never had any steady paying job," recalled Ingrid's first husband years later, "and [he] seemed to have lived largely on income from [Justus's] photographic store."

At least twice, to the astonishment of everyone in the family, Aunt Ellen sprang to her niece's defense. She protested that Ingrid was not wicked, that the girl simply had a gift for innocent recitations. Perhaps, Ellen reasoned, Ingrid's talent might serve true religion, after all. She might grow up to be a missionary. The world, especially in the Jazz Age that spread wild American music and shocking American movies across Europe, certainly needed missionaries. Ingrid listened, having learned very early to say nothing in response to such promptings from Aunt Ellen.

The reaction at school was not so pious, much less censorious. In fifth grade, Ingrid impressed her classmates with a dramatic reading of lines from "Sveaborg," a portion of Johan Ludvig Runeberg's *The Stories of Fänrik Stål*. This poem she delivered, according to one student, "with such pathos that the whole class sat shivering and with tears in their eyes." Other poems gave her rich opportunities for dramatic interpretation, too, as did her delivery of the Song of the Winds from Strindberg's *Dream Play*: "Winds are

blowing and whistling, woe, woe, woe . . ." The girls could almost
feel the keening moan of winter wind in the room, and no one at
the Lyceum was surprised when Ingrid won a public verse-reading
competition in the spring of 1925. Sten Selander, one of the judges,
delivered the prize certificate and pronounced that "Miss Bergman
will surely go far."

In late August 1925, just after Ingrid returned from her visit to
Aunt Mutti Adler in Hamburg, Justus docked in Stockholm. Among
some presents for his daughter, that which most fascinated her was
a dried California orange, which she kept for years: "It was my first
touch with America and I thought it wonderful." Shortly thereafter,
they moved to a top-floor apartment at 34 Birger Jarlsgatan, a very
elegant building in the business district.

Papa's journey had confirmed him in his devotion to music. That
autumn, he continued his own piano practice and his conducting
lessons, and he also enrolled Ingrid in private sessions with a voice
coach. She was now ten years old, he said, and the future was clear:
she would become a great opera singer. "He took me to the opera a
lot, and that bored me," she recalled years later. A segment of Papa's
home movies shows Ingrid, holding sheet music and singing as her
father accompanies her on the piano. She smiles at the camera, but
there is not much enthusiasm: her gaze seems to beg for release. At
the time, desperate to please her father, she kept still.

But she could not suppress her delight when he took her to the
Royal Dramatic Theater for the first time, two months after her
birthday, in autumn 1926. She borrowed a dress from a cousin—
cherry red, her father's favorite color—and asked Aunt Ellen to
iron it three times that afternoon.

Ingrid's earliest memories of the neighborhood around Strandvägen were dominated by the image of the theater, completed in
1908 and certainly one of the most elegant and eloquent architectural statements celebrating the drama. Papa and Greta had pointed
out to Ingrid its grand exterior marble staircase, the allegorical figures of the arts, the friezes of Dionysus and of the Commedia del-
l'Arte, the statues of Tragedy and Comedy. From her window, Ingrid
watched, season after season, as ladies and gentlemen arrived in formal dress for the opening nights. Now she was entering the place
for the first time, gazing upward at Carl Larsson's ceiling painting,

The Birth of Drama, an art nouveau masterpiece in which a lightly veiled maiden is crowned with laurel by a male figure—clearly the spirit of criticism, for he also wields in his other hand the alternate compensation, a murderous sword.

That autumn evening was crucial in Ingrid's life. The play was *Patrasket (The Rabble)* by Hjalmar Bergman (related neither to her father nor to the local pastor), a contemporary novelist and playwright best known for works that revealed a bitter despair about human life and destiny, and this was no exception. The narrative, which concerned a family in need of help from a wealthy Jewish relative, was billed as a comedy; but there was little cause for laughter in the story of venality and hypocrisy. But no matter the content (or the running anti-Semitic tone), eleven-year-old Ingrid had discovered the theater.

> My eyes popped out. Grownup people on that stage doing things which I did at home, all by myself, just for fun. And they were getting paid for it! They were making their living doing it! I just couldn't understand how these actors could behave like me, invent a world of make-believe, and call it work! And I turned to my father at the first intermission, and they probably heard me all over the theater I was so excited, as I said, "Papa, Papa, that's what I'm going to do."

From that evening, Ingrid's impromptu performances for her family had a fresh resolution. And Justus took her to one play after another, hoping perhaps that she would get the theater out of her blood and turn seriously to music. Together they saw several plays starring the great Gösta Ekman, and again at the Lyceum Ingrid impressed teachers and classmates with her memory. After seeing a play called *The Green Elevator*, she could recite portions of the leading character's final speech almost verbatim: the words of a drunken boy named Billy who moans over (what else?) a lost love: "Tessi, Tessi, my little morning fairy queen . . ." Doubtless the delivery was better than the text.

BY 1927, THE GIRLS AT THE LYCEUM ROUTINELY LOOKED TO INGRID for diversion whenever they were left unsupervised. On one such occasion she began to recite a speech from *The Rabble*, but the sudden return of the teacher, Ester Sund, led to the dismissal of the entire group from school for the day. Never mind: all the girls followed Ingrid to Humlegården, where she played the scene (the death of a sick old man) to the end. Passersby were perhaps alarmed at the sight of two dozen twelve-year-old girls huddled together in tears around a classmate who was feigning death on a park bench. Her successful realism gratified and amused her: acting was unalloyed pleasure.

She also loved to surprise her teachers and peers. Recitation of a tragic poem might be followed a few days later by scenes from a farce; one week she enacted the death of Joan of Arc, the next she improvised a lady who had sipped an excess of champagne and could not find her latchkey. "I remember that Ingrid had such a sense of humor," said her classmate Elisabeth Daevel. "She was one of the funniest ones in school. Like most of us, she was not very studious, but we all made it to the next grade."

That same year, the girls read in school the tale of Tristan and Isolde. "It had a strong appeal for my romantic young-girl dreams," Ingrid said later. "Earthly love was a very precious dream for the unattractive girl I was." She was, of course, nothing of the sort— but she was much taller than the others, and that is an awkward experience for anyone her age. By her thirteenth birthday in 1928, Ingrid had reached her full adult height of five feet, nine inches. As other girls were being fitted for their first pair of heeled shoes, she felt consigned to sensible flat soles.

"I hated school because I was taller than other people and awkward and shy," she recalled. "I wasn't a mute but I only spoke when I had to. If I knew the answer to a question and had to give it, just having to get off my chair and stand up in front of the class made me blush. School was hell. And I was lonely."

As for the poems and dramatic recitations: "I acted all the parts. I never wanted to act with others, and I always asked myself, What can I do alone? So I read funny poems and sad poems and I dramatized them." The lives of many actors reveal an identical conjunction: the essentially isolated personality that blossoms on stage or screen, where an uncertain ego can be affirmed. For some, too, role-playing—the assumption of other identities—is a way of exploring otherwise unrealized (or unlikely) possibilities. For Ingrid, professional endorsement mattered very much to her all her life, and indeed why should it not have when so substantial a talent was in a constant state of refinement? However, if the applause was not forthcoming, or if the critic appeared with drawn sword instead of gleaming laurel, she simply moved on to another role. Only once in her life did Ingrid publicly react to a negative judgment on a performance, and, to her everlasting distress, that occurred in Stockholm, many years later.

AT CHRISTMAS 1928, JUSTUS TOOK INGRID TO DINE AT BERNS' Salonger, a venerable city institution. Opened in 1863, Berns' was a first-class gourmet restaurant with formally attired orchestra, smaller rooms for private receptions and the famous Röda Rummet—the richly appointed Red Room, with its overstuffed chairs and polished tables, its low Gothic ceiling and stained glass windows. In this room gathered the artists and intellectuals of the 1880s and 1890s; here they debated politics and aesthetics; here, they sipped coffee, drank wine and beer, smoked, argued and scribbled notes. The atmosphere inspired one of its regular patrons, August Strindberg, to write an evocative satire named after the room. Ingrid and her father had a glass of champagne here, and she read the edifying mottoes on the wood carvings: "You can never do too much good . . . The greatest victory that ever can be won is the victory over one's self . . . Honor is the fairest tree in the wood." They then went down to the dining room, where an orchestra played for dances, and where they ordered a festive holiday dinner of roast elk.

Days later, as a bitter cold swept in with the new year 1929, Justus was confined to bed with a mysterious ailment. A week passed, but he felt no better. Pale and perspiring, he finally consulted a physician, who ordered an array of tests. By the time the results were available, the unhappy patient could scarcely keep down the smallest morsel of food and was losing weight quickly. His sister Ellen, ill with influenza, was unavailable to help, and so Ingrid located Greta Danielsson, who had found work across town and who now returned to help. After a few days in which all three avoided discussing the diagnosis, Justus sat down with his ex-mistress and his daughter. He had cancer of the stomach, and the outlook was grim. Greta burst into tears; Ingrid was mute with grief.

"I don't want Ingrid to see her father dying," Justus told his friend Gunnar Spångberg, a local florist, "and God knows how long it will take me." And with that, he made arrangements for himself and Greta to consult a specialist in Bavaria. "Maybe he will cure me. If not, I'll come back in a box."

Neither of these ensued. Instead, to the predictable outrage of his family, Justus remained an independent bohemian to the end. He and Greta spent the spring of 1929 in a quiet suburb of Munich. She prepared herb teas and thin soups and, when his strength allowed, he set up an easel, sat in a small garden and painted wild-flowers. "Then he came home," Ingrid recalled, "so thin it was dreadful." That was the only summer she did not spend with Mutti, who by now had resumed her maiden name and taken for her live-in lover a handsome and successful German fabric merchant. Mutti traveled from Germany that season and further alienated herself from the Bergman clan by refusing to join the chorus of those who wanted Greta out of the house. "She has the right," Mutti told Otto and Ellen. "So please allow it." And so they did: Frau Adler was not a woman to be withstood.

June and July were unusually warm, and as daylight lengthened, Justus Bergman's suffering became one protracted, appalling night of pain. He had enjoyed excellent health until the previous winter, when his hearty onslaught toward life was checked by sudden sickness. Now, he was so weak he could only whisper, and only a few drops of water passed for nourishment. Greta bathed him with cool compresses. Ignoring her father's appeals, Ingrid slept a few hours each afternoon and spent the nights at his bedside, holding his hand and, in perhaps her most brilliant acting so far, humming his favorite folk tunes and quietly repeating what she knew was a tragic fantasy—that if only he could get through this endless summer, if only he could take some soup, if only they could find a better doc-tor, if only . . .

Toward midnight on July 28, his breathing became labored and shallow, and four hours later, as Ingrid and Greta sat at his bedside, Justus Bergman slowly turned his head and looked lovingly at each. At 3:55 on the morning of July 29, 1929, Justus Samuel Bergman, age fifty-eight, was dead. Ingrid was one month from her fourteenth birthday.

Next day, the newspapers published a notice drafted by Ellen and Otto over Ingrid's signature. "Peacefully and quietly, my dear father expired. He is mourned by his daughter, relatives, friends and staff of many years. Funeral at the North Cemetery, Saturday, August 3, at four o'clock."

For several months, Ingrid was so withdrawn that there were fears for her health. She offered no impromptu performances for the family, no recitations or entertainments, and she would not be drawn into conversation. Greta, who stayed with her until school resumed in September, could not interest the poor girl in any-thing—neither a movie nor even, in the autumn, a play. For a time, Ingrid tried to paint, but when she daubed at the canvas, she became too sad to work or think or remember, and her father's brush slipped from her fingers. "I didn't see how I could go on liv-ing," she said of that year. "Well, I did. We all do." But throughout her life, a sudden pang of sadness often beclouded Ingrid. "As a child," recalled her oldest daughter Pia years later, "I remember my mother grieving over the loss of her mother and father."

Justus left an estate of almost half a million Swedish kronor ($100,000, adjusted for 1997 exchange). A quarter of that amount, secured as stocks in the company for which he was managing direc-tor, was assigned in trust for Ingrid, and small amounts were left to friends and relatives.

In mid-September, her relatives closed up Papa's apartment and moved Ingrid to Aunt Ellen's dark, second-floor flat at 6 Nybergs-gatan. The place was nearby and the neighborhood was familiar—and, in the coming year, so was the tragic motif that had made Ingrid Bergman, at fourteen, an orphan, unable to rely on the con-tinuance of any human affection.

Chapter Two

1929–1936

There is always one moment in childhood when the door opens
and lets the future in.

GRAHAM GREENE,
The Power and the Glory

D URING THE ACADEMIC YEAR 1929–1930, INGRID WAS GIVEN NO
leniency for mourning when it came to her classes in physics,
chemistry, mathematics and, worst of all, cooking. Quite to the
contrary, her teachers were practitioners of stern Swedish account-
ability—just like Aunt Ellen, who tried (without apparent success)
to impress upon her niece the gravity of formal religion. But as it
happened, early in 1930, Ellen Bergman could not go out to
church: she was now chronically short of breath, and her sixth-floor
walk-up apartment was an intimidating climb. If she were to avoid
aggravating her uneven heart rhythm, her physician said, excursions
up and downstairs must be severely curtailed.

But the woman's problem was more serious than arrhythmia.
One spring afternoon, after reading her Bible, she felt dizzy to the
point of fainting when she rose from her chair. Ingrid, who had just
come in from the Lyceum, comforted her aunt with a cup of strong

tea. Then, at Eastertide 1930, came the crisis. Gasping for breath, Ellen cried out for Ingrid at three o'clock one morning. "I feel really ill," she said, her face ashen as she struggled for breath and clutched her chest. "Will you call Uncle Otto?" Ingrid telephoned Otto and his family, who lived very nearby, and they said help was on the way.

"Read the Bible to me," Ellen gasped. "Read the Bible!" Ingrid found a psalm as her aunt became more gravely ill. "I'm going to die," she whispered. "Oh, why don't they come, why don't they come?" And then she pointed wildly: "Key—key!!" Ingrid realized what she meant: to avoid negotiating the stairs, Ellen routinely tossed the key from the front window to the sidewalk below, permitting visitors access through the locked main door; Ingrid had for the moment forgotten about this.

That task done, she returned to the bedroom and took her aunt in her arms. A moment later, Ellen Bergman clutched Ingrid's arm with a fierce grip, her gaze wild with pain. She then emitted one long gasp, her head fell against Ingrid's breast, and she was dead.

NOT YET FIFTEEN, INGRID BERGMAN HAD ENDURED A SERIES OF FAMILY tragedies that left her in a haze of confusion and pain. Her relatives recalled that for months she seemed almost a blank, her gaze vacant, her voice affectless and dry. She managed to get through the remaining few weeks of the school term by doggedly pursuing the necessary tasks and by trying to arrange her room at yet another new address: Otto and Hulda's second-floor apartment at 43 Artillerigatan, a short stroll from Strandvägen. It is easy to understand why she became for a while "aloof, cold even, and suspicious of everybody" (as she said later), withdrawn and wary from a fear that anyone to whom she might attach herself would be rudely taken from her.

At her uncle's apartment, Ingrid did not have to share a bedroom, as did her cousins. Her father's lawyer parceled her inheritance to the Bergmans as well as the income from Justus's shop, still operating in Strandvägen, and so in exchange for their care and lodging of Ingrid, she was given her own quarters, a sunny room large enough to accommodate her parents' piano and her father's desk and paintings. Aunt Hulda, a dark-eyed woman who looked a

decade older than her forty years, now kept house for eight and
supervised the camera shop; Otto tinkered with his inventions, certain that one day he would have a patent on a marvelous new device
and they would all retire to a villa in the country.

In the autumn of 1931, Ingrid was sixteen and known at the
Lyceum as the girl who seemed to become someone else when she
recited poetry or did a dramatic recitation. By this time, she had a
goal—to give herself "absolutely to the theater . . . [to be the] new
Sarah Bernhardt . . . I dreamed that perhaps one day I might be
able to act in a play with Gösta Ekman." Henceforth, classes at the
Lyceum were for her a round of tedium: "I thought only about my
work, my ambition for acting and wanting to travel and see new
things . . . "

> The theater was a kind of hiding place for me, I suppose. People
> who are lonely and have a difficult time finding themselves often
> go into the theater because there are masks you can put on. It
> helps you to release whatever it is you are fearful of. What you
> say onstage you haven't written, and what you pretend to be is
> not you. It is an escape.

She took the first small advance toward realizing her dream in
January 1932, a week after a Christmas reunion with Greta
Danielsson, who had lost weight, dyed her hair blond, was studying
voice and acting and got occasional work as an extra in films. So it
happened that one bitter cold day that winter, Greta took Ingrid
along to the Svensk Filmindustri studio, where they were quickly
put in a crowd scene for the film *Landskamp*, whose title refers to an
international sports competition. The girls were, of course, unbilled
(and were unrecognizable in the picture when it was released in
March that year), but that was no disappointment to Ingrid. She
believed, quite rightly, that she had made a beginning; and in the
bargain, she was surprised to be paid "ten whole kronor for having
enjoyed one of the very best days in my life."

The experience was sufficiently exciting to make Ingrid restless
to have done with the Lyceum. Eager for serious acting, she
inquired about classes at the Royal Dramatic Theater School, which
ran a highly structured program that selected a few candidates each

year from dozens of applicants who auditioned. Acceptance did not ensure a successful career, but entry to Dramaten (then the popular name for the school as well as the theater) guaranteed a first-rate education in one of Europe's most prestigious theatrical schools. Among other respected people, the great stage and screen actor Lars Hanson was an alumnus; he had gone to Hollywood and starred opposite Lillian Gish. A barbershop assistant named Greta Gustafsson had also studied at Dramaten; she had been rechristened Greta Garbo before moving to Hollywood, too. Signe Hasso, who had an important career on stage and screen in Sweden and Hollywood, was a contemporary of Ingrid. Viveca Lindfors arrived a few years later; she, too, had her greatest fame in America. And Mai Zetterling, Max von Sydow and Bibi Andersson were among many noted alumni in later years.

In 1787, King Gustaf III had directed that the Royal Theater teach dance, song and recitation to young artists. From that time, working actors and singers conducted a series of classes for apprentices, who also had the opportunity to go onstage as supernumeraries in crowd scenes, and occasionally even to assume minor speaking roles. By 1908, when the school moved into a half-dozen rooms in the newly completed Royal Theater, the subjects for study included diction, set design, deportment, dance and fencing—as well as French, German and the history of literature and theater.

Because these courses were focused on the business of acting and her classmates would be colleagues, Ingrid had quite a different attitude toward the prospect of a new and demanding set of academic requirements. The week after she completed the spring term at the Lyceum, on June 2, 1933, she chose her selections for the three auditions before Dramaten's judges. The Certificate Catalog for the Lyceum that season, which had recently changed its custom and listed grades for those completing the equivalent of secondary school, records that Ingrid Bergman received A's in deportment, industry, attention and organization; A- in church history, Swedish language and literature; B+ in German, history, art history and geography; and B's in mathematics, physics, chemistry, home economics, health, sewing, drawing, singing and gymnastics.

She then began to prepare at home for the drama school. Uncle Otto, who thought little of her intentions, said she had better also prepare an alternate career move. She was too tall and graceless as a goose, he said, adding that a girl's virtue could not withstand the wickedness of life in the theater. But a good share of his household's income came from Ingrid's trust fund, so he reluctantly permitted her to try out. Ingrid chose a speech from Rostand's *L'Aiglon*, one from Strindberg's *Dream Play* and a scene about a peasant girl that she stitched together from a rustic Hungarian comedy.

Forty-eight young beginners joined her for the first audition before the judges at the Royal Dramatic Theater that August; a fortunate seven would be chosen for the tuition-free classes beginning the following month. When her turn came, Ingrid stepped onstage and began the Rostand excerpt. But she did not proceed far before one of the judges waved her offstage; they had heard enough. That was the worst moment of her life, she said years later, for she spent the rest of the day wandering aimlessly around the harbor, ashamed to report home.

But when she did, one of her cousins had a telephone message for her. She had indeed passed the audition and was to report next day for round two: the judges had interrupted her performance, she later learned, because they needed to hear no more than the first few moments to be convinced of Ingrid's talent and potential.

And so the worst moment of her life thus far had become the best. Her two months of study paid off in the following days, for after she had presented her renditions from Strindberg and, by dazzling contrast, a comic turn as a lusty peasant girl leaping over streams in pursuit of her lover, she was granted a place in the September class. "While she has too much the appearance of a country girl," noted one of the teachers, "she is very natural and is the type that does not need makeup on her face or on her mind."

MUCH OF THE WORLD WAS MIRED IN A DREADFUL ECONOMIC DEPRESsion that autumn of 1933, but the worst of it was already behind Sweden, whose exports of iron, sewing machines, surgical and dental instruments, stoves, dynamite and paper commanded high prices. In addition, there was record tourism in Sweden that year, as the *New York Times* observed in a story on August 27. The proliferation of telephones and automobiles and the expansion of the nation's roadways united villages with cities, and the rise to power of the Social Democrats led to a range of medical, educational, pension and other programs benefiting every Swedish citizen, young and old. (President Roosevelt's strategy for recovery owed much to Sweden's programs, which were carefully studied by American officials who visited Sweden.)

In Stockholm, moreover, there was a new spirit of freedom and experimentation in the arts as well as in commerce and industry, and daily life seemed full of promise. "The streets were just full of well-dressed people," recalled the artist Dietrich, who began his career in Stockholm at that time. "The shops were thriving and the theater was going strong. There seemed to be one particular vogue—the Hungarian czarda, with gypsy violins, and it seemed that everywhere you went there was a restaurant selling goulash." The job market of Budapest, less propitious than that of Sweden, had impelled many workers to Scandinavia, and so Middle European music, dancing and cuisine were all the rage that season. Ingrid, too, recalled the sudden profusion of Hungarian cafes and Czech fashions; their exoticism appealed especially to young people eager for more colorful cosmopolitan styles than was afforded by good, sturdy Swedish simplicity.

But for Ingrid and her classmates, there was little time for patronizing the latest coffee houses or bistros. Classes at Dramaten met six days each week, and after an hour's break for supper the students went to stand in the upper balcony to watch the evening's performance. The 1933–1934 season provided them with a rich international repertory: among other plays, they saw Strindberg's *Master Olof*, O'Neill's *Mourning Becomes Electra* and *Desire Under the Elms*, John Drinkwater's *A Bird in the Hand*, Jean Giraudoux's *Amphitryon 38*, the *Medea* of Euripides, Bernard Shaw's *Too Good to Be True*, plays by Hauptmann, Sheridan, Aristophanes, Labiche and Pirandello, and *The Hundred Days*, a play about Napoleon by Benito Mussolini. Students were forbidden, however, to watch rehearsals, during which the doors to the auditorium were locked—but a hairpin took care of that, as Ingrid said years later. Sundays were devoted to reading assignments, memorization and scene study at home. For her private study, Ingrid liked to sit near the water, on a bench along Strandvägen or on the quieter banks of the Djurgården, a park in the midst of the city.

The instruction was intense. There were lectures on theater history with the grave Professor Stig Torsslow, who remembered
Ingrid's determination and her "methodical energy"; there was
fencing with the short, agile Robert Påhlman; voice and diction with
the stately, elegant Karin Alexandersson, who had acted for Strindberg; and scene study with the great Hilda Borgström, the star of
Ingeborg Holm. Later in the day, the students dashed to a barren
dressing room to change for movement class with the graceful
dancer Valbörg Franchi; then to body culture (how to sit, stand,
enter and exit a room) and rhythmic dance exercises with elegant
Ruth Kylberg and stern Jeanna Falk; and, perhaps most memorable
of all, the class in dramatic gesture with the formidable Anna Pet-
tersson-Norrie.

The aristocratic, seventy-three-year-old Madame Pettersson-
Norrie, with her pince-nez, platinum white hair and ample bosom,
was a figure primed for caricature. But no one dared to mock her.
Serious as a judge, she could be lethal as an executioner, sometimes
warmly and sometimes icily enjoining expansive postures and signals on her students. This she did in the curious belief that such was
the best way of overcoming shyness; anything exaggerated, she said,
could be toned down later, but for the present: "Young man, let me
see your hand in the air!" and "Why do you not throw your arms
open wide on that line, dear?" For all her idiosyncrasies, Anna Pet-
tersson-Norrie was a valuable teacher for Ingrid—not so much for
the learning of big gestures, but because she taught her presence:
how to listen to another actor, how to be within a scene, not simply
leaping out of it with thoughtless, unmotivated action to distract an
audience or (horrors!) to steal a scene.

After three months at Dramaten, Ingrid had won the admiration of classmates and instructors, and apparently the entire school
(eighteen students in the three years of study) knew about her confidence and talent. "She had a great natural talent, all her teachers
admitted that," said Rudolf Wendbladh, later the school's artistic
director, adding that she was "a chubby and impulsive girl who
knew exactly what she wanted."

Her self-assurance onstage and in classes (but not in social situations) was also noted by the actor Gunnar Björnstrand, a classmate
in 1933. "Perhaps she wasn't that way underneath, but she gave the

impression of total stability. She always radiated phenomenal health, strength and vitality. She had iron willpower and an unbelievable memory. Learning lines was a snap for her." Another classmate, Frank Sundstrom, recalled that she had strong opinions about her work at a time when women were not to have ideas. According to a third classmate, Ingrid Luterkort, "Ingrid was a beauty, but she was also confident—she knew there was something in her."

The talent was observed, too, by the director Alf Sjöberg, who took the unprecedented step, that autumn of 1933, of casting Ingrid in Sigfrid Siwertz's play *Ett Brott* (*A Crime*), which he was staging at the theater and which was to star one of Sweden's most popular performers, Edvin Adolphson. By hallowed tradition, only the best students in their last year of study were selected for the privilege of assuming a speaking role in the repertory. Hence, as classmates and teachers recalled years later, Sjöberg's selection of first-year student Ingrid aroused considerable controversy and personal resentment against her—even to the point that one student, ignoring the class on etiquette, accosted Ingrid in the street and hit her over the head with a book. Sjöberg's hand was forced, and Ingrid had to withdraw from the play during rehearsals that winter.

The incident might have depressed another eighteen-year-old apprentice to the point of quitting Dramaten, but Ingrid was too intent on success to yield—and a good thing, too, for in April Sjöberg succeeded in his attempt to advance Ingrid's career. This time, he put her, along with a few other first-year girls, in a crowd scene of Sheridan's classic comedy *The Rivals*, which he presented in repertory for nineteen performances from mid-May to early June 1934. The leading role (Captain Absolute) was again played by Edvin Adolphson; to her dismay, Ingrid was only an extra and had no dialogue. "She was very unhappy about that," recalled Ingrid Luterkort, "perhaps because her stage debut was no better than her film debut, which had also been as an unrecognizable extra, in *Landskamp*."

For years, Alf Sjöberg was rumored to have been Ingrid Bergman's first love—probably because he had so doggedly championed her cause at school. But, as Ingrid later confided to her first and third husbands, that role was assumed by Edvin Adolphson, a strikingly handsome man who, when the role required it, could exude an irresistible sex appeal. With his strong features, dark hair and eyes and commanding presence, he could intimidate men and reduce women to nerveless submission.

Adolphson was forty-one, married and a father. Nevertheless, that spring of 1934, he was enchanted by this exuberant, expressive eighteen-year-old ingenue whom he had noticed during the early rehearsals for *Ett Brott*. Ingrid found his poise dazzling, his authority irresistible and his interest in her flattering. Following a rehearsal of *The Rivals* one rainy afternoon, Adolphson invited Ingrid to join him and one other young player for a cup of coffee. The following Sunday, he stole a few hours to meet Ingrid alone for a walk through the narrow streets of Old Town, a route that eventually led to the bedroom of an old friend of Edvin who was conveniently away for the weekend.

Eighteen, passionate and playful, Ingrid did not fall into the trap ready for those who yield to unrealistic romantic expectations. For one thing, she took very seriously the fact that Edvin was married and a celebrated actor who might court a willing young actress more readily than he would public humiliation. She knew, in other words, that this was very much a matter of the moment for both of them, and she expected little more from the relationship than what it offered: a tender introduction to sexual intimacy and the advantage of time with an articulate and experienced actor who knew both the literature and the craft of the stage and was willing to encourage as well as caress. There is no indication that the romance, however furtively it had to be conducted, was anything but warmly remembered by the couple, and—as always in the life of Ingrid Bergman—a love affair was later transmuted into a sympathetic friendship.

The occasional assignations with Ingrid that spring and summer might have remained uncomplicated throughout the year but for the increasing presence of a rival who would not indifferently sustain opposition. Ingrid's cousin Margit (one of the five children of Uncle Otto and Aunt Hulda) had been the grateful patient of a young dentist named Lindström. She invited him to dinner one Sunday evening in November 1933, shortly after her family had moved to a new apartment at 37 Skeppargatan, a ten-minute stroll from Dramaten. "At that time, I regarded him as quite an old man," Ingrid said years later. "But I was still a bit awkward and lacking in social ease . . . [and] I felt very flattered that my company was not boring to him. He owned a car and lived in a nice apartment. All this made a strong impression on me." Lindstrom, then twenty-six (eight years Ingrid's senior), was six feet, two inches tall, blue-eyed and fair-haired. Edvin Adolphson's equal in looks, charm and confidence, he was also a man of professional achievement.

Born March 1, 1907, in Stöde, a village in rugged northeast Sweden, Petter Aron Lindström was the son of Alfred Lindström, the architectural landscape gardener for the county, and his cultured wife, Brita Lisa Söderberg. His second name honored a devoted uncle, and so from childhood he was addressed as Aron or, in the Swedish tradition, as Petter Aron. At twenty, he received a degree in dentistry from the University of Heidelberg; four years later, he was awarded an advanced degree in dental research from Leipzig. That spring of 1934, Petter had both a professorship and an active practice in dentistry and was pursuing advanced studies in medicine. A gifted and successful physician, he also had many cultural and athletic interests. Proficient on the ski slope and in the boxing ring, he was an avid hiker, an admirable swimmer and a tireless prodigy on the dance floor. But he did not seem much interested in theater or movies.*

Early in the new year, Petter was invited to join Margit and her boyfriend as the escort for Ingrid at a dinner dance at the Grand Hotel. "I like your hair," he told her that evening. "And what a beautiful voice you have." With such expressed admiration, he progressed quickly. Ironically, it was perhaps because her self-confidence was bolstered by Edvin Adolphson that Ingrid could accept the chaste wooing of the very proper young dentist that spring.

At home, Otto and Hulda knew nothing of the Adolphson affair, but they endorsed the growing friendship between their niece and the handsome young dentist. He had an established and honorable profession, he was the soul of charm, he made himself endlessly agreeable, and very soon Ingrid began to elicit his opinions and to rely on his judgment and counsel on, among other things, matters

---

*When he came to America, Petter dropped the accented vowel in his surname and thenceforth signed his name Lindstrom. That form will be used hereinafter.

of health and diet. Whereas her liaison with Edvin was uncertain and furtive, Petter represented stability, and they could date quite openly. In addition, there was much in her that still needed the approval and guidance of a father (for which Edvin, too, was a surrogate), and there was much in Petter that was paternal and mentorial. "For an orphan girl like Ingrid," said her contemporary, Bertil Lagerström, "Lindstrom must have represented real security"—especially, it might be added, in the certainty and firmness he emanated. Petter was not the only eloquent and persuasive teacher in history to deploy his talents beyond the classroom, where he was sometimes (thus one of his disciples, Alice Logardt-Timander) "very feared by the students." He tended to dominate everywhere.

"It was not love at first sight," Ingrid said later of her early attraction, "but it grew into something which, to both of us, became very important and impossible to live without." Perhaps thinking of Edvin, she added, "And although I liked the young men of the theater, I felt that I could rely more on [Lindstrom's] common sense." By early summer 1934, she was seeing much of Petter. They often dined and danced on Saturday evenings, and on Sunday afternoons they strolled along the harbor and through the quiet glades of the lush isle of Djurgården, the royal family's former hunting ground and latterly the site of mansions, an amusement park like the Tivoli Gardens in Copenhagen, history exhibits, a detailed recreation of early Swedish life and riding trails. They had Sunday luncheon or afternoon tea at Hasselbacken, an elegant place with a merry, youthful clientele and a dance band in the late afternoon and evening; alternatively, they took a picnic lunch and hiked in the woods, Petter's knapsack filled with bricks he claimed were beneficial for toning muscles as he walked. Edvin she now met perhaps once in two weeks.

"I have never been able to talk about myself to anybody before you," Ingrid told Petter, who recalled years later: "I listened to her. I learned that she had endured a very difficult childhood and that she had no one in whom to confide at home. I also felt sorry for her and wanted to help her—and of course I liked her."

But for the present, he was unaware of her continuing trysts with Adolphson, and his devotion to the duties of his career dampened, for the present, the blaze of passion. "It took [Lindstrom] a long time to realize that he was in love with me," Ingrid later wrote in her memoirs. "I don't think that falling in love with an actress was in his plans at all . . . He fell in love almost without realizing what was happening."

During the summer holiday of 1934, Ingrid did not accompany her drama school colleagues on a theater tour of Russia. Edvin Adolphson, by this time aware of his attractive rival, shifted gears, the better to maintain the comfortable continuance of his affair with Ingrid. And his strategy, irresistible to the eager young actress, was simple. Contracted to direct a film comedy that summer, he put her in the only youthful female role and, working with writer Gösta Stevens, amplified her part. At the same time, he was only too happy to cast himself as her romantic leading man.*

The film was *Munkbrogreven* (*The Count of Monk's Bridge*, which refers to a picturesque section of Stockholm's Old Town); it was loosely based on a play by Siegfried and Arthur Fischer that owed a debt to the comic inventiveness of the French film director René Clair (in, for example, *Under the Roofs of Paris* and *Le Million*). On July 12, Ingrid began work on the film, for which she was paid a little more than $150. Required to work only twelve days, she was present daily for six weeks—not only for the pleasure of seeing Edvin at work, but because she wanted to learn from the director of photography, Åke Dahlquist, everything she could about the craft of movies, from lenses and lighting to trick photography and diffusion. Her father's daughter, she had always used a small box camera to document family occasions. Now she longed to watch every kind of shot and to absorb the world of cinema from her new colleagues.

An engaging comedy of bad manners, *Munkbrogreven* gave Ingrid ample opportunity to develop the character of Elsa, the vivacious chambermaid in a cheap hotel managed by her frumpy old aunt and often visited by good-natured local bootleggers keeping two paces ahead of the police. A mysterious stranger named Åke (played by

---

*The facts were altered for publication years later. Ingrid's publicist, writing in 1958, began the fiction that was maintained for decades to come—namely, that the florist Gunnar Spångberg, her father's old friend, introduced Ingrid to Karin Swanström, a comic actress who was also a talent coordinator for the film studio. According to this respectable account, Swanström arranged a screen test for Ingrid and at once sent her over to meet Edvin Adolphson, who was having difficulty casting a role in his new picture.

Adolphson) arrives and is wrongly thought to be a jewel thief plun-
dering the neighborhood and giving the bootleggers a bad name. At
last the real culprit is unmasked and Åke (who turns out to be an
investigative reporter) seals his romance with Elsa by marrying her.

Ingrid made an impressive debut, and Edvin was delighted for
both of them. Meeting the handsome stranger who intrigues her,
she registers fear, curiosity and erotic fascination. Nowhere is there
any sign of overreaction, of exaggerated grimace or scene-stealing;
instead—especially when she accompanies herself on the piano and
sings the jaunty lyrics of "Golden Chains Are Love's Bands"—
Ingrid gives a polished, natural portrait of a smitten girl eager to
believe the best about her young man. Carefully photographed by
Adolphson and lit by Dahlquist to take full advantage of her fair skin
and light brown hair in contrast with Adolphson's seductive, darkly
handsome features, Ingrid smiled naturally, radiated artless charm
and was at every moment a capable and confident ensemble player
among the cast of older veterans.

Much later, some chroniclers misrepresented Ingrid Bergman's
performances in Swedish films of the 1930s, thus diminishing the
significance of her European achievements before she went to
America. But with *Munkbrogreven*, audiences and the press recognized the presence of an alluring new actress. When the film was
released in January 1935, two reviewers summarized the critical
reaction. "In her film debut, Ingrid Bergman shows great talent and
confidence," wrote one, while another praised her as "a refreshing
and straightforward young lady, altogether an asset to the film."
From the start of her career, she appealed to audiences with her
unaffected vivacity and buoyant, lucid shift of emotions. There was
always, it seemed, an inner life provoking her character's outer
reactions; yet there was also something tentative about her display
of emotions. In other words, she seemed a real person, not a pur-
veyor of counterfeit sentiments.

She made a decision at once. On August 20, just before the students at Dramaten were to receive class assignments for the new
year, Ingrid arrived at the office of the new theater director, Olof
Molander, to announce her withdrawal. She had just completed a
picture, she said, adding that she had also begun a second and was
contracted for a third, to be directed by none other than Olof's

brother, the respected and successful Gustav Molander. "That surely took some initiative and some guts," Lindstrom recalled years later. "Olof Molander got furious and told her she would ruin a promising dramatic career. But she stuck to her guns." Rudolf Wendbladh, later the school's superintendent, agreed with the shortsighted view of Ingrid's teachers in 1934: "What a pity! To think what a fine actress she might have been!" He never recanted.

Racing back to the studio of the Swedish Film Industry, Ingrid was delighted to assume, in the program melodrama *Bränningar* (released fifteen years later in America as *The Surf*), a role very different from that of the girlish, lovestruck Elsa. As Karin, she played a poor fisherman's daughter, attacked by a lustful minister who leaves her pregnant and then quits town. Literally struck by lightning, he returns after his convalescence and is moved by the girl's courage as a devoted mother, despite public ostracism. The minister publicly confesses his guilt and renounces the clerical life, taking Karin and their child to a new life on a farm.

For the first time, Ingrid endured the rigors of location shooting, from which she learned even more about the craft of movies. On the small island of Prästgrund, off the northern coast of Sweden, there was the pervasive smell of rotting fish, but this she could ignore. "I was a prima donna two hours out to sea," Ingrid wrote in her diary.

> For the very first time people asked for my autograph. [The crew] all praise me, and I must keep my head with all these compliments. I only wish I had been really good in every scene. In the rehearsals I think it is good, but then there is a take and somehow it is not the same. One thing that made me happy was that Sten Lindgren, the actor who plays my clergyman lover, believes our love scenes are so passionate that possibly they will not get past the censor.

Those problem shots were not expurgated, but neither, alas, was the somewhat damp and overripe scenario. Not for the last time, Ingrid dignified indifferent material (written by the director, Ivar Johansson) and made a rather dreary, one-note character both credible and sympathetic without a touch of nagging sentimentality. "She is superb!" acclaimed one typical review when the film was released, just a month after *The Count of Monk's Bridge*. "Her acting is well balanced and tender, and she is gracious and true."

Back at the Stockholm soundstages, word circulated about the genial nineteen-year-old ingenue who memorized quickly, never complained about retakes or the rigors of location work and found everything interesting. "Because in the background was always [Lindstrom]," she said, "I went ahead full of confidence. Even when I didn't see him for some time, I knew he was always there to help and advise me." Even Otto and Hulda were impressed with their niece's success.

Before she rushed into her third picture, in November 1934, the film company added to Ingrid's contract a $500 annual guarantee and the incentive of a 20 percent raise each succeeding year. This was nothing like the compensation given to seasoned professionals like Edvin Adolphson or Karin Swanström, but Ingrid was— then and forever—more concerned for good work and professional growth than for high wages. Stage work, as she had been repeatedly told, rarely made actors wealthy, nor was great wealth ever a factor in her negotiations. As long as she was reasonably comfortable (which she certainly was at home with her relatives) and had a variety of roles (which her employers were certainly providing), Ingrid left to fate the matter of money. If she was effective, she would be paid well: that was her reasoning. She sought excellence, not riches. Popularity, on the other hand, she saw as a sign of public approval, and for that she was avid.

The year ended with her participation in a film of Hjalmar Bergman's story of an eccentric family, *Swedenhielms*, directed by Gustav Molander. Depression-era comedies the world over offered tales of rich families suddenly reduced to penury but muddling happily along; there were also unlikely narratives of the happy poor struggling alongside the troubled rich. The Swedenhielms have another dilemma: Papa, a scientist, covets the Nobel Prize, while his three children are adult only in age and covet the perquisites of such a status. Capricious, self-righteous and vain, they finally learn the meaning of true honor from their housekeeper (an affecting and comic character played by Karin Swanström). Simultaneously, Papa, Job-like, is awarded his heart's desire after learning the painful lesson that he has ignored his family's honor. Everyone—including Astrid (Ingrid), a rich girl willing to support a penniless scientist's shiftless son—thus learns the meaning of true responsibility and gets rich in the bargain.

Ingrid's role was certainly tangential, but her real happiness was the realization of her teenage dream—"to act in a play with Gösta Ekman," whom she had so adored on stage and screen. "As if he was my father," she observed plaintively, "he inspired me in a very mystical way. I adore him more than ever." For his part, Ekman was impressed with her professionalism and promised they would work together again. "You are really very talented," he told her. "You help me to play because your face and expressions reflect every word I say. That is very rare nowadays." And as critics noted, Ingrid's scenes with co-star Håkan Westergren united the ardor of a lovestruck girl with the fear of a woman who may lose her man.

"I found working with Gustav [Molander] wonderful," Ingrid said later of the director who

taught me how to underplay, to be absolutely sincere and natural. "Never try and be cute," he said. "Always be yourself and always learn your lines." On the set he gave me a great sense of security. He was never rushing off to telephone or attending to a dozen other details like some directors I've known. He was always concentrating on you.

But grateful and cooperative as she was, Ingrid was often restless with details. After many retakes for a scene in *Swedenhielms* (necessary because of camera problems), she finally finished and was told to go by Molander. But then the cinematographer called out, "Don't leave, Ingrid! We're changing the lights for the next scene—stay right on your mark."

"It's hot in here," she replied, "and I have to get some rest."

INGRID BEGAN THE NEW YEAR 1935 WITH HOPE AND ANXIETY: SHE longed for and dreaded her first premiere, the opening night of *Munkbrogreven* at the Skandia Theater on January 21. "I am insecure and secure at the same time," she confided in her diary. "I am unsure about all the publicity there has been. I hope the public will think I can live up to it. What would Mama and Papa have said if they could see me here in my loneliness? I long to be able to creep into someone's arms to find protection and comfort and love."

This comfort was offered by Lindstrom, who managed a week's holiday that winter: he and Ingrid went skiing in Norway. A break from work was, then as later, very rare indeed for him: focused on his career, he saw private life as only one part of life—and that, perhaps, was not the most important. Dedicated to his science and devoted to his patients, he was ambitious to contribute his talents to the fullest extent—thus his concern for the poor as much as for his own good reputation. From Lindstrom as from her teachers and directors, Ingrid Bergman learned the primacy of work in her life. Acting for her was a vocation as much as medicine was for him: not merely a job, it was a calling to a high and worthy art, not merely a route to solvency or celebrity.

"She is not very intelligent, but she is special," Lindstrom said of Ingrid, perhaps assessing only her formal education, her inexperience of the world; perhaps, too, he referred to her girlish candor and the ease with which she both laughed and expressed her opinions. But he was wrong, for she had a quick intelligence, a facility for learning languages and an alacrity for memorizing complicated scripts. That year, a news article coolly observed that "Lindstrom's parents' house at Stöde has become a second home for the orphan Ingrid Bergman."

The closer the young couple drew together, the more Lindstrom became protector, guardian and counselor to his willing girlfriend. By this time, he was regularly, according to a journalist friend, "giving Ingrid good advice—and not one movie scene with Ingrid left the laboratories that had not been passed by the art-loving dentist." Surely this overstates the case, for neither of them had any influence at all in the final cut of her films. She was a contract player, such decisions were made by higher authorities, and in any case a beau's opinion would have been disregarded even more quickly than a husband's. Still, Lindstrom's lifelong disclaimer that he made any impression at all on Ingrid's career decisions is contradicted by the facts of the matter.

Certainly she elicited his feelings, and just as certainly he offered them. Additionally, Lindstrom had a wise business sense, and Ingrid was aware of her deficiency in this regard. His later protestations of diffidence and uninvolvement in her professional life disregarded his dedication, both in Sweden and later in America, to her career. "From the very beginning," according to Ingrid's old friend, the columnist Marianne Höök, "Ingrid was a strong woman always looking for a stronger man." Such indeed was Petter Aron Lindstrom.

Her personal happiness was augmented by good work in 1935. After working with her idol Gösta Ekman, Ingrid continued to advance rapidly when she appeared in films with Lars Hanson, Victor Sjöström and, again, with Edvin Adolphson and Karin Swanström. To the first, Gustaf Edgren's *Valborgsmässoafton* (*Walpurgis Night*), she brought a strength and conviction that prevented the part of the secretary-as-faithful-lover from becoming a cliché. The film, a bold story for its time, was not released in America until January 1941, when the censors made ample cuts: it concerned a woman (Karin Carlsson) who aborts a pregnancy rather than defile her youthful good looks. This act outrages her husband (Hanson), who is already attracted to his secretary Lena (Ingrid), daughter of a powerful and highly moral newspaper publisher (Sjöström). In scenes of both love and confrontation, Ingrid—at the peak of her youthful beauty and lovingly photographed by Martin Bodin— showed how well she had learned from Molander the art of under- playing and acting with pellucid sincerity.

By this time, Ingrid's confidence had increased. On her way to work one day, she met Karin Swanström, whose presence was not required on the set and who was doing her double duty as studio casting agent. "What a dreadful hat you've put on, Miss Bergman!" said Swanström, peering through her lorgnette. "That isn't for the scene, is it?"

Ingrid replied that it was: "You're the only one who doesn't like it!"

"Not only that," said Swanström. "Here I make the decisions. We shall have another hat."

"And I am the one who is playing the part, which gives me the right to have an opinion."

The lorgnette, according to one eyewitness, fell from Swanström's hand as Ingrid, proudly wearing the hat, continued her way to work.

In more delicate situations she held her ground, too. A particularly powerful studio executive, aware of the Adolphson affair, decided he would make his own move, and so he informed Ingrid that she was required for a press junket in Gothenburg to promote *Walpurgis Night*. Ready for bed in her sleeping compartment on the train, she heard a tap at her door and opened to find the executive, wearing long underwear and carrying a bottle of champagne. "I thought we should say 'Du,'" he announced with a smile, referring to the familiar, second-person singular form of the verb not casually used in professional situations at the time.

"Nothing doing," said Ingrid in English, punning cleverly and then closing the door in his face.

HER NEXT PICTURE, *PÅ SOLSIDAN* (*ON THE SUNNY SIDE*), WAS A TRIFLE OF a romance, but with co-stars Hanson and Adolphson she completed an exceedingly attractive triangle. On and off the set, Ingrid was as cordial to Adolphson as to the others in the production, but although she continued to consider him both an ally and a friend, she was now deeply involved with Lindstrom and no longer accepted invitations from Edvin. Of Adolphson's reaction to the end of the affair nothing is known, although afterward he never lacked the esteem and company of other appreciative women.

With this movie, Ingrid's star and stock among Swedish critics continued to rise: "Ingrid Bergman is blindingly beautiful and acts with strong inspiration," wrote one enamored journalist when the movie was released in February 1936—her fifth picture in one year. "She handles every line to perfection." Added a colleague: "Ingrid Bergman has matured as an actress and a woman. One simply must surrender to her beauty and talent." When it began a New York run in the summer of 1936, Ingrid was reviewed for the first time in the American press—and favorably, too, as an actress who "rates a Hollywood berth" (*Variety*). The *New York Times* critic, who found the film tedious, nevertheless praised her "natural charm [that] makes it all worthwhile . . . Miss Bergman dominates the field."

There was no Greta Garbo feature released in America that year, and Marlene Dietrich's career had begun an uncertain dip after a tight alliance with director Josef von Sternberg. In New York, therefore, crowds lined up that season outside the Cinéma de Paris to see the new Swedish beauty "whose star [thus concluded the *Times* review] has risen so rapidly in the Scandinavian film firmament."

MEANTIME, IN EARLY 1936, MISS BERGMAN AND DR. LINDSTROM marked two years of unofficial courting—a relationship sealed by Petter's kindness when Uncle Otto died suddenly on March 12. "I remember how attentive Petter was," Ingrid said later.

> His kindness and consideration touched me deeply. I soon discovered that this was not unusual in him. He was very generous and always ready to help. Old and young came to him for advice or just to cry out their troubles on his shoulder. Everybody said how happy they were for me to have found such a fine man. And so was I.

Now it was time for Ingrid to introduce Petter to Aunt Mutti, and so they ferried to Germany. Frau Adler was duly impressed with Dr. Lindstrom's credentials, his manner and bearing, his charm and his excellent German, and she endorsed the attraction between her niece—a Kindernatur, as she called Ingrid (a child of nature, of the moment), well balanced by a young scholar.

But from the first hour of their arrival, he was alarmed. Frau Adler had become, as he said, "an ardent Nazi—and her boyfriend now manufactured uniforms for the SS! In Mutti's home, the salute and the cries of 'Heil Hitler!' were not only common but also essential. And Ingrid, to please her aunt and to avoid trouble, routinely used the salute with her arm outstretched." For the moment, Lindstrom said nothing, although he refused to affect the same political enthusiasm. His apprehension deepened, when he was told by Frau Adler that he would have to drop his second name: "In our family, we cannot have someone with the Jewish name Aron." This was an odd assertion from one who bore so obviously a German Jewish name as Adler, but perhaps her connection to her lover was enough to establish her dedication to the Reich.

There was more. At a dinner party that evening, Mutti's boyfriend proclaimed that Herr Goebbels, minister of propaganda and thus head of the German film industry headquartered at UFA

Studios in Berlin, was an admirer of Ingrid; as the daughter of a German mother, she might anticipate a future as a major German film star. There was the clink of champagne glasses, a wish for good luck—and then her aunt's lover clicked his heels and gave the Nazi salute.

Chapter Three

1936–1938

Marriage: a community consisting of a master, a mistress,
and two slaves—making, in all, two.

AMBROSE BIERCE,
The Devil's Dictionary

I NGRID MOST CERTAINLY WAS NOT A NAZI," PETTER LINDSTROM SAID.
"She just wasn't interested in politics and she knew little about
the basic issues of Nazism. But she spent a lot of time with her aunt,
who was a fanatic Nazi."

Nor had Ingrid taken any interest in such discussions in Sweden, as attested by students she had known at Dramaten. "We were
all politically ignorant at that time," said actress Lilli (Mrs. Gunnar)
Björnstrand. According to Irma Christensson, "Never once did I
hear Ingrid utter any positive feelings about Nazism or Hitler. But
none of us discussed politics in those days. We were artists, and as
such we felt that we were above politics."

From a desire to please her aunt and to advance her prospective
career in Germany, Ingrid adopted the salute and the cry of "Heil
Hitler!" when they were expected of her at Mutti Adler's home.
The deeper symbolism of these gestures, and how they might be

interpreted, seem never to have occurred to her. Completely cen-
tered on her career, she was bored by discourses on politics and
politicians, whether Swedish, German, American or others. Proud
of her mother's German roots and grateful to her aunt, Ingrid was
happy to appear a good German in Germany, just as she was a good
Swede in Sweden. "Everybody around her was saluting Hitler in all
personal contacts—and even in telephone calls," Petter recalled
years later. "She thought nothing of it." But later, Petter used
Ingrid's pro forma Nazi customs of that time as censure, and so she
felt an enormous conflict—the pressure simultaneously to please
her family and Lindstrom even while her real concern was reserved
for her career. Thus there were sown the deep seeds of a guilt she
would eventually have to confront, for at this time she closed herself
off from acknowledging the horrific menace that was growing
clearer to the entire world.

Petter and Ingrid returned to Stockholm, and on March 28 she
began work on the film that would change her life forever. Director
Gustav Molander and his writing partner Gösta Stevens had prepared an original screenplay called *Intermezzo*, and for Ingrid's leading man, they had again signed Gösta Ekman, who was delighted to
be working with her once more.

THE STORY WAS SIMPLE, AND MOLANDER KNEW AUDIENCES WOULD FIND
it irresistible. With an original musical score that included a romance
for violin that has endured in popularity for over sixty years, *Intermezzo*
concerns Holger Brandt (Ekman), a concert violinist who spends
most of his life on tour and is virtually a stranger to his wife and children. Returning home in time for his young daughter's birthday, Holger meets her piano teacher, the lovely and talented Anita Hoffman
(Ingrid). One evening soon after, they both happen to attend the
same concert, and afterward he invites her for a champagne supper.
In what would later be called a midlife crisis, the bored and restless
Holger (at least twenty years Anita's senior) is at once smitten with
her, and he sets an atmosphere of frank seduction: strolling by the
harbor after supper, they watch the winter ice floes break up and drift
out to sea. For this scene, Molander and Stevens wrote in the spirit of
German nature-romanticism: the images and dialogue suggest the
melting of repression and the imminent explosion of springtime.

HOLGER (Ekman): The ice floes are on their way to the sea—a marvelous journey!

ANITA (Bergman): But the depths below are dark and cold.

HOLGER: But it's danger that gives joy to the journey.

ANITA: It will melt long before it reaches the open sea.

HOLGER: Exactly. That's what's so wonderful. Just drift with the
stream—carried away by the storm of spring. Become one with
the sea! Melt into life itself—take life by storm!

ANITA: Take life by storm!

HOLGER: Are you afraid of life?

ANITA: No—tonight I could do—anything.

Well, "anything" does not occur that night, but soon enough
Holger and Anita are lovers, and she agrees to put her own career on
hiatus to travel with him around the world as his piano accompanist.
His wife sues for divorce, and this coincides with the news that Anita
has won a competition that will advance her own career. She also
sees clearly that Holger desperately misses his wife and children. "He
thinks he still loves me," Anita tells Holger's manager, "and maybe
he does, in his way. But this is just an intermezzo in his life."

Very few actresses could negotiate the thickets of the film's
florid dialogue or make credible the romantic clichés to which
Anita's character is subjected. But Ingrid's natural approach to the
role created the impression that, minute by minute, this woman was
both ecstatically in love and fearful of being abandoned.

Caught between her need to love and her resolve to let go of her
lover, Ingrid summarized the character in one moment. Embracing
Holger in farewell, she glances over his shoulder toward his manager, who nods at her as if to say, "You're doing the right thing." But
her sad, knowing gaze conveys something else: "The intermezzo is
over," she seems to be thinking. Ingrid's sensitivity to the role of
Anita gave the film a subtle emotional structure. In the first third of
the picture, Anita seems to fall in love with Holger as the devoted
teacher and father of a young daughter (the father, it is implied, that
Anita herself lacks). Then her sentiments shift from teacher-father
to musician-father, and then to father-figure as lover.

"She always moved with wonderful grace and self-control,"
according to Gustav Molander.

She spoke her lines beautifully and her radiant beauty struck me the first time I saw her. She appreciated compliments, accepted them shyly, but they never altered the three totally original characteristics of her work: truth, naturalness and fantasy. I created *Intermezzo* for her, but I was not responsible for its success. Ingrid herself made it successful through her performance. The truth is, nobody discovered her. Nobody launched her. She discovered herself.

The circumstances of filming were exhausting for everyone. Because Ekman was also appearing in the theater each night, the cast and crew rehearsed scenes for *Intermezzo* by day and filmed from midnight to dawn. "At five o'clock one morning, I was really tired," Molander recalled, "but there was Ingrid, ready and eager as usual for the shot that was required of her. I told her about my problem with the script at that point, she thought for a while, and then she played the scene in a manner that completely solved my problem. She had an intuition and imagination that never failed."

Throughout, her performance was never less than compelling, and decades later it still seems remarkably unselfconscious—and herein lies the key to her lifetime of character creations. Ingrid Bergman seemed, in the final analysis, to have no formal technique, and neither an intellectual approach nor a critical analysis attended her preparation. She never partook of learned or pretentious conversations about the psychology of acting.

On the contrary, Ingrid always approached a role simply and without affectation, then went away quietly, memorized the lines and returned—having at some point simply understood. And with that, she had a fully realized character ready. Certainly, she benefited from the counsel of sensitive directors and from discussions with them and a company of good actors. But from the start of each project she had a discerning grasp of the women she enlivened. The greatness of her achievements came not from academic analysis or psychological examination but from the rare gift of empathetic and imaginative awareness.

FOR *INTERMEZZO*, INGRID TRANSFERRED TO ANITA THE BURDENSOME challenge—the frequent clash between career and relationships—

that she herself confronted throughout her own life. Her portrait, in other words, was powerful precisely because it drew (however unconsciously) from her own experience. Ingrid's fierce devotion to her craft, even at the age of twenty, was based not only on a confidence about her gifts but also on the conviction (based on the experience of the deaths of her parents, aunt and uncle) that relationships were transitory. Like Anita, Ingrid could, in other words, count only on the compensations derived from dedication to talent. "I long to be able to creep into someone's arms to find protection and comfort and love," she had written in her diary. But artistic achievement gave her life its surest mooring. Ingrid was a realist, not a cynic.

The impossible moral idealism at the final fadeout of *Intermezzo*, with Holger in the arms of a forgiving wife, was nicely blunted by the preceding final close-up of Ingrid's face seen through the window of a departing train. But she also turns this cliché to her advantage. Her gaze is directed at something beyond the horizon, and this is not the image of noble self-sacrifice or self-pity. Quite the contrary: she provides the only emotional, adult realism—the picture of a woman whose integrity and future lie in an inevitable acceptance of her truest self. Thanks to her muted, convincing emotions, audiences were deeply moved and critics again agreed that the young actress could do no wrong. "Ingrid Bergman adds a new victory to her past ones," ran a typical notice.

As the production of *Intermezzo* concluded on June 19, Gustav Molander sent her a bouquet of flowers with a note: "You lift and clean and beautify my movie." As for Gösta Ekman, Ingrid wrote in her diary: "I know he is married and twenty years older than me [actually, twenty-five]. I know he has a son exactly my own age, born in August, too. Once I thought, If only I could marry his son, that would be heaven." Although (as with Edvin Adolphson) she had evidently found another father-mentor to love and trust—and who apparently loved her, too—the relationship seems to have remained platonic. That spring, Ekman was often ill and tired, and in fact *Intermezzo* was his last film: he died in January 1938 just after his forty-seventh birthday.

IMMEDIATELY AFTER *INTERMEZZO*, INGRID AND PETTER TRAVELED AGAIN to Frau Adler in Germany, where they announced their engagement and, on July 7, went to the church where her parents were married; there, in a quiet ceremony, she accepted a ring from Petter. He then returned to Stockholm and his studies, while Ingrid prolonged her visit with Aunt Mutti in Hamburg for over three months late in 1936.

During this time, she perfected her German, as Ingrid wrote enthusiastically to Petter, adding that she was devoting some private time to advanced lessons in English, too. An actress, she reasoned, could not have too much language proficiency. Petter replied, urging her not to become "too German" and to remember that she ought always to be a good Swede. Nonsense, said Mutti when Ingrid read his letter aloud: Frieda Adler Bergman was German, so Ingrid was as much German as she was Swedish. Still, Ingrid thought of herself most of all as an actress, and to hell with politics and international relations.

There was something of a role model for her that season in the case of Zarah Leander, the Swedish actress who came to Germany in the fall of 1936 and was at once groomed to replace Marlene Dietrich (who had departed for Hollywood in 1930) and to substitute for Greta Garbo (who had persistently refused every offer to work in Germany). Leander, who became one of the great stars of the Third Reich's culture, had the wistful melancholy and the "exotic" Scandinavian lilt of Garbo, the sexual ambiguity projected by Dietrich and the erotic forthrightness (and the figure) of Mae West. Playing singers and courtesans, faithful wives and forlorn mistresses, she was launched with a major advertising campaign and numerous press conferences. The studio even conceded to her demand for script approval and for the right to have 53 percent of her salary deposited in Swedish kronor at her Stockholm bank— two concessions granted to no German or foreign actor working at the studio.

IN MID-AUTUMN, INGRID RETURNED TO STOCKHOLM, AND ON JANUARY 15, 1937, she also returned to the theater, appearing at the Komediteatern in a Swedish production of the French play *L'Heure H* (*The Hour "H"*) by Pierre Chaine. *Timman H*, as it was called, was a rather limp satire on Communist revolutionaries planning sabotage in a factory. Ingrid, in a small role, "was pretty and pleasant to look at," as one critic wrote, "and she gave rich promise of future dramatic performances." The play ran for 128 performances.

Her film routine then resumed in early May, when Gustav Molander (by then her champion and mentor as much as D. W. Griffith was for Lillian Gish, Mauritz Stiller for Greta Garbo and Josef von Sternberg for Marlene Dietrich) put her in the leading role of a high-spirited actress named Julia in *Dollar*, a comedy of marital bad manners in which three couples flirt shamelessly in a rondo of silliness. Perhaps reaching for the combined energy and sophisticated sexual highjinks of Ernst Lubitsch, Clare Booth Luce and even Noël Coward, *Dollar* is, at the last, a windy business about people for whom it is difficult to care. The strong suit of the Swedish cinema was never screwball comedy, after all, and *Dollar* remains noteworthy only for Ingrid's evident lively flair for comic timing, and for hilariously spontaneous gestures and glances that kept her director, colleagues and crew merrily surprised each day.

She also surprised them and her audiences, as when she inserted just the right pause between a comic moment and a sudden realization of her character's essential longing for her business-obsessed husband: "Sometimes I feel so poor that I gladly beg for small lies." Even more affecting, because delivered unhysterically amid the prevalent dizzy spirit of the picture, is the melancholy tone of her speech to a friend, as Ingrid/Julia says of herself:

> You think you have fun, think you're in love, think you are loved. Like candles at a party. You stare blindly at the flames and forget that they soon go out. Belief after belief goes out—until at last only belief itself and death are left.

The final cut of the picture so clearly revealed Ingrid as the star that Molander placed her first in the credits—even above the name of Edvin Adolphson. "Owing to her superb comedy timing and her lustrous appearance," wrote a senior newspaper critic when the film was released, "Ingrid Bergman overshadows them all."

SHE CONTINUED TO ECLIPSE OTHERS FIVE DAYS AFTER THE PRODUCTION of *Dollar* was completed. Displacing from primary position every other news event of July 11, Sweden's most famous and admired movie star married a respectable dentist and physician. Hoping for a ceremony undisturbed by a media circus, they chose the remote parish church of Stöde and invited only friends and relatives. The press, however, had been alerted by a starry-eyed local, and so reporters and cameramen pitched camp, and the couple's exit from the church was photographed and wired round the world. It is no exaggeration to say that the Bergman-Lindstrom nuptial was a social event reported throughout Europe only slightly less comprehensively than the June wedding of His Royal Highness (and former Majesty) the Duke of Windsor to the American divorcée Wallis Warfield Simpson.

"My lover!" Ingrid wrote to Petter shortly before the wedding. "My sweetheart! My everything on this earth. How I adore you! I could burst . . . On our first church announcement of [the banns of the forthcoming] marriage, this little card I am writing in my bed. I am yours in every way. Longing for you all the time, I am only happy close to you. Come and stay with me. I love you for eternity.—Yours forever, Ingrid." She was scarcely, as some later claimed, a dispassionate bride; nor, her attitude implied, was he a disappointing companion.

But Ingrid could not accurately be described as living entirely in the grip of a romantic fantasy.

> Before the wedding, my thoughts were mixed up with a lot of questions. My work meant everything to me. I loved it very much and I wondered what marriage might do to it. There were no simple answers, but I was sure of one thing—I didn't want to lose Petter.

At thirty, Lindstrom was certainly ready to settle down at last with the girl he had courted for four years. For one thing, they were exquisitely attractive people and both loved a good time when they could retreat from their demanding professional schedules: they both liked dancing at nightclubs, skiing holidays, parties and games with congenial colleagues and acquaintances. These were not very frequent indulgences, but they seized every possibility and enjoyed privately each other's buoyant spirits and boundless energies.

Petter was fundamentally a man of earnest character who did

not suffer fools gladly, and much of the theatrical social life he saw
as folly. "My father," said Pia Lindstrom years later, "represented
stability and knowledge and somebody who seemed intelligent and
capable"—someone, in other words, who saw the academic life as
superior.

Before the wedding day, had Petter any hesitation similar to
Ingrid's? So it seems. In June, he asked an older female friend if he
dared marry a beautiful young actress: would this not be a disastrous mismatch of personalities and interests? The friend met
Ingrid and confidently told Petter, "Yes, with a woman like this, you
dare it indeed." And so he did, despite the fact that he knew the
risks to which the performer's life, insecurities and complex ego
were prey. "When my husband married me," Ingrid said, "he knew
he had a selfish actress on his hands." Devotion to her craft was
bound to make it a jealous third party to their commitment—as, it
might be said, was Petter's dedication to his. Their commitments to
their careers, they both suspected, might jeopardize their commitment to each other.

As for subtler emotional issues, Ingrid (fun-loving, casual, less
formal and eight years younger than her earnest spouse) was candid:
"Well, yes, perhaps he was a continuation of my father," she said
years later,

> and I suppose I was looking for a second father. [Petter] trained
> and organized me . . . I had always been managed by men—first
> by my father, then by Uncle Otto, then by my directors. And
> then by Petter, who exercised a very strong control over me.
> Instead of teaching me to be independent, to act for myself, he
> tied me down by being helpful, by doing everything for me, mak-
> ing all the decisions for me. But I have to admit it: I was some-
> what to blame, for in the beginning I constantly asked Petter for
> advice and guidance and completely relied on him.

In this regard, of course, the Lindstrom marriage was not at all
unusual.

At the outset, things proceeded smoothly enough. After a motor
trip to Norway and England, the newlyweds moved into Lindstrom's Stockholm apartment in the same neighborhood that Ingrid

had known all her life. Located at 14 Grev Magnigatan, the flat was a smart penthouse with a large terrace facing west—certainly the most elegant home she had since her father's on Strandvägen. Here, the Lindstroms welcomed acquaintances from the worlds of film and theater, medicine and journalism. The reporter Barbro Alving (who in the press called herself "Bang") often visited, along with the satiric cartoonist Einar Nerman and a few colleagues of Petter's. On such casual occasions, they engaged a cook, for while Ingrid kept a tidy and ordered household and did not mind scrubbing and cleaning, she was still hopeless in the kitchen and resolutely refused to learn about anything that required an icebox, oven or stove. "Preparing for dinner" meant dressing for a restaurant.

ON OCTOBER 2, INGRID BEGAN HER EIGHTH PICTURE AND THE FIFTH under Gustav Molander's direction: En Enda Natt (Only One Night), which Ingrid thought, immediately after reading the script, was "a piece of junk." To please Molander—and to play a better role that loomed on the horizon—she cut a bargain. The remarkably fecund Gösta Stevens had just completed the outline for another script, based on a French play, about a beautiful woman whose face and character had become grotesquely disfigured after a dreadful fire. Ingrid agreed, therefore, to do Only One Night for Molander on condition that he convince the reluctant studio executives to allow her to play in A Woman's Face. The deal was made—and, Molander added, Ingrid's name would appear first in the billing for both pictures.

En Enda Natt was a curious film that dared to deny audience expectations. As Eva Beckman, a doctoral candidate in philosophy, a gifted pianist, a sportswoman and the ward of a wealthy aristocrat, Ingrid had never been so lavishly outfitted or radiantly photographed. Her leading man was none other than Edvin Adolphson, as a circus barker named Waldemar, who turns out to be the illegitimate son of the aristocrat. But once he has been groomed and trained to assume his rightful inheritance, he finds that his passionate nature is unappreciated by the cool (even perhaps frigid) Eva. Socially miscast and romantically rejected, he returns to his former life (and girlfriend), and Ingrid as Eva is left alone with her piano and her philosophy books—Anita Hoffman as scholar-in-residence.

But if Molander and the production team certainly knew how to beguile moviegoers with a luminous rendering of a comely couple, writer Gösta Stevens had something else in mind: Ingrid as a woman who so idealizes love that she is repulsed by the idea of its sexual expression. The progress of a torrid love scene, for example, is abruptly terminated when Waldemar's insistent kisses send Eva into a tantrum of tears and angry recriminations. Decades later, it is still difficult to know just how these characters are to be assessed: is *En Enda Natt* a plea for premarital chastity (a gloss, as it were, on *Walpurgis Night*) or for psychoanalysis (a gloss on latent lesbianism or the pathology of the frigid woman)? Is Eva Beckman to be praised as the guardian of her destiny, virtue and class? Or is she to be scolded because she is not Lady Chatterley? In any case, Ingrid Bergman was too lovely for the good of the film, whatever that was.

Stevens and Molander struggled to tell a story contradicting the facile happy resolutions of the American screwball comedies of the 1930s (*It Happened One Night* and *My Man Godfrey*, for example), which maintained that romance would make everything just fine, thank you, and that divergent social and cultural backgrounds could be quickly transformed in the sea of true love. But the thesis of Molander and Stevens simply did not work. Because Ingrid did, however, she almost made it possible for viewers to believe in her confused character. And the choice of Adolphson was fascinating, since he was still a strikingly handsome matinee idol, whether dressed in the work clothes of a circus barker or the white tie required for dinner with the aristocracy. He and Ingrid, no longer lovers offscreen, much enjoyed their collaboration and sealed a life-long friendship; with their humor and mutual goodwill, it is easy to imagine them amused rather than embarrassed by their contrived dialogue and aborted love scene.

Production was completed on December 20, and Ingrid had a free month before beginning *A Woman's Face*. Two days before Christmas, Petter regretfully told her that the press of clinic duties short-circuited their plans for a ski trip to Norway; he was now, besides his private practice, busy as associate professor of dentistry at the Karolinska Institute. Whatever disappointment she may have felt was quickly compensated when Petter presented her with a luxurious fur coat and the promise of a long summer holiday in the coming year.

But even more welcome was professional news. A poll of Swedish moviegoers put Ingrid ahead of Greta Garbo as the most admired movie star of the year 1937 (15,208 votes for Ingrid and 10,949 for Garbo, whose stock in Sweden had declined steadily each year after her departure for Hollywood). Furthermore, *Intermezzo* had opened on Christmas Eve in New York, where Ingrid's popularity at once required additional screenings in the holiday movie schedule. "The sincerity of the acting, especially on the part of the young charming Ingrid Bergman," wrote the *New York Times* reviewer, "confirms the good opinions she has won at home and abroad." Summarizing the unanimous opinion of American reviewers, *Variety* proclaimed her "a talented, beautiful actress [whose] star is destined for Hollywood." And so it was—but the journey was delayed by a detour to Germany.

OTHER ARTISTS HAD BEEN WOOED TO THE VAST AND TECHNICALLY superior resources of Universum Film-Aktiengesellschaft (UFA, located at the Neubabelsberg studios, outside Berlin), where from 1917 to 1933 some of the great international cinema masterworks were produced. Among the directors who had worked there earlier were Ernst Lubitsch, Fritz Lang, Alfred Hitchcock, Erich Pommer, Robert Wiene, Josef von Sternberg, F. W. Murnau and G. W. Pabst. Zarah Leander was the leading actress at the studio in 1937.

Everything had changed with the Third Reich. Jews were unemployable, and so many talented writers, directors, designers and actors were no longer at the studio. In July 1933, it was decreed that everyone in German film had to be a German citizen or prove German ancestry, but soon Goebbels amended the law and allowed "non-Aryan" artists when necessary for the studio's political or economic advantage. That was the beginning of various adaptations that even the propaganda minister had to make to the film industry. Jews could be outlawed, but the idiosyncrasies of an entire industry could not be easily regulated. Criticism of the Nazis was openly voiced at UFA, and the censorship imposed on production was constantly decried. Even the click of heels and "Heil Hitler!" were considered vulgar at UFA and were routinely ignored.

This lapse from what was elsewhere strict practice had to be sustained, for Goebbels and company needed a variety of people to work in German films.

In addition, the Führer's empire tried to secure the services of an international array of players—hence the warm reaction Aunt Mutti and her lover received when they spoke of their beloved Ingrid (known as a Swedish star) to a friend at UFA and arranged to have one of Ingrid's films privately screened there. "The idea to sign her up happened as soon as Goebbels and his associates saw one of her Swedish pictures," reported a Swedish correspondent from Berlin on November 30, 1937. "Seldom had they seen an actress with such spontaneity. 'She's as good an actress as she is charming in appearance,' they said."

Ingrid's work in Sweden had been arranged each year by a simple letter contract with Svensk Filmindustri, but Petter recognized that negotiations for a German picture must be very carefully handled. And so, early in the new year 1938, he brought in an old friend, the artists' agent Helmer Enwall, who assisted with the contract details, and soon Ingrid signed a deal for two films to be made in Berlin, the first that spring. "With this contract, Ingrid Bergman begins a new artistic development in her career," announced UFA's international press bulletin.

As it happened, the ground of her career and the direction of her life were being altered by developments thousands of miles away and without her immediate awareness. Like many Hollywood producers, David O. Selznick also maintained a New York office. There, two savvy women named Katharine Brown and her assistant Elsa Neuberger had the task of scouting plays, securing literary rights, viewing foreign films and suggesting new talent for Selznick to add to his roster. One afternoon in January, a young Swedish elevator operator mentioned to Elsa that his parents had just seen *Intermezzo*. "I know you're always looking for properties," the boy told her, "and my parents are just crazy about the picture and a nice girl in it. Maybe you should look at her."

The rest, as the saying goes, is history. Elsa saw *Intermezzo* at the Cinéma de Paris in Manhattan, and she reported enthusiastically to Kay Brown, who also saw it and was similarly impressed. Kay at

once sent a cable to Selznick suggesting that he secure the rights to
Intermezzo and plan an American version of it (perhaps even with
Bergman), and she followed that recommendation with the reviews,
some photos and (after considerable negotiations with the New
York distributor for Svensk Filmindustri) a print of the picture. But
Selznick was submerged in the preparations for a film version of
Gone With the Wind, and so he delegated the viewing of *Intermezzo* to
a small team of senior employees. "A group of us ran the picture,"
according to production manager Raymond Klune.

> We didn't know precisely what we were looking at, but we were
> fascinated with it, even though it was all in Swedish with English
> subtitles. It was sort of a romantic soap opera type of thing, but
> we were all impressed with Ingrid Bergman and we told him that
> we all thought she was great, sensational, let's get her by all
> means.

To this Selznick replied that he thought they were looking at the
picture to determine its suitability for an American remake, not to
bring over a new star. "Yes, by all means," replied Klune, "but
remake it with her." Selznick then sat through half the film, liked
what he saw and realized that, as with many foreign pictures and
actors, he could probably secure rights and import actors for rela-
tively little money. But *Gone With the Wind* and plans for a film of the
equally popular novel *Rebecca* occupied Selznick virtually around the
clock (thanks to both his hyperactive personality and his habit of
taking the amphetamine Benzedrine), and so for the first several
months of 1938, discussions of an American *Intermezzo* and the
importing of Ingrid Bergman slipped to a lower place on Selznick's
agenda. Kay Brown continued gently to badger her boss with polite
reminders about Miss Bergman, who was already receiving offers
from London and from other Hollywood producers.

Miss Bergman had a very full life that season, and she especially
anticipated working at UFA. Before her departure for Berlin that
spring of 1938, she created one of her most intense and complex
portrayals, that of Anna Holm in *A Woman's Face*, which began filming on January 18. Then, during production, Ingrid learned that she

was pregnant. She and Petter celebrated with a champagne supper and dancing at the Café Royale of the Grand Hotel.

A character to challenge the most accomplished actress, Anna would have been easy for Ingrid to misrepresent as a romantic cliché; instead, she brought contours and shadings that humanized a role alternately grotesque and incredible—and thus dismissed forever any doubt about her eminence as an actress. Facially disfigured in childhood when a fire killed her alcoholic parents, Anna has inherited her family's dissolute character: at the center of a ring of crooks, she is a woman without conscience or warmth. But when a plastic surgeon, the husband of one of her intended blackmail victims, restores her beauty, a slow spiritual transformation begins as well. Risking herself to save a child for whom she has become governess, she also redeems herself.

Petter stepped in to help his wife with the problem of her makeup. "He did something quite brilliant," she noted years later, detailing how he invented "a sort of brace which fitted inside my mouth and pushed out my cheek. Then, with glue, we pulled the eye down on the other side—it wasn't possible to get the right effect with ordinary makeup—and then, oh, did I look a fright!"*

THE PLOT OF *A WOMAN'S FACE* WAS (AS SO OFTEN IN THE MOLANDER-Stevens collaboration) needlessly complicated and often inhibited by repetitious, attenuated episodes. But the final effect is both chilling in its depiction of evil and poignant in the revelation of a long-buried yearning for love in the soul of an embittered woman. It is a well-known fact of filmmaking that the sequences of motion pictures are almost always photographed out of narrative order, for producers and directors must depend on such variables as actors' schedules and the need to complete in one time unit all shots in each set or at a given exterior location, regardless of their various places in the scenario. There is also the unpredictability of the

---

*Ingrid's published memoirs were patched together by writer Alan Burgess, whose errors were both numerous and significant. In the discussion of *A Woman's Face*, for example, Burgess wrote that Anna Holm goes on trial for murder, and that this moment ends the film, leaving her fate to the audience's guess. But nothing remotely like this occurs.

weather and the demands of the approved budget. These exigencies, requiring films to be made out of sequence, have always imposed on film actors a unique challenge—that of creating a credible character in small bits and pieces of film, and the day's work is sometimes a jumble of sudden and confusing shifts in the emotions required. The first day's work may involve one of the final scenes; the second day may require an early scene, and so on. More than one screen actor has slipped badly on these rocky shoals.

From such necessities sometimes emerge artistic virtues, and audiences, who often feel indifferent to a character or an entire picture, can look to this predicament and even to the occasional miscalculation or incompetence of actors for the reason that a movie experience has been so deeply unsatisfying. Continuity may be expert in terms of matched shots; emotional coherence is another matter entirely.

In this regard, Ingrid did very little wrong throughout her career. Her subtle construction of Anna Holm was a prime example of a talent that could conceive a character moment by moment and could, therefore, represent the separate instances in a woman's life as self-contained carriers—as microcosms—of an entire identity. As the wretched crook, a woman who hates the world, she seemed to spit out her lines, plotting revenge against someone simply because of her advantages: "Doesn't she have everything a woman wants? Isn't she loved, admired, adored? Isn't she beautiful?—Well, then! Shouldn't she pay for it?" Later, this motif is carried forward: she resents a child (and even briefly considers harming him) simply because "You have everything! You're spoiled! You get whatever you want and get away with everything you can!" But the tearstained face of this child, as needy of a mother as of Anna (his new governess), causes the first crack in the hard heart of this woman whose face has been restored and whose spiritual recovery may now begin.

Crude and masculine as the criminal Anna, Ingrid gradually softened her, so that as the physical beauty is revealed, she makes it plausible that this, too, is an emblem of inner transformation. *A Woman's Face* thus became, with her expert understanding and her impeccable, subtle glances and reactions, a small gem, a drama in the tradition of Arthur Wing Pinero's haunting English play *The*

Enchanted Cottage. The deepest logic of these works is the need for spiritual metamorphosis, not the artifice of outer rejuvenation.*

INGRID'S PREGNANCY FORCED THE ADVANCEMENT OF THE PRODUCTION of her upcoming German film, originally scheduled for late May. Immediately after the conclusion of *A Woman's Face* on March 29, she proceeded to the UFA studios and was lodged in a comfortable rented, suburban house with the three German women signed to be her co-stars in *Die vier Gesellen* (*The Four Companions*), which began shooting in the second week of April.

Sweden's history of respect for Germany's sense of social order, artistic achievement and Lutheran tradition was much compromised after Hitler's rise to power in 1933, and the Swedish nostalgia for Germany caused serious ethical problems in the years before and during World War II. Many Swedes rejected anti-Semitism as well as the evident desire of the Reich to extend its empire beyond the frontiers of Germany. Several prominent Swedes, led by the king, an archbishop and a literary scholar, even believed they could persuade Hitler to modify his stance, but their journey to the Führer was futile. For one thing, he scorned Sweden's neutrality; for another, he promised to help Sweden greatly by purchasing matériel for German "defense"; at least two major Swedish manufacturers of armaments did massive business with Germany. In 1937, for example, twenty shipments of Swedish iron ore were exported to Germany. But the apparent collusion was diluted: even as Sweden allowed German troops to enter Norway via Swedish borders, Norwegians and Danes were given refuge in Sweden from Nazi persecution. Dual sympathies, in other words, were everywhere evident.

So much had been clear as early as 1933, when the Swedish parliament forbade the wearing of political insignia—meaning that

---

*Joan Crawford tried very hard, as usual, to enliven Anna Holm two years later in a glossy American remake of *A Woman's Face*; alas, she and director George Cukor seemed to have misperceived the Swedish original. Contrariwise, the 1945 American film *The Enchanted Cottage* (starring Dorothy McGuire and Robert Young, written by DeWitt Bodeen and Herman J. Mankiewicz and directed by John Cromwell) retained its poetic and emotional integrity decades later precisely because it was unafraid to affirm that love is never a matter of reliance on physical charm. Both stories concern the problem of disfigurement in a world increasingly obsessed with mere cosmetic appeal.

uniformed Nazis were unwelcome in public. Nor did the government remain silent when it was discovered that Germany was inter-
cepting and censoring mail from Germany to Sweden. In 1934,
Swedish police closed a Nazi office in a Stockholm hotel on the correct pretext that it was "an institution likely to disturb general
order." As it happened, the hotel director himself was a fervent
Nazi. A year later, eleven Nazis were jailed in a raid to enforce the
law against political groups that were military in character. The
stated opposition to Nazism by the Swedish parliament further
informed Swedes of the dangers of Nazism—and the threat to their
own security.

INGRID COULD HARDLY HAVE BEEN UNAWARE OF ALL THIS, AND SHE WAS
forthright about her decision to work in Germany:

> I took the German offer because I spoke the language—but not
> with the intention of staying in Germany at all. I had my eyes set
> on Hollywood, of course, but it was a question of waiting for the
> right opportunity. I'd never had any interest in politics, so I didn't
> know what I was doing . . . If I knew anything about politics, I
> would have had more sense than to go to Germany to make a
> picture in 1938.

Still, she added significantly, "You could feel there was something brewing [during the production of *Die vier Gesellen*], and the
fear was something unbelievable. But I wasn't interested and just
went there to make a movie." Perhaps with good reason, then,
Ingrid Bergman later nurtured a real guilt for a kind of passive
acquiescence in the terrible tenor of that time.*

Ironically, *Die vier Gesellen* was a dismal failure. The pallid story
of four young women who have no luck with their advertising
agency, it was a romantic comedy, a genre even less suited to the
German than to the Swedish temperament. Self-righteous about

---

*Petter Lindstrom's assertions about a meeting between Ingrid and Goebbels were
inconsistent. In a letter to her dated March 26, 1980, he admitted his agreement with Ingrid
that she never met Goebbels. But in a letter he drafted after her death, he wrote, "Through
Mutti, Ingrid met Goebbels." In fact, she never did.

sex, it also censured women's independent thinking—two issues which Nazi supervisors at UFA resolutely condemned. The pregnant Ingrid, who endured several weeks of morning sickness during production, looked vague and distracted for much of the film, as if she were as nauseated by the dialogue as by the normal trials of childbearing.

She was also troubled by the odd priority of the director, Carl Froelich, who continually stopped her in mid-scene when she made the slightest error in her German pronunciation. But everyone knew she was a Swedish import, Ingrid replied—and besides, she had acted the scene well. Still, her German was more important, Froelich insisted: she had to repeat the scene.

The picture was finished in late May, when Ingrid was five months pregnant. Petter came to Berlin, and together they drove to Paris and then down to Monte Carlo for a holiday. By early July, they were back in Stockholm, where Ingrid prepared for the birth of their baby and considered her future. As usual, Petter was at the ready with Helmer Enwall. "I asked him if he could find a studio in England or the USA that might offer Ingrid a job," Petter recalled. "Enwall obtained one offer from London and three from Hollywood, but the financial terms of these contracts were unexciting," and nothing came of the contacts. Ingrid signed with UFA to make two more films the following year.

On September 20, 1938, a girl was born to the Lindstroms, who named her Friedel Pia: the first name honored Ingrid's mother, the second was an arrangement of the parents' initials (Petter, Ingrid, Aron).* Later, the child was baptized by Pastor Bergman, still in service to the local parish.

The day after the baby's birth, while Ingrid was still confined in a clinic, she kept an appointment she and Petter had made two weeks earlier. To her room came a cultivated, intelligent lady named Jenia Reissar, who worked for David O. Selznick in London and Europe, in much the same capacity as Kay Brown in New York. Born to an educated and influential family in Russia, she had at first

*Ever the scientist, Petter observed that although "we made up the name Pia from our initials, the superficial, fine and soft cover of the brain is called 'pia,' a Latin name, and [because] brain anatomy fascinated me, Pia seemed okay as a second name."

studied medicine in London, but this was a profession in which women were unwelcome, and so Reissar had turned her considerable abilities to the arts. David Selznick was prudent enough to recognize her quickness and her helpful social contacts in Britain.

Reissar had received a wire from Selznick instructing her to proceed to Stockholm, buy the rights to *Intermezzo*, sign Ingrid Bergman to a contract and Gustaf Molander to direct. "The Lindstroms were very nice to deal with," Reissar said, "very reasonable and honest. If they said something, that was it—they didn't go back on their word." But with the excitement over the baby, no promises were made for the present and discussions were postponed for a few days. Meantime, Molander declined the offer. He spoke little English and had no desire to leave his family in Sweden for the uncertainties of Hollywood filmmaking.

A few days later, Ingrid invited Jenia Reissar to her apartment and said she was indeed very keen on going to Hollywood, where other Swedes had much success. After nine Swedish films, she had become one of Sweden's most admired and popular screen actresses, but as always she was not inclined to easy satisfaction. In addition, Ingrid knew that scripts like *A Woman's Face* were exceptional: whatever their charms, *Dollar* and *Only One Night* were artistically unchallenging. Work in America would, she believed, at least broaden her experience.

The offer was made even more attractive when Reissar said that Selznick would very likely engage the actor Leslie Howard, then at work in *Gone With the Wind*, as her leading man. "I will go to Hollywood for that!" said Ingrid at once.

"Her husband wasn't terribly pleased with the financial terms," Reissar said years later, and after some discussions Ingrid said that while she was most enthusiastic to go to America, she would not leave her infant daughter at once. Fine, said Reissar, who had been told to yield in the matter of timing—and with that she produced the standard seven-year contract for Ingrid's signature.

"She wouldn't sign right away," according to Jenia Reissar. "We met several more times, she and her husband wanted to know about every term in the contract, and she had many questions about the conditions of movie-making in America and about Selznick as a producer." And then Lindstrom addressed the major sticking point:

"He objected to her signing a long-term contract with options and he objected to the clause that could dismiss Ingrid if she got pregnant. So I removed those stipulations and we agreed on a one-picture deal. If she liked Hollywood, she and Selznick could discuss terms after *Intermezzo*."

By mid-October, Reissar had a new draft of the contract ready for Ingrid's signature. "I thought that by now it would be easy to get her to sign—which required her husband's approval, because he was the one who raised quite a lot of problems." And so for several days, the discussions continued. By that time, Selznick—unduly anxious that Ingrid was temporizing, and that he might indeed be displaced by another producer—had instructed Kay Brown to sail to Stockholm "and not come home without a contract with Miss Bergman," as he wrote later. The negotiations were complicated, and Petter insisted on bringing in Helmer Enwall and attorney Cyril Holm.

Petter might have delayed Ingrid's signature even longer had he known what confusions had swirled in Selznick's head. "A cold shudder has just run through me," he had written to Kay that summer. "Maybe we are dealing for the wrong girl. Maybe the girl we are after is Gosta [sic] Stevens. You had better check on this." Then Selznick waffled on the matter of assigning Ingrid to the remake of *Intermezzo*: for several weeks that autumn, he was committed to the idea of co-starring Loretta Young with Charles Boyer. But he still wanted Bergman under contract and instructed Kay Brown to supervise the final negotiations. Jenia Reissar, who had efficiently prepared the way, returned to her assignments in London.

BORN IN 1902, KATHARINE BROWN GRADUATED FROM WELLESLEY College in 1924 and then worked at a theater academy in New Hampshire. Joseph P. Kennedy was a patron of the school, and when he bought the Film Booking Offices of America (FBO), a movie production and distribution company, Kay accepted a job in the editorial and story department in 1926. Kennedy eventually merged FBO with the Radio-Keith-Orpheum enterprise and hired Kay to scout and purchase literary rights for the studio (*Cimarron* was among her first acquisitions).

In 1935, David Selznick engaged her as his New York associate, and Kay continued to bring to term some of the most important deals in movie history. The following year, she read Margaret Mitchell's novel *Gone With the Wind* before publication and prevailed on the diffident Selznick (who at first could not envision it as a successful picture) to buy the rights for $50,000 (at that time, the highest price ever paid for a book). Then, in 1937, Kay convinced Selznick to negotiate for the services of England's most popular director, Alfred Hitchcock, whose pictures were financially successful worldwide.

Kay, who had two young daughters back home, wanted Ingrid to assess the impact on her family of such a critical development in her career, and to be certain of the step she was about to take. But with Petter's approval, Ingrid was confident. Besides, as her husband said, "Ingrid really did not like Sweden"—an attitude to which she later admitted. "I am happy I was born Swedish because this means having a tough education—at least it was in my time. But I couldn't live there, even when I was in my twenties. Sweden is too far from the rest of the world psychologically. There you feel confined on an island."

But by the end of 1938, she had agreed to go to America the following spring to star in a Hollywood remake of *Intermezzo*, for which she would be paid the handsome sum of $2,500 weekly— one of the highest of the time and twice Vivien Leigh's salary for *Gone With the Wind*. If she or the picture was unsuccessful, she reasoned, she could return to Sweden or Germany.

"It was really Petter Lindstrom who supervised everything and made Ingrid accept Selznick's offer," recalled the Swedish actress Signe Hasso, who was also successful in America on stage and screen and later as a writer. "He deserves the credit for her coming to America. He helped her tremendously in her career and was always a great influence on her." Her husband, Ingrid confirmed, "trained and organized me . . . and if it hadn't been for him, I would never have gone to Hollywood." Petter also encouraged her to use English as much as possible before she departed Stockholm—and in these lessons she was much aided by Kay, who made three trips from New York to conclude negotiations and then to accompany Ingrid to America. As the time for departure drew near, the Lindstroms agreed that, since his wife would be absent only for a few months, it would be prudent to leave Pia behind and not subject her to transatlantic steamship travel. Petter engaged a nanny.

In all the discussions, Kay was impressed by Ingrid's lack of affectation, her directness, her warmth, good humor and conviction that refining her talent mattered much more than creating a false sense of movie-star glamour, which she knew was subject to the winds of time and fashion in any case. For her part, Ingrid admired and trusted the neat, elegant and bright Kay, thirteen years her senior. She could see things from every possible business and personal perspective, and, utterly without bogus charm or icy ruthlessness, she was very like a mother to Ingrid—guiding and urging, protecting and suggesting. Laurence Evans, later Ingrid's London agent, fairly summarized Kay Brown: "She was an altogether remarkable woman with a keen intelligence and personality. She was also a born leader, and of course that would have much appealed to Ingrid, especially at this stage of her career."

As for Ingrid, she was both thrilled with the thought of working in America and nervous about the outcome. "Sweden seemed too small and I felt I had to get to a bigger country . . . But I was scared to death that Hollywood would not like me."

Chapter Four

1939

Tomorrow I will discover Sunset Boulevard.

HENRY MILLER, "SOIRÉE IN HOLLYWOOD"

On Thursday morning, April 20, 1939, the *Queen Mary* docked in New York; aboard were Ingrid and Kay, who had made another journey abroad to help her new friend prepare for the journey. Installed, at Selznick's expense, in a room at the Chatham Hotel, Ingrid told Kay that she intended to waste no time in perfecting her English and her familiarity with American life. She wanted to have lunch and dinner at typical cafeterias and restaurants; she wanted to read the newspapers, listen to the radio and scan the comics; and most of all she wanted to go to the theater.

As for her first few meals, they were monotonous—a glass of wine and steak or a hamburger, inevitably washed down with strong coffee and topped off with her first exciting discovery, the American ice cream sundae: henceforth, she often ducked into Schrafft's, Child's, Louis Sherry or the Automat for two scoops of vanilla, a double serving of hot fudge and a generous peak of whipped cream ("I never did get sick, I only got fat!"). Forever after, ice cream remained a major indulgence, to be foregone only when she was about to begin work in a new production and had to lose pounds quickly.

She also learned about the American cocktail, and in no time she developed a taste for gin martinis, rum drinks, whiskey sours—virtually anything offered. "When I came to America and saw all the names—stingers, daiquiris—I just started with 'A' and went down the list!" Happily, Ingrid had a strong constitution and held her liquor well; a liberal tippler all her life, she could stop drinking for a diet, and she was never anything like an alcoholic. Discipline and pride would never have permitted her to be controlled by any appetite.

As for improving her English, Ingrid was too restless to settle down with newspapers, which she rarely studied in any case, and Kay agreed that the theater was the place to go. After a week, she had seen *Abe Lincoln in Illinois*, *The Little Foxes*, *The Philadelphia Story* and *No Time for Comedy*—but she was no nearer to understanding ordinary American speech. When Kay spoke slowly, clearly and used only elementary phrases, everything was fine. But Ingrid was stymied by the pace of dramatic dialogue, by dialect and by anything more complicated than a simple declarative sentence. Kay agreed the situation required an immediate remedy, since filming on *Intermezzo* was set to begin in May. She cabled Selznick, who replied that he would have a dialogue coach ready for her in Hollywood.

That arrival occurred early Saturday afternoon, May 6. Kay accompanied Ingrid on the train from New York to Pasadena, where a car and driver waited to transport them to David Selznick's mansion on Summit Drive in Beverly Hills. With a swimming pool, a huge formal dining room, multiple parlors, a library and a screening room, the Selznick estate was something unimaginable for a Swedish actress quite content with a tidy apartment. Ingrid had seen such grand luxury in American movies and magazines, but she was far too sensible to equate the perquisites with professionalism.

She was at once introduced to David's wife, Irene (daughter of MGM mogul Louis B. Mayer), who was listening to the Kentucky Derby; her husband, she said, was in Culver City working on *Gone With the Wind*. Amazed to see Ingrid with a few modest pieces of luggage and minus the customary movie-star steamer trunks, Irene showed her to the guest quarters at the Selznick residence, which she was to occupy for the present. Ingrid was astonished to find a lavish three-room suite with its own bath and sitting room.

That evening, Irene Selznick invited Ingrid to join her and some friends for dinner at the Beachcomber, a Hollywood restaurant that affected the atmosphere of the South Pacific. Kay was not included, for she was an employee and therefore not to be considered acceptable Hollywood royalty. Also on hand that evening were Miriam Hopkins, Richard Barthelmess and Grace Moore, and Ingrid, confused by their musket-fire conversation, was literally speechless in their presence. But after one of the Beachcomber's lethal daiquiris (served in a ceramic coconut and topped with a tiny pink parasol), she attempted a joke about her height, and from that moment (as Irene Selznick recalled), everyone was beguiled by her.

Although Ingrid's English was limited, she had a remarkable capacity for communication: everything she felt was somehow quickly conveyed with a glance, a subtle but direct expression and an economy of gesture—an amalgam of qualities, it must be added, that made her feelings so immediate on the screen. "Her lack of affectation was monumental," according to Irene (who was not easily touched by her husband's stars). "Simple and direct, she had a totally refreshing quality. In fact, she didn't seem like any other actress I ever knew. I hadn't planned to be more than hospitable to my houseguest, but I immediately took her under my wing and tried to teach her Hollywood."

After dinner at the Beachcomber, the group repaired to the projection room at the home of Miriam Hopkins, and at about one in the morning, someone tapped Ingrid's shoulder: Selznick had joined the party at last and awaited her in the kitchen. As he leaned across a table and wolfed down leftovers from Miriam's refrigerator, Selznick—owlish, lumbering, hypertensive and as garrulous as his memos indicated—squinted at her through thick glasses and was alarmed at her height (five feet, nine inches). "God! Take your shoes off!" he mumbled after a perfunctory greeting.

"It won't help," Ingrid replied coolly. "I'm wearing flat-heeled shoes." The producer speared a piece of cold lamb and reached for a bottle of whiskey.

*   *   *

DAVID O. SELZNICK WAS ONE OF THE GREAT POWERS IN HOLLYWOOD. Then thirty-seven, he had already been a successful producer at RKO, Paramount and Metro-Goldwyn-Mayer, where his father-in-law, Louis B. Mayer, installed him as vice-president in charge of production. By 1939, Selznick had produced dozens of hits, among them *What Price Hollywood?*, *A Bill of Divorcement*, *King Kong*, *Little Women*, *Dinner at Eight*, *David Copperfield*, *Anna Karenina* and *A Star Is Born*. *Gone With the Wind* was soon to be released, and *Rebecca* was on schedule for imminent production. *Intermezzo* was to be his fifty-fifth production.

With financial backing from the Whitney family, Selznick now had his own studio, a move designed not only to expand the empire but also to facilitate his supervision of every detail in every film he produced. Tens of thousands of memos and cables, dictated day and night throughout his career, testify to his corporate zeal. Sensual and brooding, a man of keen intelligence and voracious appetites, Selznick was also an endless source of ideas, many of them generated during long nights of whiskey, poker and pills. Involved in every aspect of his productions, from casting to hair and makeup and advertising, he could also drive his staff and his contracted artists to the brink of madness with his demands on their time, energies and attention.

THE FIRST MEETING BETWEEN INGRID AND DAVID, OVER COLD LAMB and whiskey, continued as he returned to the subject of her name, which he said was too German. What about renaming her Ingrid Berryman? "Bergman is a good name and I like it," she replied. "If I fail in America, I can go back to Sweden and still be Ingrid Bergman."

Well, besides her name, there was a problem with her eyebrows, Selznick continued: they were too thick by far. Another splash of whiskey in his glass. And her teeth obviously needed fixing, and as for her makeup, something had to be done, and—were there any leftover potatoes in Miriam's icebox? some bread and butter?

"I think you've made a big mistake, Mr. Selznick," Ingrid interrupted, speaking with quiet deliberation. "I thought you saw me in the movie *Intermezzo* and liked me and sent Kay Brown to Sweden to get me. Now you've seen me, you want to change everything. So I'd rather not do the movie. We'll say no more about it. No trouble of any kind. We'll just forget it. I'll take the next train and go back home." And with that, David O. Selznick, who was accustomed to getting what he wanted, stopped munching and sipping. He had met his match. In fact, he realized the astonishing good sense of her reply.

"He said it sounded fantastic," Ingrid recalled,

—the best publicity angle ever—and that he'd work on the idea of a natural girl, that nothing was changed. He told the people in the makeup department not to touch my eyebrows, and although I had to have some makeup on for the camera—my face turned red under the hot lights—it was all designed to look very natural and un-madeup. So I became the "natural" star. And it was just at the right time, because everything had become very artificial in movies—all those plucked and repainted eyebrows, all that heavy lip rouge and the ridiculous plastered hairdos. I looked very simple, my hair would blow in the wind, and I acted like the girl next door.

Suddenly Selznick was on her side. It was brilliant, he said: her real name, her real features, her real hair and teeth. In Hollywood, this was about as uncommon as snow.

As she said, Ingrid's courage in confronting Selznick derived from a simple conviction: if she was not liked or accepted in Hollywood, she could easily return to work in Sweden or Germany. She had seen enough American movies to know that by 1939 most actresses were coiffed and cosmeticized beyond all resemblance to normal life. To be sure, she was restless in the Swedish cinema and appreciated the enormous technical resources and apparently infinite budgets of American moviemaking; in addition, she knew that many foreigners had succeeded in their careers in America, where there was a particular predilection for German-Scandinavian women (among many others, Greta Garbo, Marlene Dietrich, Hedy Lamarr, Ilona Massey and Anna Sten).

But she was also shrewd enough to know that glamour could be distracting (beautiful women were rarely praised for their acting genius), that mere artifice could secure her popularity only temporarily (until the age of thirty-five if she was very lucky), and that only a talent maturing with the help of good scripts would secure her career. Finally, she harbored the hope that she would one day be able to act onstage again.

INGRID'S THEATRICAL AMBITIONS WERE PART OF A LARGER WORLD SHE envisioned for herself. In the months after Pia's birth, she had gone several times weekly to the Stockholm cinemas, had seen everything she could and realized the astonishing possibilities of working in the international cinema. Her time in Germany had not satisfied a constant appetite for new methods, new tasks, new settings, new venues in which to work. She also saw Swedish life as restrictive ("confined on an island," as she had said), but at the root of this ennui may also have been the suspicion that the deepest satisfaction of her life would not come from marriage and motherhood but from good work. Her character had been formed by two unassailable experiences that led her to a remarkable self-reliance: the deaths of relatives and unshakable confidence about her talents. At twenty-three, she had traveled thousands of miles to a foreign culture, where she had nothing to rely on except her inner strength and an unaffected self-composure that allowed the emergence, at a moment's notice, of her extraordinary gifts as an actress. Hence she seemed neither homesick nor unsure of herself. Adjectives and verbs she could easily learn; audacity and vigor were hers already.

A week after her arrival, Ingrid was guest of honor at a Selznick dinner party, where the two dozen guests included Tyrone Power, Loretta Young, Errol Flynn, Claudette Colbert, Gary Cooper, Joan Bennett, Cary Grant, Spencer Tracy, Charles Boyer, Clark Gable and Ann Sheridan—the last-named being promoted by Warner Bros. as "The Oomph Girl." No one could explain to Ingrid the definition of that coined word, nor was any help available in her Swedish-English lexicon. She despaired, she said, unable to learn the meaning of "oomph," of ever mastering American English. But help was on the way, for within a few days Ingrid was introduced to her language and dialogue coach—Ruth Roberts, a calm, perceptive woman who taught English to a number of immigrants. Sister of the writer and director George Seaton, Ruth became Ingrid's lifelong instructor and later her trusted friend and companion on location shootings.

By mid-May, Selznick had leased a house for Ingrid—a charming Spanish-style villa at 260 South Camden Drive, Beverly Hills. Selznick was again shocked at her reaction to the news of her move: this was an unnecessary expense, Ingrid said. Since a furnished trailer was waiting for her at the Selznick studios, she would be very happy there. Irene quietly advised Ingrid that this was not appropriate for her new status as a Selznick leading lady.

Her new neighborhood was nothing like Summit Drive, high above Sunset Boulevard, where estates with swimming pools, guest cottages, tennis courts and servants' quarters often occupied several acres. Ingrid's temporary residence was now two blocks south of Wilshire Boulevard, on a small tract of land without a pool—and so with less of a glamorous cachet. But it was certainly more opulent than anywhere she had ever lived, and she adored both the charm and the sheer exoticism of it all: the red tile roof, the pale stucco walls and beamed ceilings, the arched porticoes, the lush plantings of yucca, cactus, lemon, olive and eucalyptus trees, the sweet aroma of night-blooming jasmine—all of it gracing a spacious four-bedroom home for Ingrid and a woman Selznick hired as her cook, driver and personal assistant.

As for her contract with Selznick International Pictures (later amended in her favor), Ingrid was to receive $2,500 per week during the filming of *Intermezzo*. Selznick stipulated options, according to which she might be further engaged to appear in two pictures annually, and she would be paid $2,812.50 weekly with a guarantee of sixteen weeks for the second year; annual increments would raise that fee to $5,000 weekly by the sixth year. With a sixteen-week work schedule, Ingrid was guaranteed a minimum annual salary of $80,000 by 1946—if she was happy with the results of *Intermezzo*.

In the end, between 1939 and 1946, Ingrid received a gross income of over $750,000 from Selznick, which made her (with Irene Dunne) one of the highest-paid women in Hollywood but not one of the richest women in the country. Although she was a registered "resident alien," she had to pay American taxes on that income; at the time, the government taxed her level of income at 90 percent, and so her actual net compensation hovered at about $20,000 annually.

*   *   *

For three days in early May, Ingrid was required for silent tests as her hair, light makeup and natural coloring were assessed by cinematographer Harry Stradling and director William Wyler, on loanout from producer Samuel Goldwyn to direct *Intermezzo*. On Wednesday, May 24, Wyler began rehearsals, and things proceeded smoothly through Saturday. But on Monday, Memorial Day, Wyler—a meticulous craftsman known for multiple retakes of each scene—sent word to Selznick that he was leaving the picture: the requirement that he finish *Intermezzo* in six weeks was intolerable to him, he said, and so he pleaded his prior commitment to Samuel Goldwyn as an excuse; the truth was, the script was not at all to Wyler's liking.

Selznick was not alarmed at this news. The budget for *Gone With the Wind* had already climbed to the unimaginable level of $4 million, and although Selznick had planned *Intermezzo* as an economical project, Wyler's reputation for multiple retakes spelled disaster in Selznick's nervy imagination. Never mind that Wyler's *Jezebel* had just earned Bette Davis her second Oscar, or that his *Wuthering Heights* was one of the year's great successes. As it happened, Selznick's original choice to direct *Intermezzo* had been Gregory Ratoff, the Russian immigrant actor-director who was an old gambling buddy and who owed Selznick a tidy sum from poker games. And so on Thursday, June 1, he arranged to borrow him from Darryl Zanuck at Twentieth Century-Fox, where Ratoff was under contract. Barking commands in a thick Slavic-Yiddish accent often incomprehensible to his cast and crew, the new director of *Intermezzo* assumed the attitude of a stern taskmaster with everyone— except Ingrid, whom he adored.

At first, she was disturbed by this sudden transfer of such an important duty from one man to another, but then, as she realized, it was not really Ratoff's movie. Selznick, as eager for haste and economy as he was to repeat the success of the Swedish *Intermezzo*, had each scene of the first version screened on the set. And somehow, to the amazement and annoyance of virtually everyone involved, he managed to scurry back and forth from supervising *Gone With the Wind* to controlling every take of *Intermezzo*. Ratoff, therefore, seemed (even to himself) mostly an aide to Selznick. "He was temperamental, but he was also a dear, sweet man," Ingrid said of the director. "His accent was very funny to listen to. He used to come up to me and say, 'You don't read ze line right. Lizzen to me and do eet zees vay!' And then Ruth came up and said, 'For God's sake, don't listen to him! Listen to me!'" This, as everyone might have predicted, led to considerable confusion for Ingrid, who was fearful that whatever she said, she would not be understood. No cause for worry, Selznick told her: anything muddy in the recording could be dubbed later.

Whereas Ingrid's diction could be corrected, her appearance, once recorded, could not, and four days after Ratoff began shooting, Selznick was convinced that now Harry Stradling (who had already worked successfully in Hollywood, England and France) was incompetent to photograph Bergman's American debut. "There is no single thing about the physical production of the picture," wrote Selznick in a cautionary memo to Stradling,

> that even compares in importance with the photography of Miss Bergman. Unless we can bring off our photography so that she really looks divine, the whole picture can fall apart. It is entirely possible that we haven't yet learned enough about her angles or about exactly how to light her. The curious charm she had in the Swedish version of *Intermezzo*—the combination of exciting beauty and fresh purity—certainly ought to be within our abilities to capture. It would be shocking indeed if some cameraman in a small Stockholm studio was proven to be able to do so much more superior work with her than we are.

(It is hard to know, after reviewing the Stradling scenes that have survived, just what Selznick had in mind. He had told Stradling he wanted a natural look, and that is what the cinematographer provided.)

Apart from her height, which could be easily compensated by adjusting angles and by the proper positioning of shorter players, Ingrid was not a difficult subject for the camera. But the rumor that she wore no makeup for *Intermezzo* was a pleasant fiction devised by Selznick to support his publicity about the arrival of a Swedish milkmaid who was so lovely she needed no help from cosmeticians. The truth is that she was very fair-skinned and the bright lights evoked a

ruddy gleam that had to be expertly matted with the proper pow-
ders.

Regarding Stradling, however, Selznick was frantic: he saw what
he had to see in that second week of dailies, which was a series of
visual disasters that threatened to sabotage the picture. And so
Stradling was the next to be dismissed from the production and was
replaced by Gregg Toland (who had photographed *Wuthering Heights*
for Wyler and Goldwyn).* But now it was Ingrid who became anxious. "Tears came to her eyes," Selznick wrote with astonishment in
a memo to William Hebert, his director of advertising and publicity.
"She wanted to know whether it would hurt [Stradling's] standing
[to be let go], because after all he was a very good cameraman and
it didn't matter if she was photographed a little worse—she would
rather have this than hurt him."

Selznick, a man not easily impressed (especially by actors), was
learning, as he told Hebert, that Ingrid was "the most completely
conscientious actress with whom I have ever worked." For evidence,
Selznick detailed the fact that she subordinated her entire life to the
needs of the production. "She practically never leaves the studio
and never for a minute suggests quitting at six o'clock . . . and on
the contrary is very unhappy if the company doesn't work until
midnight."

His astonishment continued: Ingrid was anxious about expenses
regarding her clothes for the picture, too. When a dress was discarded because it was not becoming to her, she asked the wardrobe
department if a collar might be added, or the color or cut changed,
so that money would not be wasted. Furthermore, she was so
pleased with her small dressing room (the larger suites having been
assigned to the quartet of stars in *Gone With the Wind*) that she suggested to Selznick that he cancel the lease on Camden Drive and
save money by allowing her to live at the studio.

"All of this is completely unaffected," wrote Selznick—and in
this, too, he saw the seeds of beneficial publicity, "so that her natural sweetness and consideration and conscientiousness [are already]
something of a legend . . . particularly in view of the growing non-

---

*Typically, Selznick changed his mind about Stradling's talents within days and (wisely)
assigned him to the even more arduous task of photographing *Rebecca*.

sense that stars are forcing us to put up with." Ingrid wanted to be a successful, serious actor; the trappings of stardom were not her ultimate goal. "I'm a down-to-earth person," she said somewhat wearily years later when asked how she rated herself among stars. "I want to be right here on the ground. I do my job, that's all."

So did Toland, who gave Selznick what was required: a natural Bergman who was nevertheless cunningly rendered with every resource available to the professional—shade and shadows, scrims and key lights, angles and distances measured to the millimeter. In *Intermezzo*, there are certainly moments when a surprisingly realistic representation fills the frame—in the boating scene, for example, when her hair blows in the wind (a scene not in the Swedish version). But the most natural element of all was her acting.

The film was not much of an improvement on the romantic gaucheries of the original. Maintaining the Swedish setting (and lifting many long shots directly from Molander's version), the Anglophile Selznick and the English Leslie Howard (associate producer on the film) somehow decided to infuse the film with a British spirit, British teacups, manners, decor and accents. Little more than a moral gloss on the titillating story of a middle-aged husband and father who has a romantic interlude with a much younger woman, *Intermezzo* suffered much from the constant intrusions and interference of Selznick, who was (thus Ingrid), "always sending notes down. We'd get these rewrites and reply, 'We've already shot it, for heaven's sake!' He was impossible. He could never make up his mind. We went over and over my entrance—I can't tell you how many times I did it and redid it. He said he wanted my arrival in the American film world to be like a shock."

In addition—as if he had made a vow to invent the visual equivalent of the adverb—Selznick demanded a profusion of scenes with the appallingly adorable daughter of the morbidly self-absorbed violinist (Leslie Howard) and the terribly responsive dog (little girls and puppies being always irresistible to American audiences). He also augmented the role of the terrifically noble and long-suffering wife (Edna Best); and he gave his writer, George O'Neil, wearisome ideas for scenes with admirably devoted friends and servants. The movie was, in other words, a bundle of saccharine clichés, memorable only for Ingrid, who alone rises above the level of cuteness.

Credible in every sequence, she communicated the feelings of a young lover as much by her silences as by her speech: her gestures seemed unfeigned and ingenuous, her reactions and timing the spontaneous attributes of an authentic person—not the embellished construct that might have been presented by a less gifted actor. Even more than in the Swedish version, she created an Anita Hoffman who came to life from moment to moment, a young woman whose character emerges only when she is suspended between the height of rapture and the depth of guilt. Something tentative was added to the performance here—hence Ingrid's universal appeal: women in the audience could identify with her vulnerability, while men could endorse her longing to overcome her vacillation and to live passionately as well as professionally.

INTRODUCED TO THE AMERICAN WAY OF FILMMAKING, INGRID WAS surprised to find that "it's so much easier to make films here than in Europe . . . There are more people on the set, more clothes, more stand-ins—which we didn't have in Sweden—more makeup men and electricians. Whereas on the average set in Sweden you'd find twelve people, in America there would be fifty. The only other difference is that here things are a bit glossier and the sets more expensive." Very quickly, she was learning about every aesthetic and technical aspect of filmmaking.

Intermezzo was completed by the end of July, there were several days of dubbing inaudible bits of dialogue, and then, on August 3, Selznick ordered color film tests of Ingrid on the Gone With the Wind set of Rhett Butler's bedroom. Selznick promised her that when (he did not say "if") she and Intermezzo were successful, he would offer her a new contract and a prime role in a Technicolor picture. She replied that her dream was to play Joan of Arc, and he agreed it was a perfect project for her. The next afternoon, after one final retake of her first appearance in Intermezzo, Ingrid boarded the train for New York, and from there she sailed at once for Stockholm.

SHE HAD TO BE HOME BEFORE THE END OF AUGUST, AS PETTER HAD informed both her and Daniel O'Shea (vice-president of Selznick International), if she was to honor her commitment to make another German picture. She had rejected so many scripts from

UFA, Petter reminded Ingrid, that it would have been unwise for her to reject another; Lindstrom's point, relayed to Kay through Ingrid, had been confirmed in a memorandum to O'Shea on June 29. But then, as deftly as any agent, Petter wrote to Kay Brown on July 28, "I have cabled UFA that my wife cancels forthwith her contract [which she did not]—but I did not specify whether the cancellation was for one or both films she had agreed to do!" With that letter, Petter ensured that Selznick would know that Ingrid had other career offers than Selznick and Hollywood. He was, in other words, setting up a virtual auction for her services.

More to the point, Petter was negotiating directly with Carl Froelich (who had directed Ingrid in *Die vier Gesellen*). In a letter to Kay Brown from Stockholm on July 19, Petter wrote that he "felt a certain safety from the fact that my wife's former director in Germany, Mr. Froelich, has now become a very influential person in German film as president of the combined German interests . . . She will do everything [she can] to accept, without conditions, the [screen]play now suggested . . . and my wife ought to be in Berlin" as soon as possible. Four days later, he added that he was "still negotiating with UFA," and that "my wife should be careful about not trying UFA's patience too far."

Ingrid left all these matters to her husband. For one thing, she understood that she ought not to be directly involved in negotiations; for another, she asked herself who could be more trustworthy than her own husband, who by now had assumed the central place of manager and agent. Kay saw a further point Petter had made: "I suppose when Dr. Lindstrom so quickly cancelled out of the German picture, they [UFA] decided to meet the terms of the contract which allowed Miss Bergman to take out most of her [German] money"—as Zarah Leander had managed to do.

"WHAT A MARVELOUS TIME I HAVE HAD IN HOLLYWOOD!" INGRID wrote to Ruth Roberts as the Super Chief rattled eastward from Los Angeles to New York on August 4. "So many nice people. If you return to the studio, please give them all my love."

"I prayed that I had done well and that David would want me back," she said later. "I had loved the experience of working in Hollywood and I loved the people I worked with. I wanted so much to come back, but I had to think of my baby and Petter's studies. It all seemed so complicated." As indeed it was. But an answer to her prayer reached her by cable on the *Queen Mary* as she sailed to Sweden: "Dear Ingrid—You are a very lovely person and you warm all our lives. Have a marvelous time but come back soon. Your Boss." When he saw that message, Petter fired off another cable to Kay: he was trying to negotiate a deal for an English picture, he reported, so whatever Selznick offered should take this into account.

Petter met Ingrid in Cherbourg on Saturday night, August 19, and they went straight on to Stockholm, where he had rented an old and unmodernized but very charming house, the Villa Sunnanlid in the city's park Djurgården. She welcomed one reporter from a newspaper, to whom she said that yes, she was late for her arrival on the set of her new film at UFA, where she was to play Charlotte Corday in a historical drama—but her agent (that is, Petter) had obtained an extension for her, and she would proceed to Berlin in October. Meantime, she looked forward to a family reunion. Pia, almost a year old, wailed in the unfamiliar presence of her mother; Petter offered a more cordial welcome, but much later she realized that the four months apart had revealed serious differences of personality and perspective between them. Later, Ingrid admitted that from this initial separation her marriage "never really recovered." With distance had come the first sense that their tastes and temperament were so divergent as to make them virtually incompatible partners. Furthermore, each was committed to a difficult and demanding career, and while Petter affected to know what was right for Ingrid, she had an unshakable sense that he was patronizing her; on the other hand, she could not enter (even by conversation) into his field at all.

Close to the heart of the problem was Ingrid's desire to be free to work wherever opportunities occurred—an aspiration that clashed with the stability her marriage, motherhood and the ethos of the time required. In her early life, after all, she had known a series of dislocations: the deaths in her family, the many relocations from one home to another, the isolation often felt by someone with ambition and an imaginative personality—all these had molded the young Ingrid to be, in some profound inner way, independent. But at the same time, her emotional neediness encouraged her to be dependent on a man. As long as she had known Petter, she had relied entirely on his counsel.

Of course, she had also counted on Kay and Irene for professional and social introductions in Hollywood, and on David Selznick for the employment. But once *Intermezzo* was under way, Ingrid was very much on her own, and she learned from her dealings with everyone from the director to the sound technician, and from Ruth Roberts to her maid, that she could negotiate the waters of ordinary social discourse, even in English, without drowning in a sea of humiliation and confusion. She had understood, in other words, that her talent was something people admired, and that she had considerable inner resources on which to base her own solid opinions and make her artistic decisions when it came to both the choice and the interpretation of roles.

Three days later, German troops marched into Poland, and two days after that Britain and France declared war on Germany. Sweden remained neutral, although for how long no one dared predict, and everything was uncertain in diplomatic and commercial relations with Germany. No sensible Swede wanted to work in a country at war, and UFA's production schedule was, for the present, frozen. "My German picture cancelled," Ingrid cabled Selznick on September 29, with no reaction about the war. But she was not without prospects: her husband and Helmer Enwall had landed for her a role in a forthcoming Swedish picture. Then, on October 6, *Intermezzo* opened in America, and Selznick relayed the news they had all hoped for: the press and public had found a new star in Ingrid Bergman.

"Sweden's Ingrid Bergman is so lovely a person and so gracious an actress," began the review in the *New York Times*, which went on to praise her "freshness, simplicity and natural dignity . . . Her acting is surprisingly mature, yet singularly free from the stylistic traits—the mannerisms, postures, precise inflections—that become the stock in trade of the matured actress . . . There is that incandescence about Miss Bergman, that spiritual spark which makes us believe that Selznick has found another great lady of the screen."

Selznick continued to read the reviews to her in a long, often indistinct transatlantic telephone call (a very expensive and infrequent method of communication in 1939):

"David O. Selznick was exceedingly smart in sticking to the lovely
leading lady of the original. Ingrid Bergman is her name, and
her presence [in the film] is its chief distinction. She has natural
assurance and dignity as well as an exciting talent . . . Using
scarcely any makeup but playing with mobile intensity, she creates the character so vividly and credibly that it becomes the
core of what narrative there is . . . To my mind, she is the most
gifted and attractive recruit that the studios have enlisted from
abroad in many a moon."

"Tall, beautiful, emotional and a superb actress, Ingrid Bergman is a
new addition to the American screen worth raving about."

"She is beautiful, talented and convincing—a warm personality that
introduces a new stellar asset to Hollywood."

"She is the finest thing that has come to Hollywood from anywhere
in many a day. It is extremely unfair to call her a second Garbo
just because she hails from Sweden. She has a combination of
rare beauty, freshness, vitality and ability that is as uncommon as
a century plant in bloom."*

And so they went, page after page of ecstatic notices. "I told you
so," said David O. Selznick again and again. More prints were being
shipped to additional theaters, he added, and long lines were forming everywhere as audiences flocked to see Selznick's new star.
Vivien Leigh had been working on *Gone With the Wind* longer (and
under far more demanding conditions), but that picture was not yet
released. Ingrid Bergman was the most incandescent entertainment
news of the year thus far.[†]
    "I cried all that day in Stockholm," she recalled. "When we
were making the picture, I had seen some of the rushes. David and
Gregory Ratoff and other people said I was good, but I didn't trust

---

*When a reporter asked Garbo's opinion of Bergman after she had seen the American
version of *Intermezzo*, she replied, "Oh, please!" She was not smiling.
    [†]Leigh won the best actress Oscar; the other nominees were Bette Davis for *Dark Victory*,
Irene Dunne for *Love Affair*, Greta Garbo for *Ninotchka* and Greer Garson for *Goodbye Mr.
Chips*.

them. It was wicked to feel that way, but when I learned that audiences were pleased, then—and then only—was I convinced and satisfied." On October 9, with Petter's approval noted in a letter to Selznick, Ingrid signed the option for a second year of employment with Selznick International, to begin the following April. She noted, somewhat dubiously, that she was bound to Selznick whether he produced films for her, loaned her out to other studios (for any weekly price he could negotiate for himself, although she would always receive only her contracted salary) or kept her idle and awaiting a Selznick project.

Of his profits on loaning her out, Ingrid spoke matter-of-factly: "I was never unhappy about him selling me for such high prices to other studios and me not seeing a cent of it. People tried to make me angry about it, but I just said that I signed the contract, and if he could get $250,000 to my $50,000, it was all right by me because he was clever and I was not!" But idleness was a situation she could not endure.

For her salary, she would be required to appear in two pictures each year if Selznick so wished, but she had the right to do one stage play annually as well—provided it had his approval. He also had the right to sell her for radio plays. All this understood, Ingrid made plans to return to Hollywood in the new year 1940.

FIRST, THERE WAS THE PRODUCTION OF *JUNINATTEN* (*JUNE NIGHT*), which began filming in Stockholm on October 18. The lyrical title is deliberately ironic, for the finished film (directed by Per Lindberg from a script by Ragnar Hylten-Cavallius) remains one of the cinema's bitterest indictments of sexual exploitation and misguided passion. *June Night* also broadened the range of Ingrid's gallery of characters: assessed years later, this performance must be placed very high in her catalog of achievements.

She was cast as Kerstin Nordback, a free-spirited woman in a small Swedish town, involved with Nils, a violent and abusive man who very nearly kills her with a gunshot to the heart as she prepares to leave him. Saved by delicate heart surgery, she appears at the trial and pleads for leniency on her ex-lover's behalf, claiming that she must bear the responsibility: "All I wanted was an affair . . . "—a courageous and frank admission that wins her nothing but public shame. She changes her name to Sara, moves to Stockholm, takes a job in a pharmacy and (in a gloss on *Die vier Gesellen*) shares quarters in a boardinghouse with three other working women who also have man trouble.

At this point, the film's intentions become clear, for each woman she meets is the victim of rude sexual pressure from her boyfriend. Even a gentle and humane physician named Stefan (Carl Ström) exploits his nurse for easy erotic satisfaction, and when he learns about Sara's history, he becomes obsessed with meeting and knowing her. She later endures a near-lethal heart spasm from the shock of Nils's reappearance and renewed violent passion, and Stefan cares for her; eventually, he is so precipitous in his declaration of love that she succumbs. The finale, as they drive away to a countryside shimmering with June's full flower, suggests that Kerstin, once numbed, has rediscovered the possibility of love in her life. But the other women, whose relationships have been failures, must find the right man as Kerstin has—thus their wish, at the end, on the legendary June night.

Ingrid made Kerstin/Sara a sympathetic character whose wounds are symptomatic of the harshness of sexual exploitation, and in this regard *June Night* (which could never have been produced in America in 1939) is relentless in its emotional honesty. Longing for love, Kerstin sees quickly—as Ingrid indicates with a raised eyebrow, a slight grimace or the proper hesitation on a key word—the easy perfidy behind amatory advances.

A single sequence near the end of the picture synthesizes all the destructive selfishness behind the brutal sexual pawings of the men in the story; here, even a gentlemanly doctor shares the crazed passion of the drunken, sexually driven male characters.

STEFAN (Ström): I've thought about you so much.
KERSTIN (Bergman): Have you? We just met!
STEFAN: I've seen you everywhere.
KERSTIN: Just imagination and a wishful dream—that's all you have.
[On that line, Ingrid pauses and slightly turns her head, so that one senses that Kerstin, too, understands what it means to imagine and dream.]

STEFAN: When you pass someone, something happens. They become
    another person.—Don't look so skeptical. You get men to think
    strange and dangerous thoughts. Your little heart—are you care-
    ful of it?
KERSTIN: Yes, it's become a habit. I don't notice it myself. I have a
    scar.
[Her tone is wise and wistful: she appreciates the irony, yet she can-
    not escape the situation of dependence.]
STEFAN: I want to kiss you.
KERSTIN: No—not today.
STEFAN: Say it—say that you want me.
KERSTIN: But you know nothing about me. I've made such a mess of
    things.
STEFAN: Don't I? I know you stir my fantasy. That's enough for me.

Carl Ström, in the role of the benevolent but misguided doctor,
provided the proper admixture of humane intent and protracted
adolescent delusion. But Ingrid took the complex role of Kerstin
and infused it with a deep sense of tragedy, raising the cliché of the
tarnished woman into a portrait of an unjustly dishonored soul,
racked by guilt and at the mercy of cruel reporters and pathetic
suitors. Decades later, her courtroom scene, the sequences in the
pharmacy, with the doctor and at the finale, reveal just how instinctively she understood, at the age of twenty-four, the complex range
of twisted emotions that pass for feelings in an adult world. Per
Lindberg, who refused to overdirect his star, sensibly allowed Ingrid
the freedom to seek and find the core of the character. He and the
film's audiences were perhaps amazed that she found Kerstin's
home base to be nowhere until she risks everything at the end—
and this, of course, was the deepest logic of the remarkable *June
Night*.

FILMING CONCLUDED ON DECEMBER 5. WHEN SELZNICK CABLED
Ingrid, asking when she planned to return to Hollywood, Petter was
ready with a reply. He had volunteered to serve for several months,
beginning in January, in the Swedish army—as, of all things, a documentary filmmaker; he would supervise the production of several
important short features about advances in dental surgery. At the

same time, he and Ingrid shared the general anxiety about Sweden's strategic position and its possible involvement in the war. She and Pia would certainly be safer in America, and Petter would join them later.

"Leaving Petter behind was a very difficult decision for me to make," Ingrid later told a friend, but "in the end, [he] made the final decision, as always." He accompanied his wife, daughter and a nursemaid as far as Genoa, where, on January 2, 1940, he put them on the Italian liner *Rex*, bound for New York.

Chapter Five

1940

Fie upon this quiet life! I want work.

SHAKESPEARE,
King Henry the Fourth, Part I

D URING INGRID'S LAST WEEKS IN SWEDEN, DAVID O. SELZNICK HAD
sweetened the prospect of work in Hollywood by promising
her that he would fulfill her dream by producing a film about her
beloved Joan of Arc. In happy anticipation of that prospect, she dis-
embarked in New York on January 12—an arrival duly noted next
morning when the *New York Times*, on page one, dropped a few
notable names on the *Rex*'s passenger list. But Kay Brown, on
instructions from her boss, enjoined silence on the matter of the
Maid of Orleans: Selznick would announce plans for the picture in
his own good time—which in fact never came. Nor did he have a
substitute project for her.

"Although I was shy, I had a lion roaring inside me that wouldn't
sit down and shut up," said Ingrid. During the first two months of
the year, she never ceased to badger Selznick to put her back to
work, which was the great reality of her life. Indeed, she would neither sit still nor keep silence, as her producer quickly learned. "I

was going mad for lack of work," she recalled years later.

Idleness was intolerable to Ingrid, whose theatergoing that winter only increased her appetite for a job. As so often in the next decade, inactivity produced anxiety, and anxiety induced another kind of hunger—for all sorts of fattening dishes, especially ice cream sundaes. That season, she quickly gained fifteen pounds. These she tried to shed by strolling in Central Park or rowing a boat on its lake, by walking through Harlem's flea markets on Sunday afternoon, and by exploring every exhibit at the World's Fair. Occasionally on her outings, moviegoers who had seen *Intermezzo* recognized her, and although she willingly signed autographs, she was unnerved by mere flattery. One boy, about eleven years old, pestered her and Kay for two blocks and leaped with them into a taxi, where he pressed his requests for still more autographs until Kay booted the intruder back onto the curb.

"Oh, you may have hurt him!" cried Ingrid, gazing at the boy (who was unharmed) as Kay ordered the driver to speed on.

"Hurt him, nothing," said Kay with a wink at Ingrid. "I've killed him. But I didn't use a gun, so it was legal. You're going to like America—it's a great country."

ALERT TO INGRID'S DESIRE FOR WORK, KAY STORMED SELZNICK WITH cables and phone calls from her Park Avenue apartment, where Ingrid, Pia and the maid were temporarily lodging. Finally, Selznick summoned his new star to Hollywood on January 22, where she would join a cast hired for a radio adaptation of *Intermezzo*. Ingrid left Pia with Kay and boarded the train, but only after a new maid arrived to care for the child. The Swedish girl they had brought along had fallen in with a bad New York crowd, had taken to drugs and routinely slipped into a stupor. Ingrid fired her, and Kay engaged a robust replacement, also a Swedish immigrant.

In California, Selznick explained to Ingrid why the Joan of Arc project had to be indefinitely postponed. Five hundred years ago, the English and French had conspired to betray the girl, but now those countries were at war with Germany. According to the peculiar logic of the time, a strict neutrality had to be maintained in every Hollywood story about European nations—even if the narrative itself took place five hundred years earlier. But Selznick's real

reason, she learned later, was not quite so diplomatic: his share of
the income from *Gone With the Wind* had to be divided with his
father-in-law, Louis B. Mayer, at MGM (who, in exchange for the
loan of Clark Gable for the picture, got the right to release it and
took half the profits); in addition, *Rebecca* was not yet released. A
film about Joan of Arc was going to be another expensive epic, and
Selznick's accountants urged caution.

But if, for the present, there was to be no production concerning St. Joan of Arc, Selznick was carefully orchestrating publicity on
behalf of St. Ingrid of Stockholm. Bosley Crowther, film critic for
the *New York Times*, was granted the sole Manhattan interview that
month, and on the twenty-first of January (the day before her
departure from New York for Hollywood), the editors published a
story entitled "The Lady from Sweden."

"Picture the sweetheart of a Viking," Crowther began,

> freshly scrubbed with Ivory soap, eating peaches and cream from
> a Dresden china bowl on the first warm day of Spring atop a sea-
> scarred cliff and you have a fair impression of Ingrid Bergman
> . . . This reporter would like to go on record that he has never
> met a star who compares in the slightest degree with this incredi-
> ble newcomer from Sweden.

She was, he continued rhapsodically, "a Scandinavian dream girl
. . . as simple and genuine an article—the legendary Garbo
included—as has ever been imported to these shores by the sometimes fallible film industry." Crowther raved about her lack of affectation and her childlike smile, her good spirits and simplicity, and
he admired her beauty, which he devotedly detailed ("light brown
hair, pale blue eyes, a fair complexion which radiates health and a
strong, athletic figure"). He also reported that she wanted to play a
variety of roles, "even comedy and a fallen woman."

During the following two years, Selznick's press campaign continued, becoming virtually a running theme in American journalism
that both reflected and augmented the country's growing love affair
with Ingrid Bergman. "Lunching with her," sighed commentator
Thornton Delehanty in an excess of schoolboyish infatuation, "is
like sitting down to an hour or so of conversation with a charming

and highly intelligent orchid." Another reporter considered that she was "as unspoiled as a fresh Swedish snowfall." Orchids, snowfalls, peaches and cream, Ivory soap in Dresden china: such was the power of Ingrid's evident charm that even jaded New York writers dipped their pens in purple, creating outrageously adoring metaphors and stitching together similes that were hilariously over-wrought.

Even the more sober and perceptive accounts were uniformly positive. "The first time I met her was on the set of *Intermezzo*," recalled the writer and university professor Åke Sandler, son of Swe-den's prime minister and himself an immigrant at the time. He had visited Ingrid at the Selznick studio in Culver City with Walter Danielson, the Swedish vice-consul, and had written a graceful account of Ingrid for the Swedish-American press. "Seldom had I seen a more innocent face," according to Sandler. "She actually radiated a kind of purity and she was extremely charming and accommodating. I understood why Petter had fallen for her." How-ever welcome, all this veneration made Ingrid wary: could not such sudden and extravagant praise be just as precipitously reversed by a reporter's whim or by an incautious public word from her? Well, said Selznick, you just have to behave: watch your step, play by the rules, and do what I tell you. She promised to try.

BY LATE JANUARY, INGRID WAS BACK IN NEW YORK WITH PIA, THE maid, Kay and Jim Barrett and Kay's two young daughters, Kate and Laurinda, who were just about to enter grade school and who wel-comed Pia, not yet two, into their lives. But whereas the children were happy, Ingrid grew more and more miserable in her idleness. Aware that Vinton Freedley (who had produced several Gershwin musicals) was about to revive Ferenc Molnár's romantic fantasy *Lil-iom*, Kay leaped to reverse Ingrid's nervous indolence.

Best known to audiences through its later 1945 transformation into the Rodgers and Hammerstein musical *Carousel*, *Liliom* was the story of a shiftless, irresponsible fairground barker famous for his powers of romantic seduction. Liliom marries the gentle Julie, whom he loves but frequently abuses and attacks; when she is preg-nant, he turns to crime for easy money and kills himself rather than face arrest. Tried before the heavenly court, Liliom repents and after a term in purgatory is allowed to return to earth to perform one good, redeeming deed.

Julie was one of the most sympathetic roles in modern European literature, Kay explained to Selznick in a long memorandum. It would do him no harm, she said, to loan out one of his new stars to Broadway during a hiatus in her film assignments, and it would make Ingrid very happy to be working again. Selznick reluctantly agreed when he learned that the play was to have a limited run of six weeks, and that he would make a little profit on the deal. At once, Kay telephoned Freedley and director Benno Schneider, and Ingrid made an appointment to read for the part. As for her Swedish-tinted diction, a New York-based dialogue coach had been engaged to work with her four hours daily, and the play—set in Hungary—would not be compromised by the accent as long as the actress delivered her lines clearly.

Freedley was delighted at Kay's suggestion of Selznick's client, and after a deeply affecting audition, Ingrid was signed. Two weeks into rehearsal, she thought it only fair to remind Freedley that she had very little experience as a theater actress; furthermore, she promised to master the details of stage business before opening night.

"What are you talking about?" Freedley asked, ticking off plays by Ibsen, O'Neill and many others in which he believed she had appeared.

"No," Ingrid replied quietly, "that was Signe Hasso."

Freedley suddenly realized his mistake and, enraged, turned to Kay. "Well," she replied, unfazed, "how were we supposed to know who you wanted? Signe is out in California now, and you asked for Ingrid." Kay was not, she insisted, responsible for Freedley's confusion; in any case, it was by that time too late to rectify the situation.

The playwright was just as skeptical about the cast when he met the leading lady (whose tall, frankly plump figure had to be camouflaged with petticoats and aprons) and leading man Burgess Meredith, who was four inches shorter than Ingrid. "Why don't you play Liliom?" Molnár asked her sarcastically before turning away in disgust. Most other newcomers, especially those assaying a key role in a foreign language, might have been intimidated to the point of resignation, but not Ingrid. Fearful though she was, she never doubted

her ability, and she saw Julie as the role that would win her the favor
of the New York theater world and revive Selznick's apparently flag-
ging interest in her.

Producer, cast, director and crew plodded through rehearsals
toward an opening night of March 25 at the Forty-fourth Street
Theatre; none of them had any idea of the impression Ingrid would
make. At the first performance, her speech over the dead Liliom
had the audience hushed, her every phrase timed perfectly, her
pauses natural and pitched in a range of tender emotions.

"Sleep, Liliom, sleep," she said, cradling Meredith's head in her
hands. "I never even told you—but now I'll tell you—you bad,
quick-tempered, rough, unhappy, wicked, dear boy. Sleep peacefully,
Liliom. They can't understand how I feel—I can't even explain it to
you—not even to you—how I feel. You'd only laugh at me. But you
can't hear me."

Conveying the character's combination of tenderness and
reproach, Ingrid's voice became dry with grief, as if she were
beyond tears; then, as she opened the Bible to read, her voice
became undulant, her tone liquid. Many in the audience that night
began to weep as she read the verses from chapter five of St.
Matthew, in which Jesus enjoined loving forgiveness for enemies.

"The part of Julie," wrote Brooks Atkinson in the *Times*, "introduces us to a young actress of extraordinary gifts and ability . . . She
has a slight accent. She also has a clean-cut beauty of figure and
manner, responsive eyes, a sensitive mouth, a pleasant voice that can
be heard and modulated. And more than that, she seems to have
complete command of the part she is playing . . . Miss Bergman
keeps the part wholly alive and lightens it from within with luminous beauty."

Atkinson, not easily persuaded of any beginner's talents, added
an additional endorsement a few days later:

Ingrid Bergman, who is making her first appearance on the
English-speaking stage, acts with incomparable loveliness. She is
personally beautiful and endows Julie with an awakened, pulsing
grace of spirit. One is timidly reluctant to praise an actress too
highly on her first appearance, but the time will come when it
will be hard to praise Miss Bergman enough. There is something

wonderfully enkindling about the way she illuminates Julie's character.

The general critical acclaim was summarized by Ernest Lehman, a writer then contributing drama reviews to the *Hollywood Reporter* and *Dance* magazine (and who, in the next decade, became one of Hollywood's most distinguished screenwriters): "Miss Bergman scored a brilliant triumph by her magnetic personality, her fresh beauty and her solid, splendid performance."

DURING THE RUN OF *LILIOM* THAT SPRING, INGRID SEALED FRIENDSHIPS with the cast and with the New York press, whom she continued to charm into worshipful, babbling submission by the simple expedient of being herself and speaking her mind on everything. In 1940, newsmen were given mostly prepared statements by actors' agents and studios, and when the stars spoke publicly it was in carefully measured, unrealistically polite phrases. In this regard, Ingrid was her own person. "Put it down that I love New York," she told a reporter from the *Journal-American*. "I love the drugstores. And next the double[-decker] buses. There is nothing like that in Stockholm."

That was fine—but she continued: "There are only two disagreeable things in New York. The subway goes too fast and they close the doors on your neck. And the air is not good. It is so full of motor car gasoline it stinks!" Celebrities simply did not speak so frankly at that time. They were ambassadors of endless goodwill, spreading the gospel of cheerful perfection wherever they went and avoiding controversy (not to say opinions) at all cost. Far away in Culver City, David Selznick rattled the *Journal-American* and fired off a long memo to his chief publicist, urging him to tell Miss Bergman to be more discreet in broadcasting her notions about urban life. What, she asked Kay when she got this message, would be Selznick's reaction if he knew that Ingrid had just met the playwright Maxwell Anderson at a party given by Burgess Meredith? Ingrid had spoken passionately about Joan of Arc, and Anderson, of course beguiled by her, promised Ingrid that he would write a play about the saint for her. Unlike Selznick, he was true to his word.

*   *   *

BEFORE THE END OF MAY, THE RUN OF *LILIOM* HAD BEEN CONCLUDED, and Kay opened her summer cottage near the ocean in Amagansett, Long Island, where she installed her two girls with Ingrid, Pia and the maid. "They were a part of our family—that's how I remember Ingrid and Pia when I was growing up," recalled Kay's daughter, Laurinda Barrett. "The predominant memory I have is ice cream—they were all nuts for ice cream."

The extended family was augmented in early June, when Petter arrived for a holiday. Leaving Pia for a few days with the maid and the Barrett girls, Ingrid met him at the airport, and they went to a hotel room she had booked on a high floor overlooking Central Park. "Look at this beautiful town," Ingrid said to her husband, pointing out the trees, the horse-drawn carriages and the strollers far below. "This is the most exciting town in the world!" But Petter could see only the dust and grime of the city. Pacing without shoes, he complained, "Look—the carpets are filthy and my socks are filthy." More to his liking was Amagansett, where, as Laurinda Barrett added, "he could do all sorts of acrobatic stunts. He walked on his hands all over the front lawn, and he carried us around on his back for a ride." Her sister Kate also recalled that Pia and the girls dressed up in Scandinavian costumes and sold to neighbors little Swedish toys they had made under Ingrid's tutelage.

After three weeks in America, Petter returned to Sweden to arrange for the family's permanent relocation in America. He intended to keep them far away from the conflict in Europe, and he wanted to obtain his medical degree at a prestigious American university like Harvard, Yale or Columbia.

The Lindstroms' brief reunion once again exposed the cracks just beneath the facade. Engaged in their separate careers and more different than ever in temperament, Petter and Ingrid were polite friends that June, united only by a shared delight in their baby daughter. Never given to elaborating on unpleasant relations, Ingrid simply said that the visit was "not a success."

Besides her professional idleness, an additional source of her unhappiness that summer was a basic loneliness. No matter her admirable progress with American English, Ingrid Bergman was still an alien in a society that, despite its self-description as the world's melting pot, regarded foreign women either as morally suspect

exotics or as potential saboteurs. This may help to explain why, during her time in New York, Ingrid had many professional admirers
and was considered a welcome addition to any party list but, despite
her best efforts, she gained no lifelong friendships apart from Kay.

INGRID TURNED TWENTY-FIVE THAT SUMMER, AND SHE HAD DEVELOPED
a sparkling social grace, a lively sense of humor, a taste for gin ton-
ics, good wine and Scotch whisky; she also had a growing awareness
of the frank sexual aura she projected. But for all that, she was
mostly fearful that her career might be forever stymied. Ever aware
of herself and her compulsions, she understood that dietary indiscretion, at such times, was a refuge. "I gain [weight] because I feel
sorry for myself," she wrote on September 2 to Ruth Roberts in
California, "so I must give her a little ice cream." Like many
actresses (among others, Bette Davis, Marlene Dietrich and Marilyn
Monroe), Ingrid often referred to her professional self in the third
person. "I always look at myself in a detached way," she said the following year, "as though I were watching a stranger for whom I am
responsible; in that way, I can be critical." She understood the distinction between the private woman and the public figure, and that
season Ingrid Bergman, the unemployed actress, had to be pampered a bit.

In addition, because she accepted friendly gestures and hospitality from many acquaintances, there was the inevitable prattle about
her love life. Gossips reasoned that obviously a beautiful woman
who had successfully negotiated the dangers of New York theater
society must have had a score of gentleman callers. But if that was
the case, she and they kept their counsel.

DURING THE FIRST COOL DAYS OF AUTUMN 1940, INGRID BEGAN TO
find life in New York unendurable: "Dear God, if only I could make
Joan come to life instead of this disgusting idleness and ice cream
eating," she confided to Ruth Roberts. "Work, please, work."

At last Selznick heard her plea. For Columbia Pictures, Gregory
Ratoff was to direct *Adam Had Four Sons*, a screen version of Charles
Bonner's novel *Legacy*, about a French governess who serves a widower and his sons for more than a decade; finally, Papa realizes his
repressed love for her, and family conflicts are marvelously resolved

by a happy Hollywood ending. Ratoff begged Selznick to loan him Ingrid, and in early October she and Pia headed for California, but without the maid, who decided that America was not for her and (European war or no) returned to Sweden.

Selznick's staff helped Ingrid find a modest, bright and furnished two-bedroom apartment on Shirley Place, south of Olympic Boulevard at the western extremity of Beverly Hills—a convenient location equidistant to the Selznick studios, Metro and Columbia. They also found a gem of a housekeeper-cook named Mabel, who began work on Pia's second birthday and won the child over by whipping up an angel cake and finding two pink candles. Then, a few days later, Ingrid was laced into early-twentieth-century corsets and period costumes and outfitted with an uncomfortable wig for her role in *Adam Had Four Sons*.

Although it benefited from the work of a few successful directors like Frank Capra, Columbia Pictures in 1940 was unofficially rated as a grade B studio, a less prestigious cousin to Metro, Paramount, Warner Bros. and Fox. But Ingrid cared less for its reputation than for the chance to be back at work. "I am one of the few actresses who really thinks movies are wonderful, and absolutely with no eye to money," she said. "A good part on the screen is just as good [as on the stage]—that's my idea." And with that thought, she made credible a script thick with clichés. "She survived *Adam Had Four Sons*," said Kay Brown dryly, "and anyone who could come through a stinker like that is destined for success."

Ingrid's performance in this sentimental picture made on the cheap reveals precisely the source of her professionalism and the degree to which she instinctively understood the subtleties of screen acting. Into the role of Emilie Gallatin, a French governess imported to raise the four sons of Adam Stoddard (played by Warner Baxter) after the death of their mother (Fay Wray), she infused a kind of strong, Gallic wisdom that prevented the sweetness of the role from turning into treacle. Her half-smile of compassionate recognition about human folly, her knowing glance about human psychology, her insistence to director Ratoff that she would underplay scenes of appallingly cheap sentiment: these were the qualities that made Ingrid's portrait of Emilie affecting where it might otherwise have been insupportably coy.

At her own suggestion, and with Ratoff's hearty approval, she humanized the saintly character wherever she could, adding scenes in which she played basketball and did gymnastic exercises with the boys. These were grace notes in a turgid, lugubrious scenario that was, as Ingrid recalled, "made up minute by minute as we went along," and so she had the challenge and opportunity to make a virtue of necessity. Fay Wray summarized the convictions of the cast and crew on this picture: "Ingrid had a quality that was spiritual and physical at the same time. She seemed very real, not like she was performing at all." When the picture was released in 1941, the critical and popular consensus was that Ingrid had lent her considerable gifts to an inferior film, that she was "completely believable and engaging," and that "such a gift as her magnificent acting deserves a far better break" than *Adam Had Four Sons*.

The break certainly did not come with her next picture, *Rage In Heaven*, into which she was rushed in late autumn, a day after completing *Adam*. Christopher Isherwood and Robert Thoeren had stitched a humorless, improbable scenario from a novel by James Hilton, whose earlier works had been the bases for the Hollywood hits *Lost Horizon* and *Goodbye Mr. Chips*. Metro, to whom Selznick loaned Ingrid, had wrongly counted on another success—especially since the leading man was Robert Montgomery, one of their great stars; but when she read the script, Ingrid could have tempered their enthusiasm. The story concerns a paranoid schizophrenic (Montgomery, in a variation of his role in *Night Must Fall*) who terrorizes his wife (Ingrid) and exploits the loyalty of an old friend (George Sanders). *Rage In Heaven* was almost comically incredible.

The disappointing script Ingrid could endure, for once again she found the proper dramatic mechanisms to mold a compelling character from a paper cliché. Her portrayal of Stella Bergen, an elderly woman's companion who becomes mistress of the manor and wife of the madman (darker shades of her previous role in *Adam*), was remarkable for nuance and a fine balance between confidence and terror.

Ingrid could not endure the barking rudeness of director W. S. ("Woody") Van Dyke, a martinet who strutted around the set in boots and knee breeches and shouted commands like a drill sergeant. The director of seventy-six films in twenty years, he was much in demand at the time—but not among actors, who dubbed him "One-Shot Woody" because he rarely gave them a chance to repeat a take. He brought pictures in under budget, and that endeared him to moguls like Louis B. Mayer—if not to serious colleagues like Ingrid. "Let's get this thing moving!" Van Dyke cried at one moment, and "Get this picture off the ground!" the next. "I want that next scene ready in five minutes!" The filming of *Rage In Heaven* was for her a nightmare of incivility and unprofessionalism, and these qualities she could tolerate no more patiently than she could the director's airy unconcern for the fine points of character development. Van Dyke had been hired to take over from a slower director, and he saw his task as simple expediency—to finish the stupid picture in a way that would satisfy Mayer, and to hell with the actors.

Her only recourse that November was to approach Selznick. What should she do against such a man as Van Dyke? Her performance was of no interest to him and she feared the end result would be a picture that would help neither her nor Selznick as he tried to find future projects for her. Hesitant to interfere, Selznick patted her hand and sent her back to Metro with a promise of big things to come—after *Rage In Heaven*.

Next day at Metro, Van Dyke, who resembled nothing so much as an angry prizefighter, began with his usual tactics, snarling and stomping on the soundstage, dashing from one corner to another and verbally beating everyone into submission. Ingrid had had enough, and for the first time it was clear that (however submissive she was to her husband) she indeed had a lion roaring inside her, and with that strength she had developed considerable confidence regarding her art.

"Why don't you stay with the army, the way you go on marching and yelling?" she cried indignantly, her voice rising so that everyone on the set fell silent. "You don't know anything about people's feelings! You certainly can't direct a woman! You are certainly not interested in anything but 'Finish the picture,' no matter what sort of picture it is! You don't give us any possibility of acting." No one had ever dared confront the formidable Van Dyke so directly—and Ingrid was not finished: "Why don't you put on roller skates so you can go quicker from one place to another?"

Well, said Van Dyke, with an attitude like that she was going to be fired. That was fine with her, Ingrid retorted, and she swept away to confer with George Sanders, who also hated the production. And then, to everyone's surprise, Van Dyke slipped quietly into Ingrid's dressing room later that day, apologized for his behavior, said that she was doing a splendid job and promised to develop a more humane attitude. With that, she had the gratitude of everyone connected with *Rage In Heaven*. Van Dyke had not much opportunity to mend his ways: after a few more unexceptional films, he died in 1943 at the age of fifty-four, the memory of "that young Swede" still stinging his memory. Like Selznick, he had met his match.

Coincidentally, that young Swede, establishing herself as a first-rate actress in everything she did, was working that autumn at the same studio as the older Swede: Greta Garbo, ten years her senior, was then working on *Two-Faced Woman* (which turned out to be her last movie). Ingrid tried, unsuccessfully, to arrange a meeting with her detached, unsociable colleague, but a common heritage and language meant nothing to Garbo, who rebuffed Ingrid's every attempt at friendliness.

"Can you imagine that?" Ingrid later asked. "She was only thirty-five years old and a most beautiful and talented actress, and she never worked again from that day on. Can you imagine all those years? You get up in the morning and what do you do? If you have children and grandchildren that's a different thing—but to be so lonely!" For her part, Ingrid could not imagine not working for-ever—good scripts or bad, on stage or screen: "I do not care what kind of parts I play, big or small. As long as a part makes sense and the character is a human being, I will try."

Her directness, her lack of guile and artifice and her openness were, reporters in Hollywood noted, a stark contrast to the sphinx-like withdrawal of Greta Garbo, who would never have been seen (as Ingrid was) jumping up and down on the bumper of her car to untangle it after it had copulated with another. "Darnedest thing I ever saw," said the studio policeman who ran to Ingrid's assistance. "First film star I ever knew who didn't mind getting her hands dirty, or didn't cuss out the other fellow for leaving his car parked right in her way."

Just in time for Christmas, Petter arrived in America, exhausted after traveling from Stockholm to Berlin to Lisbon and then, via a Portuguese freighter, to New York, where Ingrid and Pia met him. He was eager to hear news of Ingrid's work, and also to further his own career in the United States, for which he had to enroll in medical school and work for a proper American medical degree.

The holidays in New York were made festive mostly by Kay Brown and her family, who gave a series of elegant parties culminating on New Year's Eve. But as Petter sought Kay's advice on his applications to medical schools, Ingrid was again bored to distraction by her inactivity. From her suite at the Carlyle Hotel, Ingrid wrote to Selznick, pleading heartbreak for a lack of work. "I feel like a race horse," she told a reporter. "I can work day and night without feeling any need for sleep. In Hollywood, they laugh at me because I arrive at the studio ahead of time!"

Petter, meantime, was assessing his options. His drive for success, which matched her own, only highlighted what they soon realized during Ingrid's latest period of inactivity. For most of the last two years, the Lindstroms had lived apart. This had been a critical period in their careers, and it was perhaps asking too much for their marriage to sustain both the protracted absence and the fact that they had emotionally and professionally grown independently. No matter how much they attempted to encourage each other and to share the nurturing of Pia, it was evident to Ingrid and Petter that not only their interests diverged: they also had very dissimilar attitudes about almost everything. For one thing, Ingrid spoke her mind, and her bemused manner of doing so enabled her to utter astonishingly forthright comments on just about anything. While becoming Americanized, Ingrid was also developing into a highly cosmopolitan, articulate woman of the world; Petter retained the proprieties of a middle-class Swede, his demeanor characterized by the utmost gravity and reliance on cool intelligence. It would be too facile to describe her as a creative artist, him as a cautious scientist; but these designations, however incomplete, say something about their respective talents.

Very near the center of their differences was Petter's unfortunate belief that his wife's gifts, no matter how they ought to be gauged, did not endow her with much intelligence, common sense or the ability to make the best decisions. His most serious miscalculation was that this adorable young woman did not have much of a head on her shoulders; he presumed, in other words, that her evident wish to rely on a man's counsel signified a girlish lack of maturity and resolve. With the energy that always characterized his actions on her behalf, he added the supervision of her career to his own, and she allowed him to do so—and this, as neither of them could have foreseen, was the fatal mistake that eventually drove them forever apart.

At work, Ingrid Bergman was a woman who could make remarkably correct judgments about a role, a production, the coherence of a narrative and the artistry of a script. Never inclined to analyze or intellectualize, she relied on an enlightened intuition, while at home she slipped easily into the habit of submission to the guidance of a persuasive, powerful husband. What she did not realize was that she did not need Petter Lindstrom quite as much as he needed her to need him.

Chapter Six

1941

Nothing is so good as it seems beforehand.

GEORGE ELIOT,
Silas Marner

THE LINDSTROMS RETURNED FROM NEW YORK TO BEVERLY HILLS on January 22, and Ingrid intently combed the news and trade papers for items about Broadway and Hollywood casting. Among the items that most interested her was one concerning Ernest Hemingway's recent novel, *For Whom the Bell Tolls*, which she had read in New York. Paramount had snapped up movie rights to the story of an unlikely love affair during the Spanish Civil War, and there was a constant buzz that winter about who would play the fiery Spanish girl Maria opposite Gary Cooper, who had starred in an earlier Hemingway-based movie (*A Farewell to Arms*, 1932) and was the author's choice to play Robert Jordan, the laconic, idealistic American hero. Before she and Petter left for a brief ski holiday, Ingrid hurried into Selznick's office and asked to be loaned out to Paramount for the part of Maria. Yes, she said, forestalling his objections, she knew she neither looked nor sounded Spanish, but could not the right makeup, lighting and haircut cover these details? And had she not been praised for her turns as a French governess and a German refugee? It was not simply the story that had gripped Ingrid, she admitted: she wanted to do a film with Gary Cooper.

Selznick listened, without saying that he had already thought of her for this role; had put his brother, the agent Myron Selznick, on the phone to Paramount to sniff out the studio's possible cast list; and had gone so far as to canvass Hemingway himself for his feeling about Ingrid as Maria. Well, Selznick said simply, reaching for a pick-me-up pill and a beaker of water, we would just have to see, wouldn't we?

On January 25, Ingrid and Petter drove north for a ski holiday at June Lake, near the California-Nevada border. Selznick, with an eye on the men at Paramount, had approved the idea of a photo-story for *Life* magazine ("Ingrid Bergman Takes a Short Holiday From Hollywood"), and while the Lindstroms posed smilingly on the slopes and popped snowballs at each other, he plotted virtually around the clock from his office in Culver City. Ingrid, meantime, had no idea that the article for *Life* was part of Selznick's campaign strategy. "To keep you up to date on the situation on Ingrid and *For Whom the Bell Tolls*," he wrote to Kay Brown on January 31,

> I pinned Hemingway down today and he told me clearly and frankly that he would like to see her play the part. He also said this to the press today. However, he tells me also that at Paramount he was told she was wooden, untalented, and various other things. Needless to say, I answered these various charges. Myron is working on it very hard.
>
> I am also personally supervising a publicity campaign to try to jockey Paramount into a position where they will almost have to use her. You will be seeing these items from time to time. Incidentally, Ingrid wasn't in town today, or I could have brought her together with Hemingway. However, we are arranging for her to fly today to see Hemingway in San Francisco before he sails for China. If he likes her, I am asking him to go to town with Paramount on it. If she doesn't get the part, it won't be because there hasn't been a systematic campaign to get it for her!

As he wrote, Ingrid was indeed about to meet Hemingway. She and Petter had driven, during the night of January 30–31, from

June Lake to Reno, where she boarded a morning flight for San Francisco. That afternoon, she, her husband and—lo!—another photographer from *Life* magazine went to Jack's Restaurant on Sacramento Street, where they joined Ernest Hemingway and his new wife, the journalist Martha Gellhorn. Over salads and a few bottles of white wine, they discussed *For Whom the Bell Tolls*, Hemingway describing his characters and themes with expansive gestures and boozy bravado.

And then, with a curiously violent motion, he reached out and grabbed a fistful of Ingrid's long, light brown hair: all this would have to go if she was to play Maria, described in the novel as having "blond hair cropped short like a boy."

This element of transgender confusion was an obsession for Hemingway. Many of his leading ladies in fiction and in life, from Lady Brett Ashley in *The Sun Also Rises* to the author's own wives, were short-haired androgynes—thus his great friendship with, for example, the bisexual Marlene Dietrich, who always wore her trademark gentleman's suits in Hemingway's presence. As with the rest of Hemingway's favorite women on and offscreen, he thought Ingrid would be much more appealing as a boyish girl—in this case, smitten with love for his close friend, Gary Cooper.

The long luncheon ended as waiters were preparing to reset the tables for dinner. In parting, Hemingway pushed into Ingrid's hand a copy of the novel, signed "To Ingrid Bergman, who is the Maria of this book." But for all this, and despite Selznick's drum-beating, Paramount announced that the first screen test for the role of Maria would be made in ten days by Betty Field, who had just co-starred in the film of John Steinbeck's *Of Mice and Men*. The studio was in no hurry to announce a complete cast: taking a page from Selznick's publicity angle during his 1938 search for the perfect Scarlett O'Hara, Paramount happily temporized about a final choice for Maria while Dudley Nichols tried to hammer out a shootable screenplay from Hemingway's sprawling novel. And with that, Ingrid, only momentarily elated, was now once again without purpose.

Never mind, said Selznick when she returned to Beverly Hills. He had arranged for her to go over to Metro again, this time for a lovely role in a major production with Victor Fleming, who had

directed *Gone With the Wind* and *The Wizard of Oz*. Ingrid was to be
the sweetly innocent, loyal, lovestruck fiancée to Spencer Tracy in
Dr. Jekyll and Mr. Hyde. Robert Louis Stevenson's famous story of a
man's split personality (based, it later became clear, on the author's
own harrowing experience with mind-altering drugs) had often
been brought to stage and screen since its publication in 1885.
Among the most celebrated actors who had undertaken the role
with considerable success were Richard Mansfield, Daniel Band-
man, John Barrymore and Fredric March. Coaxed into the picture
by his buddy Victor Fleming (who had directed him in *Captains
Courageous* and *Test Pilot*), Tracy saw it as a startling opportunity, for
he was an actor best known for less disturbing, more appealing
parts. Surprise would be the most important element of his attack
on it.

Ingrid was not going to assume her assigned task without a fight,
for as she read the role of Beatrix Emery, she grew more bored and
exasperated with the turn of each page. For one thing, the role had
no depth. In love with Henry Jekyll and oblivious to the dark implications of his experiments, the fiancée paled by comparison with
Ivy, the Cockney tart who fancies the doctor and is victimized and
finally killed by his alter ego.

The characters played by Ingrid thus far in her American career
had nothing of the variety she had enjoyed in Sweden. In her own
language, she had played comic, dramatic, tragic and romantic roles;
Selznick, however, had allowed her little scope. Although she made
each role her own and could find the truth in any character, there
had been a tedious identity to her American repertoire. In *Intermezzo*, *Adam Had Four Sons* and *Rage In Heaven*, she had been an
admirably self-sacrificing governess or companion. Now she longed
to portray someone else—even a fallen woman, as she had told
Bosley Crowther.

Selznick and Fleming brushed aside this idea, the producer
because he did not want to tarnish her screen image, the director
because he doubted her ability to portray a barmaid who meets a
bad end. Besides, they told Ingrid, the role she coveted was to be
played by Metro's resident sweater girl, Lana Turner, who had just
turned twenty-one and was being groomed for sexy stardom.

But Ingrid gently applied pressure until Fleming finally agreed to test her for Ivy, and on February 20, he was compelled to report to Selznick that Ingrid had surprised him. In just one scene—when a grateful Ivy, rescued from a beating in the street, tries to seduce Dr. Jekyll by slowly removing her blouse under pretext of a physical examination—she shone with a rare combination of sexual sophistication and pathetic innocence. If they put Lana Turner in the less demanding part, Fleming told Selznick and Louis B. Mayer, then both Tracy and Bergman would be seen in startling new roles.

That was the outcome. By the time filming began at the end of February, Ingrid was being fitted for Victorian dresses and screenwriter John Lee Mahin had given Ivy the last name Petersen, to explain her Swedish-tinted Cockney burr. "Ingrid is not only going to be the most important factor in making Hyde believable," said Spencer Tracy during production—and then he tempered his praise with some concern: "But no one is going to know that I am in the picture! She's that good!"

And so she was. Ingrid is first heard twenty minutes into the picture, screaming off-camera as Ivy is rescued by Jekyll from attack by a passerby in a London alley. Feigning a twisted ankle, she embraces the doctor, her wary smile conveying both innocence and attraction. Moments later, Jekyll escorts her home, and she plays her seduction scene—unrolling her stocking, removing her jacket and blouse—as if this were her wedding night. Tracy's Jekyll is fascinated but reserved: repaying his kindness by the mere gift of her garter, she whispers, "doesn't seem near enough to me." And so the atmosphere is set for her to get much more than she bargains for.

In Mahin's acute screenplay and Fleming's careful direction of it, perhaps never before had Stevenson's story of spiritual dislocation been so deftly sketched within the frame of sexual threat. The first transformation of Jekyll into Hyde is accomplished in a hallucinatory episode in which Tracy is seen whipping a white horse and a black horse that at once change into discreetly naked images of Bergman (taking the place of the black horse) and Turner (in place of the white). Jekyll/Hyde then slowly unscrews a cork from a bottle—but the cork changes into the head of Ingrid, who is at once seen supine on a floor of waves. "It must have been Fleming who designed that," said Ingrid years later, aware of the director's fascination with Freudian sexual emblems. For the first time in an

American picture, Ingrid Bergman conveyed a frankly carnal nature.

The motif of the popping cork was inserted, much to Fleming's pleasure, into the subsequent episode by Ingrid herself, when Ivy is seen tending bar, singing and flirting at the Palace of Frivolities. Fascinated and frightened, attracted and repelled by Tracy as Hyde, she tries to appear tough and independent but is wary and nervous. Tripping on her syllables, averting her gaze and drawn back by the awful power of his, Ingrid's Ivy achieves a depth unmarked in the script alone. "I got to love this girl," she said after filming was complete, and that level of understanding enabled her to vanish into the role.

Tracy/Hyde compliments Ivy on her singing (Ingrid herself recorded the jaunty lyrics of "You Should See Me Dance the Polka") and Fleming rightly demanded a close-up of his lascivious gaze. And then, in a remarkable shot, Ingrid gave her director something unexpected and uncanny: to show both the flattery and the fear she felt, she momentarily dilated her nostrils as the dialogue continued:

HYDE (Tracy): And where does the lovely sound [of your singing] come from?

IVY (Bergman, pleased but uneasy): I don't know sir. [She sets down the bottle of champagne and tries to leave his table quickly.] Half a quid, sir.

HYDE (as if hypnotizing her with his low, threatening but sensual tone): Half a quid?

IVY (her lips slightly curling in disgust, but her brow feigning unconcern): Yes, sir. [She tries to depart but he restrains her.] Well, I'll just take a sip of champagne—of course, I shouldn't stay too long.

HYDE (moving closer to her): Where did you get such a pretty voice?

IVY (her intense gaze suggesting she half-recognizes him as the benevolent Dr. Jekyll): Oh—I—don't—know.

HYDE (surveying her throat, breasts and torso): Perhaps it's the pretty place it comes from?

[Like the mare in the hallucination, she half-opens her mouth and dilates her nostrils once again.]

From here, the tragedy moves quickly and agonizingly to the entrapment of poor Ivy by Hyde, who sets her up in elegant concubinage only to brutalize and torture her very near to the point of madness. The horror of sexual enslavement, perhaps never so chillingly rendered in a movie, begins as he takes her away in a horse-drawn carriage:

HYDE (seething): You belong with the immortals! Come with me to Mount Olympus! Drink nectar with the gods! Sing the ancient songs of pleasure and put Athena and Diana to shame!
[The poor girl does not understand his classical references and wants to believe in his protection—even as she is disquieted by his brutal lovemaking.]
HYDE: Don't be frightened of me, Ivy. When a botanist finds a rare flower, he shouts his triumph, doesn't he?
IVY (nodding slowly, although her expression indicates her complete lack of comprehension): Are you one of them [a botanist]?
HYDE (leaning forward for the kiss): You like a man who sees a girl and makes up his mind, don't you?
[The sound of the horses' hooves is heard more insistently, recalling the nightmare.]
IVY (quivering, her voice breaking with a sob of anxiety): Oh—I don't know what you're talking about!
HYDE (contemptuously): Oh—she doesn't know what I'm talking about!

Here begins the dreadful emotional center of this extraordinary film, as the scene cuts to Ivy, kept in claustrophobic isolation by her murderous mentor, beaten into submission by a man she must always address as "Sir," who cruelly demands that she read aloud portions of *Paradise Lost* to him. Promised the freedom of a night out only to have it cruelly denied, Bergman's Ivy is a portrait in abject terror, a heartbreaking character made painfully recognizable because her own attempt at seducing him had, alas, been all too successful. Her life with Hyde becomes a fetid, lurid imprisonment, a grotesque cycle of suffering even as she desperately longs for human contact.

Ingrid's dry-mouthed, wide-eyed reactions, appropriate for a
character constantly kept off guard by her lover-captor, were created
spontaneously, and there is perhaps no more poignant scene of
anguish in the Bergman film catalog than that in which her demonic
suitor forces her to sing a reprise of "You Should See Me Dance the
Polka." Now no longer the carefree barmaid joyously floating a
melody, she tries to sing, in a voice tremulous with fear and
remorse—but the freedom of the dance is lost to her forever.
Pinned to the wall by a vicious, all too human monster, she seems
nearly to break down when he springs back, grasps pieces of rotten
fruit and throws them viciously against her face and body.

From there, it is a direct and short route to the character's
death. Thanks to Ingrid's delineation of Ivy's inner life, of the girl's
longing to survive, her recognition scene with Dr. Jekyll (whom she
manages to visit briefly in search of medical attention) is given an
almost unbearable envelope of despair. Her final scene, when she
sees all too well that her Mr. Hyde is Dr. Jekyll, remains, more than
a half-century later, almost impossible to watch without flinching.
Aware that her own repentance, her desire to be free and to begin
anew have now undone her, Ingrid's Ivy becomes a completely
human amalgam of desire and desperation.

For his part, Fleming was speechless with admiration but mostly
praised Tracy; Selznick, to no one's surprise, said he had predicted
the film would be a triumph. Only Ingrid ended the picture with a
characteristically modest assessment: "I'm a little surprised at how
well it came out." But Tracy was very nearly correct: expert as his
acting was, audiences were and remain stung to silence by the
haunted agony disclosed by his unpretentious, astonishing co-star.

"I WOULD HAVE PAID ANYTHING FOR THIS PICTURE," SHE WROTE IN
her diary late that winter.

> Shall I ever be happier in my work? Will I ever get a better part
> than the little girl Ivy Petersen, a better director than Victor
> Fleming, a more wonderful leading man than Spencer Tracy, and
> a better cameraman than Joe Ruttenberg? I have never been hap-
> pier. Never have I given myself so completely. For the first time, I
> have broken out from the cage which encloses me, and opened a

shutter to the outside world. I have touched things which I hoped were there but I have never dared to show. I am so happy for this picture. It is as if I were flying. I feel no chains. I can fly higher and higher because the bars of my cage are broken.

And the reason for her happiness, her flight, her achievement of new heights beyond her previous cage? It was very simple: she was in love.

But not as most people thought. Perhaps inevitably, rumors began during the production, and by the time of its release in August, many in Hollywood believed that the onscreen passion of Spencer Tracy for Ingrid Bergman was realized in life. Alas for the gossip mongers: not a single person connected to the picture could, then or ever, confirm the idle talk. On the contrary: Billy Grady, a Metro executive charged with supervision of *Dr. Jekyll and Mr. Hyde*, knew that Tracy adored Bergman, "but Spence was too discreet, and he knew this was one girl he couldn't have. So he settled for a nice, professional relationship." Years later, Tracy elaborated: "The only thing Ingrid and I did was to have hamburgers at a drive-in [restaurant] in Beverly Hills." So much for illusion.

As it was, the source of Ingrid's soaring happiness was an unrequited and (for the present) unconsummated infatuation: "By the time the film was over, I was deeply in love with Victor Fleming. But he wasn't in love with me. I was just part of another picture he'd directed." That season, Ingrid was twenty-five, her fantasy lover fifty-eight—like Edvin Adolphson and Petter Lindstrom, he was father, mentor, protector and lover. During the filming of *Dr. Jekyll and Mr. Hyde*, he began calling her "Angel," and this she took for a declaration of love.

Victor Fleming was a rough-and-tumble racing-car addict with a limited education but infinite arrogance, a craggy-handsome face and a reputation as a Hollywood Casanova. If a neighbor's whining cat or barking dog disturbed his sleep, he reached for a rifle and with one clean shot stopped the noise. Committed to a bachelorlike independence and emotionally inaccessible except to drinking buddies like Clark Gable, Spencer Tracy and John Lee Mahin, Fleming ordered the word "love" excised from his marriage ceremony and then, as further witness to his spirit of blithe convenience, refused to bring his wife into his home until she became pregnant a year later.

After that, the hapless Mrs. Fleming was alarmingly often the butt of what can only be called his sadistic manipulations: he treated her, according to their daughter Victoria, "like a cat with a mouse" and routinely she was ordered to attend a movie premiere ten paces behind her husband and his female star of the moment. If his wife annoyed him, he had curious ways of showing his displeasure. A favorite gesture was to catch a fly or insect at the dinner table, season it, pop it into his mouth and chew noisily. If the poor woman left the table in tears, Fleming considered his stunt successful. He was not, to put the matter succinctly, all charm—although at least some women seem to have thought him irresistible. His life was often complicated by a remarkable number of simultaneous liaisons with beautiful women.

Compared to Edvin Adolphson or Petter Lindstrom, Victor Fleming might seem an anomalous quasi-lover for Ingrid, although at the time she knew little about his family life. Furthermore, with her he was almost a gentleman. Once she had passed the screen test for Ivy, Fleming's appreciation of her talent earned her devotion, and his paternal care of her through the rigors of filming counterpoised what she perceived as Petter's rank indifference to her role in (as he considered it) a cheap penny dreadful of a movie. More than once, Ingrid caught Victor spinning a line of risqué stories for the boys in the crew, yet he could be courtly in guiding her through a scene: here was an entirely new breed of American male, and she was fascinated.

Indeed, as she learned more of his tough diction and tougher lifestyle, Fleming may have seemed exciting precisely because his demeanor was in such stark contrast with her husband's. Fleming approved of her and he was in charge; but he was also inaccessible, and according to the strange pique and paradox of romantic obsession, remoteness is, for many people, precisely the defining quality of attraction. Certainly for Ingrid, Fleming's intensely perverse direction of the picture was as appealing to her as his somewhat leonine control, and he earned her lifelong gratitude. "He got things out of me that were different from anything I had done before," she reflected thirty years later. "People said about *Dr. Jekyll and Mr. Hyde*

that they did not recognize me. What more can an actor want?"
And so, until circumstances changed dramatically several years later,
Ingrid Bergman settled for friendship with Victor Fleming.

Love energized her that season, as her friends recognized. Even
when she was not required on the set and had worked late the previous night, Ingrid arrived at seven in the morning to watch Fleming's thoughtful, crisp direction of other players. In addition, she
prepared her own scenes intensively, reading about the mores and
carriage of Victorian women across a wide spectrum of society. "She
always looked as if she was bursting with health and vigor," recalled
Ruth Roberts, who worked with Ingrid on her accent and diction
throughout filming. "Once, she made me stay up all night with her
so she'd look haggard the next day for a scene in *Dr. Jekyll and Mr.
Hyde*. In the morning she was as blooming as ever, but I looked like
the wrath of God!"

AS SUCH THINGS DO, WORD OF INGRID'S STUNNING PERFORMANCE
went around Hollywood even while Fleming and his editor were
giving *Jekyll and Hyde* its final form. A number of directors, having
followed her progress through three films, were eager to see the latest—and none of them was more avid, in this regard, than the
Englishman Alfred Hitchcock, another immigrant artist under contract to David Selznick. That spring of 1941, *Rebecca*, Hitchcock's
first American film, received the Oscar for best picture of the year
1940. The statuette, of course, went to producer Selznick, who was
now loaning out Hitchcock to United Artists, RKO, Universal and
Fox, and at profits even more gigantic than his fees for Ingrid.
Hitchcock had to have Selznick's approval for any project (as did
Ingrid), and he regularly met with him to review story ideas.

"Hitch told me," Selznick wrote on April 2 to Val Lewton, his
West Coast story editor,

> what sounded like a very interesting, if rather erotic story, that he
> thought would be wonderful for Bergman, and that I think he
> would like to direct. He says Joan Harrison [one of Hitchcock's
> team of personal assistants and writers] has the whole story
> which is based on the true account of a couple that were kid-
> napped by Chinese brigands—I guess they would be Japanese in

our picture!—the young wife of a military attache or something
of the sort and a close male friend, who after being kidnapped
were kept chained together by the Chinese for six months.

I can understand the appeal of this to Hitchcock, and I am
not sure but what it might prove to be something very interesting. Obviously the thing we need most of all is a combination
starring vehicle for Ingrid and a picture for Hitch to direct.
Would you please get hold of Miss Harrison and get the dope on
this for me.

For several months, even while directing other pictures, Hitchcock and two writers tried to fashion a scenario based on this kernel
of an idea, but in the end they prudently abandoned it as ineffectual. Still, his desire to work with Ingrid only increased, and over
the next two years his team scoured libraries and story files for
something Selznick might approve. To assure himself of Ingrid's
willingness to work with him, Hitchcock invited the Lindstroms to
several small dinner parties at his snug, unpretentious home in the
wealthy Bel-Air Estates section of Los Angeles. There, Hitchcock
reigned—portly, proper and endlessly witty, alternating risqué stories and accounts of the most gruesome murders with detailed
instructions on how to prepare the finest soufflés.

Forty-one-year-old Hitchcock was the most genial and ebullient
host, sometimes like a naughty boy with his crude jokes designed to
shock the ladies, but always a fascinating raconteur with a mind of
crystal. Ingrid listened to every word—there was no doubt in her
mind that she wanted to work with him—and even Petter had to
admit that yes, Hitchcock had a prodigious memory and a constantly creative imagination, and that Ingrid would do well under his
direction.

After dinner, Hitch and his wife, Alma, rolled back the living
room carpet and snapped on the phonograph, and the house on
Bellagio Road became an impromptu dance hall. No one was more
active at this than Petter, who whirled Ingrid round and round,
through the jitterbug, the samba, the polka and the rhumba. Appreciating the fun as well as the exercise, he inevitably arrived with at
least two or three shirts he could change, so energetic was he
throughout the evening. Other guests—among them Joan Fontaine,

Cary Grant, George Sanders, Teresa Wright and their spouses—found it hard to keep up with Petter; they marveled, too, at Ingrid, who needed only a splash of cold water and not a single dab of makeup to refresh herself and look radiant once again after a particularly energetic turn on the dance floor.

But by the spring of 1941, Petter had little time for dancing. Anxious to obtain his American degree and to begin medical practice, he readily accepted the help and contacts offered by Kay Brown and David Selznick. "Here is a report of the expedition you started for me," he wrote to Selznick from New York on April 18. "Kay arranged an appointment for me at Yale. She has made heroic efforts to help me in this, [and then] I called on the Dean of Columbia University." But Petter's final choice was the University of Rochester, where administrators agreed to accept more of his Swedish credits than the other schools, and because they would confer the M.D. degree after only sixteen months of study rather than the normal two years of American university residency. This expeditious schedule was facilitated by Rochester's dean, Dr. Alan Valentine, a close friend of Selznick and John Hay Whitney, who contacted him on Lindstrom's behalf. "Thanks for all your good help," wrote Petter to Selznick after his official acceptance at Rochester.

This development meant that northern New York State would, for the next year and more, be Petter's residence; he forthwith decided that Pia, soon to turn three, would be better off with him and a nanny in Rochester rather than with Ingrid in Beverly Hills. "My mother had to face the dilemma, over and over," said Pia years later, "whether to stay with her children or pursue her career. The career was in Hollywood, but it was deemed best for me to be with my father, who was in medical school in Rochester. My mother came to visit occasionally, but she spent most of her time in California. Real family life was never as real to her as what was happening on the set. When she wasn't working, she felt she was wasting time."

Ingrid was scheduled to tour in a play that summer, and so Petter reasoned that only God and Selznick knew what was to occur after that (in fact, only God knew). Before the academic year began in autumn 1941, Petter, Pia and Mabel settled into a characterless stucco house at 985 South Avenue, Rochester, a twenty-minute walk from the University Medical School. Ingrid would visit when her obligations permitted.

WITH THE EVIDENT DELAY OF *FOR WHOM THE BELL TOLLS* AND NO immediate suitable project to offer her, Selznick decided to put Ingrid to good dramatic use onstage, a concession so unexpectedly successful the previous year. Summer theater was the perfect venue, Selznick reasoned: he could move his star across the country as the premiere of *Dr. Jekyll and Mr. Hyde* drew near, thus earning both cash and publicity. The play, which both Ingrid and Kay proposed to Selznick, was a 1920 drama by Eugene O'Neill that seemed a perfect career sequel to Ivy Petersen. And the role, which Garbo had undertaken for her first talkie in 1930, would present Ingrid strongly, and so Selznick agreed to expand his empire into the so-called straw hat circuit of summer theater that year, presenting the play under John Houseman's direction in Santa Barbara, San Francisco and Maplewood, New Jersey.

Anna Christie charts the title character's journey as she discovers the possibility of love in a loveless society. Chris Christopherson, a former sea captain who has come to hate the sea and has settled for the helm of a coal barge, learns that his daughter Anna, whom he abandoned fifteen years earlier in Sweden, is soon to visit from Minnesota. Unaware that she has turned to prostitution after being raped, Chris must confront the fact that she has suffered from his neglect. Convinced that she will forever be unloved, Anna at first rejects even the passion she shared with the sailor Mat Burke, but finally she tries to face a new life, free of illusions, with him—as does Chris, who will undertake his first real ocean journey in years. But the sea, O'Neill implies, controls everyone's final destiny.

O'Neill had described Anna as a tall blond of twenty, "handsome after a large, Viking-daughter fashion but now run down in health and plainly showing all the outward evidence of belonging to the world's oldest profession." But Ingrid managed to look only slightly ravaged, for no pale makeup could entirely remove the glow of fitness from her features and the predominant image of health and common sense that she projected. "Ingrid was a joy to work with," recalled Houseman. "She was eager, passionate, well prepared, and she gave me everything I asked for except the feeling that Anna was sick and corrupted and destroyed; one had the conviction that beneath her period skirt, her underclothes were starched, clean and sweet-smelling."

"I see Anna Christie as I am myself, a strong healthy girl from Sweden," Ingrid told a reporter that summer, as if responding to Houseman's notes during rehearsals. "I do not make her very lost or dreary—sick, bitter, yes—she is just a country girl going wrong in the city. I do think that in the famous scene where she swears on the cross that she will never [as a prostitute] love another man and will be good, you must believe her. It wouldn't make sense if you thought she would go back [to her old life]." That was certainly an interpretation that could be read in the text (and doubtless one appealing to summer theatergoers), but it also removed some of the grit from the play.

Her entrance on July 30 at the Lobero Theater, Santa Barbara, where *Anna Christie* ran through August 2, focused the inherent problem of perceiving Ingrid Bergman as a ruined whore. Sinking wearily into a chair at "Johnny the Priest's Bar," she uttered the immortal line, "Gimme a whisky—ginger ale on the side. And don't be stingy, baby." Whereupon the audience—which included Lana Turner, Tony Martin, George Raft, Samuel Goldwyn, Alfred Hitchcock, Olivia de Havilland and an oversubscribed crowd—burst out laughing. "They expected, I suppose, for me to say, 'Give me a glass of milk,'" Ingrid recalled with amusement years later. "Oh well, we got over that."

Once they did, playgoers in the three cities that August and September found her portrait starkly compelling. Ingrid's natural restlessness and high-strung temperament found its locus in Anna's roughness, and she projected a certain stillness at the center of the role that came from something toward which she always strove. In this, too, Anna and Ingrid were, as she insisted, alike: both tried to meet others' high opinions of them, however romanticized. There was a special autobiographical poignancy to some of her lines, too. "I don't remember nothing about my mother. What was she like?" and "Kids . . . always listening to their bawling and crying . . . caged in, when you're only a kid yourself and want to go out and see things."

But her final lines had the audience motionless: "Cut out the gloom," she said to her lover Mat, with a tone of determined gaiety that turned into an expressed hope. "We're all fixed now, ain't we, me and you?" She poured beer for them both. "Come on! Here's to the sea, no matter what! Be a game sport and drink to that!" Never before and rarely since had O'Neill's long, structurally problematic play been given so clear a possibility of redemption. "She has given O'Neill's drama a poetic interpretation and a new life," ran a typical review, "and in doing so she made a place for herself in the history of the theater in the United States."

At the same time, crowds were flocking to movie theaters all over the country, for *Dr. Jekyll and Mr. Hyde* opened on August 13, and the raves for Ingrid's performance were past counting. In the twenty months since her return to America, she had appeared in two plays and three films, a prodigious achievement for any actress, but not enough to satisfy Ingrid Bergman, who saw every accomplishment as a challenge compelling her to refine her gifts with the next project. Purposeful activity defined her life, and the routines of quotidian reality bored, angered and alienated her from her family, her friends and herself. The women she played taught her about women; the scripts she read infused her imagination and sparked a native intelligence.

During the run of the play at the Curran Theater, San Francisco, Ingrid received an invitation from Carlotta Monterey O'Neill to join the playwright for Sunday lunch at Tao House, his home on a great cliff overlooking the ocean. "He took me to his study," Ingrid remembered, "and he had nine plays lying around. He was going to do his famous saga of an American family through one hundred fifty years—a cycle about America's growth and especially its greed, how we ruin our lives with greed." O'Neill then said he wanted Ingrid to be part of a repertory company, in which she and the other players would appear in one city in one role and another in the next. But when he said this project would require a six-year commitment, the conversation went no further. Her obligations to Selznick could not be ignored, nor would she wish to do so.

INGRID WAS GROWING, AT TWENTY-SIX, INTO A WOMAN NOT EASILY SAT-isfied with trivia. She was, in other words, the best example of the actress as creative personality: she did not merely "play at" roles; rather, they moved her to a deeper focus and concentration on life itself. Her natural timidity, her refusal to appear pretentious or grand, her lack of guile—all these would never allow her to discuss her art in florid rhetoric or to hold forth on the subtleties of the artist's life. She had no patience with such self-referential talk, no matter the source. Ingrid Bergman had a job to do: that was the ethos she shared with Duse and Bernhardt, whose biographies she devoured later that year while idle and awaiting Selznick's pleasure.

"It was unbearably dull, with nothing to do," said Ingrid of her time in Rochester during the autumn of 1941. It is not difficult to understand her disappointment and boredom. Household duties were not enough to sustain her talent and interests, and the only people she met were Petter's colleagues. "When they came to the house all the conversation was medicine. This was surely natural and the way it should be, but for me it was not easy." To Ruth Roberts she confided, "In all our married life [over four years], we have been together only for about twelve months."

As for the routines of motherhood, she was simply too intent on her career to give it all up for the doubtful joys of daily parenting. She loved her child, and when she was with her in Rochester she gave Pia the attention she deserved and wanted. But soon she felt not only bored but also unnecessary at home: Mabel had been trained to perfection by Petter, who generally found fault with Ingrid's methods and style, and so Mama could only hanker more than ever for the opportunity to get back to work. One might ask if this was very different from the lot of many gifted women who became mothers but did not wish the daily routine to be their only career.

In addition, Ingrid herself had never known the ministrations of an attentive mother and therefore never knew what comprised its fulfillment. Greta Danielsson was a genial sister-figure but nothing as stable as a mother substitute; Aunt Ellen had died after six months of harboring Ingrid; and Kay was, after all, her boss's employee and had a life of her own as wife and mother. With every element of her life as with her art, Ingrid created the role according to her own intuition, never merely modeling herself on an existing pattern. Pia Lindstrom, whose assessment should be taken as central to any consideration of Ingrid's qualities as a mother, certainly reached adulthood with a tangle of confused feelings about her mother. But she also understood, as she said, that "although it's wonderful to have a parent around, you can be raised without having a parent around every minute. I think all of us children realized the things she had to contend with—the forces in her life, the call to perform, her need to be in a contented family which she knew on the set of her movies."

But there was no call to perform in Hollywood or onstage from September 1941 to the spring of 1942. Irked by inactivity, Ingrid was further annoyed by the good people of Rochester, who invaded the privacy of their local celebrity day and night. The *Times-Union* and the *Democrat and Chronicle* reported that citizens crowded outside the house and rang the Lindstrom telephone constantly. "I have a good-looking daughter, Miss Bergman. Would you look at her to see if she's good enough for a screen test? . . . " "Miss Bergman, I have a friend . . . I wonder if . . . " "Miss Bergman, may we come over and get your autograph? It's for my cousin . . ." An unlisted number was installed, but strangers still felt free to ring their doorbell, and the Rochester police had to patrol the house several times daily. "It's nice and comfortable here," Ingrid wrote to Selznick on September 29, "like in prison."

Her journeys to New York (to Kay's Manhattan apartment on East Eighty-sixth Street, to the theater, to museums) became more and more frequent. And when she was in Rochester, boredom led her, as so often, to overindulge her appetite: ice cream, knäckebröd and goat cheese—"I think I have tried everything to stop eating. Well, it doesn't help." The best thing about Rochester, according to Ingrid, was the railway station, where she boarded trains for escape.

She tried to plan her days in Rochester, as she told friends, as if she were back in school. She wrote letters in the morning, took Pia for a walk, played piano, kept her album of clippings, had her English lesson. At both the piano and the English she was really quite proficient by this time; her musical repertoire expanded to include a few Chopin preludes, and the command of her new language was impressive, her vocabulary varied, her letters invariably correct and surprisingly stylish.

"Only my reading and knitting save me," Ingrid confided in a letter to Ruth.

I am knitting Pia's doll, sweaters and skirts. She is an extraordinary child. I told her that for Christmas we were going to give away all the toys she didn't like or she thought other children would like. But she should collect them and choose which ones herself because they were hers and I would have nothing to say. And Ruth, I nearly cried. I saw her for an hour go very carefully through all her things . . . She was so sweet. Very good things she gave away, saying, "I don't think I play very much with that." But an old dolly, very, very dirty, she kept, saying: "Yes, she is dirty but she really was a very good girl." And her mother was quiet. All this from a three-year-old!

Christmas was only a brief respite from the snail's pace of life. "Having a home, husband and child ought to be enough for any woman's life—I mean, that's what we are meant for, isn't it?" asked Ingrid at the time, confiding plaintively in Ruth Roberts and expressing a dilemma more common than she knew. "But still I think every day is a lost day. As if only half of me is alive. The other half is pressed down in a bag and suffocated. What shall I do? If only I saw some light."

Chapter Seven

1942

Love, and a cough, cannot be hid.

GEORGE HERBERT,
Jacula Prudentum

OR ALMOST NINE MONTHS, FROM EARLY SEPTEMBER 1941 TO LATE
May 1942, Ingrid Bergman's major occupation was knitting.
Good heavens, she complained to Kay Brown and Ruth Roberts,
soon she would be able to outfit every soldier in the world with a
sweater. As she sat quietly in Rochester, welcoming local ladies to
tea and her husband's colleagues to dinner, her cultural life limited
and her career apparently stymied, Ingrid's patience was worn
down; never had she felt so useless.

No good news was forthcoming from David Selznick, who had
briefly considered dressing her as a nun for a forthcoming film version of A. J. Cronin's novel *The Keys of the Kingdom*. He then changed
his mind and announced that she would appear in something called
She Walks in Beauty, based on Henry James's novel *The Wings of the
Dove*—and then that idea vanished into oblivion also. John Houseman suggested to Selznick that he team Ingrid with Alfred Hitchcock in a film of Stefan Zweig's novel *Letter From an Unknown*

Woman, but Selznick (acting on the astute counsel of Kay Brown), replied that this was not Hitchcock's kind of material. (Houseman later produced the film himself.)

Selznick had ceaselessly and vigorously campaigned for Ingrid to play Maria in *For Whom the Bell Tolls*, but the new year brought the announcement that those hopes, too, had been scuttled. Paramount, acceding to Hemingway's demand for Gary Cooper, had paid a great deal of money to borrow him from Samuel Goldwyn, and so they were inclined to cast one of their own contract players as Maria—the Norwegian dancer and actress Vera Zorina, a veteran of several unexceptional film musicals; she was then completing a Broadway engagement. Olivia de Havilland, her sister Joan Fontaine, Susan Hayward and a score of others also tested for the role, but Paramount, economizing, assigned it to Zorina, a great beauty from whom, it was hoped, a great performance could be coaxed.

"I'm down now," Ingrid wrote dejectedly to Selznick when she learned the news about Zorina. "Since your cable of 1940 regarding [the suspension of] *Joan of Arc*, I have experienced a series of postponements and changes in your plans . . . I cannot stand being idle. In these days [of war] more than ever, I feel one has to work, one must accomplish something. I feel very sad."

Irene Selznick knew of Ingrid's displeasure with inactivity: "Hard work is not the indulgence most people crave, but to Ingrid it was a necessity." In fact, with that winter's darkness and confinement, Ingrid was soon very close to something like clinical depression. Even on sunny days, she sat listlessly, asking Mabel to take her place on outings with Pia and arousing Petter's impatience with her sullen withdrawal. At the end of March, she and Petter met with the Hollywood agent Charles K. Feldman, and after Petter had investigated his company's credentials, Ingrid signed with the Feldman-Blum agency in Hollywood. But because her career was entirely subject to Selznick, Feldman could essentially act only as her manager and adviser. Petter still approved every annual renewal of her Selznick contract, counseled her about wardrobe, weight, comportment and speech and scrutinized radio roles offered to his wife.

He also began to act as her de facto agent, and this created predictable problems with Selznick and Feldman. On April 10, for example, Ingrid was to go to New York to read in a radio play, but Selznick withdrew his permission for this; the reason, as he wrote in a memorandum to his vice-president and general manager, Dan O'Shea, was "because Petter would not agree to give us half of the $1750" to which Selznick was contractually entitled. For his part, Petter figured that since he had set up the radio deal, he and Selznick need not split the compensation. Furthermore, Petter wrote to O'Shea, "We are going to decide about [Ingrid's wishes to return to the] theater not later than September"—by which he meant that he would decide and Selznick would be duly informed. With this development, the skein of the Bergman-Selznick-Lindstrom relationship began to be very tangled indeed. Still, Selznick knew that he had to placate Petter to ingratiate himself with Ingrid—thus his promise to pay $500, the cost of Petter's California medical license.

AT LAST, ON APRIL 24, SELZNICK INFORMED INGRID THAT HE HAD A movie for her. This he did because he could earn a great deal of money on the deal—$125,000 from Warner Bros., while he paid Ingrid her contracted salary of $35,000—and because, with the possibility of Sweden's alliance with Germany and Italy, he felt it necessary to use Ingrid before Hollywood became chilly to the idea of using a Swedish actress who had taken no steps to acquire American citizenship.

And so it happened that Ingrid was to be loaned out to producer Hal Wallis at Warner Bros., and that studio, in turn, would provide Selznick with their contracted player, Olivia de Havilland, for a Selznick picture. "The picture is called Casablanca and I really don't know what it's all about," Ingrid wrote to Ruth Roberts. In this she was not alone: at every stage of its development, everyone involved in the picture was similarly in the dark about its political and romantic logic. On May 2, having left Petter and Pia in Rochester, Ingrid returned to Hollywood for the first time in a year. Selznick's assistants had found her a snug little apartment at 413 South Spalding Drive, Beverly Hills, in the same modest complex as her former residence around the corner on Shirley Place.

Casablanca, Gone With the Wind and Citizen Kane have perhaps been the subjects of more exhaustive study than any other American movies. The production of each was an uncertain undertaking begun against terrific creative odds and completed with no sure idea of just how the final product should be marketed. *Casablanca*, the movie for which Ingrid Bergman is perhaps best known to moviegoers, was, in the making, one of the most difficult and frustrating experiences of her life. A classic in spite of itself, it was improvised daily by many authorial hands, and its success is entirely due to a certain kind of haphazard good fortune that sometimes occurs in Hollywood.

Casting was not the major problem, but the writing was. Warner Bros. production files clarify that the brothers Julius and Philip Epstein worked more than others on the screenplay, but Howard Koch is also credited, and a number of uncredited writers made important contributions (Willy Kline, Aeneas McKenzie, Casey Robinson and Lenore Coffee among them). The director, producer and cast also had a hand in adding some dialogue. Contrary to the academic understanding of moviemaking, this is not as rare as it may seem.

The genesis of *Casablanca* may be briefly outlined. In late 1938, New York schoolteacher Murray Burnett visited a French nightclub called La Belle Aurore, whose music and general atmosphere reminded him of a Broadway show called *Everybody's Welcome*; this musical had featured a song by Herman Hupfeld called "As Time Goes By." By the summer of 1940, Burnett and his writing partner Joan Alison had written a play called *Everybody Comes to Rick's*, which, at the end of the following year, was still unstaged when producer Hal Wallis at Warner Bros. bought the film rights for $20,000, the largest sum ever paid for an unproduced play.

Mindful of the recent success of Charles Boyer and Hedy Lamarr in the exotic romance *Algiers*, Wallis took the play to writers Julius and Philip Epstein, renamed the project *Casablanca* and, in early 1942, announced that the leading roles would be played by Ronald Reagan, Ann Sheridan and Dennis Morgan.

By the end of April, a third draft of the script had been delivered to Wallis and Warner, and Michael Curtiz, the Hungarian director chosen for *Casablanca*, was busy at work. He had collaborated with Victor Sjöström and Mauritz Stiller in Sweden and was so prolific in Hollywood that he sometimes directed as many as five pictures in a year.

But the script problems continued and were of much concern to Ingrid when she read the fourth draft in early May. Selznick assured her that the final version would make her forever one of Hollywood's unforgettable romantic heroines, that she could do no better than to play opposite Humphrey Bogart (now cast as the leading man) and—could she ask for more?—that she would look stunning photographed by Arthur Edeson in the smart and flattering wardrobe designed by Orry-Kelly. Still, Ingrid could not grasp the fuzzy logic of the story at this point: she would have to understand the woman before she could enliven her. And in this regard, an extraordinary thing took place.

On May 22 and 23, Ingrid asked for confidential meetings with Wallis, Curtiz, Warner and Selznick, before whom she set forth a number of questions about *Casablanca*. Who precisely was this Ilsa Lund? What was the emotional background of a woman who falls so passionately in love with two such different men? How deeply does she feel a clash between love and duty? What was the meaning of this line after you looked at this other one, a few pages later? How can this scene be reconciled with that one? Her insistence on answers to these questions, according to Warner Bros. production files, enabled the writers, producer and director to take their script the last important mile. With the writers still typing away, filming began on May 25 at the Warner Bros. studio and back lot.

CASABLANCA HAS, AT ITS CENTER, THE RELATIONSHIP BETWEEN THE ENIG-matic expatriate American Rick Blaine (Bogart) and Ilsa Lund (Ingrid), once his lover but now married to the anti-Nazi freedom fighter Victor Laszlo (Paul Henreid, who had torn up a lucrative contract with UFA in 1936). Around them all swirls a tangle of spies and opportunists, German officers and Vichy officials—prime among them the chief of Casablanca police, Louis Renault (Claude Rains).

"No one had the slightest idea of where the picture was going," recalled Ingrid.

We were handed new pages of dialogue every morning and after-noon, and we had to run off and memorize little bits and pieces of it—and re-think the character in the bargain! Every time I asked

Curtiz who I was in this picture, what I felt, what I was doing, he
said, "Well, we're not really sure, but let's do this scene and
tomorrow we'll let you know!" Really, it was quite impossible!

And so, that hot summer of 1942, Casablanca plodded erratically
toward completion, with a cast and crew working overtime and with
dogged efficiency to offer their best work. Ingrid, who turned in a
haunting performance, was miserable during the entire production,
and no one had the remotest idea that the picture would become
one of the most popular and enduring films in American history.
    For one thing, the idealistic-romantic finale, in which Rick sac-
rifices his love for Ilsa and convinces her to go with her husband
and fight for freedom, was not decided on until the end of production. Under orders from Curtiz, Wallis and Jack Warner, the writers
had prepared the alternative that Ilsa would remain with Rick. This
version was to have been filmed later, but the first conclusion
looked so good to everyone that the other was omitted—especially
in light of the final line of the picture (devised by Hal Wallis), which
bonds Bogart to Rains: "Louis, I think this is the beginning of a
beautiful friendship," which was recorded two weeks after the cast
had been dismissed. As for the film's most famous words—"Here's
looking at you, kid"—Bogart borrowed them and slipped them in
on the spot: he had picked up the line from Ruth Roberts, who was
simultaneously teaching Ingrid poker and slang one day during a
lunch break.
    A very different idea might have permanently derailed the pic-
ture's popularity. After filming was completed, composer Max
Steiner urged Wallis to drop "As Time Goes By." But this decision
would have necessitated the reshooting of all scenes in which the
melody is sung or played, for it was a romantic link between Rick
and Ilsa. Also, Ingrid had begun work on another film the day after
completing Casablanca, and her return to reshoot scenes would have
been a logistical nightmare. Hence "As Times Goes By" was
retained. The alternative proposed by Steiner, countless fans have
maintained ever since, would have been too terrible to contemplate.

RADIATING A COMPLEX SET OF EMOTIONS—REAWAKENED LOVE, VULNER-
ability, honor with insecurity—Ingrid brought to the film a sense of

the fragility of romance that spoke directly to the heart of a wartime audience. With this picture, her image on film was forever transformed, although the making of it provided not one pleasant or memorable day. Ilsa was all banked fires, desire clashing with devotion, heart with head—and somehow, from 1942 and each year thereafter, audiences recognized that here was a woman whom a moral aristocrat like Henreid could fight for, yet a woman whom the most cynical scrapper like Bogart could never root out of his cool, untamed heart.

Casablanca gave Ingrid Bergman her first role as a great lover (if not her first great role). But because the memory of it was always irksome to her—and ever more so with the passing of years, as the film acquired cult status and she became identified with it—she never relied on this image to bear her along, never wanted to return to the terribly pretty iconography of Ilsa Lund.

As usual she triumphed against all odds, and her performance is justly admired. For the first two-thirds of the picture, she gave Ilsa an extraordinary stillness, and it is this quality that gives the character's romantic hesitation its poignancy and its maturity. There are an extraordinary number of long close-ups on Ingrid in *Casablanca*, yet these do not retard the picture's momentum or its emotional energy. Her "friend" the camera (as she always called it) caught every nuance, and unlike many mere performers, this actress somehow rendered the suggestion of tangled feelings, the network of emotions that comprise any adult's inner life.

Especially in the last third of the picture, she gave Ilsa a heightened, rarefied passion that cut its way through confusion. For the scene in which she attempts to extricate letters of transit from Bogart so that she and Henreid may leave Casablanca, Curtiz kept his camera almost entirely on Ingrid, who knew the precise pauses and the shifting tremors of emotion with which the character's range of feeling had to be conveyed as she moves from threats to a declaration of love.

ILSA (Bergman): You want to feel sorry for yourself, don't you? There's so much at stake, and all you can think of is your own feeling. One woman is hurting you. You take your revenge on the rest of the world. You're a—you're a coward and weak. [She does not mean this, and her eyes begin to glaze with tears.] No, no, Richard—I'm sorry. I'm sorry—but you are our last hope. [Her voice falls to a whisper.] If you don't help us, Victor Laszlo will die in Casablanca.

RICK (Bogart): What of it? I'm gonna die in Casablanca. It's a good place for it. Now, if you—

ILSA (interrupting, suddenly pointing a revolver): All right—I tried to reason with you. I tried everything. Now I want those letters. Get them for me.

RICK: I don't have to. I've got them right here.

ILSA (her eyes brimming with tears): Put them on the table.

RICK: If Laszlo and the cause mean so much to you, you won't stop at anything. [He walks toward her.] All right. I'll make it easier for you. Go ahead and shoot. You'll be doing me a favor.

ILSA (trembling): Richard, I tried to stay away. I thought I would never see you again That you were out of my life. [They embrace.] The day you left Paris—if you knew what I went through—if you knew how much I loved you—how much I still love you. [They kiss.]

On paper, the scene is, as the great screenwriter Ben Hecht said in another context, a lot of romantic hooey; but thanks to Ingrid's thoroughly credible delivery—she is all tremulous poetry confronting Bogart's stolid prose—it works perfectly.

Onscreen romance notwithstanding, there were no friendly associations to encourage and unite the cast during production. "In *Casablanca*, I kissed Bogart," Ingrid said, "but I never really knew him. He came out of his dressing room, did his scene, then fled away again. It was all very strange and distant." Only much later did she learn that Bogart's wife, the eccentric actress Mayo Methot, was pathologically jealous of her husband and routinely threatened all sorts of violence if he even befriended a female co-star. Bogart, the image of independent, self-confident machismo, obeyed. He may have been glad to do so, for he also confided to colleagues (as did Spencer Tracy before him), that he felt Ingrid was stealing the entire focus of the film away from every other performer.

Petter visited Hollywood on a brief holiday, from June 14 to July 4 (having left Pia in Rochester with Mabel). He went directly to the

Warner set, bearing—to everyone's surprise—ten reels of sixteen-millimeter film he had taken of the Lindstrom life in Rochester, much of it featuring the antics of Pia, who was an engaging little charmer almost four years old. Ingrid, delighted, invited a few cast and crew members to watch the impromptu screening at the end of the day.

DESPITE THE PROFESSIONAL DIFFICULTIES ATTENDING CASABLANCA, IT was an immediate success, beginning with an accident of history. On November 8, the Allied forces landed in Casablanca, and at once Jack Warner's publicists prevailed on him to rush the picture to an early release in New York. After a sold-out premiere, every standing-room ticket was gone for subsequent performances during the limited end-of-the-year run. When President Roosevelt returned from the Casablanca Conference in January 1943, the film's success was guaranteed: it was as timely as the world's head-lines, and by mid-February it was on two hundred American movie screens. Indeed, among the fans was the president himself, who ordered a print for his guests at a New Year's Eve party he hosted at the country's own casa blanca, located at 1600 Pennsylvania Avenue.

Long lines formed at every theater in the country, and it was perhaps inevitable that this irresistible story of love and nobility—though laced with errors of fact, logic and character consistency—would be nominated for eight Academy Awards (Ingrid was not named among them). It won three (for best picture, director and screenplay of the year 1942), and more than a half-century later was still counted as one of the most popular movies of all time—not for its historic timeliness but because it remains superior enter-tainment. But Ingrid Bergman, for one, could never understand why. When complimented on her performance, she smiled patiently, laughed and said, "Well, it was a very strange experience. Let me tell you, we were never certain what was going on . . . "

ONE DAY AT THE END OF JULY, PAUL HENREID NOTICED INGRID'S quiet glumness during a break in filming. Well, she explained, she had nothing to look forward to. Selznick kept her idle too often, she found life without work intolerable, and despite a strong-arm campaign, she had lost the role of Maria to Vera Zorina. Even as they spoke, *For Whom the Bell Tolls* had begun filming in northern California. She honestly (and rightly) believed the part would have been better off with her. "I don't think she was taken by her own beauty at all," Henreid said years later. "She was taken only by the desire to do the best work possible in her profession."

But as she poured out her unhappiness to Henreid, Ingrid was unaware that, hundreds of miles away on location, the bell was tolling disastrously on a production that was as riddled with problems as *Casablanca* and would, in the end, be far less popular and successful.

First of all, there were problems with director Sam Wood, not the most sensitive director under even the best of circumstances, a technician more interested in arranging the horses than working with actors. But Wood had just directed Gary Cooper in *Pride of the Yankees* and was Cooper's good buddy, so there was no question of engaging a replacement. In addition, neither Cooper nor Wood much liked Vera Zorina, an exquisite beauty but far too refined for either the role of Maria or the rigors of filming in the California mountains. Together, Cooper and Wood reported to Paramount's production chief, B. G. De Sylva, that they agreed with Hemingway and Selznick: Ingrid Bergman was the right one for the role. Zorina would have to go.

This presented an indelicate dilemma, for Wood—without regard for his truest feelings—had already told Zorina that, yes, her test had been magnificent, and that the single scene he had filmed with her showed that she was a marvelous actress. This prevarication, doubtless uttered to flatter and encourage, now backfired loudly, for the poor woman had believed it. Trained as a ballerina and at the time the wife of choreographer George Balanchine, she was a Paramount contract player with no major movie credits and, until Wood spoke on her behalf, she was terrified of appearing in so major a production as *For Whom the Bell Tolls*. Wood's adulation infused her with unrealistic hopes—and made the blow of dismissal all the more shattering. As it happened, Zorina should have lit candles of gratitude not to have appeared in a film that was, in its final realization, one of the most boring pieces of nonentertainment in Hollywood history.

By the last of July, *Bell* had been delayed several weeks while Cooper (and Wood, doing his bidding) quietly awaited news that *Casablanca* was complete and Bergman available. Then, three days before the wrap of that production, Zorina was summoned to De Sylva's office. Cooper and Wood had given him an ultimatum, he said: Bergman would replace her, or they would quit the production. For the rest of her life, Zorina felt betrayed, furious at what she later called the "ultimatum ruthlessly engineered by David O. Selznick."

But this was not the truth, and no one had the courage to be forthright with her. The screenplay was far too long and its problems were magnifying daily; she could not project sufficient star power to carry the picture opposite Cooper; and no one, as *Life* magazine put it with uncharacteristic sarcasm, "could get her to stop being a first-rate ballet dancer." Hemingway, who wielded enormous unofficial power, was not surprised: Ingrid had been his choice from day one, after all.

And so De Sylva, who could not risk losing Cooper, Wood, Hemingway's endorsement and perhaps all the money he had authorized for *Bell* thus far, called Selznick. Would Ingrid be willing to cut off most of her hair? Selznick, on July 31, then rhetorically put the question to Ingrid. She would cut off her head if she had to, she cried excitedly. Eager to have done with *Casablanca*, she was ignorant of worse problems to come. Selznick was fairly eager, too: he made a quick, slick deal with Paramount, who paid him $150,000 for Ingrid (who, with a bonus for overtime, received $34,895).

ON AUGUST 5, INGRID AND RUTH ROBERTS ARRIVED IN SONORA, AT the foothills of the Sierra Nevada Mountains, near the Stanislaus National Forest. Next day, Ruth wrote to Dan O'Shea that Ingrid looked wonderful "and [was] happy to the bursting point." She looked forward to realizing her dream role, to having her hair cut and dyed and her pale skin made up to look olive. It was her first color film, and most of all she looked forward to the learning process—and to the company of Gary Cooper, whose natural style of acting she so admired.

Ingrid would not have been pleased to hear of some difficulties that were unwittingly being caused by Petter's good intentions.

Someone in Selznick's legal department had wrongly sent to Rochester the option papers she had to sign to formalize her release for *Bell*. Petter, reading the various clauses that July, had some objections, and this began a volley of letters and cables between Rochester and Culver City. Without consulting Charles Feldman, Petter simply began to negotiate on Ingrid's behalf, seeking better bonus clauses, more time off and other concessions she had never requested and which Selznick found unreasonable. "The only thing that can stand between Ingrid and both her great happiness and her great success is your fantastic attempt to manage her," Selznick wrote to Lindstrom in a letter drafted on August 6.

Two weeks later, Petter wrote to O'Shea, "I am sorry I promised to rush the contract back to you . . . I cannot ask Ingrid to sign a contract which I have seen for only half an hour . . . I would like to call you tonight." Selznick, furious, complained to Feldman: "Lindstrom is still doing tricks and attempting to take advantage of the increased value Ingrid will have because of *Bell* . . . If Lindstrom persists in his attitude and tries to outsmart Ingrid's friends and producers as well as her agents, Ingrid is going to have to pay the penalty." Her reliance on her husband and willingness to have him handle even her private finances had already created some hardships for her: "She didn't even dare to buy herself a dress without his okay," said their friend Michel Bernheim, a French film producer.

"I personally would have told Dr. Lindstrom to go fly a kite," Selznick said to his publicity director Whitney Bolton, who complained that Petter had opinions about every aspect of Selznick's management of Ingrid. Selznick had a personal reason to resent the management style of Petter, who, during the June visit to Hollywood, had spoken rather undiplomatically to Selznick. "David seemed ill at ease with me," Petter wrote to David's wife, Irene, "and [he] evidently resented it when I told him that his biggest assets were his wife and father-in-law." Such frankness did not win Petter an ally.

FOR THE PRESENT, THESE DEVELOPMENTS WERE NOT CONVEYED TO Ingrid, and this was much to Selznick's credit; he knew she had sufficiently hard work demanding her attention high up in the Sierra

Nevadas. Life there from early August to late September was harsh
in some ways and enormously gratifying in others; as so often,
Ingrid made a virtue of necessity with the first and embraced the
second.

First, there were living conditions that few stars would have
uncomplainingly sustained. Near the Stanislaus River, she and Ruth
were assigned a small vacation cabin, leased by Paramount from a
California family. Trout swam picturesquely in the rapids just
beneath the back porch, and when they had time, Ingrid and Ruth
stopped to hook one for Gary Cooper or Sam Wood. But this was
no Hollywood bungalow: there was very little water and no electricity, heat or telephone. The production manager feared the wrath of
his leading lady, but he was surprised to find Ingrid actually enjoying
the simple rustic life. Her wardrobe for the part called for little
more than a man's shirt, old pants and rope-soled shoes, and she
was quite content to wear these off-camera. It was a new experience, a simpler life, and she took it in good humor, making no
demands. "I love being out in the sun," Ingrid wrote to Irene
Selznick on August 23, "and climbing and riding make me feel so
much better than sitting in a dressing room in a comfortable chair."

Then there were the rigors of filming. The entire picture was
designed by William Cameron Menzies, who had been responsible
for the look of every scene in Gone With the Wind, Our Town, Kings
Row and Pride of the Yankees, and he chose whatever most resembled
the rugged Spanish terrain. For the most part, that meant the cast
and crew proceeded almost fifteen miles farther into the mountains,
among sheer granite boulders eight and nine thousand feet above
sea level. There, the company arrived in the frosty mornings,
worked through the hot afternoons and warmed themselves with
mugs of coffee in the cold evenings before bundling into cars and
heading back to town. Ingrid loved every minute.

Not because she knew she was in a masterpiece, however. The
least alert crew member knew, fairly early, that For Whom the Bell
Tolls, with its endless talk and endless close-ups, was becoming a
crushingly tiresome and emotionally flat picture that bled the life
and love (not to say the crucial political angle) out of the Hemingway novel. It was 1942, and Hollywood had to play everything safe:
there was no condemnation of Spanish Fascism, no mention of

Franco and his forces, very little back story for the guerrillas, and only the politest gestures to indicate the problematic, passionate affair between the freedom fighter Robert Jordan and the benighted peasant girl Maria. (Fifty years later, some of the cuts were restored for home video: this only gave the picture, now no longer timely and still coy in its love story, more of its muchness.)

But it was not only the Motion Picture Code's censors that diluted the story: Sam Wood utterly lacked a sense of pacing and was uninterested in every player except his friend Gary Cooper. This performance is of considerable interest, for Ingrid seemed to have coaxed an animated performance from the usually wooden Cooper, apparently touched by her presence in a way he was not often by his female co-stars. There are spontaneous smiles and chuckles here, suggesting his enjoyment of her, and a glow of agitation in the love scenes that is otherwise absent in the Cooper canon. Watching his films decades later, it is clear that his popularity derived precisely from his aloofness and finely chiseled features— qualities often confused with talent. But Gary Cooper was always Gary Cooper, tall in the saddle but short in the range of histrionic ability.

Wood was indeed fortunate in these rare moments when *Bell* caught fire; but for them and the talents of Bill Menzies, Katina Paxinou and a team of seasoned professionals in supporting roles, the picture might have had not much distinction at all. Paxinou, alone among eight nominations for *Bell*, won an Oscar as best supporting actress; Ingrid was also nominated, as best actress of the year. But in the end, *Bell* turned out to be a very pretty but massive Technicolor travel documentary of the California mountains, a preposterously inflated bore that could have narcotized even the hyperactive, pill-popping Selznick.

The production was unintentionally steeped in the spirit of Disney's "Pirates of the Caribbean." Menzies yielded to Wood's demands and glamorized *Bell*, each scene resembling a painting too pretty for the rough story. In the winter scenes, for example, the film is as appealing as a pack of Hallmark Christmas cards; the only absentee is old St. Nick, bobsledding around the mountain. Nor is Victor Young's romantic score always appropriate—indeed, his major motif is too often repeated and every acting beat is supported by intrusive incidental music. In one scene, as a Republican taunts Pablo, Young scores a chord burst with every punch the man delivers to the traitor. The picture, at such moments, is dangerously close to satire. In the final analysis, war never looked so attractive as here in Paramount, Spain.

In one of the two starring roles of the film, even the resourceful Ingrid Bergman could find nowhere to attach her talent, and although in her memoirs she fondly recalled working with Cooper, she confided to friends years later that the months of working on *Bell* were among the most frustrating and disappointing of her career: "I hated every moment of it," she said flatly, for she knew from the start that the script gave her nothing to work with—even her two dramatic monologues came from left field and provided no context in which the audience could find its logical empathy.

Ingrid's best performances were delivered in consort with first-rate players and inspired directors, who created an atmosphere in which her talents could flourish. Cooper, the perfect physical embodiment of the character of Jordan, gave her nothing to work with except his charm, and for *Bell* that was largely insufficient. Ultimately, Cooper played Cooper (as only Cooper could), and his inability to inflect his diction made his overwritten, repetitive final injunction to Ingrid maddening for audiences then and later: "You must go because you are me and I am you, and where you go I go—don't you see?—and if you stay I cannot go because we can never be separated, because I go only where you go and if you go then I am free to go even though I stay—because I am you and you are me."

The mind reels at this sort of bogus mysticism, wrapped in sophomoric syllogisms of the sort undergraduates use to seduce coeds, as unconvincing as a politician's promise to cut taxes. Never mind that it also contains a grave logical flaw: if she is he and he is she, then she ought to stay and be killed with him—because she is he! Or words to that effect. Cooper mutters the scene as if he were suffering brain deterioration rather than a broken leg.

As for Ingrid, she had been so powerful in *Walpurgis Night, A Woman's Face, Dr. Jekyll and Mr. Hyde* and *Casablanca* that here she could, by default, only glide along the surface of Maria's character. With no guidance from her script, her director or her co-star, the otherwise harrowing account of Maria's past and the uncertainty of her future become a muddle. Bergman's choices in these revelatory scenes are filled with an uncharacteristically superficial anguish that seem unrelated to the brutal honesty of a woman who has survived monstrous treachery. She turns away from her friend the camera, pulls at her shorn locks and embraces a tree trunk in her efforts to show her discomfort. But the restless staging of these scenes cannot hide the emptiness of her emotions—and no one was more aware of this than Ingrid herself.

It is impossible to acquit Sam Wood, for he had not the skill to take his cast into dark waters; instead, the picture glorified the war Hemingway condemned. A film must communicate the ravages of war to imply the sanctity of peace; *For Whom the Bell Tolls* homogenizes both. Thus Ingrid's neat, stylish haircut and careful pancake makeup are ineffectual, and she seems more Nordic than ever— perhaps because she could not lose herself in Maria. In her first Technicolor picture, she appeared to be ravishingly slumming, right along with her fellow players, not one of whom was Spanish. Sam Wood, who loved the scenery and the horses much more than the story or his actors, presented a Never-Never-Land where the bells of patriotism rang loudly but emptily. "It was all very difficult," Ingrid said years later, "with Sam Wood screaming and upset and yelling. He was completely out of control so much of the time— really, I had never experienced anything of this sort before."

The critics were respectful but disappointed. She really knew how to act, they insisted, but she bore only a passing resemblance to a real human being. A young girl who has suffered gang rape and witnessed mass murder cannot leap into a scene looking like a refugee from a Palmolive ad. As for Gary Cooper, James Agee spoke for many: he was fine to behold "but generally a little faint."

Ingrid's only happy memories of the picture owed to one fact. Within hours of joining the company, she was very much in love with Gary Cooper.

Ever discreet, Ingrid spoke mostly of his acting ability. "He was one of the most natural actors ever," she said later,

so natural that you didn't know if he was acting—you had to go and look at the script to see if he was saying the lines or just talk-

ing to you! And he was very shy and timid, but also very sweet.
And how handsome! Looking at Gary Cooper was so wonderful.
It was unbelievable that I was there working with him. What was
wrong was that my happiness showed on the screen. I was far too
happy to honestly portray Maria's tragic figure.

Ingrid's remarks, which certainly suggested a romantic infatuation but never offered any unambiguous indication of a consummated affair, were taken, after her death, to indicate just that. But is
there evidence for this conventional wisdom?

To be sure, Cooper, then forty-one, had an uneven marriage
with a woman who refused him a divorce, and his life was heavily
spiced with a series of tempestuous love affairs. He had documented liaisons with, among others, some of the most alluring and
promiscuous women in Hollywood—among them, Clara Bow, Marlene Dietrich and Lupe Velez, whose lists of conquests could have
formed a small telephone directory. (Patricia Neal, it should be
added, also had a long, later intimacy with Cooper, but she did not
fit the pattern of these other ravenous personalities.)

Certainly the less scrupulous Hollywood tale-tellers, after the
deaths of Cooper and Bergman, longed to believe that she would
find irresistible this lanky, laconic man with an intense sexual aura
that derived as much from apparent diffidence as from his six-and-
a-half-foot frame and pellucid blue eyes. The gossips, in other
words, too often saw what they had to see, and from this longing for
scandal came a settled belief that such an affair, because possible,
was actual—despite the fact that neither of the principals, nor a
single person associated with the two films they made together, ever
flatly asserted that there was a realized romance. In those pre-
tabloid days of 1943, of course, people did not publicize their intimacies, and transient intrigues were not broadcast on afternoon talk
shows. But it is also significant that neither Cooper nor Bergman
ever confided such a relationship to friends, as they did in other
cases.

It is possible that love blazed that summer in the Sierra
Nevadas, and if it did one ought not make much of it. Perhaps it is
even likely that these two people found a measure of warmth and
comfort together against the absent charm of the production and

the predicaments of their respective marriages. Cooper's amorous whispers to Bergman onscreen and his insistently affectionate attention toward her when the camera stopped rolling may indeed indicate a brief fling. In addition, Ingrid was a responsive twenty-seven-year-old denied both the companionship and the understanding of her husband. There may be a clue, too, in a remark to Ruth the following winter (between her two films with Cooper), when Ingrid visited a Midwest farm: "You should see those farmer's sons. If it wasn't for Petter and Gary Cooper, I think I should like to be a farmer's wife." The implication, however lightly expressed, was that, were she not committed to both these men, she might have considered a change, or at least a new romance, in her life.

But Ingrid always had a byronic attitude toward leading men and directors throughout her life, and this tendency was part of her sentimental approach to men in general—that is to say, her intimacies were like Gallic idylls, tender and romantic connections, sometimes erotic but more often not. Whether she and Cooper were lovers during 1942 and 1943 is, in the final analysis, less important than the fact that her adoration of him sprang something free in her nature. Even more than with the unresponsive Victor Fleming, Ingrid, in the California wilderness, certainly felt a passionate attachment to Cooper, and this improved her self-confidence considerably and enlivened her performance. Forever after, she was grateful to him for enabling her to fall in love (chastely or not)—a condition she required in order to replicate Maria, and one she had not felt for any man since Fleming.

Whatever the form of expression, or for however long it continued, Ingrid's last summary must be taken seriously: "I never got to be a really close friend to Gary Cooper." For their various reasons, the sentimentalists and the moralists may have to ignore this and assert a frankly sexual affair. But the historian must have firmer grounds than the quicksands of rumor, and in this case there is simply no point from which to see clearly that Ingrid Bergman and Gary Cooper were lovers in fact, although they certainly seem to have been in spirit. Like many such stories, simple repetition of the less complex version has given it the substance of action.

The romance was further taken to be a physical reality especially by those making much of the fact that, during the filming of *Bell*,

Ingrid asked Selznick's permission to loan her again the following spring to Warner Bros., where Wood and Cooper had made a deal for a film based on Edna Ferber's novel *Saratoga Trunk*. But she was unaware that her co-star and director mentioned her as only one on a list of possible leading ladies, along with Vivien Leigh, Olivia de Havilland, Hedy Lamarr and others.

IN OCTOBER, THE PRODUCTION MOVED TO THE PARAMOUNT STUDIOS in Hollywood, for the filming of dozens (and dozens) of scenes and of the process shots involving players and filmed backgrounds. Since July 16, Petter had exchanged a lively correspondence with David Selznick and Kay Brown about Ingrid's options for the coming year and obtained clauses beneficial to his wife's future income. More and more, Petter felt it necessary to protect Ingrid from industry wolves—to the point where he now prepared to have himself legally designated her attorney-in-fact. On November 7, Selznick was strong-armed by Petter into paying for his train journey from Rochester to New York, and his hotel expenses there, where Ingrid's contract was the subject of a meeting with Ernest L. Scanlon, Selznick's treasurer.

As the holidays began, Petter was in a mood to celebrate: he had won, with distinction, his American medical degree (officially granted in January 1943) from the University of Rochester. And so he decided to invite a small platoon of movie people to celebrate at the apartment on Shirley Place.

"He was the perfect host, of course," recalled the artist Dietrich, then working at Paramount and one of the Swedish-American community frequently invited to the Lindstroms. "But he was terribly tough on Ingrid. She returned from a day's work at the studio tired but happy, and he said, 'Well, are you going to do something worthwhile now?' Whatever she replied, he seemed to say, 'No, you should do such-and-such instead.' I wondered how he could be that way with her. After all, he was not yet set up in practice, and she was bringing in all the money."

Alfred Hitchcock, constantly trying to find the right project for which Selznick could not deny him Ingrid, agreed. "The Lindstroms were delightful to be with, but one sensed a kind of undertow of tension. Somebody, one thought, had to come along and rescue

Ingrid." Professionally, it would be Hitchcock himself; romantically, to his dismay, it would be someone else.

After the holiday parties, Ingrid, Petter, Pia and Mabel returned to Rochester to close up the house. Petter would now continue his internship and residencies, and seek staff positions in California medical schools.

Chapter Eight

1943

The real offense, as she ultimately perceived, was her having a
mind of her own at all.

HENRY JAMES,
The Portrait of a Lady

IF SWEDEN SHOULD BE OVERRUN BY THE NAZIS," INGRID TOLD THE
press, "I hope that the people of America would not turn against
my people. Sweden, like Switzerland, is surrounded, cut off, made
helpless by the enemy. There is very little she could do. If the tragic
moment of attack should come, I hope the people of America will
not forget this."

In 1943, her plea was taken seriously by none other than the
Overseas Bureau of the Office of War Information, charged with
spreading the good word about the efforts of the various con-
stituents of the melting pot, uniting in a common effort against the
enemy. To this end, during the war, documentarist Irving Lerner
was directing various short films, made in foreign languages, for
export to allies and neutrals abroad. This entire propaganda effort
was under the supervision of Robert Riskin, the Oscar-winning

screenwriter of Frank Capra's screwball comedy *It Happened One Night* and a man now concerned with sterner realities.

So it was that in January, Ingrid received a diplomatic courier from Washington by way of Selznick, inviting her to travel a few weeks later to Swedish communities in Minnesota. There she would be filmed visiting the farms and homes of typical immigrants, and then, in Hollywood, she would narrate (in Swedish for export and in English for the bureau's archives) a tribute to the patriotism of her countrymen in the New World. Thus would be achieved the goal of enabling Swedes abroad to see the nobility of (as it was to be titled) Swedes in America.

On February 2, 1943, Ingrid, Pia and Mabel left Rochester by train (Petter stayed behind to continue packing up); they stopped over briefly in Chicago and arrived next day in frigid Minneapolis, where the temperature hovered at about twenty degrees below zero. They were met by Selznick's new publicity director, Joseph H. Steele, who at once became one of Ingrid's greatest admirers. Tall, slender, intelligent and not at all the image of the vulgar Hollywood "flack" (the industry word for a publicist), Joe at once fell in love with Ingrid—but chastely, for he was married and Ingrid had no romantic interest in him.

She much admired Joe's facility for languages. His father had been a missionary in Turkey, and Joe's childhood had been peripatetic: by the time he was six, he could speak Turkish, Arabic, Armenian and English, and to these he later added French and Italian. She was adept in this area, too: her English was remarkably fluent and she was practicing her French; these, with Swedish and German, would eventually be augmented by fluent Italian. Ingrid also liked Joe's manners, his ethics, his devotion to her and his refusal to submit her to the demands of an increasingly voracious press and public. At first, her gentle rejection of his subtle pass pitched him into a romantic gloom, rather like a forlorn schoolboy, but very quickly he realized that the bond of lifelong fellowship— which he enjoyed forever after—was preferable to a transient affair. He was, in other words, a man of some maturity and character.

Next morning, February 4, Joe collected Ingrid at the Nicollet Hotel and drove her the two-hour journey to Chisago County. There she lived for a few days and was filmed with the C. E. Swanson family, Swedish immigrants who at appropriate seasons farmed and milked, spun wool and sheared sheep. Ingrid, donning the simplest garb, shared in all of it. She shoveled snow and made snowmen for Pia. She helped pitch ice-frosted hay, cuddled piglets and sat with old ladies at looms. *Look* magazine also documented it (Selznick knew a good thing when it passed his way), but Steele sensed that this was something Ingrid wanted to do as a good cause. She sought no movie-star comfort and took an interest in everything of concern for the Swedish immigrants. By coincidence, the four-day tour concluded in, of all places, a town called Lindstrom, Minnesota.

ON FEBRUARY 8, JOE ESCORTED INGRID, PIA AND MABEL BY TRAIN TO Los Angeles, where the star was due for makeup and wardrobe tests for *Saratoga Trunk*. Selznick had approved this only because (along with everyone else in Hollywood who had not visited the set of the picture), he believed Ingrid's work with Wood and Cooper on *For Whom the Bell Tolls* was going to be an enormous success—and because, while he paid Ingrid her usual salary of $2,250 each week, he negotiated to receive $15,625 each week for the loanout of eight weeks. The trio of Cooper-Bergman-Wood could not lose, Selznick argued; one might have said that at least he could not lose.

In fact, everyone except Selznick lost on the deal. *Saratoga Trunk* was the most expensive Warner Bros. picture to date, with ninety-six sets, over eleven thousand props, dozens of lavish nineteenth-century gowns for Ingrid, two hundred stuntmen for a one-minute nighttime train wreck sequence and an array of crinoline, carriages, gas lamps and ferns that stuffed the movie's trunk to overflowing. Spectacular it certainly would be, and that, in the end, would be the major point of sale, for it was also a very overfed turkey in which no one could rationally take pride except the studio seamstresses.

The source was a difficult one—a rambling Edna Ferber romance novel that sashayed from New Orleans to Saratoga Springs to tell its tale of a glamorous, illegitimate sorceress named Clio Dulaine (Ingrid) who returns from Paris to avenge society's mal-treatment of her family by shocking polite society up and down the East Coast. Money is her god, men her acolytes. She abuses her mulatto maid (white Flora Robson, in offensive blackface), barks

orders at her servant, an ornery dwarf named Cupidon (Jerry
Austin), exploits a decent man (John Warburton) and finally accepts
a lanky Texan named Clint Maroon (Cooper).

But the veteran screenwriter Casey Robinson (late of *Captain
Blood*, *Dark Victory*, *Kings Row* and *Now, Voyager*) could not redeem the
narrative's problems or make this mash palatable or even interesting. It is, in the final analysis, a movie in search of coherence: at first
Saratoga Trunk is a thriller, then it is a comedy of manners, next a
romance and finally a Western shootout.

Ingrid had badgered Selznick for the role, but to her horror she
turned the last of the script's two hundred pages the day before
filming began and promptly burst into tears as she fell into Ruth
Roberts's arms. Never mind that she now had glowing notices for
Casablanca: all she could count, among her six American films, was
one to make her proud (*Dr. Jekyll and Mr. Hyde*). From her apartment
at Shirley Place, Beverly Hills, she drove six days each week, with a
very heavy heart indeed, to Burbank for filming, and from late
February through mid-May the production trudged on. The
romance with Cooper, whatever expression it had taken, was evidently over, and to the dismay of the wardrobe department, Ingrid
gained eleven pounds during filming. Larger bustles and more voluminous layers of silk had to be added to several of her gowns, for
she had never been heavier in any picture.

As the petulant, often hysterical Clio, Ingrid was forced into
heavy brunette wigs, and the makeup department was instructed to
apply thick eyeliner and sticky paint high over the lip line. At times,
it seemed (as Vivien Leigh once said of Laurence Olivier's grotesque
makeup for *Macbeth*) as if her makeup came on the screen, then her
costumes appeared, and finally Ingrid herself marched on, more or
less discerned beneath the sludge. "If they thought less about how
much money they are spending on sets and costumes and makeup,
and more about creating real, believable human beings, it would be
better," she said a few years later; she may well have had *Saratoga
Trunk* in mind. Her prescription for good moviemaking, and her
implicit criticisms of its empty excesses, remain valid decades later.

To distract herself from the rigors of filming this expensive bore
of a picture, Ingrid bought a new eight-millimeter camera and
advanced her skills as an amateur cinematographer, documenting

everything Sam Wood did with crowd scenes (and rightly asserting, only to good friends, that she could well have done better as director). But however sharp Ingrid's dismay, her collegial goodwill was uncompromised: Ingrid's stand-in, Betty Brooks, had to do double time for the film's complicated lighting cues, and Ingrid complained loudly on the young woman's behalf until Brooks received a substantial bonus for her tiring tasks.

She also agreed to meet Joe Steele every Sunday, to discuss events and activities Selznick might approve for publicity. This addition to her schedule prompted an important letter from Selznick to Steele, dated May 17:

> I appreciate your working on Sunday with Ingrid, and even though she has not complained about working on Sunday, I still would like to urge you to give her Sundays off without any interruption for publicity purposes . . . until the end of *Saratoga Trunk*.
>
> Ingrid is so extraordinarily cooperative that I think we must lean over backwards not to take advantage of her good nature or someday even her wonderful character will rare up [sic] and react against us, just as happened with Garbo at Metro as the result of early lack of consideration of her by their publicity department.
>
> In all the years I have been in the picture business, I have never heard of a girl going through so tough a schedule as Ingrid has had in recent months, and even though this has been entirely by her own wish, I think it behooves us to be very sure that she at least gets her Sundays for rest and for her child . . . In *Saratoga Trunk*, there is also the extraordinary circumstance of her having worked for over ten weeks without one single day free in the schedule . . . I tried very hard to force rest on Ingrid but she wouldn't do it, and the very least we can do is to be certain that her Sundays are not cut into.
>
> It must also be borne in mind that Ingrid doesn't even take the one day off monthly that is the habit of feminine stars, once they achieve stardom—and as you know, some of them insist on two or three days.

She had sought the role of Clio Dulaine for the opportunity to play an amoral schemer after the lovestruck Ilsa and the battered

Maria. Instead, she now had to serve a bloated film with not a shred of character consistency. Jack Warner himself recognized this when he saw the final cut, for *Saratoga Trunk*, completed in early June 1943, was sent overseas for the entertainment of servicemen (who at the screenings may have had their first good sleep in months) and it was shipped for general release in America only in early 1946. "There is a steady song in my heart," Ingrid had said when Selznick gave his approval for her to do the picture. Of the final product, she had nothing to say, even in her published memoirs almost forty years later, except that she was unrecognizable in her flouncy getups. The steady song had, almost at once, gone resoundingly flat.

It is easy to understand, then, that by summertime Ingrid was desperate; indeed, she had been so depressed during the final weeks of filming that, for the first time in her career, she fell ill (perhaps, not surprisingly, with laryngitis); her doctors kept her from working for more than a week. Then Gary Cooper, his scenes finished, loped out of her life, and Petter moved to San Francisco to begin an internship in surgery at Stanford University Hospital; his absence deprived her only of an escort to parties.* Selznick, with *Saratoga Trunk* concluded, wanted to put her at once into something called *Valley of Decision*, in which she would play a courageous, self-sacrificing, virtuous bore—"so good all the time it makes you ill," as Ingrid said. For such soap-opera caricatures she had only one response: "Where is my gun?" Instead, she convinced Selznick that her misery in the role would make her patently incredible.

Ingrid was wise not to leap at these offerings simply to be sure of work. At Metro, George Cukor had been signed to direct and Charles Boyer to co-star in the second film version of Patrick Hamilton's stage thriller *Angel Street*, and the studio executives negotiated with Selznick for Ingrid to play the difficult leading role. (Cukor had also wanted Ingrid for the American version of *A Woman's Face*, but Metro insisted on Joan Crawford.) Selznick, at

---

*In the late 1970s, years after Cooper's death, some gossip attributed the following statement to him: "No one loved me more than Ingrid Bergman, but the day after filming concluded, I couldn't even get her on the phone." Such a frank statement would have been uncharacteristic of Cooper, and the rudeness very unlike Ingrid.

first, refused, because Boyer's name was to appear first in the billing. When Ingrid learned of this, she stormed into Selznick's office, sobbing that he was hindering her career. She cared not at all whether her name was first or eighth: this was a marvelous role and he must not sabotage the deal by such an unreasonable demand. Selznick reluctantly yielded (and pocketed $253,750 in the bargain), and in early July Ingrid reported to Metro for preproduction on *Gaslight*.*

Hamilton's play had been hugely successful in London and New York, and a British film version had been much praised. Columbia Pictures bought remake rights, intending to cast Irene Dunne in the role of the woman whose husband attempts to drive her insane so that he can steal jewels hidden by her aunt, whom he had murdered. But Louis B. Mayer jumped into the deal with a heftier offer; he had Hedy Lamarr in mind for a Metro version. At the same time, Mayer bought the negative of the British film and as many prints as could be located; all these were destroyed so that Metro's new *Gaslight* would have no competition.

But it would not have a rival in any case, for the finished picture, set in fog-shrouded Victorian London (all of it recreated in Culver City) was a brilliant achievement by everyone involved—everything, in other words, that had been unrealized in *For Whom the Bell Tolls* and *Saratoga Trunk*. The screenplay (by John Van Druten, Walter Reisch and John L. Balderston) built its suspense methodically and limned its characters with shrewd economy. Cukor, accustomed mostly to haute couture comedies or airy vehicles for established Hollywood ladies, directed his cast calmly but with meticulous attention to detail. Boyer gave the role of the malevolent husband an oily, basso charm that was chillingly credible. Joseph Cotten nicely underplayed the part of a detective. And in her movie debut, the untrained and inexperienced Angela Lansbury, then seventeen, turned the role of a cheeky housemaid into a brilliant miniature of sassy wickedness.

But Ingrid had the thorniest job, for the role of Paula Alquist had to be shaded with considerable nuance to be credible and sympathetic, not merely melodramatic in her hysteria and irritating in

---

*Selznick realized exactly the same profit for the loanout of Ingrid for *Saratoga Trunk*. Her total earnings for that picture were $69,562, and for *Gaslight*, $74,156.

her fragility. From the first day, Ingrid realized that the woman could not be portrayed as a willing accomplice in her own torture—that she was not, in other words, an anemic Gothic-Victorian heroine. There would have to be flashes of the young Paula, the girl who loved dancing and song and who fell rapturously in love with her piano accompanist when she was studying voice. She would have to infuse the pain of psychological suffering into a woman of established strength who had clear memories of earlier happiness— only then could her plight be more agonizing and her final triumph more resounding.

In this regard, there was something pointedly brave in Ingrid Bergman's nature. Perhaps partly from her multiple experiences of loss in childhood and the consequent necessity for her to do something worthwhile on her own, she had become a woman whom mere adversity could not break. Reading the role of Paula Alquist, who adores a man bent on her destruction, Ingrid may well have read something of her own emotional history. Like Paula, she had lost her mother in infancy, her father had died when she was young, and she had been raised by an aunt. Also like Paula, Ingrid had been trained as a singer. And like the heroine she was about to play, Ingrid had just inherited money from her Aunt Hulda Bergman, Uncle Otto's widow (the sum was but a few thousand dollars, but it was a testament from her family nonetheless). She found something of herself in the character. And because the makeup department was pleased to let Ingrid look like Ingrid, she was freer, before her old friend the camera, than she had felt in a year.

Also like Paula, Ingrid knew what it was to be hurt by those she loved—knew, too, what it was like for a woman to put herself so close to the fire that she risked danger. To be sure, there was never an ounce of cruelty in the character or actions of Petter Lindstrom and Gary Cooper. But it is likely neither of them ever understood the tangle of her complexity, her fusion of dependence and self-reliance, of chary insecurity and unwavering confidence in her gifts. Her complete openness to these men, her need of their endorsement, her reliance on their collaboration and her vulnerable trust in their decisions—these feelings were part of her sensitivity as a woman and as an artist rich in imagination.

That summer, Ingrid was still formally within the confines of a marriage that had evaporated into a distant, polite strain, and she had just come from the emotional and professional mortification of the Cooper/Wood films. Disappointment and dissociation can embitter, but they can also clarify and even ennoble, and that is exactly what Ingrid brought to her portrayal of Paula Alquist. *Gaslight* was her way of rising above the flames—of becoming, in a way, the victorious soldier. As friends knew, Joan of Arc was never closer to her thoughts or more frequently in her conversation than that season. Ingrid never saw herself as a martyr (much less as a saint), but she understood the terrible loneliness of a woman whose ideals had only recently proved so unattainable. For neither the first nor the last time in her life, she would make something work—no, not merely work, but prosper.

To prepare, she was as judicious and precise as ever. After reading a formidable number of books and articles on hallucinations, delusions and genetic schizophrenia, Ingrid insisted that Cukor and Metro arrange for her to visit a psychiatric asylum. Somehow, she was permitted to visit repeatedly a forlorn patient who, despite occasional periods of complete lucidity, was subject to the most agonizing fits of dementia. Ingrid watched the woman's eyes, alternately full of hope and then cloudy with fear, her manner warm with welcome and then dark with anxiety. But the actress was no prying user; she brought games and diversions for the patient and became a reliable friend until the poor woman died of tuberculosis the following year.

INGRID'S PERFORMANCE IN THE PICTURE, FED BY SO MANY TRIBUTARIES, was inspired. Instead of wild eyes and hysterical outbursts, she simply shifted her gaze, blinked her eyes, affected a dry mouth, moistened her lips, stumbled on the occasional word. Cukor had no trouble with her, for she was always accessible and welcomed his reactions. He knew, too, when to stress a close-up of her querulous brows and unknowing glance. When Gregory (Boyer) insists that Paula is becoming forgetful and delusional, there is something in her appearance that resists the diagnosis even as she is alarmed at the possible truth of it. Her strangulated outburst at the musical soirée, when she is duped into believing that she has filched her husband's watch, is a masterpiece of improvisation—a muffled sob, a brief outpouring of grief, a reining in of fear, and then the dreadful breakdown, all the more poignant because so bravely resisted.

More than a half-century later, Ingrid's Paula remains a deeply affecting portrait of a woman torn between a fear of madness and a solid sense that she is really quite sane. In her last great scene—when she taunts her captured torturer, pretending to be as mad as he wished her—Ingrid called on every subtle, natural ability within her. Nothing was overacted; nothing seemed calculated. When she finished the scene, the crew's applause echoed from above the cat-walks to behind the camera; well, she said, maybe it was all right. That winter, she was nominated by the Academy as one of the best actresses of the year, and *Gaslight* received six other such citations—for best picture, actor (Boyer), supporting actress (Lansbury), screenplay, cinematography (Joseph Ruttenberg) and art direction (Cedric Gibbons, William Ferrari, Edwin B. Willis and Paul Huld-schinsky).

As for Ingrid, the critics ransacked their vocabularies for superlatives: "Miss Bergman is superb in her nerve-wracking part. Her sympathetic and emotional performance cannot fail to hold the spectator engrossed" ran a typical review. The public agreed: *Gaslight* had confirmed her as an actress of the first rank, and she now topped movie magazine polls as America's favorite actress. Such was the point of *Time* magazine's August 2 issue, which featured her on the cover: "INGRID BERGMAN (AS MARIA)—Whatever Hollywood's bell tolled for, she rang it."

Inside was a rhapsodic article that recounted the general outline of her life and career thus far and summarized everything: "Not only is Ingrid Bergman without an enemy in the whole community: people like the way she works, too . . . Her particular kind of beauty comes from within; it is the beauty of an individual . . . She is an uncommonly well-balanced and charming woman [of] poise, sincerity, reticence, sensitiveness, charm and talent." And so it went, page after laudatory page, including the undiluted encomia of those two harpies, Hedda Hopper and Louella Parsons. No living person could long survive such a canonization process; Ingrid, most of all, distrusted it.

*   *   *

THE FILMING OF GASLIGHT, WHICH LASTED FROM EARLY JULY THROUGH October, was not an unrelievedly intense affair, no matter the fervor of her preparation and rehearsals or the emotional demands of each scene. One evening, Selznick had scheduled a party for a large contingent of potential investors, and he expected his most important contract stars to attend. Joseph Cotten was ordered to escort Ingrid to the Selznick mansion. They were both exhausted, had an early call next day, and were in no mood to be elegantly polite for their boss's benefit.

On the spot, Ingrid came up with a plan for an innocent practical joke, and she and Cotten raced to Metro's wardrobe department. There they found a waitress's costume that fit her (complete with black dress and white apron, cuffs and cap) and a butler's uniform for him. An hour later, they slipped quietly through the Selznicks' kitchen door, cautioned the majordomo not to give away their secret, swept up a platter of hors d'oeuvres and a tray of drinks and began making their way, with necessary Hollywood deference, through the swanky gathering. "That maid bears a striking resemblance to Ingrid Bergman," whispered Irene Selznick's sister, Edie Goetz.

Moments later, the actors went further. They conspired to gulp down, with a great flourish and in full view of a crowd of guests, a couple of glasses of champagne and to affect instant inebriation. And then, thick of speech but ever courteous, Cotten-as-butler called across to Ingrid, "Come along, Martha! We only agreed to work for an hour. Remember, all our children are waiting up for us!" With all eyes now trained on her, Ingrid took two more drinks, knocked them back and giggled so uncontrollably that Selznick, summoned to the scene, at once recognized her. Alas, only the jokers appreciated the joke.

AT LAST, THAT AUTUMN, INGRID HAD TIME TO CATCH HER BREATH. SHE spent more time with her daughter, now a pretty, alert child of five, and she wrote to Petter, asking his reactions to her idea that they might think of buying a house in Beverly Hills—a place with a yard for Pia and space for entertaining friends and colleagues. After all, her gross earnings for 1943 were almost $100,000, and after taxes and commissions she would have almost $25,000 remaining—

surely enough for a major down payment on a nice house north of Sunset Boulevard. Her husband replied that they might begin searching when he returned to Los Angeles for a holiday.

Years later, Petter admitted that the emotional distance separating them ever more at this time derived as much from his career as hers: the marriage was rocky, he said, because "not only Ingrid but I too was somewhat obsessed with professional work . . . I did not hesitate to move away from Southern California when that facilitated or advanced my professional work." Years later, he was even more forthright in a letter to Ingrid: "The simple truth is that I was not a perfect husband and I was too involved in my very own demanding work; and moreover our marriage was not ideal, although the first two years I think there was a complete trust and honesty between us." In this regard, his honesty was as admirable as hers; the gradual dissipation of the bond between them can hardly be called the fault of a so-called Hollywood lifestyle.

But the fact is that Petter's professional work very much included Ingrid's, and by 1943—despite the demands on his time and energy—he was more than ever involved in controlling every detail of her career, and this alienated those who did not think such management appropriate. "He knew that he was in the driver's seat in undisputed control of the hottest star in all filmdom," said Joe Steele, who described Petter as "harsh and obdurate in his dealings, [and a man] whose disenchantment lay in an egregious distrust of everybody and everything."

TO BUILD PUBLICITY, STUDIOS OFTEN LOANED STARS TO RADIO NETworks that broadcast condensed versions of popular films. So it was that, in September, Selznick sent Ingrid a script for a radio version of *Casablanca*. This she took along on one of her frequent visits to Petter in San Francisco; he quickly read it and, to Ingrid's surprise, made some emendations in the dialogue. "I have changed the script the best I can," wrote Petter to Dan O'Shea when he returned the script on September 20. One can imagine the extensive raising of corporate eyebrows along the corridors of Selznick International Pictures. A star might suggest changes, an agent could make inquiries, a manager was free to register objections. But such a blunt gesture as Petter's was simply beyond his competence.

He may have felt free to exercise this bold extension of his influence over Ingrid's career because of a negotiation he had concluded with Selznick earlier that year. To augment the small stipend he had for his studies, Petter offered Selznick his language talents and his business contacts as a Swede. In a deal co-signed by Lindstrom and Selznick on May 2, Petter was to be paid $5,000 a year "to make synopses of current Swedish fiction deemed suitable for motion pictures for Miss Bergman, to obtain publishers' lists on Swedish fiction and to buy up former pictures in which Miss Bergman acted." Neither party expected these tasks to be done, but many such deals were made in Hollywood, and spouses, friends and lovers of stars thus benefited from the studio coffers.*

By year's end, Petter had taken a step that astonished his wife, David Selznick, Charles Feldman, Kay Brown and everyone else who learned of it. In a letter he sent to O'Shea dated December 30, Petter again spoke for her, agreeing that "in consideration of your payment to Ingrid of the full amount due her for the fourth picture [in eighteen months], I agree that the date of January 6, 1944, as provided in the contract, shall be postponed for a period of five weeks." Then came the astonishing signature: "Petter Lindstrom, Attorney-in-Fact for Ingrid Bergman."† As Selznick and company immediately learned, Petter had himself declared her official representative—and with that, he unwittingly contributed as much to the final dissolution of his marriage as any step taken later by Ingrid herself. A week after that, he further directed Selznick to forward all correspondence and contracts for Ingrid to him "as Attorney-in-Fact, at 414-C Shirley Place, Beverly Hills." Ingrid learned of it when Selznick informed her.

Also in December, Petter told his wife that, since she had no immediate project after *Gaslight*, she ought to do something on behalf of the American war effort. She agreed, and he arranged for her to entertain American troops at Alaskan army bases. For five

---

*In this case, the Internal Revenue Service, perhaps because Ingrid's salary was already handsome, investigated the matter in December. Nothing irregular was found, and Lindstrom kept his $5,000.

†The five-week extension ran until July, when at last Ingrid began a film with Alfred Hitchcock.

weeks, from the end of December, she hopped from one remote outpost to another, doing dramatic readings, singing Swedish folk songs and signing photographs for idle or recuperating soldiers.

"Like everyone else," recalled one veteran, "she had to endure temperatures of twenty below and more, had to dress in uniforms and spend her night in sleeping bags, often on the floor. At one place, it was so cold that her eau de cologne turned to ice! During the bus trips there were no facilities, and for several weeks there was no possibility of a bath. But Ingrid Bergman never complained and was never too tired to entertain the soldiers."

"We danced with the soldiers," she recalled, "and we ate with them and visited the hospitals. They're so thankful for anything you do." But then Ingrid fell ill with a terrible chest cold and high fever, and on January 20 she was flown to a Seattle hospital, where physicians diagnosed double pneumonia. As soon as she could submit to the rigors of an airplane trip, she was whisked back to Los Angeles and ordered to bed for a month. Thanks to the ministrations of Mabel, Petter and her personal physician Dr. Culley, the pneumonia responded to treatment without complications.

Chapter Nine

1944

When lovely woman stoops to folly,
And finds too late that men betray,
What charm can soothe her melancholy?
What art can wash her guilt away?

OLIVER GOLDSMITH,
"Song"

FOR THE FIRST MONTHS OF THE NEW YEAR, INGRID WAS EXHAUSTED.
Pia, returning from nursery school each afternoon, was often
ushered away from Mama's room, and friends like Ruth Roberts
and Kay Brown had to be reassured: her illness left Ingrid uncharacteristically weary, and she needed a great deal of sleep.

Everyone urged her not to rush back to her normal round of
activity, and so she yielded and allowed herself a favorite way to
relax: she drove out to the ocean—either to the beach at Malibu or
the high cliffs of the Santa Monica Palisades—and sat reading and
studying scripts, just as she had done as a girl, sitting on a bench
along Strandvägen. Throughout her life, closeness to the ocean
revived and calmed her.

But usually she was in a hurry.

"People tell me, 'Take it easy!' but I feel all the time I must do something," she said.

> That is why I hate Sundays. Other people can't wait for Sunday because they sail boats or play poker or hunt. But I have no hobby. I can't wait for Monday. I have always felt this. I want to work, I cannot relax, and I am unhappy when a picture is over— so I read scripts and take lessons all the time. French lessons, lessons in tennis and swimming and riding—not for exercise but only to learn something well enough to fake it in a picture, and then I lose interest. I also read many books, plays and fiction and biographies. If you took the stage away from me, I would stop breathing. I hope they will put on my gravestone, "She acted to the last day of her life. Here rests a good actress."

That winter, management of Ingrid's life was ceded more and more to her husband. "He told me what to do and what to say, and I leaned on him for everything. He meant well. He took burdens off my shoulders." He also corrected her posture, advised her on her hair and makeup, scolded her caloric indulgences. "Of course what he said has helped me an awful lot through the years. Petter did me a lot of good by nagging me, but in those days it irritated me beyond measure."

By 1944, he was more manager and mentor than husband, and Ingrid was nurturing a silent resentment. For one thing, with no work that spring, she felt she had no reason to watch her diet as she recovered from pneumonia.

> Petter wanted me very slender and thin. He always complained that he couldn't understand, with all the diets I was on, how come I didn't lose weight? What he didn't know was that, though at the table I ate just the right things—a little salad, juice—I had a jar of cookies in my bedroom, and right after dinner I'd go and eat them all up. And in the middle of the night I'd go down to the icebox and eat everything that was edible just to fill in after my slenderizing dinner.

The stories of celebrated women harassed or humiliated into diets are, of course, legion; this was not the fatal blow to the mar-

riage, but it was, as she said, "all the small things" that had accumulated and wore away respect and, with that erosion, love. Ingrid
admitted her mistakes, and when she asked forgiveness, reminded
her husband that he, too, was human. "I make mistakes?" he asked.
"I? I certainly do not! I think a thing over very carefully before acting!" Honorable in so many things, Petter Lindstrom may be for-
given an egregious lack of humor.

Ingrid was put on so small an allowance by her husband that she
had no cash to buy clothes when an opportune moment occurred.
More than once, Joe Steele was frustrated when Ingrid had to ring
Petter for permission to do an interview, or to ask for money for a
new dress or suit. "She was always the subservient wife," said
Selznick, echoing the impression of Michel Bernheim. "Lindstrom
managed all the money, and she couldn't spend a penny on herself
or the house without getting his okay first." Joe Steele knew that,
too: "Her husband handled all the finances." This much was true in
most American families, but most American families were not
entirely supported by the wife's income.

Petter's supervision and organization of her life now extended
beyond contractual details and dealings with Selznick. "Often, in
the interviews I gave, he told me I didn't say the right thing," Ingrid
recalled. "And sometimes when Petter and I came back from a party,
he would say, 'You shouldn't talk so much. You have a very intelligent face, so let people think you are intelligent, because when you
start to chatter it's just a lot of nonsense.'"

But no matter how he tended to underrate her charm, and
intelligence, Petter was convinced that Ingrid was at least appealing
enough to be having affairs with all her leading men. "Some I was
very attracted to, and I think they were attracted to me," she said.
"But there were certainly no love affairs." In the absence of evidence to the contrary (and there is none) and because Ingrid was
forthright regarding men in her later life, there is no reason to
doubt her. But Petter believed what, for his own reasons, he had to
believe.

Years later, Ingrid admitted to herself that despite her confidence in her craft, she was, like many women of her time, completely intimidated by her husband. Raised in a culture that presumed masculine superiority and the natural dependence of women

on the greater abilities of men, Ingrid never questioned those assumptions. Much of the conflict in her first and second marriages derived from the fact that she was unable to transfer to her private life the acuity of her professional self-confidence and her keen judgment about her abilities and career choices. "To be truthful, I was afraid of him—and certainly it was craziness to be married to someone I was afraid of."

Irene Selznick clearly sensed Ingrid's dilemma. Her lifelong memory of Petter was of a righteous and strict man who dominated the Lindstroms' life in Hollywood as he had in Sweden. Irene tried once to encourage Ingrid to buy a new dress for an important premiere, but she could not convince Petter it was necessary.

As for her relationship to Pia, it would be easy to judge Ingrid a failure as a mother because her career was of central concern to her. "But when we were together," Pia said years later, "we spent happy hours playing children's games, pillow-fighting, sitting up late, talking." Pia did not aspire to her mother's profession. When a visitor asked her if she wanted to grow up to be an actress, too, she asked, "Do I have to?"

In retrospect, Pia characterized her childhood as a time of benign neglect: "My mother was super-devoted to her career, and my father was very busy with his, so I was alone a great deal of the time—and lonely. I have no vivid memories of family happiness."

Years later, Ingrid was severe about herself at this time: "I felt guilty, but not guilty enough to stop working.

> I was too young to be a mother—not so much young in years as immature. I was so wound up in my career and Hollywood's star system and all that, that I didn't find time for the little girl in my house. She'd wait all day for me to come home from the studio, and then when I did arrive, often much later than expected, I was either too tired to give her much time or hurriedly dressing for some function or other. There's no doubt in my mind, I neglected her, and for that I have a lasting sense of guilt.

Irene Selznick, for one, believed that Ingrid's remorse was ill founded. "I couldn't understand why Ingrid had such guilt about her child just because she worked," Irene Selznick recalled. "No matter what Ingrid did with her and for her, she never felt it was quite enough. I hadn't known any other woman who had this anxiety." Indeed, Ingrid Bergman was supporting her family, and millions of women then and later had little time for their children for precisely the same reasons.

Ingrid's feeling is perhaps understandable since she herself recalled the deprivations of maternal attention in her own childhood and resolved that her daughter would not mature with the same memories. But in some cases, a mother's death may be more readily integrated within a child's life than a mother's occasional presence for a course or two at dinner.

Though Ingrid believed she neglected her daughter, this harsh judgment of self may derive from another source—the same emotional equipment that led her too readily to believe Petter's severe assessments of her. The truth is that Pia's lot in the 1940s was not much different from that of many other children then and always (especially, it may be argued, in Hollywood). Often materially privileged, children were sometimes denied much parental attention, but this is not necessarily fatal and did not cause any remarkable suffering; many less than wealthy families cannot have as much "togetherness" as happy tales take for granted, and children in such cases are often astonishingly resourceful (Ingrid herself was one).

It is easy to imagine, on the other hand, what resentments against children could be harbored by a mother who had an opportunity for significant work but who was denied it (or denied herself) under the pretext that she was "needed at home." Some parents and children do indeed have such an overwhelming need; others, for economic reasons, cannot afford the luxury of responding to that need; and other parents and children are much better off without constant contact. Unlike many societies, America has—but only since World War II—marketed the curious myth of the wondrous mother, caring for Dick and Jane, calling them and their dog home for dinner and easily managing the impossible balancing act of her duties as cook, maid, nurse and teacher. Of her obligations to be a faithful, satisfying wife, nothing was ever discussed: this was all "natural."

For many, to be sure, it was. But for countless others it was the stuff of elementary school readers. In this regard, it is interesting to observe that American culture presumed that fathers would be mostly absent from home, supporting their families each day, often traveling on business, preoccupied with the climb up corporate ladders and ordinarily able to devote only small parcels of time to their children. That was fine, that was "natural," too. Mothers were expected to be brilliant chocolate-chip cookie bakers, maids-of-all-work, ever ready with Band-Aids, glasses of milk, the answers to questions in geography and arithmetic and endless patience for the kiddies' demands.

But at the same time, some industries (like the movie business) always had good jobs for women, and society approved their entrance into such work. How, one might ask, could a woman undertake such a demanding career and fulfill the storybook ideal of a full-time mother with apron and spatula? During the war, especially, few could. In this regard, many mothers in the 1940s were perforce absent from their children: the wives of many men fighting abroad were at work for long hours; many women served in airplane factories and munitions plants; and "Rosie the Riveter"—the culture's designation for women contributing to the war effort— was found in profusion in every city and hamlet of America.

Pia Lindstrom was not an abused child. But that she was effectively deprived of attention is unassailable, and the absence of siblings made her early life all the more lonely. Two factors fed the harsh judgment of Ingrid by herself and others: the hypocritical condemnation America later issued against her in 1949 and 1950, and the subsequent emergence of a more affluent middle class in the 1950s. By that time, many mothers did not have to work and were free to slave—at home, where the hours were longer and the compensation less. The presumption of the omnipotent, omniscient Mommy was, it may be argued, largely an invention of the authors of *Fun with Dick and Jane*, with a little help from Dr. Benjamin Spock. Television, most of all, captured the mood of the times: Mommy was the most important person in the life of a child, and she would never have to do anything wrong at all if she just followed the rules (whatever they were). This was the home of the brave, after all, and, like Dr. Lindstrom, no one had to make a mistake.

Finally, in the entire matter of Ingrid's sense of responsibility for her family, it must be kept in mind that she was supporting herself, her husband and her daughter. Petter had only the smallest monthly stipend as a medical student, intern and resident—an amount entirely insufficient to care for a family; they were all kept comfortable only by Ingrid's income. It is not easy to understand why she should be considered a negligent mother because she was a movie star and not a corporate tycoon—or a doctor.

SELZNICK EXPECTED INGRID AND PETTER TO ATTEND THE ACADEMY Award presentation on March 2 at Grauman's Chinese Theatre in Hollywood, especially since she had been nominated for her performance in For Whom the Bell Tolls. Jean Arthur, Joan Fontaine, Greer Garson and Jennifer Jones were also in the running. When Jones won (for The Song of Bernadette), Ingrid raced back to honor her. "I apologize, Ingrid," said Jennifer Jones. "You should have won." But Ingrid would have none of it: "No, Jennifer, your Bernadette was better than my Maria." She was right, and she knew it.

That month, Petter completed his internship in surgery at Stanford and began a three-month residency in otorhinolarynology (specializing in ailments of the ear, nose and throat) at County Hospital in Los Angeles. He then undertook a residency in neurosurgery, completed it in 1947, and began a lifetime career as a neurosurgeon.

Still, he did not ignore Ingrid's career, and for once David Selznick had to dictate one of his extended letters to Petter to correct the harsh judgments Petter had expressed about Ingrid's boss in a letter dated April 6.

Petter had complained (a) that Ingrid would have been better off with another producer who would have kept her busier (and perhaps made her richer); (b) that she had made only mediocre films when Selznick loaned her out; (c) that there had been numerous changes to the original contracts of 1939 and 1940; (d) that Selznick still had not fulfilled his promise to star Ingrid in Joan of Arc; and (e) that circumstances had led Ingrid to the point that she was looking elsewhere after the expiration of the Selznick contract, but that she "would not sign elsewhere without notification [to Selznick] in advance." In fact, Ingrid had (thus Petter) "got hold of [this letter] and, with her usual common sense, bawled me out."

Selznick's reply ran to seven pages; one by one, he responded to Petter's objections.

"You have a tendency," Selznick began acidly but accurately, "to discount our greater knowledge of the picture business than yours. I would not presume to say that you would be better off if you stayed at Stanford than at County Hospital, or gone to Columbia instead of Rochester. I assume you know your medicine and what you are doing. But you are not willing to assume that I know my pictures and what I am doing." He knew what was best for Ingrid, Selznick continued; Ingrid and Dan O'Shea knew "second best." But Petter was "a very bad third!"

As for Petter's objections to mediocre films, the producer dealt with that easily, simply by referring to the popularity and profits of *Dr. Jekyll and Mr. Hyde*, *Casablanca* and *For Whom the Bell Tolls* (which, despite the critics, drew enormous crowds nationwide); furthermore, *Gaslight* was scheduled for release that May, and advance word was more than encouraging.

The third complaint was also specious, Selznick insisted: all the changes to Ingrid's contract, protracted though they were (usually because of Petter's temporizing), gave her more per-picture fees and greater bonuses—so what was the problem?

As for *Joan of Arc*: that was very nearly impossible in light of the war. "The feeling in this country for a while was none too friendly to the French, and even when this passed there was a grave doubt as to whether we wouldn't actually be fighting with Vichy [the collaborationist French puppet government during the German occupation of France]. Even today, the international situation is so uncertain that a picture glorifying the French at the expense of the English (and/or of the Catholic Church: somebody burned her!) is a pretty difficult thing to contemplate."

Finally, the threat that Ingrid would go elsewhere rankled Selznick. "This is the equivalent of a military tribunal advising a prisoner that he will not be shot at dawn without being notified in advance . . . Your whole letter, Petter, confuses me in view of Ingrid's statements that she would be with me as long as she was in pictures." Selznick concluded in the tone with which he began: "My association with Ingrid is an unmitigated joy except for your persistent refusal to understand the skill that has gone into the handling of her . . . I have the deepest confidence in your great success—as a doctor."

Selznick's no-nonsense reply hit its mark. On May 13, Petter replied:

> As I said in December, we feel Ingrid should not decide on any new contracts for quite some time. I wanted to tell you, however, that I enjoyed reading your last letter very much.
>
> Ingrid certainly is anxious to make pictures with you. In the intervals, when you are not using her in your productions, we will endeavour to arrange her work so that we will know approximately when she is on and off.
>
> Ingrid has talked to you a little about those "outside pictures." . . . For that reason, I thought I should specify the date— January 1, 1945. I had not in mind that she should sign any exclusive contract with any "outsider," neither before nor after that date.

Where in hell (or Beverly Hills) was Charles Feldman, Selznick wanted to know? Had Ingrid's agent no influence here? To which the only reply was that Feldman, try though he might, had none.

"It amounted to complete submission [to Petter] on my part," Ingrid said years later. "He insisted on managing all my business affairs, and it was not Petter's nature to trust anyone, especially in business dealings. He would often say that no man ever gave his wife more freedom. That was true. But I was always free away from him, not with him."

UNDER ANY OTHER CIRCUMSTANCES, SELZNICK MIGHT HAVE PURSUED the matter of Petter's management even further. But he wanted only to please Ingrid that spring: Alfred Hitchcock was at work with screenwriter Ben Hecht on a project for Ingrid Bergman and Gregory Peck, now also under contract to Selznick. Peck's first two films had quickly established him as a major star. "I'd like to stress," wrote Selznick to his story editor Margaret McDonell, "that I'm almost desperately anxious to do this psychological or psychiatric story with Hitch." As it happened, both Selznick and Hecht were undergoing psychoanalysis at the time. Hitchcock, who had no interest in it, considered Selznick's insistence on psychiatric jargon and Freudian dream theory as an excuse for a love story.

The basis for it was a 1927 novel, *The House of Dr. Edwardes* by John Leslie Palmer and Hilary Aidan St. George Saunders (writing under the joint pseudonym Francis Beeding), a bizarre tale of witchcraft, satanic cults and murder, all of it set in a Swiss lunatic asylum. Hitchcock had convinced Selznick that this odd property (the rights to which Hitchcock had bought for a pittance and then cannily sold them to Selznick for a tidy profit) could be substantially reworked to become a thriller in which a lady psychoanalyst solved a murder mystery and so saved the life of her patient, with whom she has fallen in love.

Like Ingrid, Hitchcock (who had earned Selznick the Oscar for *Rebecca*) had made only one picture for Selznick before being loaned out to other studios, where he had made a number of popular and successful pictures (among them *Foreign Correspondent, Suspicion, Shadow of a Doubt* and *Lifeboat*). Hecht was a journalist, playwright, novelist and probably the quickest screenwriter in the history of Hollywood. Most of his seventy movies were written in less than three weeks, and on those that he "doctored," he was happy to work without credit for compensation as high as $125,000 (a sum about ten times greater than the normal fees paid to screenwriters in Hecht's time). His most noted movies (or those whose problems he helped resolve but for which he took no credit) included *Twentieth Century, Nothing Sacred, Gunga Din, Wuthering Heights, Queen Christina* and *Gone With the Wind*.

The Hitchcock-Hecht collaboration was a fruitful one. Both shared an interest in the darker corridors of the human mind, both wanted to spin a hefty yarn, both wanted to interweave a love story. Selznick, when he read the final draft (with some changes by his psychiatrist, Dr. May E. Romm), was thrilled.

Begun as *The House of Dr. Edwardes*, the movie was eventually rechristened *Spellbound*. The narrative begins as Dr. Murchison (played by Leo G. Carroll), the director of the mental asylum Green Manors, in Vermont, has suffered a breakdown and is to be succeeded by the famous Dr. Anthony Edwardes (Peck), who immediately falls in love with his new colleague, Dr. Constance Petersen (Ingrid). But then Edwardes begins to behave strangely: emotional outbursts are curiously triggered whenever he sees parallel lines on white surfaces. Constance discovers that Edwardes is not Edwardes

but an amnesiac impostor who, along with the police, believes he
has killed the real Edwardes. Soon the law is on his trail.

Unwilling to accept that the man she loves is a killer, Constance
hides him away from the police with her former professor, Dr. Alex
Brulov (Michael Chekhov), and together the two analysts attempt to
untangle their patient's strange dreams. It turns out that the young
man had repressed the memory of the accidental death of his
brother when they were children, and it was not he but the
demented Dr. Murchison who murdered the real Dr. Edwardes to
save his own position. When Constance puts all these pieces
together at the conclusion, Murchison kills himself. She and her
patient—freed of his legal and psychological guilt—are now able to
marry.

INGRID LIKED THE DESCRIPTION OF DR. PETERSEN IN THE NOVEL
("Constance regarded herself very steadily and without prejudice
. . . She prided herself above all on being clear") and she liked Constance's generous loyalty. But she found incredible the mingling of
professional psychiatric duty with romance: "I won't do this movie
because I don't believe the love story," she told Selznick. "The
heroine is an intellectual woman, and an intellectual woman simply
can't fall in love so deeply."

To allay her misgivings, Selznick, Hitchcock and Hecht met with
her. After all, said Hitchcock, everyone likes a good love story, and
if they wanted to commit to realism, they ought to make documentaries. This argument did not carry nearly as much weight for her as
Hitchcock's thoroughgoing professionalism, his ability to entertain
as he spun the complexities of the plot, and his extraordinary talent
for enabling her to "see" the whole picture as he spoke. Ingrid had
of course heard of Hitchcock's wizardry, and she had especially
admired his taut, dense picture *Shadow of a Doubt*, starring her colleague and friend Teresa Wright.

Furthermore, the love story and the technical innovations
Hitchcock planned for *Spellbound* would be their real focus and challenge. As for the psychiatric jargon, Hitchcock also reminded Ingrid
that audiences had very little precedent or context for movies about
psychoanalysis. Sigmund Freud had died only five years earlier, and
such technical language (guilt complexes, father-fixations, dream

symbolism) was not widely used or understood by the general public. Hence what appeared in the script as a simplistic solution to the story's mystery by a sort of sophomoric interpretation of dream images would be something fresh and fascinating in 1944.

After two hours of discussion, Ingrid was won over. On June 20, she reported to the Selznick Studios for makeup and wardrobe tests, and the first scenes were shot on July 10, Ingrid's seventh wedding anniversary; in her honor, Hitchcock ordered a huge cake wheeled out for the cast and crew after the day's work. Doubtless she was more festive over resuming work than being reminded of her marriage.

"I remember that we had some disagreements during filming," Ingrid recalled years later.

> I said, "I don't think I can give you that kind of emotion." And he [Hitchcock] sat there and said, "Ingrid, fake it!" Well, that was the best advice I've had in my whole life, because in all the years to come there were many directors who gave me what I thought were quite impossible instructions and many difficult things to do, and just when I was on the verge of starting to argue with them, I heard his voice coming to me through the air saying, "Ingrid, fake it!" It saved a lot of unpleasant situations and waste of time.

With *Spellbound*, Ingrid Bergman and Alfred Hitchcock began a historic collaboration that resulted in three films and a friendship that endured until Hitchcock's death in 1980. But however mutually rewarding, this was one of the most problematic relationships in their lives, for Hitchcock very soon fell deeply in love with his leading lady. But he did not arouse similar romantic emotions in her: she greatly respected his genius and had enormous affection for him as a mentor, father-figure and friend, but there her feelings stopped. This made their work together, over a period of four years, both a great joy and a painful trial for Hitchcock.

During those preproduction discussions about *Spellbound*, he was at first merely fascinated by Ingrid; but by the time he began filming, Hitch was a doomed romantic—thus the extraordinary tenderness of his direction of her and the far greater genius of their next picture, *Notorious*. Just as Ingrid had to live within a world of imagination to create credible feelings for her characters, so the power of Hitchcock's masterworks owed to his unassailable genius as a visual storyteller who worked with the raw material of his own fantasies. During his long creative life, he lived within the prison of the haunted lover manqué: his frustrated passion for several of his leading ladies brought him great pain. But it was precisely that anguish that also gave the world great art, which is sometimes realized in the furnace of romantic discontent. In this regard, he left a profound spiritual testament in a series of remarkably self-revealing motion pictures.

"There was certainly something ailing Hitchcock that year," according to Gregory Peck, whose performance as a vulnerable patient gave the picture much of its appeal, "but it was difficult to know exactly the cause of his suffering." He could not have been aware that it was the director's acute, unrequited passion for Ingrid.

Hitchcock, who turned forty-five that summer, had been married since 1926 to Alma Reville, his closest collaborator. Entirely dependent on her counsel, approval and ministrations, Hitchcock would never have contemplated divorce. His emotional life was tangled and intricate, his repressions deep, his spirit tormented. But somehow his private fears and feelings were transmuted into romances that touched millions all over the world and continued to do so long after his death. In this regard, it is a tenable hypothesis that, had he been able to live out his fantasies, he might well have been incapable of dealing with them—much less of changing them into art.

For the rest of his life, Hitchcock frequently confided to friends an elaborate tale, forged in the workshop of his fervent imagination: it was the fantastic account of Ingrid's hysterical refusal to leave his bedroom, after a dinner party at his home, until he agreed to make love to her. If this fiction were not so pathetic, it would be amusing, but Hitchcock told what he considered the emotional (if not the literal) truth of their relationship. He and Ingrid (he believed with all his heart) would be the perfect couple, if only—well, after all, as he wrote for her to say in *Spellbound*, "We're all just bundles of inhibitions."

*   *   *

THROUGHOUT FILMING, SHE OF COURSE DID NOTHING TO ENCOURAGE his amorous inclinations, but her restraint had the opposite effect. This he took for cautious diplomacy, and so he redoubled his efforts to attach her permanently to his life. To that end, he spun for her the outlines of *Notorious*, and she committed to it at once. Hearing of this, Selznick politely reminded them that, since they were both under contract to him, project approval and casting decisions were his prerogatives—although he, too, was beguiled by Hitchcock's ideas.

"Hitchcock was one of the few directors who really stood up to Selznick," Ingrid recalled,

> and Selznick for the most part left him alone. When he came down to the set, the camera suddenly stopped, and Hitchcock said the cameraman couldn't get it going again. "I don't know what's wrong with it," he would tell Selznick. "They're working on it, they're working on it." And finally Selznick would leave, and miraculously the camera would start rolling again. It was Hitch's way of dealing with interference, and although I think Selznick finally guessed that it was a ruse, he said nothing. Selznick left him alone after that. They were two strong men, but they had great respect for each other.

Gregory Peck agreed, adding that "Selznick believed in treating his actors like little tin gods, but he was a little hard on directors. Hitchcock, I think, learned to take it all in his stride."

During the production of *Spellbound*, Hitchcock was courtly and attentive to his leading lady but never effusive in the presence of others. Disallowing the emergence of his deepest feelings and, as so often, dropping them into his scripts, he added at the last moment a telling exchange for Ingrid and John Emery, in the role of a colleague whose infatuation (like Hitchcock's) she does not reciprocate:

DR. FLEUROT (Emery): You're a sweet, pulsing, adorable woman underneath. I sense it every time I come near to you.
CONSTANCE (Bergman): You sense only your own desires and pulsations—I assure you, mine in no way resemble them.

The basic idea of *Spellbound*—love-smitten lady analyst plays detective to prove the innocence of haunted patient accused of a crime—was constantly refined by Hitchcock during shooting to emphasize ever more clearly the change in Constance Petersen from unworldly professional to ardent lover. Quite concretely, *Spellbound* became the story of a twofold transformation—the treatment of the disturbed Peck/Hitchcock by Ingrid and, concomitantly, her release to explore her deepest womanly feelings for this troubled man. To this point in her career, the deepest attachment in Constance's life has been to her mentor, the fatherly Dr. Brulov (a kind of Petter Lindstrom), and she needs her tormented patient to free her for passion. In *Spellbound*, therefore, the characters played by both Bergman and Peck must escape certain emotional blocks to establish a loving commitment.

One of the hooks Hitchcock devised to lure the audience's fascination for this bizarre situation was a series of dream images designed in collaboration with the surrealist painter Salvador Dalí. He gave Hitchcock the De Chirico–like effects he wanted, but however provocative these images remain, they are but a few of the total Dalí provided. For years, Hitchcock mentioned only that there was also a statue that would "crack like a shell falling apart, with ants crawling all over it, and underneath, there would be Ingrid Bergman." Most of that sequence was filmed, and still photographs of it survive. But Selznick ordered the entire business cut from the finished film.

Ingrid's recollections were quite precise.

It was a wonderful, twenty-minute sequence that really belongs in a museum. The idea for a major part of it was that I would become, in Gregory Peck's mind, a statue. To do this, we shot the film in the reverse way in which it would appear on the screen. They put a straw in my mouth so I could breathe, and then a statue was actually made around me. I was dressed in a draped, Grecian gown, with a crown on my head and an arrow positioned so it seemed to be through my neck. Then the cameras rolled. I was in this statue, I broke out and the action continued. We ran it backward, so it would appear as if I became a statue. It was marvelous, but someone went to Selznick and said,

"What is all this drivel?" and so they cut it. It was such a pity. It could have had that touch of real art.

At the time, her protests went unheeded. She understood that what fell to the cutting room floor was more than gimmickry, for the piercing of Constance's neck with an arrow suggests just how far, in his own mind, the patient's anger and guilt may go: there is a clear connection between his belief in his capacity for murder and his ambivalent feelings about Constance as healer and lover. The statue also represents his image of her as a mother-goddess figure (thus the Venus/Cybele costume), with the arrows reminiscent of the spiked fence that caused the death of the patient's young brother in their childhood. Constance-as-statue also suggests that he sees her as classically cold, artificial, remote, untouchable. The unedited original, as Ingrid rightly perceived, might have conveyed even more powerfully the paradoxically compatible emotions of love and hate, desire for help and mistrust of helpers, and the overarching fear of discovery.

THE ENDURING EMOTIONAL APPEAL OF SPELLBOUND NEVER DERIVES from its Byzantine plot but rather from the entirely natural and understated performances by Ingrid Bergman and Gregory Peck, both of whom portray with a kind of ingenuous astonishment their discovery of previously unrecognized needs. Each of them embarks on a frightening journey of self-realization—and that this dual journey is so unlikely was precisely Hitchcock's point. He created the proper atmosphere in which these performances could emerge, and with films like Spellbound it became clear how very much an actor's director he was.

In the naturalness and fragility of Ingrid's portrayal of Constance, in the way she turned her head, folded her hands and stifled an inchoate sob, there was virtually a handbook on modulated, adult screen acting. Of all that Hitchcock taught her, the most valuable lesson was perhaps the significance of the close-up image of her gaze: her shifting glance downward, or to the left or right, would reveal a thought or anxiety or moment of grave reflection.

A good example of this occurs in the first evening scene, when Ingrid comes to Peck's room with a copy of Dr. Edwardes's book.

He is slumped in a chair, asleep, and awakens to see her standing before him. She admits that she has come to his room to discuss not the book but the sudden bond between them. Their subsequent kiss and embrace are full of charged feeling but are still somewhat restrained gestures, freighted with anxiety—an effect somewhat diminished for later audiences by Selznick's insistence on a symbolic overlay of a number of doors opening down a long corridor during the kiss.

Even more moving is Constance's final departure from her teacher, Dr. Brulov. As Ingrid, completely absorbed in her role, sobbed over having failed to win the release of her beloved, she is comforted by her teacher. "It is very sad to love and lose somebody," he says (just before the dénouement saves the day). "But in a while you will forget and you will take up the threads of your life where you left off not long ago. And you will work hard. There is lots of happiness in working hard—maybe the most." Alfred Hitchcock was, as so often, presenting himself. There is enormous tenderness here, and the scene became a perfect metaphor for the delicacy of Ingrid's relationship to her director.

Spellbound was a far greater success than any of its participants anticipated. It cost $1.7 million to produce and grossed $8 million in its first release, thus making it one of the two or three most lucrative movies of the 1940s. It also received six Oscar nominations—for best picture, director, supporting actor, cinematography, special effects and score; only Miklos Rozsa took home the statuette, for the music. This was also the first American film in which Ingrid Bergman received first star billing onscreen.

NOT LONG AFTER SHE BEGAN WORK ON *SPELLBOUND* THAT JULY, INGRID and Petter, who had been looking for a house to buy, found one they liked. Built like a chalet or mountain lodge, it was located at 1220 Benedict Canyon Drive, north of Sunset Boulevard in Beverly Hills. Built in 1920 of chiseled fieldstone and redwood, the house was reached at the end of a short, steep driveway and was surrounded by lush plantings and old trees. There were a vast beamed and vaulted living-dining room with a large stone fireplace; an antique copper bar; a master suite; a large country kitchen; an office; a small bedroom for Pia; and a tiny guest cottage. Eventually, a swimming pool was installed on the property, and there were plans for the addition of other rooms.

"Imagine! We moved in yesterday," Ingrid wrote in Swedish to her father-in-law in Sweden, on August 3.

How happy we are. I couldn't sleep a wink, I only walked around and patted my furniture and my packed trunks. I am so happy, and I don't believe Petter has been this happy in many, many years. We were lucky to buy the house with a good deal of its furniture, just the kind I wanted and so difficult to buy new these days. But because I didn't sleep, they complained that I wasn't beautiful enough when they took closeups today . . . As soon as we can, we will install a swimming pool and even a tennis court. First Petter wants to build a sauna . . .

I have started my new movie, and all is well. I'm playing a doctor, and again this is different from the films I have acted in before. I like it, that I can play different roles. That is seldom done by actors in Hollywood—they usually play the same types over and over again until they die.

Pia is well now that she got rid of her tonsils . . . She will start regular school this fall. I can't believe that we are aging, too—I don't feel a day over 19! But Petter is too busy. I feel he looks so run down, and there's no hope of a vacation for a long time.

On October 10, she again wrote to her father-in-law:

I finished my film, "Spellbound," and I believe it will be an interesting film. I really enjoyed working with Alfred Hitchcock, and I am so happy that his next film also will be with me. It is a spy story . . .

I would really like another film before this, but it doesn't look like something suitable is coming up, so I'm planning a tour around America for bonds and for blood donations for the wounded. One makes speeches and speeches and more speeches, and I hope it doesn't go in one ear and out the other.

The "tour around America" took her, with Joe Steele as escort, to Indiana, Pennsylvania, Minnesota, Wisconsin and Canada. Steele

sensed that Ingrid was "like a race horse at the starting gate, eager
to be off [because of] her deeply ingrained restlessness." As for her
husband, Steele noted that time and again Petter agreed to Ingrid's
departures without complaint. Steele was quite aware of the reason
for this bland acquiescence—namely, that the Lindstroms found it
increasingly hard to be together. By 1944, there was virtually no
marriage.

At each stop on the bond tour (which she undertook at the invitation of the War Department), Ingrid read speeches prepared in
Hollywood by writers engaged by the War Department—lengthy
and grandiose comments entirely unsuited to her personality. Often,
she simply put aside these tedious pages and spoke directly to her
audiences in school halls, baseball parks and ballrooms, telling them
of life in Sweden and of her gratitude to be working in America.
Then she did a short dramatic reading from a little collection of stories and verses she had assembled: excerpts from Paul Gallico's
"The Snow Goose," poems by Carl Sandburg or a story by Ben
Hecht.

Her expressive, liquid voice and her evident warmth and sincerity won over every group she met, and her presence meant a successful contribution. Besides the rallies, there were civic luncheons
and cocktail parties, visits to hospitals, radio interviews and press
conferences for the war bond cause. She put in long days and then
went on to the next city for more long days, "but there was never a
peep [of complaint] from Ingrid Bergman," according to Steele—
only "an astonishing, unflagging zest for the job to be done."

At Thanksgiving, Ingrid and Joe revisited the Swedish immigrants they had met in Minnesota during the making of *Swedes in
America*, and then she was back home before Christmas, shopping
for Pia and planning decorations for her house. Because of Petter's
insistence on economy, Ingrid bought from Selznick portions of her
Spellbound wardrobe, for which she wrote the studio a check for
$122.77. After all, Petter's own closet was not extravagantly
stocked, he said, and he made one or two suits last for season after
season.

But there were no such economies when it came to facilitating
life in their new home. Within a year, the Lindstroms had, in addition to Mabel, Pia's nanny Mary Jackson and a part-time secretary

With her father, Justus Bergman (c. 1921).

Summer 1923.

At the Lyceum for Girls (1925).

At the Royal Dramatic
Theater School (1933).
Ingrid Luterkort stands
far left, Signe Hasso is to
right of Bergman and
Edvin Adolphson stands
fifth from right.
(*From the collection of
Ingrid Luterkort*)

In her first film, *Munkbrogreven/
The Count of Monk's Bridge* (1934).

In *Ocean Breakers/
Bränningar* (1934).

In *Swedenhielms* (1934).

With Victor Sjöström
in *Valborgsmässoafton/*
Walpurgis Night (1935).

With Gösta Ekman,
in *Intermezzo* (1936).

Publicity for the Swedish
Film Industry (1936).

OPPOSITE:
Dr. and Mrs. Petter A. Lindstrom,
July 10, 1937.

With Edvin Adolphson, in *En Enda Natt/Only One Night* (1937).

With Anders Henrikson, in *En Kvinnas Ansikte/A Woman's Face* (1938).

Presented as a
"daughter of Germany"
for UFA publicity (1938).

In *Juninatten/June Night* (1939).

Presented to America as a
Swedish milkmaid (1939).

On Broadway, in *Liliom* (1940).
(Culver Pictures)

With Leslie Howard, in
the American version of
Intermezzo (1939).
(*Museum of Modern Art/
Film Stills Archive*)

As Ivy Petersen, in
*Dr. Jekyll and Mr.
Hyde* (1941).
(*Courtesy of the
Academy of Motion
Picture Arts and
Sciences*)

With Humphrey Bogart,
in *Casablanca* (1942).
(Warner Bros.)

With Charles Boyer,
in *Gaslight* (1943).
(*Culver Pictures*)

Arriving in Alaska
to entertain
troops (1943).

With David O. Selznick (1944).
(*IMS Bildbyra*)

With Gregory Peck
and Alfred Hitchcock
during the production
of *Spellbound* (1944).
(*Museum of Modern
Art/Film Stills Archive*)

During *Spellbound*.

named Doris Collup. The house (named Hillhaven Lodge by its previous owners) cost $65,000; the cash for this, the additions and the household staff was provided entirely by Ingrid's salary: Petter's residency in neurosurgery was not concluded until 1947, and only then could he begin his practice and expect a respectable income.

The focus of the Lindstroms' new home was a large round table backed against a built-in sofa in front of the living room fireplace. When friends and colleagues visited during the Christmas holidays, Ingrid entertained casually (her usual outfit was a simple sweater and tweed skirt). After greeting her guests, she went off to the kitchen, hastily arranged a tray of biscuits and cheese, and served these with cocktails. But often people had to be patient: her incompetence at the bar and in the kitchen invariably forced her to rely on hired help, although she was always uncomfortable giving orders.

Because of his long working hours, Petter usually arrived late in the evening, but then he became a good host. He switched on the gramophone, popular music filled the house, and Petter led the guests in an evening of energetic dancing. At such times, he was the life of the party and cut a dashing figure; no woman turned down the chance to hoof it with the tireless Dr. Lindstrom.

As for the guest list, this was, at first, a problem. Ingrid thought that a party of friends meant just that—and so she invited Irene and David Selznick; Ruth Roberts; Alfred and Alma Hitchcock; the French director Jean Renoir and his wife; Teresa Wright and her husband; Ben Hecht; and several crew members from *Spellbound* with whom she had become especially friendly. "This is impossible—quite impossible," said Irene when she saw the list: mixing stars with technicians and language coaches with studio chiefs simply was not done in the highly stratified world of filmland aristocracy. (Ingrid may well have remembered that Kay Brown, after escorting her to the Selznicks in 1939, was pointedly excluded from a welcome dinner that same evening.)

So much for the myth of classless America. "That was a great shock," Ingrid said, and when she mentioned the matter to Hitchcock, he just smiled and welcomed her to the realities of Hollywood social life. "Thank goodness there was the Hitchcock group," Ingrid added years later. "Hitch and Alma mixed a lot with actors they liked and didn't care if they were stars or not." After acceding to

Irene's demand at that first winter party, Ingrid went her own way, giving small, informal buffet parties to which she invited Charles Boyer, Gary Cooper, Clark Gable, Ernst Lubitsch, Gregory Peck, Joseph Cotten and their wives.

But Petter's efforts to manage Ingrid's world began to affect even the spirit of their parties, no matter how genial he tried to be. He greeted their guests effusively, Joe Steele recalled, and worked hard to share the prevailing spirit of relaxed camaraderie. But something was wrong: he was too formal, too managerial, too opinionated on everything relative to Hollywood, when after all he knew so little—as, indeed, why should so serious and gifted a surgeon know much about the occasional artistry and pervasive pettiness of Hollywood? More and more on such occasions, Ingrid (thus Steele) became "suddenly subdued, the atmosphere leaden [and] the disharmony too pronounced, his interests too divergent from theirs. The doctor tried hard, exceedingly hard, but the end result was hollow."

AUSTERITY PERVADED THE AIR, AND NO MORE SO THAN WHEN THE TALK turned to Ingrid's roles or publicity assignments. "No, I don't think that is good for you to do," said Petter more than once when Steele mentioned an upcoming event or appearance.

"Oh, I don't see any harm in it, Petter," Ingrid said lightly.

"I said it is not good," insisted Petter calmly. "And you will not do it."

That same season, Ingrid had Selznick to contend with, too. While Ingrid was on tour, he had been approached by director Leo McCarey, who had a big hit that year with the heartwarming religious comedy *Going My Way*. McCarey very much wanted Ingrid to play the devoted, sensible, down-to-earth nun in the sequel, *The Bells of Saint Mary's*, which would again feature Bing Crosby as the devoted, sensible, down-to-earth Father O'Malley. Nonsense, said Selznick: sequels are never popular. The best way to a producer's heart, figured McCarey, was through his most insistent star, and so McCarey took an ad in the Minnesota newspapers when Ingrid was on tour: "Wait till Ingrid Bergman hears the idea Leo McCarey has for her!"

Back home, she at once rang Selznick, who told her he had read the script and yes, it was a nice part, but he was very unsure. Ingrid rang McCarey's office at RKO, arranged to read the script and began to importune Selznick. "If you don't let me do this, I'll go back to Sweden!"

McCarey got Ingrid, and Selznick got $175,000 cash on the loanout, as well as the return to him of two RKO pictures he had produced more than a decade earlier, *A Bill of Divorcement* and *Little Women*.

And so Ingrid began her research, which in this case meant visiting a convent of teaching nuns in Los Angeles, where she met McCarey's aunt, a member of the order and in many ways the inspiration for the role she was to play. From her visits with the sisters, Ingrid took away concrete ideas about how and how not to portray Sister Benedict in *The Bells of St. Mary's*. She was delighted to have every cliché about nuns shattered: she saw no sentimental, saccharine piety in the lives of these women. Instead, she saw quiet devotion, hard work, strength of purpose and a refreshing sense of humor. These women were in many ways, Ingrid was surprised to learn, very like herself.

BUT THE NUNS WERE HAPPY IN THEIR COMMITMENT; INGRID WAS NOT. At the end of that year, with her marriage in disarray, she finally asked Petter for a divorce. But they had never had a quarrel, he protested: why should they separate? Quarrels would be useless, Ingrid replied, because there was never any discussion between them. Their life, her career, the management of home and child: everything was subject to his control. "I won't argue with you," Ingrid said sadly. "I'll just go away." But he persuaded her that it was absurd for them to live in separate homes: no one had competitive claims on their affections, and they were, after all, bound by devotion to Pia.

The child had evidently inherited her parents' alertness.

"You always do what Papa wants you to do," Pia told her mother one afternoon.

"Certainly I do," Ingrid replied, doubtless startled by the keen assessment of a seven-year-old. "Papa is very intelligent, and he is head of the house."

"But does Papa ever do anything you want him to do?" Well did she ask.

A few days later, Ingrid was munching chocolate while reading a magazine. "Oh," Pia said, pointing to the candy, "does Papa know about it?"

On still another embarrassing occasion, Ingrid said that of course Pia could join some friends at the movies. "But what's the use of you telling me?" Pia asked plaintively. "I have to wait for Papa's permission." And so it went.

"I think I was just waiting for someone to come along and help me out of that marriage," Ingrid said later, "because I didn't have the strength to go."

Chapter Ten

1945

A lover without indiscretion is no lover at all.

THOMAS HARDY,
THE HAND OF ETHELBERTA

THE EARLY WEEKS OF THE NEW YEAR WERE SPENT IN LONG PREPRO-
duction meetings with Leo McCarey, to whom Ingrid laid out
her ideas for the role of Sister Benedict. Sometimes, Bing Crosby
appeared, sucking on a pipe, nodding occasionally but saying very
little. As for her wardrobe and makeup tests, that was of course no
problem in *The Bells of St. Mary's*. Her garb throughout the picture
would be only a black nun's habit (which conveniently concealed
Ingrid's Christmastime weight gain). The makeup department,
which often had trouble applying the right cosmetics so that "nuns"
would appear neither glamorous nor sickly, found that Ingrid's
complexion was as rumor had it. With a light dab of powder and
the merest tint to her lips, she looked both unadorned and healthy.

On March 15, 1945, the Academy Awards were distributed at
Grauman's Chinese Theater on Hollywood Boulevard; the statuettes
were not of bronze but plaster that year, in keeping with wartime
restrictions. To no one's surprise, Leo McCarey's blockbuster *Going*

My Way received seven Oscars—for best picture, director, actor (Bing Crosby), supporting actor (Barry Fitzgerald), story (McCarey), screenplay (Frank Butler and Frank Cavett) and song ("Swinging on a Star," by James Van Heusen and Johnny Burke). Jennifer Jones read the nominees for the best performance by an actress, and to prolonged applause, Ingrid came forward to receive the award for *Gaslight*.* "Your artistry has won our vote and your graciousness has won our hearts," said Jennifer, who spoke spontaneously in those days before everything was neatly scripted for presenters.

"I am deeply grateful," said Ingrid, wearing the same simple frock she had worn the previous year. "In fact, I'm particularly glad to get it this time, because tomorrow I go to work in a picture with Mr. Crosby and Mr. McCarey, and I'm afraid that if I went on the set without an award, neither of them would speak to me!" Letters, flowers and cards arrived at Benedict Canyon in wild profusion for weeks, but Ingrid's first note of thanks was to her director, George Cukor: "I am still in a daze about my Oscar and I can hardly express myself in any language," she wrote, "but I wanted very much to tell you how grateful I am to you for your help and understanding of my poor Paula in 'Gaslight.'"

In the case of the genial and admiring McCarey, Ingrid did not have to worry about him not speaking to her on the set next day. But from the very next morning at RKO, she found Bing Crosby an enigmatic co-star, professionally pleasant but distant and always surrounded by a small team of lackeys and retainers. Since his start at age eighteen in 1922, Crosby had quickly become one of the most influential and popular crooners in the world, and to this he added an enormously successful movie career beginning in 1930. His unpretentious affability was precisely what America wanted, especially during wartime. With Bob Hope and Dorothy Lamour, Crosby had already filmed the first three of the *Road* comedies; and movie magazine polls voted him the most popular male star several times during the 1940s.

But Crosby's virtues had few counterparts in real life; indeed, he was to his sons an abusive tyrant with a very different private char-

*The four men credited with the film's art direction were also winners.

acter. "Bing Crosby was one of the most charming, most relaxed persons I have ever worked with," Ingrid said later, "but I never knew him—or his wife or his children." Such was the identical experience of many who worked with Crosby, with the notable exception of a few men who joined him on the golf course. But however warmhearted and even droll the tone of *The Bells of St. Mary's*, the picture was nothing like a romance, and so Ingrid's wariness of Crosby contributed, although accidentally, to her performance and their onscreen chemistry.

The narrative was uncomplicated, even predictable, but it had a wit and charm not often seen in movies with religious characters. Sister Mary Benedict (Ingrid) welcomes the new pastor Father O'Malley (Crosby) to St. Mary's, where the school is in dire need of repair. The priest and nun clash amiably over standards of education, children with family problems are nurtured into maturity, and St. Mary's School is saved by the conversion of a wealthy and ultimately benevolent curmudgeon (Henry Travers). When Sister Benedict is summarily transferred, she believes it is because of Father O'Malley's dislike of her tactics. Only at the last minute does he tell her that she is being sent away to cure her incipient tuberculosis. Relieved that she is merely ill and not rejected, Sister Benedict can depart serene in the knowledge of her achievement, as O'Malley reminds her that if she ever needs help, she should "dial 'O' for O'Malley."

Decades later, there emerged a somewhat fatuous snobbism about this movie, perhaps because, beginning with the cynicism of the 1960s, all institutionally religious men and women in America became figures fit only for conversational target practice. In addition, nuns' garb eventually became (also in the 1960s) more sensibly adapted for work in the modern world, and so figures in earlier films, dressed in ancient attire, were seen as simply comical anachronisms.

Hollywood has been as uneasy with chastity as with promiscuity: hence the image of the sweetly desiccated, sexless spinster who appeared only occasionally in the 1940s and 1950s. But the nun created by McCarey and Bergman—no wizened maiden but a clearheaded beauty shining with tranquillity, inner wisdom and a spirit of genuine self-sacrifice—remains an exception to the lot, especially when contrasted with the later array of movie and television clichés. The portrayals of nuns, even after Ingrid's anomalous Sister Benedict, were for the most part so dipped in honey that they became desperately darling caricatures of mature women, silly examples of girls caught in a protracted preadolescence.*

Contrariwise, *The Bells of St. Mary's* has few clichés in its clerical and religious figures, and Ingrid was so patently human, so natural in the role, that McCarey marveled at how wonderful Dudley Nichols's script sounded on her lips: "When she walks onscreen and says 'Hello,' people ask, 'Who wrote that wonderful line of dialogue?!'"

In fact, she wrote several lines and suggested a few scenes that tightened and leavened the picture. Hers was the idea to feint and parry a bit more zealously during her boxing lesson with the shy schoolboy needing to learn self-defense. She stepped lively, almost dancing, evoking humor but not tipping into burlesque. And she put her soprano to good use when she sang an old Swedish tune for the nuns—gliding from a high note into an embarrassed giggle when Crosby arrives and asks, "What was that song, Sister?"—"Oh," she replies, a worldly smile of remembrance lighting her face, "it's just a—about—spring." But her little laugh suggests that the Swedish lyrics perhaps concern more than just the darling buds of May, and so they do: "Spring breezes whisper and caress loving couples," runs the lyric. "Streams rush by, but they are not as swift as my heart . . ." Not great poetry, but not something she could have got away with in English.

Crosby's reserve notwithstanding, the filming was for Ingrid a happy experience. The last day of shooting, in late May, found her in such good humor that she risked a joke on Crosby, McCarey and the entire production team. The scene was the final one, in which Sister Benedict learns of her illness. Instead of simply saying "Thank you, Father O'Malley" and turning away with a smile, Ingrid said,

---

*The exceptions in film history have been few and noteworthy: Deborah Kerr in *Black Narcissus* (1946) and *Heaven Knows, Mr. Allison* (1957); Audrey Hepburn in *The Nun's Story* (1959); and Susan Sarandon in *Dead Man Walking* (1995). Perhaps the most ludicrous example of the sweet little sister was television's *The Flying Nun*, in which lithe young Sally Field was nothing more than Gidget with aerodynamically remarkable headgear.

"Thank you, Father—oh, thank you with all my heart!" And with that she threw her arms around Crosby's neck and planted a violent kiss on his lips. Crosby stepped back, shocked, McCarey's eyes widened as he shouted "Cut! Cut!" and a priest, engaged as technical consultant to the movie, rushed over: "Now, now, Miss Bergman—we simply can't—no, this will not do!" Then Ingrid burst out with her infectious, irrepressible laugh as everyone caught on to the joke. She put the company in such a good mood that four more takes were necessary: as soon as they came to the last crucial seconds, someone snorted with laughter and ruined the shot.

The role of a warm, sensible nun widened still further the range of women in Ingrid's repertoire. Over the last six years in American films, she had played women who become teachers, companions and wives (*Intermezzo*, *Adam Had Four Sons*, *Rage In Heaven*); a tortured barmaid (*Dr. Jekyll and Mr. Hyde*); the bewildered but idealistic lover of two men (*Casablanca*); the brutalized girl who finds love amid political terrorism (*For Whom the Bell Tolls*); an implacable adventuress (*Saratoga Trunk*); the intended victim of a murderous thief (*Gaslight*) and a psychiatrist who releases her lover from the effects of obsessive guilt (*Spellbound*). Sister Benedict added still another different jewel to her crown, and later in 1945, for the third straight year, she was nominated for the Oscar as best actress for her performance. "Exquisitely serene . . . radiantly beautiful . . . luminous"—the critics trotted out the usual lexicon for Ingrid Bergman.

But she was not pleased with the romantic fantasy being spun about Ingrid Bergman, especially after the release of *Bells*. Many Catholic mothers stopped her in her travels, announcing that they wanted their daughters to become just like Sister Benedict; non-Catholics were, according to the same national movie magazine polls that year, just as enthusiastic—Ingrid Bergman onscreen, whatever the role, was the model of American womanhood. (Did they not know that Ingrid had resolutely retained her Swedish citizenship?) *Look* magazine chose Ingrid for its lush color cover on September 18—but it was a photo of Ingrid in the nun's habit. The distinction between the role and the woman was increasingly blurred. St. Ingrid was the real Ingrid Bergman, the public believed.

*   *   *

HAD THAT PUBLIC KNOWN ABOUT HER PRIVATE LIFE THE SEASON AFTER she completed *The Bells of St. Mary's*, she would have toppled at once from her unwelcome pedestal. But even if newsmen or gossip columnists had been aware, in 1945, it is unlikely that anyone would have reported that Ingrid Bergman, who had brought so much joy to a world at war, was so starved for affection that she took not one but two lovers.

"One side of me is very bohemian," she said later, "the other side is the reverse." Her vie bohémienne began, appropriately, in Paris, where Ingrid arrived in early June 1945, a month after V-E Day. Her success in Alaska and on the bond tours had inspired the United Service Organization (USO) to ask Selznick to release Ingrid for an entertainment tour of Allied troops in Europe. In Paris, she awaited instructions for her transfer to Germany, where she was to join comedian Jack Benny, singer Martha Tilton and musician Larry Adler.

Ingrid was assigned a room at the Ritz, then less a luxury hotel than a crowded madhouse that billeted generals and journalists, artists, entertainers and the international press corps. Within days of her arrival, Ingrid was the light and life of the international set in Paris, eclipsing even the popularity of the formidable Marlene Dietrich, who had been near the front lines and now sniffed unwelcome competition in the air. "Ah, now you're coming—when the war's over!" she said with a dubious smile as Ingrid stepped into the hotel foyer one morning.

But a more genial welcome, also at the Ritz, came from the photographer Robert Capa, then best known for having fearlessly and brilliantly documented the most notable episodes of the war, including the landing at Anzio, the invasion of Normandy and the liberation of Paris; he would also blaze a trail through Germany with paratroopers. He invited her to a modest supper, they strolled along the Seine, he talked about the art and craft of photography, took candid snapshots of her—and very quickly she was in love.

Capa, born Andrei Friedmann in Hungary, was just two years older than Ingrid, but life, work and liquor had taken a heavy toll; he seemed older and, with a terrible sadness, unhappier. Early in the war, he had emigrated to New York, where he worked at various photojournalism jobs before distinguishing himself as the premier documentarist of the Allied effort. A somber and tense man with thick, unmanageable hair and heavy brows that sometimes gave him a sinister mien, Capa had many romantic liaisons, enjoyed several daily beakers of whiskey, had an acerbic wit and impressed women with his continental sophistication. He spoke five languages but said he dreamed in images, most of which were of battle and filled him with disgust. The awfulness of armed conflict had touched him personally when Gerda Taro, his wife and assistant, was crushed by a tank during the Spanish Civil War. She died in his arms.

"Capa is wonderful and crazy and has a beautiful mind," Ingrid told Joe Steele later. She did not add that he was also penniless and depressed, for he had lost every cent at the gambling table, at the bar and in payment for the apartments of his mistresses. He was also, at thirty-two, in a severe emotional crisis, for although he welcomed peacetime as much as anyone, he also had to find new work, and mere magazine, social or portrait photography held no interest for him.

For both of them, romance came under trying circumstances and at a time of particular loneliness and emptiness. He was very likely her first lover since her marriage, and he represented the possibility of escape from it. For Capa, Ingrid's humor, her bubbly laughter and her frank sensuality tempered his melancholy. "It was, it is, your merry mind that I love," he wrote to her later, "and there are very few merry minds in a man's life." Evidently, more than her merry mind preoccupied his downcast spirit that summer, for their torrid affair blazed brightly and, for the time being, without complication. After all, she was far from home and Hollywood, and Paris itself at the end of the war—not bombed, and still the place for lovers—seemed full of promise after so much deprivation. They sipped champagne at Fouquet's, where they were invited several times by an understanding American officer friendly to Capa; they had late suppers at quiet bistros within sight of Notre-Dame; they sat in a corner of the Ritz bar, holding hands, sometimes whispering, sometimes silent. And for almost six weeks they shared his or her room each night.

"Outwardly, he seemed more charming and exuberant than ever," wrote Capa's biographer, Richard Whelan, "for only by emphasizing those qualities could he find some relief from the unhappiness and the sense of being lost that tormented him." Cynical to the core, Capa was (according to his friend Hal Boyle), "the most romantic-looking guy in the press corps," and from her first meeting with Capa, Ingrid was desperately addicted to his presence. Prodigal and passionate, he lived from moment to moment, was confident of his fierce sexual aura, and deemed Ingrid worthy of every night; he was, in other words, the kind of man she had known only in movie scripts but who had now sprung magically to life. For two months that summer and irregularly for the next two years, Ingrid and Capa (she called him only that) conducted a discreet but intense adventure. But he forestalled any talk of serious commitment, and for the time being she posed no ultimatum. She was simply content with the present.

BUT IN MID-JULY, INGRID WAS AT LAST SUMMONED TO GERMANY, AND Capa, who had to remain on assignment in Paris, promised they would reunite in Berlin. Her first visit to her mother's homeland, the country of Aunt Mutti and the place where she had to finesse her contract with UFA, seems to have evoked no feelings from Ingrid, or at least none that she expressed then or later to friends. In a letter to Petter's family after she returned to America in September, Ingrid simply expressed sympathy for the civilians who were victims of war: "Poor people, one has to say when one sees those destroyed German cities, even though one is happy that they finally received their punishment." As for her family, her aunt's Nazi lover had died since their last visit, and Mutti herself had somehow managed to emigrate to Copenhagen, but there was no postwar contact between aunt and niece.

Her first stop was Bavaria, where she met her colleagues. Ingrid admired Jack Benny enormously and joined him in satiric sketches for the soldiers; with Martha Tilton she cheerfully sang duets; and in Larry Adler she found an amusing, gifted admirer. Baltimore-born Adler, married and a year older than Ingrid, was a slim, dark-haired, bright-eyed genius who could not read music but created and played it magnificently. Ingrid found Adler "so romantic, so much fun to be with, and his simple but wonderful music wrapped you up in warmth." The music precipitated something complicated. Believing either that she would never see Capa again or that he was

delicately trying to break off their relationship, Ingrid was susceptible to the considerable charm of Larry Adler.

The entertainers had been lodged in a private house on the out-
skirts of Augsburg, northwest of Munich. There, Adler was sitting at
a piano when Ingrid entered and complimented him on the little
tune he had improvised. When she asked him to write it down, he
readily admitted he could neither read nor write music.

"You're very proud of your ignorance, aren't you?" she asked
with a smile, and with this directness (thus Adler), "I fell in love
with Ingrid immediately, although at first I wasn't sure it was Ingrid.
I hadn't seen her most recent movies, after all. Only after a minute
or two, and hearing that voice, did I realize it was definitely she."

Adler soon had a chance to reacquaint himself with her career: a
special service officer screened *Saratoga Trunk*, still making its European rounds before an American premiere. "Ingrid," Adler said
when the lights went up, "you're a healthy Swedish girl—you are
not a French courtesan. You were not right for the part!" She
protested that it was her best work so far, and for several days she
avoided him. But the distance was soon bridged, when Adler's good
humor got through to her. She also insisted that, when he returned
to America, he must find a good teacher and learn to write music.
This he did: Adler studied with no less a composer and musician
than Ernst Toch and for the rest of his life credited Ingrid Bergman
for his career: "If it wasn't for her, I wouldn't have composed." Best
known as the virtuoso of the harmonica, Adler elevated that instrument to concert status, wrote the scores for seven films and was
much in demand by the world's symphony orchestras.

From mid-July to mid-August, and occasionally thereafter, the
intimacy flourished, and so for the second time in two months—
after so long without warm male companionship—Ingrid became a
complaisant lover. Adler was present, Adler was attentive, Adler was
of the moment. And so, more than ever a natural child of the
moment (a Kindernatur, as Aunt Mutti had called her), she easily
gave herself up to the satisfactions of love.

FOR YEARS, MANY WHO KNEW OF THE SIMULTANEOUS AFFAIRS (AND
later, the prelude to her second marriage) took them to be the pattern of Ingrid Bergman's life—namely, that she was an irresponsible

woman who blithely abandoned her family, indulged every carnal caprice and took whichever attractive lovers presented themselves. In time, this presumption went further: she was a cold-hearted exploiter of men, ran the gossip, a woman who used others' impressions of her fame and their attraction to her to supply her own insufficiencies and her inability to be alone. Such a portrait is grotesquely at variance with the reality of her character.

Ingrid turned thirty that summer of 1945, but there was still, to be sure, a girlish and callow aspect of her personality; in many ways, she was not at all the worldly woman misperceived by the public. Her early life, of course, had been spent on emotionally unstable ground that had often shifted with the deaths of those near to her, and then she had relied entirely on her husband for life's practical matters, so that she would be free to refine her art. Uninterested in matters financial throughout her life, she readily left the management and decisions about them to whatever man she trusted. Completely dedicated to her craft, she was thus free to order everything else in second place. At the same time, the intuitive mechanisms within her, the talent that enabled her to deliver brilliant performances on stage and screen, were hers and hers alone, and so only on these did she count unerringly.

Her career was, then, successfully managed, her marriage controlled by her husband. Fame was a burden, but she bore its fickleness with remarkable simplicity and grace, and her refusal to prevaricate or affect airs and graces endeared her to all her colleagues as much as to the press and public. If people adored her, the cult was of their own invention—she did nothing except good work to provoke their devotion, and even her beauty was prized more by admirers than by herself. From the time of A Woman's Face to the end of her life, Ingrid was unafraid to appear plain (or worse) for the truth of a role.

Marriage had, at first, brought her great consolation. But matrimony cannot, however wonderfully realized by a couple, supply every human need: that fiction, she quickly learned, was the stuff of American movies. In the case of the Lindstroms, it might be said that in a way their union was so successful that both of them had grown a great deal. Years later, they might have been admired for maintaining successful, separate careers. But nothing in the culture

of the time, or in the backgrounds from which they came, freed
Petter or Ingrid for any belief other than the supremacy of the husband's rank, and in some way she knew this—thus her flight from
the stifling boredom of inactivity and the narrow range allowed by
housewifery. Every season of her life, Ingrid Bergman was like a
young woman starting out in pursuit of an exciting new career. Each
role marked a fresh departure into uncharted territory, a novel discovery of inner resources.

ESPECIALLY WITH REGARD TO LOVE, INGRID WAS A CURIOUS COMBINA-
tion of romantic and pragmatist. On the one hand, she longed for a
man to take charge, for the security that a stable union offered, and
she knew the difference between an easy connection of the flesh
and the intimacy, at its best, that sex betokened. She certainly never
gave herself indiscriminately to anyone, nor was her life in any way
controlled by sexual impulse. The realist in her prevented any easy
identification between a grand passion and a little lust. She could
have enticed perhaps any man she wanted, and there was a legion of
adorers throughout her life ready to offer transient or enduring
love. But she was not indiscreet. Even her fantasy romances were
checked by common sense.

Her relations with Capa and Adler, then, might be seen within
the context of a young woman of extraordinarily intense inner
resources who mimicked love in art but felt deprived of it in life. It
was not the convenience of sex that drew her to them, it was—as
always in her life—their creative gifts that fascinated her. Capa, with
his keen eye and Gothic philosophical disposition, swept her away
with his sheer desire for life. "You have become an industry," he
told her. "Your husband is driving you; the film companies are driving you; you let everybody drive you." He wanted not the film star
but the woman. But he did not want her for a wife, and this was the
brake on the velocity of their relationship.

As for Adler, she saw him as a delightful companion and a man
whose music consoled and elevated her. The subject of marriage
was left unaddressed, but both of them realized that their affection
was destined to evolve into friendship, and so it would later become
and remain until her death. Ingrid was, Adler thought, the least
affected person and performer he had ever met, and the most gen-

erous who came to entertain the troops—but he also felt that she
was not exactly right for the task. "The boys wanted comic book
humor, burlesque, raw stuff—and there was Ingrid, reading mostly
from plays and poems."

One night was especially embarrassing. She finished her little
performance and came off the makeshift stage in tears, for the soldiers had mooed romantically and then hooted rudely, waving con-
doms in the air. ("Too bad you fellows haven't got a better use for
those things," said Adler, scolding them a few minutes later.)

Although she was always invited to dine with the military brass,
Ingrid never did. "She always went out and ate with the enlisted
men, took down their names and addresses and called their families
when she got back to America," Adler recalled. "I saw it for myself."
Nor did she exploit her fame to meet the generals. Invited to lunch
with Eisenhower, she declined: "I really have nothing to say to
him," and that was that. Her practical nature, always counterpoised
with her romantic side, was again evident when she and Adler rode
in an open car through the German countryside. Their driver failed
to observe a roadblock order to halt, a shot rang out, and Adler felt
a twinge in his back. Fearing that he had sustained a fatal wound, he
slid to the floor and asked Ingrid to tell his family that he loved
them to the end. But she saw that there was neither blood nor any
sign of a wound. "Larry, stop this nonsense," she said, and a moment
later she fished a bullet from the car's upholstery, where it had
lodged and freed a spring that had merely poked Adler in the back.

HER DISCERNMENT THAT SEASON WENT FAR DEEPER THAN THAT, AS
Adler soon learned—indeed, Ingrid Bergman was keenly aware of
the profoundest lineaments of her own character. This facet of self-
awareness was clearly revealed when she gave Larry Adler a copy of
a novel she had read, saying that the title character was the closest
she had ever read to a portrait of herself—"warts and all," as the
saying was—and that one day she hoped to produce and star in a
film version of it.

The book was *Of Lena Geyer*, a long and deeply affecting novel by
Marcia Davenport published in 1936. The story, set in Europe and
America from the 1870s to the 1930s, tells of a poor Bohemian
girl, an emigrant from Europe to America who through talent and

ambition becomes the world's most famous and brilliant opera singer. She also knows that intimate relationships are far more difficult to negotiate than the thorniest cadenza or the most elaborate contract. In each chapter of this colorful, dramatic and poignant story, Ingrid read passages that reflected herself:

"Lena could not cook a thing . . . she claimed she didn't know how to break an egg . . . But she was vitally in earnest about her work [and] had a great resource of self-discipline . . . She was physically a big, broad-hipped, free-moving animal, strong, with magnificent muscular development and bones as big and square as a man's . . . 'Work could not kill me,' she often said."

"She had an absolute disregard of how much work she did. All her life she had tremendous energy. She could rehearse all day and sing in a performance at night . . . she was full of animation and mischief . . . and she was childishly delighted with jokes and pranks and nonsense. She used to be like a big, jolly breeze."

"'I have traveled a great deal and have never thought of myself as the citizen of any particular country. Art is international, and the distinctions of birthplace and language should not have any bearing upon the artist's point of view.'"

"'I shall try to be yours and live for my art too,' Lena said, 'but I must be fair with you. If I cannot do both, you know what my choice will have to be?' How great was her psychological dependence upon the art in which she had made herself supreme."

"She said she knew nothing about accounts, all she could do was keep track of her pocket money."

"If you were to ask me to sum up her life in America in a few words, I'd say that it consisted chiefly of closing up this big gap between what she thought she liked and what she really did like."

"'This isn't a question of career or money or anything,' Lena said. 'It's my life, it's art, the one thing I've given up everything on earth for.'"

Of Lena Geyer, a remarkable novel about a remarkable woman, haunted Ingrid Bergman for the rest of her life; one of her keenest disappointments was her failure, in the late 1940s and 1950s, to evoke any interest in having it rendered onscreen.

COMPLICATIONS AROSE WHEN ROBERT CAPA ARRIVED IN BERLIN AT THE same time as Benny, Tilton, Adler and Bergman. "Of course it was uncomfortable for all of us, and there was some difficulty at the time," according to Adler, "because Capa and I were aware of how Ingrid was juggling us both around. I think we both tried to be good sports about it. And I couldn't blame her. She had met Capa first and he was a very attractive guy, and he was single and I was married."* Mercifully, the awkward situation (but not the romances) ended after ten days, when they returned to Paris. From there, Martha Tilton and Jack Benny flew back to America and their families, and Adler, too, soon felt compelled to return.

Capa now had Ingrid entirely to himself, and he was apparently so persuasive a lover that Ingrid spoke of leaving her husband for him. This was invariably his signal to change the subject, and this saddened and depressed her. Ingrid may have relished the role of unfaithful woman onscreen, but in life she was uneasy with it. In her world, one married the beloved; she had once loved Petter but now only feared him; there had been no one in real life to provide the necessary escape hatch; and now here was the unattached, available, seductive Capa. She saw no reason that they should not be together forever.

There was something blithe about Capa's attitude to her. He boasted to anyone who would listen that Ingrid Bergman was his mistress, then added quickly that this was a secret. Besides, he said, the relationship seemed headed nowhere, mainly because his future was so uncertain. Ingrid would have to return to California, but who was beckoning Capa? She had urged him to come to Hollywood, where she was certain he would find an important position as a still photographer documenting films in progress for magazine stories and studio publicity. When she departed Paris for Los Angeles, he promised to consider this option.

Ingrid was home in Beverly Hills by early September, settling

---

*In her published memoirs, Ingrid never hinted at a romance with Adler, doubtless because she had decided to discuss her simultaneous affair that same year with Capa.

Pia into the new school year and awaiting a call from Selznick about the new Hitchcock picture promised for her that autumn. Capa and Adler were not mentioned, and because the Hollywood gossips heard no reports of any suspicious behavior (nor would they have sought it in Ingrid's case), life resumed its normal dull, affectless routine at 1220 Benedict Canyon. She and Petter saw each other for a quick cup of coffee at breakfast, she wrote to his relatives. Because many doctors were in wartime service, he was working longer hours than ever, and only rarely did the three Lindstroms dine together. She did not add that she and Petter had a polite, unspoken arrangement: they went to work; they occasionally entertained a few friends; they approved plans for the addition of the swimming pool, which was added to the property that winter; and they looked after the welfare of their daughter—and all of this without any pretense of devotion for each other.

While the world continued to believe that Ingrid Bergman's successful career was conjoined to a perfect home life, she was miserably lonely, and a rueful smile may have crossed her features when she read the results of one interview that year: "Miss Bergman just can't help being a good girl on the screen because that's the way she is." That was bad enough, but then the fictions multiplied: "She does not drink, does not smoke, does not stay out late nights"—all of which she did quite prodigally. For the time being, the press continued its Bergman cantata, and the rhapsodies over her proliferated.

Hitchcock, who had been counting the days until her return, asked Selznick to summon her for a story conference with him and Ben Hecht, who was again providing the script. She was delighted to be back home, she told them, and eager to begin the new film. Hitchcock believed the second assertion but not the first, for he saw on her features a somewhat forlorn look and noted the absence of her usual ebullient good humor. Ingrid's evident distraction Hitchcock rightly took for emotional turmoil, but he knew not the precise cause of it until Ingrid confided in him a few days later, when they were alone one boozy afternoon after a session of script study.

She was in love with Robert Capa, she said as Hitchcock poured hefty drinks for them, and although Capa was expected to arrive in Hollywood that autumn, she saw no hope for the fulfillment of that love. She felt a prisoner of her marriage, of her image, even of her sense of duty and propriety; and she felt abandoned because of Capa's inability to make a commitment to her. Hitchcock, at once a sympathetic friend and ever more desperately her secret fantasy lover, of course repressed his own feelings. And, as usual, he made them serve the forthcoming film. Over the next three days, he asked Hecht to help him focus Ingrid's character, a woman forced by duty into a loveless marriage. The early and late scenes of the picture, Hitchcock insisted, would hinge entirely on this woman's need to be told she is loved, and at last to be redeemed by both an avowal and an action of romantic commitment.

But Hitchcock's immediate response that warm September afternoon in his office was to remind Ingrid of the final scene in *Spellbound* between her and Michael Chekhov, who had played her mentor. "It is very sad to love and lose somebody," Hitchcock quoted, repeating the dialogue of Dr. Brulov as he embraced the weeping Dr. Petersen, who fears she has lost her lover forever. "But in a while you will forget and you will take up the threads of your life where you left off not long ago. And you will work hard. There is lots of happiness in working hard—maybe the most." The speech now had a different application.

Ingrid at once recognized the words, and her eyes filled with tears. Hitchcock had offered her comfort with the same words he spoke for himself: what other refuge had they, these two lovers, but the work that lay before them? She might not have Capa, but she had her work, and now her work was with him; as for Hitchcock, he knew all too poignantly that yes, indeed, her work was with him, but her heart was not—or rather that her heart was with him as a daughter and a friend. They were both, in a way, lost souls. That quiet afternoon, they sat—allies in distress, sipping gin martinis, smoking too much and finding in their unspoken sympathies for each other the courage that comes from the deepest kind of love, a caring beyond the jungle of sex and into the clearer field of affection.

Preproduction meetings that week assembled Hitchcock, Hecht, Selznick, Bergman and her leading man, Cary Grant, and their sessions were friendly, efficient and businesslike: rarely had there been so auspicious a beginning for any Selznick picture. But then, having contracted all the major participants for the film, Selznick sold it as a package to another studio and so realized the largest profit of his career.* On October 15, the new Hitchcock-Hecht-Bergman film went before the cameras at RKO Studios.

THAT SAME DAY, PETTER WROTE TO A LAWYER HE HAD ENGAGED AS intermediary regarding the imminent expiration of Ingrid's contract with David Selznick. The reason for Petter's letter was the delay in starting the Hitchcock picture, and the awkwardness this caused in New York, where playwright Maxwell Anderson had completed most of *Joan of Lorraine*. As he had promised Ingrid when they met in 1940 at the home of Burgess Meredith, he had indeed written a play about St. Joan of Arc for her. Now Anderson and his colleagues at the Playwrights Company wanted to know Ingrid's availability for Broadway.

"It has cost us great embarrassment that we have not been able to tell when Miss Bergman will be available on Broadway," Petter wrote, adding that Selznick had as yet not told them whether there would be a second picture (to which he was entitled) should Hitch-cock's be completed before year's end. "We have never had anything against two pictures during this option period, [but] we have been figuring out together how much Miss Bergman would be paid if only one picture were made. As far as I remember, we came to a minimum of about $130,000 and the maximum of about $180,000. That salary I suggested to be changed to $100,000 plus 3% in case of a new deal." As for the expiration of Ingrid's contract, Petter wanted that confirmed unless an entirely new set of financial terms could be negotiated forthwith, since "Miss Bergman gets a compensation far below her standard" and because Selznick "has not used Miss Bergman in any of his productions for over six years" (which was, of course, not at all the case).

He then adopted a new tone, which may well have brought a smile to its reader's lips: "As far as the salary goes, we are not much concerned. We are here to work and to work under pleasant condi-

---

*RKO paid Selznick $25,000 a week for Hitchcock's services and $20,000 a week for Ingrid's; they received their usual salary from Selznick, slightly more than 10 percent of those amounts.

tions and not just to make money"—the "we" being, presumably, Dr. Lindstrom as attorney-in-fact for his client, Ingrid Bergman. Finally, Petter addressed the matter of Charles Feldman, who had been made useless because of Petter's involvement. "Please find out how much [Selznick's people] are willing to pay of their obligations to Feldman. Also how much Feldman thinks he is entitled to. The difference Miss Bergman will probably pay"—the point being that he wished to have done with Feldman so that sole management of Ingrid would be ceded to Lindstrom.

The lawyer (John O'Melveny) sent a copy of Petter's letter to Selznick, who, as might have been expected, read it and fired off a lengthy and angry reply. "As to Dr. Lindstrom, I have long since become aware of his habit of misinterpreting and often of refusing to acknowledge friendly and unselfish gestures made toward him." Now, he continued, Selznick recognized that the subtext of Lindstrom's letter was his desire that Ingrid not renew her contract with him unless an entire new set of financial terms were negotiated at once.

Selznick's frank wrath had been aroused over two matters. First, there was Petter's implication that Ingrid had been an indentured slave. "She has done everything she wanted to do in the way of appearances, tours, pictures, plays and everything else," Selznick pointed out. Second: "Dr. Lindstrom had the consummate and unprecedented gall to ask for payment for a picture which Miss Bergman had requested be called off [*The Scarlet Lily*, which was to have been filmed in England and Palestine]." Selznick should not have been so indulgent, he added, when Ingrid declined the offer of two other projects.* He had a right to her services for a final picture, and he was willing to draft a new contract "at two or three times" her earlier compensation. Lindstrom had stalled negotiations on these items, and now—using Anderson's play as primary bait— he was implying that Selznick had reneged on an agreement.

"I have met many irrational and unreasonable people in my relations with great stars and with those who attach their wagons to them," Selznick concluded, "but I have never encountered the like

---

*These were roles in *The Spiral Staircase* and *The Farmer's Daughter*, which were ultimately acted by Dorothy McGuire and Loretta Young.

of Dr. Lindstrom's behavior and attitude ... Please wish Miss Bergman luck for me in her new associations, whatever they may be, and please express my hope that her career will continue brilliantly."

It was, then, a fortuitous coincidence that Selznick had abandoned his involvement in the new Hitchcock production: daily contact with Ingrid would, at this time, have been something close to intolerable for both of them. As her contract expired, there was the inevitable distance between them. But because Ingrid's statements about Selznick were laudatory and effusive, they were able to maintain, after all, a solid friendship, and later Selznick came to her aid in a critical situation when she was called an unfit mother.

EVEN BEFORE *SPELLBOUND* WAS COMPLETED, A YEAR EARLIER, HITCHcock had discussed with Hecht the contours of a movie he longed to create, in which Ingrid would portray a woman somewhat like Mata Hari, carefully trained for a complicated espionage assignment. Her character would even go so far as to marry a man she did not love—while the man she did love, her partner in spying, seemed to reject her romantically even while he needed her professionally. The transformation of a theme into a dramatic narrative took the entire year, and although there was some inspiration from a 1921 *Saturday Evening Post* short story that had been first noticed by Selznick, the final narrative was pure Hitchcock. But it could not be completed until Ingrid returned late that summer: Hitchcock had the solutions to his thorniest problems when he learned of the Capa affair. This did not alter the structure of the screenplay he had hammered out with Hecht; on the contrary, it sharpened everything already present.

Whenever possible, Hitchcock preferred to use one-word titles, and this time he had it from day one: *Notorious.** The finished film remains one of Hitchcock's purest masterworks; at the same time, it is a testament to Ingrid Bergman's genius as an actress, for although she was cited for more incandescent roles, many of her admirers

---

*Others in the Hitchcock catalog: *Downhill, Champagne, Blackmail, Murder!, Sabotage, Suspicion, Saboteur, Lifeboat, Spellbound, Rope, Vertigo* and *Frenzy.* (*Rebecca, Psycho, Marnie* and *Topaz* were the original titles of novels on which his film versions were based.)

consider *Notorious* her most deeply felt performance. The tale of a lovelorn woman and a frightened man—and of another man betrayed both by his own devotion and by the political expediency of the couple—*Notorious* is a profound exploration of adult confusions.

The story is straightforward, yet even a brief plot summary hints at deeper concerns just below the surface. Alicia Huberman (Ingrid), a hard-drinking woman of easy virtue and the daughter of a German spy, is impressed into service as part of America's efforts to outwit a group of Nazis in Brazil. Although in love with the American agent T. R. Devlin (Cary Grant), who engages her for this patriotic task, Alicia agrees to marry Alexander Sebastian (Claude Rains), an old acquaintance who still loves her and now heads the German spy ring in Brazil, working to develop uranium ore for the atomic bomb. When her true purpose is discovered by Sebastian, he and his tyrannical mother slowly poison Alicia, but on the verge of death she is rescued by Devlin, who at last admits that he has loved her all along.

The basic concern of *Notorious* is a twofold redemption (and thus something very common in the list of Hitchcock's fifty-three movies): a woman's need to be trusted and loved, which will enable her to transcend a life that has become empty of affection and riddled with guilt; and a man's need to open himself to love, which will enable him to overcome a life of severe emotional repression. In the case of *Notorious*, behind the man's character are Alfred Hitchcock and Robert Capa; behind the woman's is Ingrid Bergman.

Aptly, Hitchcock and Hecht chose to locate this romance about trust within the package of an espionage thriller, for spies are, of course, characterized by their exploitation of trust. Going one step further, that theme is aptly and ironically sustained in the motif of drinking. Far from representing unity, toasting health or celebrating prosperity, all the drinking in *Notorious* is either socially empty (an escape from guilt and pain) or downright poisonous—thus the opening whiskey-soaked party; Alicia's pattern of camouflaging emotional rejection by pouring herself a drink; the ingredient for the bomb hidden within a wine bottle; and the arsenic-spiked coffee served each day to kill Alicia gradually. The structure of the film, tightened by Hitchcock and Hecht even as filming began, was meticulously rendered.

But rigorous structure and carefully planted motifs do not give *Notorious* its considerable impact. That derives from the simplicity of the dialogue and the subtleties of Ingrid's complex performance—and behind it all was Hitchcock's access to his own feelings and to Ingrid's feelings about Capa.

Notorious thus became, even as it was in production, an artistic rendition of two tortured inner lives, and its story of desire versus duty, of passion versus pretense, synthesized two private lives and many public ones. The great achievement of this film may be that in going so deeply into the reservoir of anguish felt by Alfred Hitchcock and Ingrid Bergman, *Notorious* reached unusual depths. Its meditation on the nature of authentic, trusting love went further than a mere romantic cliché, for a specific real-life situation infused it—so honestly that few viewers are unmoved by its universal application.

It is also astonishing that this movie was produced at all (and that it was such an immediate success), since it contains such blunt dialogue about government-sponsored prostitution: the sexual blackmail is the idea of American intelligence agents, who are blithely willing to exploit a woman (and even to let her die) to serve their own ends. The depiction of the moral murkiness of American officials was unprecedented in Hollywood—especially in 1945, when the Allied victory ushered in an era of understandable but ultimately dangerous chauvinism in American life.

TO ACCOMPLISH THE DEEPEST LOGIC OF *NOTORIOUS*, HITCHCOCK DID something unprecedented in his career: he made Ingrid his closest collaborator on the picture. "The girl's look is wrong," Ingrid said to Hitchcock when, after several takes of her close-up in the dinner sequence, everyone knew something was awry. "You have her registering [surprise] too soon, Hitch. I think she should do it this way." And with that, Ingrid did the scene her way.

There was not a sound on the set, for Hitchcock did not suffer actors' ideas gladly: he knew what he wanted from the start. Well before filming began, every eventuality of every scene had been planned—every camera angle, every set, costume, prop, even the sound cues had been foreseen and were in the shooting script. But in this case, an actress had a good idea and, to everyone's astonishment, he said, "I think you're right, Ingrid." It was, after all, their story.

And she got it right throughout. Early on, for example, Alicia learns of her traitorous father's suicide by poison capsule. Hitchcock kept the camera fixed on the memory-swept desert of Ingrid's pale features as she speaks, her face revealing first sadness, then objective memory, then regret for a happier, lost past, and finally an odd sense of release:

> I don't know why I should feel so bad. When he told me a few years ago what he was, everything went to pot—I didn't care what happened to me. But now I remember how nice he once was—how nice we both were—very nice. It's a very curious feeling—as if something had happened to me and not to him. You see, I don't have to hate him anymore—or myself.

Heard just moments after scenes in which Ingrid played the woman roaringly drunk and then painfully hung over, the dialogue gave ample opportunity for her, despite several weeks separating the filming of these sequences, to create a complex of adult experiences and emotions. With whispers, slurred speech, dry mouth and all the signs of mental confusion, she built a character grounded in truth—an alcoholic woman of easy virtue who is made profoundly sympathetic. In this regard, it is simply unreasonable to imagine that Ingrid's fragile emotional condition did not in fact break open her deepest sentiments and contribute to the clarity of her performance.

She was much aided by Cary Grant, in a role that was remarkably calm and pointedly unusual for him. Grant was known mostly, up to that time, for screwball romantic comedies, and his career was foundering when Hitchcock chose him a second time (after *Suspicion* four years earlier) to portray a man almost pathologically afraid of women, a man who can kiss but not commit. During filming, Grant and Bergman formed a lifelong friendship. Rumors to the contrary notwithstanding, there was no affair: he was just emerging from his tumultuous marriage to heiress Barbara Hutton, and for intimacy he turned mostly to Randolph Scott, with whom he shared a weekend house on the beach at Santa Monica for more than a decade.

The dialogue of the outdoor cafe scene set in Rio, for example, was so expertly rendered by Grant and Bergman that Hitchcock needed no more than a rehearsal and two takes. Grant, tight-lipped and stony-faced, brilliantly played Devlin as a man chillingly contemptuous of the first woman to evoke love from him; Ingrid, meantime, shifted naturally from hurt to challenge, from the promise of a new life to a fear that she would be disallowed the chance for it. And Hitchcock permitted, at the last minute, the insertion by Ingrid of several touches that were markedly autobiographical, as if she were deliberately fusing her own identity with Alicia's—her hatred of cooking, for example.

ALICIA (Bergman): I wonder if at the embassy someone can get me a maid. It's a nice apartment and I don't mind dusting and sweeping, but I hate cooking.
DEVLIN (Grant): I'll ask them.
ALICIA: And while you're at it, find out when I go to work.
DEVLIN: Yes, ma'am.
[A waiter asks if they want another round of cocktails.]
DEVLIN: Have another drink?
ALICIA: No, thank you—I've had enough.
[He orders one for himself.]
ALICIA (slightly tossing her head back and smiling with almost childish pride): Did you hear that? I'm practically on the wagon—that's quite a change!
DEVLIN (sarcastically): It's a phase.
ALICIA (her smile fading): You don't think a woman can change?
DEVLIN (more bitterly): Sure—change is fun—for a while.
ALICIA: "For a while." What a rat you are, Dev.
DEVLIN: All right. You've been sober for eight days. And as far as I know, you've made no new conquests.
ALICIA (trying to hide her hurt): Well, that's something.
DEVLIN (even more sarcastically): Eight days! Practically white-washed!
ALICIA (almost pleading as she begins to show her feelings for him): I'm very happy here. Why won't you let me be happy? . . . I'm pretending I'm a nice, unspoiled child whose heart is full of daisies and buttercups.
DEVLIN: Nice daydream. Then what?

ALICIA (with a short intake of breath, as if struck by a blow—and as the waiter arrives): I think I will have another drink—make it a double!

DEVLIN: I thought you'd get around to it!

ALICIA: Why won't you believe in me, Dev—just a little? [She starts to ask the question again, but the words stick in her throat and she pauses. She gazes down, then finally puts it to him again, almost begging.] Why won't you?

The supper scene, at night on the balcony (which reverses the earlier daytime kissing scene in the same location), reveals most clearly the terrible clash between these two characters. Grant must tell Bergman of her espionage assignment, which is to go to bed with Rains to learn about Nazi activities in Rio. But although this is against his will, Grant cannot bring himself to save her from this step—which he could easily do by the declaration of love for which she longs and waits.

ALICIA: Well, handsome, I think you better tell Mama what's going on, or all this secrecy is going to ruin my little dinner. Come on, Mr. D., what is darkening your brow?

DEVLIN: After dinner.

ALICIA: No, now. [No reply from him.] Look, I'll make it easy for you. The time has come when you must tell me that you have a wife and two adorable children, and this madness between us can't go on any longer.

DEVLIN: I'll bet you've heard that line often enough.

[A flash of pain crosses Ingrid's brow, a thrust of her lower lip, and then:]

ALICIA: Right below the belt every time. Oh, that isn't fair, Dev.

DEVLIN: Skip it. We've got other things to talk about. We've got a job . . . Do you remember a man named Sebastian?

ALICIA: One of my father's friends. Yes.

DEVLIN: He had quite a crush on you.

ALICIA: I wasn't very responsive.

DEVLIN: We have to contact him.

[She now sees that she is to be sold into sexual slavery.]

ALICIA (sitting): Go on—let's have all of it.

DEVLIN: We're meeting him tomorrow. The rest is up to you. You've
  got to work on him and land him.

ALICIA (with a sad grin): Mata Hari—she makes love for the papers.

DEVLIN: There are no papers. You land him. Find out what's going
  on inside his house, what the group around him is up to—and
  report to us.

ALICIA: I suppose you knew about this pretty little job of mine all
  the time.

DEVLIN: No, I only just found out about it.

ALICIA: Did you say anything—I mean, that maybe I wasn't the girl
  for such shenanigans?

DEVLIN (coldly): I figured that was up to you—if you'd care to back
  out . . .

ALICIA (plaintive): Not a word for that little lovesick lady you left an
  hour ago?

DEVLIN: I told you—that's the assignment!

ALICIA (covering her pain with weariness): Now don't get sore, Dev.
  I'm only fishing for a little bird call from my dream-man—one
  little remark, such as, "How dare you gentlemen suggest that
  Alicia Huberman—the new Miss Huberman—be submitted to
  so ugly a fate?"

DEVLIN: That's not funny.

ALICIA: Do you want me to take the job?

DEVLIN: It's up to you.

ALICIA: I'm asking you.

DEVLIN: It's up to you.

[Silence—and then, in a voice dry with fear and longing:]

ALICIA: Not a peep, eh?—Oh, darling, what you didn't tell them,
  tell me—that you believe I'm nice and that I love you and I'll
  never change back.

DEVLIN (icily): I'm waiting for your answer.

ALICIA (defeated, moving away from him): What a little pal you are.
  Never believing me—not a word of faith, just—down the drain
  with Alicia. [She turns aside and, wounded with rejection,
  uncorks a whiskey bottle and downs a hefty drink.]

At every moment, Ingrid's performance was startling, and
Hitchcock, who had very few suggestions for her, took note of her

excellence and always kept her at least a few moments at the end of the day's work. Never given to extravagant praise, he simply offered her a drink, shrugged his shoulders, smiled and said, "It was very good today, Ingrid. Very good." Indeed, every day was good, and they both knew it: the day they filmed the scene in which she returns Grant's scarf, a relic of the beginning of their romance; when, in the first stages of being poisoned, she feigns a hangover so that the man she loves will not be forced to her side unwillingly; the scenes in which Ingrid communicated the long, sad gazes of love denied when it is most needed—only the most ungenerous, cheerless cynic could fail to find in her performance one of the most memorable achievements in the history of film acting. "Ingrid Bergman's performance here is the best that I have seen," wrote James Agee, not a critic easily pleased, and the *Film Bulletin* summarized the reaction of the press, praising "Ingrid Bergman's brilliant portrayal [which] again makes her a candidate for an Academy Award" (for which, amazingly, she was not even nominated).

"I really don't know much about acting and I have never read anything about acting," Ingrid said later. "As for my one year of school, I'm sure I learned a lot about using the voice, using the body, listening to other people. But instinct is what I go on. The only thing I go for is simplicity and honesty, because if something isn't simple and honest, then it doesn't reach people. It's lost." Regarding the role of Alicia: "I like to portray characters whose lives have been irregular, or sometimes even a little abnormal—people who have been affected by unusual circumstances, or who have been reared in unusual environments."

Notorious is very much a film about how people conceal feelings—about how they glance aside, look down, avert a gaze to cover emotion. In this regard, dialogue is often juxtaposed with ironic images. Before the grand party, for example, Sebastian apologizes for not trusting Alicia and goes to kiss her hands in contrition. But she is unworthy of trust—she is, after all, betraying her husband's devotion to her and has just now stolen his key in an attempt to further betray him. To conceal the key, she throws her arms around his neck and passes the key surreptitiously from her left to her right hand, using the gesture of love as a ruse. Moments later, to throw Alex off the track outside the wine cellar, Devlin sets up a "scene" to convince Alex that he (Devlin) is in love with Alicia, which of course he is. The actions of lovers (this time real) are again used as a ruse. Never have gestures been so freighted with complexity nor the signs of commitment been so layered with meanings true and false.

The crucial cinematic device linking these two tense moments is the famous crane shot in which the camera at the Sebastian party descends without a cut from a vast overview of the grand foyer of the mansion to a close-up of the key held tightly in Bergman's hand. This extraordinary moment was not simply technical virtuosity on Hitchcock's part; on the contrary, it was important for him to emphasize two levels of reality within a single image. The (literal) key to something dangerous lies within this impressive and sophisti-cated setting; one spatial continuum, in other words, contains a double reality—just as the bottles of Pauillac contain uranium ore, just as single affectionate gestures contain multiple realities.

Notorious is from first frame to last a film of startling ironies and contrasts. Promiscuity and sexual exploitation are contrasted with the desire for true love. Drunken dizziness is contrasted with arsenic poisoning. Social elegance and propriety mask a murderous savagery. Giggling small talk (between Bergman and Grant, sipping champagne and exchanging information at the party) hides collu-sion. A labeled bottle is emptied of fine wine and contains ore to make a deadly bomb.

The final moments of the picture are remarkable for Hitch-cock's ability to evoke power simply from camera motion and from performances. Rarely in the history of motion pictures had an actress been so delicately, adoringly photographed as Ingrid Bergman was in the final bedroom scene. Playing a woman sick unto death, Ingrid was rendered in shadow and half-light, and Hitchcock arranged the scene so that there was a radiant tenderness surrounding her, almost a halo of enveloping desire. Hitchcock insisted that there be no music accompanying the scene, he was that sure of how it would look. Finally, just in the proverbial nick of time before her death, Grant admits his feelings of love. "Oh, you love me!" Ingrid whispers. "Why didn't you tell me before?" As the camera circles around her and Grant, he replies: "I was a fat-headed guy, full of pain. It tore me up not having you."

It is easy, when watching movies, to distinguish aesthetic distance, a simple celebration of an actor's beauty, from a deep emotional involvement. The former attitude characterized, for example, the appreciative detachment of D. W. Griffith's approach to Lillian Gish and F. W. Murnau's to Janet Gaynor. But the sentimental attachment was obvious in Josef von Sternberg's rendering of Marlene Dietrich, and Hitchcock's of Ingrid Bergman.

All the motifs of the picture coalesced in the final sequence, wherein Hitchcock created perhaps the tenderest and most deeply felt love scenc in his entire filmography. Straight from the pages of a fairy tale (the Prince saves Sleeping Beauty), it remains every romantic's ultimate fantasy: to save the beloved from the jaws of death. That it remains so compelling is a tribute to the talents and sentiments of the director, his writer—and perhaps most of all to his "little lovesick lady," who became the closest actor-collaborator of his six-decade-long career. "He was very exclusive with me all during production," Ingrid said years later. "He didn't mingle with people. But we were good friends and worked very closely together on Notorious. He was very controlled—he knew that he had to be, and that I had to be. The most awful things were going on for both of us, but he kept his temper. I never heard him raise his voice or yell or scream or be nasty to anybody, ever."

THE YEAR 1945 ENDED WITH A CELEBRATION ON THE SET OF NOTOR-*Ious*—not just a modest holiday toast, but a banquet arranged by Hitchcock to honor his leading lady. There was good reason for his extravagance: between November 2 and December 7, three films starring Ingrid Bergman had been released—*Spellbound*, *Saratoga Trunk* and *The Bells of St. Mary's*, which was breaking all records at Radio City Music Hall. As one wag noted, there was a rumor around Christmastime that someone had actually seen a movie in New York City that had not starred Ingrid Bergman. By year's end, the gross receipts for this trio of pictures had exceeded $21 million, and Ingrid Bergman was receiving more than 25,000 fan letters weekly. It was no surprise when *Box Office* magazine, which polled critics, theater owners, radio commentators, representatives of women's clubs, film councils and educational organizations, announced—for the first of two successive years, as it happened—that Ingrid was the most profitable actor in America for her employers. At once, popular publications (*Look* magazine among them) followed, bestowing on her various awards for achievement.

Invitations proliferated, some of them asking Ingrid to present honors to war heroes, and so to honor herself. One particularly pleased her, from American Youth for Democracy. On December 16, Ingrid presented a medal to Lieutenant Edwina Todd, a valiant American nurse who had worked in the Philippines. California's Attorney General was also present, along with Bill Mauldin, Dore Schary, Barney Ross, Artie Shaw, Dorothy Parker and Frank Sinatra. The event was a huge success, and Lieutenant Todd, already cited by the government, was thrilled to meet Ingrid.

But the holiday season was not undilutedly merry.

Since October, Ingrid had managed an occasional tryst with Larry Adler, and once she suggested they try to take a brief vacation together if Petter went off alone on a ski holiday. "I was being psychoanalyzed at the time," Adler said later, "and my analyst told me this would be a disaster, that it would end my marriage." But there was another reason for his denial of her request. "When I looked at the possibility of marrying Ingrid, I knew that I couldn't live my life walking four paces behind Ingrid. A film star is more important than anyone who wears a medal of honor, and my ego was too big to endure being Mr. Bergman." With that, the brief romance ended, later to be transformed into an enduring friendship.

And then, as if on cue, Robert Capa stepped back onto the scene. He arrived in Hollywood before Christmas, rented a hotel room and very quickly—with some quiet maneuvering by Ingrid—was engaged to take publicity photos on the set of *Notorious*. Adler lived in Los Angeles and was well known there, but the arrival of the famous photographer was trumpeted loudly in the movie community. Invited to every important holiday party and courted by directors and stars who knew his worth behind the camera, he had, at first, little time for Ingrid.

At RKO, Hitchcock, mindful of the risk of any indication to the contrary, introduced her to Capa as if they were strangers. But then, during the last week of December, Ingrid was not required on the set for two days, and of this Petter was unaware. She drove her Oldsmobile down Benedict Canyon early both mornings and, instead of heading east to the studio, she made a right turn and sped along the twists and turns of Sunset Boulevard to its end, at the ocean. Then she headed north on Pacific Coast Highway to Malibu, where she sat alone on the beach, reading scripts, enjoying the sea air and watching the waves. In the afternoons, she met Capa at 18 Malibu Road—the beach house of his friend, the writer Irwin Shaw, who left them alone until evening.

Chapter Eleven

1946–1947

I have only a little time,
so little that I cannot waste nights or days or half-hours.

MAXWELL ANDERSON,
Joan of Lorraine

O N JANUARY 16, 1946, INGRID RECEIVED A STRANGE TELEGRAM
from Gerald L. K. Smith, a right-wing crackpot and fierce
anti-Semite who championed the view that Hollywood was supporting a Communist takeover of America. Formerly sympathetic to
Nazi ideology, Smith was also one of many who came forward over
the next few years with the mad assertion that anyone in the arts (all
of whom he presumed to be left-wing rabble-rousers) should be
held suspect until proven innocent of sedition, treason or at least a
dangerous anti-Americanism.

"It is reported," read Smith's cable to Ingrid,

> that on December 16 you participated in a program held under
> the auspices of American Youth for Democracy at the Ambas-
> sador Hotel in Los Angeles, together with Frank Sinatra and oth-
> ers. About the same time, J. Edgar Hoover, speaking before the

Catholic Youth Organization of New York City, asserted that
[American Youth for Democracy] was the successor to the Young
Communist League, and was positively organizing a campaign to
undermine our American government. Did you appear at this
banquet with an intelligent understanding of its sponsorship or
were you an innocent victim of a slick program committee?

Ingrid tore up the telegram and sent no reply. But two weeks
later, Smith appeared before the fledgling House Un-American
Activities Committee and demanded an investigation of the lives and
activities of Walter Winchell, Eddie Cantor, Frank Sinatra, Orson
Welles, Ingrid Bergman and dozens of others. His demands were
not satisfied, and soon the request faded into oblivion. But some
people in Hollywood began to wonder about the integrity of famous
foreigners in America like Ingrid—celebrities who made a great
deal of money and yet did not swear American citizenship. Ingrid,
always proud of being Swedish, never thought to swear allegiance to
America; from the start of her Hollywood career, she in fact thought
she would one day return to Europe.

THE SELZNICK YEARS NOW BEHIND HER, SHE WAS FREE TO ACCEPT
other offers. After *Notorious* was completed in late February 1946,
she met producer David Lewis at Enterprise Pictures, a new and
independent production company that had purchased the rights to
Erich Maria Remarque's popular novel *Arch of Triumph*. Lewis Milestone, who had won the Oscar for directing the film version of
Remarque's *All Quiet on the Western Front*, had agreed to write and
direct *Arch*, and the cast already included Charles Boyer and Charles
Laughton. Everyone believed that, with her participation, success
was all but guaranteed, and so Ingrid signed a contract. Petter negotiated for her to receive the amazing sum of $175,000 and 25 per-
cent of the film's net profits. Milestone, Harry Brown and Capa's
friend Irwin Shaw (who had a share of Enterprise Pictures) began
work on the screenplay, and production was firmly set to begin in
June, since Ingrid had promised to be in New York in October for
rehearsals of *Joan of Lorraine*.

Meantime, before the cast of *Notorious* disbanded, there was the
usual send-off celebration, at which Ingrid was deeply touched by

words from Cary Grant. He had so much enjoyed acting with her, he told her privately, and he much appreciated her friendship. He felt that the experience of working with her and Hitchcock was the key that would open new doors in his career, and so he had filched an appropriate memento, a prop from the production—the wine cellar key, which is passed from her hand to his and then back to her in the film. The key, he told Ingrid, would remain a precious souvenir for him; years later, the same key would twice become an important talisman in the lives of Cary, Ingrid and Hitch.

INGRID HIRED JOE STEELE TO HANDLE PUBLICITY FOR *ARCH* WHILE ALSO functioning as her press assistant, and in early April—after Ingrid, Petter and Pia had taken a family ski holiday in Nevada—she and Joe flew to New York, where they settled into suites at the Saint Moritz Hotel. The prime reason for the trip was to confer with Maxwell Anderson and the producers of *Joan*. "Hollywood was stifling," she said later.

> It was really such a gossipy place. All people ever talked about was box-office and money, and it became tedious. I got very good parts, of course. I had the best leading men. I had the best directors. I couldn't complain. But the minute a picture was finished, I rushed off to New York because there I felt I was with real people [by which she meant theater people]. It was another life. In Hollywood it was just movies, movies, movies. I mean, I like movies, but you also have to have time to talk about something else—and meet other people. So I came to New York and worked in the theater.

But there was another motive behind the journey eastward that frigid winter: Bob Capa, weary of Hollywood, had returned to Manhattan.

Joe acted as Ingrid's guardian, but he could not run interference where Capa was concerned, and so he was often extremely anxious that the press would learn of Ingrid's absence from the hotel to be with her lover several nights each week that winter and spring. Ingrid and Bob sat in dark corners of Greenwich Village bars, sipping drinks and listening to jazz; they cuddled in the balconies of

West Side movie theaters; they strolled up Fifth Avenue at four in the morning.

Somehow, they managed to evade the gossips, and this Ingrid took as virtually a sign of heaven's approval. For her, this was the most romantic episode of her life, but the significance of it was for the most part her fantasy, as if this were an irresistible role in her best film to date. Although Capa was fond of her, he was fonder of his freedom, and he insisted he was not the marrying kind: he longed to remain a freelance photographer roving the world for stories. One night, when the whiskey had flowed freely, he told Ingrid that she had better get on with her life. Eventually she did, but for most of 1946, neither of them curtailed the affair.

Months later, Ingrid confided this unhappy conversation to her friend Hitch. Seven years later, when she was long separated from Hitch and Hollywood, he made the Capa-Bergman affair the basis for the relationship between characters played by James Stewart, as a world-traveling freelance photographer, and Grace Kelly, a beautiful socialite, in *Rear Window*. (Cornell Woolrich's short story, to which Hitchcock had purchased rights, had no such love angle.)

IN HER MEETINGS WITH MAXWELL ANDERSON, THE PLAYWRIGHT described the intriguing structure of his play-within-a-play. The story of Joan was to be staged as if it were being rehearsed by a theater troupe, the role of the maid taken by the character of actress "Mary Grey," who interacts with historical figures and with her theater colleagues. This interesting conceit gave Anderson full scope for the moral meditations he wished to make explicit, and to examine the issue of compromise—in the battle waged by Joan in the fifteenth century and in the aesthetic struggle of artists in the twentieth. The point of *Joan of Lorraine* is clarified at the conclusion, when Mary Grey learns, by playing Joan, that compromises must be made on nonessential worldly matters (and with the cooperation of less than admirable people) if real faith and heroism are to triumph in the realm of the spiritual.

Ingrid also spent time that spring with Kay Brown, who was by now one of the most important and respected agents in New York and Hollywood. Her client list was impressive, eventually including the likes of Montgomery Clift, Lillian Hellman, Fredric March,

Arthur Miller, Samuel Taylor and the American engagements of (among others) Alec Guinness, John Gielgud, Rex Harrison, Laurence Olivier and Ralph Richardson. Without consulting Petter, Ingrid joined the roster of Kay's clients, although the business aspect of their relationship had no purpose until years later. But the friendship was reconfirmed forever, and Ingrid was a frequent visitor to Kay's family. One fine day, she offered to help them with the tradition of spring cleaning, a chore that compelled Kay's astonished husband, Jim Barrett, to ask, "What are we doing? The most beautiful woman on earth is cleaning our stairs!"

But all that season, Capa remained Ingrid's most constant companion and mentor. She read books according to his advice, went to plays he recommended, attended concerts he selected for them and, for the first time in her life, began to take an interest in world affairs. In a way, Capa played the role of holiday husband, and this, in some vague way, she realized uneasily. By that time she was, as Capa told Joe Steele in March, "all tied up in a million knots. For a grown woman, she's so naive it hurts. She's afraid to let go. She hasn't the vaguest notion of what the world's about." Worst of all, Capa concluded, she knew nothing about movies except what was coming out of Hollywood in the last seven years. He had seen European films all his life and continued to do so now, even in the few so-called art houses that dotted Manhattan. If Steele wanted to do Ingrid a favor, Capa said, he ought to take her to see *Roma, città aperta—Open City—*a powerful Italian movie Capa considered a masterpiece.

Next afternoon, Joe and Ingrid bought tickets to that film at the World Theater on West Forty-ninth Street. When they emerged two hours later, Ingrid was too moved to speak. The narrative of the film was simple and its execution utterly lacked glamour and artifice, but its impact was enormous. A leader of the Resistance named Manfredi (played by Marcello Pagliero) takes refuge in the home of Pina (Anna Magnani). When she is killed by the Germans, Manfredi is hidden by his mistress (Maria Michi). But she betrays him and he is arrested along with a priest who is also a Resistance hero, and both men die without yielding up any secrets that would betray others.

Planned in secrecy and made under the pretext of being a documentary silent film (the soundtrack was added later), *Open City* is a tribute to the courage of the Italian Resistance against Fascism during the war. Filmed after the death of Mussolini, it presented a graphically realistic portrait of the misery caused by the German occupation of Rome. *Open City* also marked the renaissance of the Italian cinema.

That evening, she asked Capa to tell her about the director, Roberto Rossellini. He was the genius of modern Italian cinema, Capa said. No, he did not make films outside Italy—why did she want to know? "Because," Ingrid replied, "this movie seemed like real life. I'd rather be remembered for one great artistic film like this than all my money-making hits. Why can't Roberto Rossellini come to Hollywood and make a movie like that with someone like me?" Well, Capa explained, that was a complicated matter: for one thing, what made her think American audiences were interested in gritty neorealism?

This man Rossellini, Ingrid continued, must be an extraordinarily wonderful human being. Well yes, maybe, Capa replied, but a man and his work are two different things. That could not be in this case, Ingrid said: the movie was too magnificent for that. And from that moment, Ingrid did indeed fuse and confuse the man and his work: "I fell in love with Roberto before knowing him in person. I fell in love with him just looking at the movie!" And so she did— just as millions who did not know Ingrid fell in love with her.

For days, *Open City* haunted her, and to anyone who would listen she spoke of its simple images and its affecting drama, which featured (with the exception of two or three professionals) people Rossellini found in the streets of Rome. This, she learned later, was more for economic than artistic reasons, but his preference for amateurs conformed perfectly to Rossellini's belief that a "performance" should be avoided at all cost, that the cinema was a medium for the presentation of truth, not fiction. Stories attracted him not nearly as much as stark images of human feeling; drama concerned him only if it illuminated something in the soul; and actors interested him not at all. But for his best films (and *Open City* probably qualifies as the best of all) he did require a good storyteller: in this case, he had Sergio Amidei and the young Federico Fellini, working as a screenwriter before his own remarkable directing career.

Although they were not, in the strict sense, documentaries, Rossellini's films were visually very close to the documentary genre.

Rome's ordinary pedestrians, its avenues and narrow alleys, its monuments and the rumbling of modern trucks through the ancient city—all these become characters in the story. Rossellini certainly was never eager to make easy entertainments for mass consumption, and the narrative line in *Open City* was an excuse to capture the faces of suffering citizens. These, so memorably presented on the screen, Ingrid could not forget. She had often spoken of her own acting method as one of "simplicity and honesty," and that is precisely what she saw in *Open City*.

In late May, she returned to Los Angeles to begin *Arch of Triumph*. This time, her transportation was provided by Howard Hughes, who flew her in his own plane and zoomed over the Grand Canyon to impress her. But Ingrid dozed (it was a way of ignoring Hughes's frequent requests for a romantic evening that season), and the splendid views were left to be appreciated by the other passengers—Joe Steele, Alfred Hitchcock and Cary Grant.

"She showed up twenty pounds overweight when we started shooting!" producer David Lewis recalled. "I had to beg her husband to put a lock on the refrigerator at home," since Ingrid freely acknowledged that, although she ate cottage cheese for lunch at work, she attacked the larder at home.

Her insecurities and anxieties, of which her compulsive overeating was again a sign, were ironically sharpened when Capa followed her to Hollywood; cash poor as always, he asked her to get him the job of still photographer on the set of *Arch*, which she easily did. Almost every evening after filming, Capa joined Ingrid, Charles Boyer, Lewis Milestone and some of the crew for cocktails—Capa, as usual, drinking rather too much.

That summer, as the movie progressed, Ingrid began to grow weary of her lover's moody coolness, not to say his hangovers. How often and where they met privately cannot be determined; certainly her schedule of work (at the studios rented by Enterprise in Culver City) was sufficiently demanding that regular treks to Irwin Shaw's hideaway in Malibu were impossible, and Ingrid was reluctant to be seen as a frequent guest at Capa's hotel.* Bellboys and desk clerks

---

*In addition, Shaw did not like what *Arch of Triumph* was becoming, and he withdrew from both the production and his partnership in Enterprise Productions.

were routinely compensated for providing tidbits to the gossip columnists, and she dared not risk the consequences.

Petter knew that his marriage was irretrievably damaged. "He did the damndest things," according to David Lewis. "If Ingrid was coming home at eight, he'd have dinner with Pia at seven-thirty. If Ingrid was coming home at six, he and Pia would eat at five-thirty. I don't know—maybe he was trying to hold the child emotionally, just in case something happened. But there is no villain in this story. Their lives took such divergent paths that there was no way to bring them together again."

Work, as so often, was her refuge, and into *Arch of Triumph* she poured her emotional turmoil that summer, giving to a dark and claustrophobic picture an intensity that, in the finished film, is sometimes frightening.

The film follows closely Erich Maria Remarque's novel, set in Europe on the brink of World War II. A lightly veiled account of Remarque's tortured affair with Marlene Dietrich, it tells of an Austrian refugee surgeon named Ravic (Charles Boyer) and his anguished romance with a Romanian-Italian cabaret singer named Joan Madou (Ingrid). The sweet wine of their love turns sour when he refuses to marry her (shades of Robert Capa and Ingrid Bergman); Ravic is, after all, a man without passport who practices medicine illegally and is several times deported. During one of his absences, she takes up with a shallow new lover, who in a fit of pique shoots her. Ravic, who all along has resented his own fierce passion for her, is summoned to her bedside. But his medical skill cannot save her, and he watches her die as they protest their love for each other. He is then deported once more, this time accepting his destiny.

Like the novel, the movie has a dense, gloomy mood (all the sequences of the first half-hour are set in nighttime rainstorms) but also a certain melancholic appeal despite its torpid pace. Darkly passionate, Boyer played Ravic with an expert, ironic sensibility; he is alternately obsessive, endearing, bitter, smug and repentant. Ingrid, on the other hand, is his perfect foil—confused and vulnerable, almost pathetic in her need to be loved yet shrewd and manipulative in her efforts to attract Boyer. Her death scene is singularly effective: avoiding all the clichés of romantic movies, Ingrid (expertly mimicking paralysis) simply affects impaired breathing and unfocuses her gaze, as if she has begun to glimpse the frontiers of a far country. "Ti amo—ti amo—ti amo," she whispers to Boyer, and asks for a final kiss; the moment of death is barely noticeable.

When it was finally released after almost two years of editorial fiddling, *Arch of Triumph* was a resounding failure. Ingrid was, as usual, praised for her carefully limned portrait of a desperate woman, but the picture received a critical drubbing, moviegoers were bored, and very soon Enterprise Pictures (having lost its entire $4 million investment) was a footnote in Hollywood history. "Under Lindstrom's management," said Milestone, "Ingrid made several bad pictures, one of which I directed." Boyer put the matter succinctly when he confided to a friend that at first the film had been terrible for four hours, but thanks to careful editing it was made awful for only two.

As for postwar audiences, they apparently did not want to step back to the eve of the war; they were disappointed, too, by a doubly unhappy finale for the lovers (death for her, displacement for him); and they could not accept a neurotic romance as the symbol of a world on the brink of conflagration. Milestone's reverent fidelity to Remarque's doomed lovers—and the movie's immoderate duration—were, in the end, precisely what denied it success. Nothing, as Ingrid said forever after, could have offered a starker contrast to *Open City*.

PLANNED FOR TEN WEEKS OF FILMING, *ARCH OF TRIUMPH* WAS STILL before the cameras after sixteen, and there was something of a frantic shuffle to complete all Ingrid's scenes before she left for New York in late September to begin rehearsals as another Joan. At the same time, Petter was going to visit his relatives in Sweden. Enterprise threw a farewell party for Ingrid, at which Lewis Milestone observed the strain between the Lindstroms.

Milestone admired Petter's dedication to his medical studies. "But [Lindstrom] had some old-fashioned European ideas. He had the attitude that he had bestowed his name on a poor orphan girl [who, Milestone might have countered, never used it], and therefore she should be grateful to him for the rest of her life. There were implications all the time—he was the solid citizen who had rescued a poor waif. He never let her forget it. But how long can you operate on gratitude?" Not much longer, it seemed: a few days before their departures, Ingrid again asked Petter for a divorce, and again he brushed aside the idea. Perhaps because the Capa affair was so rocky and promised so little—and because, as Petter reminded her, she had no capacity to manage her business affairs on her own—she did not insist.

On October 1, Ingrid settled into Suite 2606 at the Hampshire House, on Central Park South, and four days later she strolled happily to the first rehearsal for *Joan of Lorraine* at the Alvin Theater on West Fifty-second Street. "At last I was playing Joan. I lost myself in the role and forgot my basic loneliness, for while my professional life was full and exciting, my life at home was secluded and empty."

From the age of seven, the Maid of Orleans had been her favorite person in history, and in preparation for the role she had so long coveted, Ingrid read everything she could about Joan. And as she did so, her identification with the girl who died at nineteen deepened. "She was a simple peasant," Ingrid told a writer years later, "and she didn't understand a great deal that was happening to her. But she remained faithful to her voices, faithful to the mysterious calling inside her. The way she dealt with all those learned men! And her courage unto death! She had such common sense." Those were, of course, precisely the qualities that Ingrid wanted to deepen in herself: simplicity in art and life, fidelity to her calling, the will to be brave.

But Ingrid had no pretensions to sanctity, nor did a tidy definition of it much interest her. Instead, she bore down heavily on Max Anderson, begging him (very like the character of Mary Grey she assumed in the play's interludes) to remain faithful to the true contours of Joan's life and not to force Joan to be too much the agent for the playwright's political philosophy. Anderson listened, altering according to her best instincts and remaining firm where that was called for.

A week after Ingrid arrived, Bob Capa turned up in New York, and until Petter arrived there from Sweden in late October, Capa and Ingrid tried to stoke the embers of a dying ardor. This time, she decided that the best way to deflect any unwelcome publicity was to be seen quite openly with Bob Capa. Her instinct was on the mark: after they took a very visible center table at Sheridan Square's trendy nightspot Café Society, reporters figured that the actress and the photographer must be friends, nothing else; hence the couple never made the gossip columns. Besides, in the minds of the vast majority of Americans, Ingrid was above suspicion—rather like the saint she was about to incarnate on Broadway.

Joan of Lorraine was written to be staged very simply, with a minimum of props and nothing like elaborate sets, so that the action could easily flow from the stage as locus of rehearsal to the stage as platform for presentation. But however economical the concept, the efforts of Margo Jones—a lady with but one directorial credit behind her—were unacceptable to the playwright and his producers, and she was replaced before opening night by cast member Sam Wanamaker and Max's son Alan Anderson. Things improved at once, although Ingrid was upset that Jones was dismissed so perfunctorily.

She did not have similar discomfort over a far more serious matter that confronted the company when they arrived in Washington, D.C., in late October for a pre-Broadway run at the Lisner Auditorium of George Washington University. Outside the theater during the days before the premiere were representatives of the Southern Conference for Human Welfare and the American Veterans Committee, protesting the traditional Washington policy of restricting ticket sales to white people. Petter, who had accompanied his wife from New York, asked Joe Steele about the regulation and was told that blacks were indeed barred from the theater. "This has been going on for years," said Max Anderson that afternoon, "and there's nothing we can do about it." As for Ingrid, she simply told them, "I am here to play Joan and I have nothing to do with theater rulings."

Fearing adverse publicity for Ingrid and the play, Steele prevailed on her publicly to denounce the tradition of discrimination. Steele's plan worked, and the wire services carried an edifying story:

Ingrid Bergman said tonight that she would not have agreed to appear in Tuesday's opening [of *Joan*] had she known that Negroes would not be permitted to see the performance.

She said she learned only ten days ago that George Washing-

ton University had reaffirmed its policy on non-admission of
Negroes . . . But it was then too late to alter her previous commitment to appear.

"I deplore racial discrimination in any form," she volunteered at a news conference. "To think that it would be permitted in the nation's capital, of all places!

"I really had not known that there were places in the United
States—entertainment places which are for all the people—
where everybody could not go."

It would take almost twenty years before the United States
made equal rights, regardless of race, a matter of law, but Steele was
sufficiently canny to force his client to see that her initial indifference was potentially harmful to her image. That, rather than the
immorality of the matter, convinced her. Larry Adler recalled a similar moment during a strike by a Hollywood union while *Notorious*
was in production: Ingrid broke a picket line, thus demoralizing a
contingent of beleaguered workers. "Larry, I'm an actress," she
replied when he criticized her. "I have nothing to do with the strike.
My duty is to make a film." Years later, Adler and Lindstrom were
united in their astonishment at her lifelong lack of concern for
social issues that went beyond mere politics. (In his memoir, the
ever constant Steele gave Ingrid all the credit for enlightened moral
superiority in both cases; she prudently followed suit in the interviews that formed the basis of her autobiography.)

Capa, who was en route to an assignment in Turkey, sent Ingrid
a single white rose on her opening night in Washington. "My white
rose is very near me," she cabled him. But emotionally, he was
much less proximate. Like many lovers who fear that their gradual
retreat may not be countered with a fierce struggle, he began to
worry. "London is so quiet and empty," he wrote to Ingrid a week
later, "but still Europe is so much more real and refreshing after the
States. Every time I go to a bar, to a play, for a walk in the foggy
streets, I want to see you there next to me." But his inability to
make of her anything more than a mistress, and her refusal to abandon her career and accompany him around the world, had taken its
toll; the affair would not long survive, but Ingrid could not have
foreseen the circumstances of its termination.

*   *   *

ON NOVEMBER 18, *JOAN OF LORRAINE* OPENED AT THE ALVIN IN NEW York, joining a remarkable Broadway season that included seventy-nine new productions: forty-six new plays (among them *State of the Union*, *Born Yesterday* and *The Iceman Cometh*), thirteen musicals (including *Call Me Mister* and *Annie Get Your Gun*), two revues, seven one-person or staged-reading shows and eleven revivals of classics.

New York's critics were virtually on their knees in veneration of Ingrid: "She is with few peers in the whole realm of make believe" was typical of the tributes offered to Ingrid. "There is no doubt about the splendor of Miss Bergman's acting," wrote Brooks Atkinson. "Her gifts have multiplied and prospered since 'Liliom,' and Miss Bergman has brought into the theatre a rare purity of spirit [and] matchless magnificence . . . [She is] a rapturously attractive maiden with pride, grace and a singularly luminous smile . . . Her appearance is a theatrical event of major importance . . . "—and so Atkinson raved in two lengthy exaltations in the *Times*, placing her firmly in the ranks of Katharine Cornell and Helen Hayes. Even *The New Yorker* took flight: hers was "a performance that may be incomparable in the theatre of our day."

In any assessment of her achievement that season, it is good to recall that Ingrid was taking an enormous risk—primarily because sophisticated New York audiences, however much they may have liked her as a movie star, were notoriously finicky about the "genuineness" of real (that is, theater) acting. Accustomed to the tiny bits and pieces of acting before the camera, which required her to memorize only a few phrases at a time, she now had to retain an entire part, including lengthy and difficult speeches—and in a language that was not her own. Eight times weekly (and without benefit of body microphones, those friendly aides for actors that came to the theater several decades later), Ingrid had to project Anderson's poetic prose, finding the proper colors in the spectrum of her voice.

But this was more than a job for her: it was the fulfillment of a long hope. "I have always wanted to play Joan," she announced each evening in the words of Mary Grey—words added by Anderson late in his revisions, when he believed that Mary and Ingrid were truly one person. "I have studied her and read about her all my life. She has a meaning for me. She means that the great things in this world are brought about by faith—that all the leaders who count are dreamers and people who see visions. The realists and the common-sense people can never begin anything." And audiences at the Alvin were invariably silent, as if in church, throughout the ringing cadences of her final monologue:

"I believe my visions to be good," she proclaimed, and it would have been natural for Ingrid to think of her own great gifts. "I know them to be good, but I do not know how to defend them. When I am brought into a court and must prove what I believe, how can I prove that they are good and not evil? Yes, and I ask myself whether I have been honest always, for when I went among men I acted a part . . . When I spoke with my own voice, nobody listened, nobody heard me—yet, was it honest to assume ways that were not my own? I know there's to be no answer."

Joan of Arc's dilemma had a modern resonance in the dilemma of Ingrid Bergman, whose life, even as she endured the monotony of acting onstage for 199 performances from November 1946 to May 1947, was changing radically. During the opening night party at the Astor Hotel, Ingrid had to slip away several times from the crush of guests and admirers. On each occasion, Kay and Ruth sought her out and reported to Petter and Joe that Ingrid was fine, that she would return to the party soon. They did not add that they had found her in the ladies' room, curled in a chair, weeping.

JOAN OF LORRAINE QUICKLY BECAME ONE OF THE HITS OF THE BROADWAY season, and its six-month run could easily have been prolonged. But the experience, although wonderful, was not unalloyed: the physical and psychological demands of eight performances a week, the complications of illness, of amorous intrigues, the uncertainty of her future in Hollywood and of her marriage—all these effected an acute nervous anxiety in Ingrid that endured throughout the year. As Ruth, Joe and Kay recalled, Ingrid seemed unable to sit still.

But for at least one brief period she was forced to. The winter of 1947 remains on record as one of the worst in the history of the country's weather, and a fierce influenza epidemic attacked millions trying to cope with a succession of storms and frigid temperatures. Ingrid was strong, but she was not immune, and several performances were canceled in January when a slight cough turned into a feverish cold and severe laryngitis. She was shivering in bed when a telephone call from the Swedish consul was put through in early January: in Stockholm, the King had awarded her Sweden's highest honor—the gold medal "Litteris et Artibus," for her "outstanding acting and her dignified way of representing Swedish art in the United States."

Other honors followed in rapid succession that year: the Drama League and the Antoinette Perry (Tony) awards for best performance of the year by an actress; the Venice Film Festival Award for best performance (in *Spellbound*, which had a delayed European release after the war); and numerous magazine, newspaper, civic and church awards. It is no exaggeration to maintain that Ingrid Bergman was at this time the least controversial, most beloved celebrity in America; indeed, the entire Western world was hurrying to add her name to the list of those most idolized and honored.

IN THE UNITED STATES, NOW UNSUBTLY ENTERING A DISTURBING TIME of self-canonization after the war, a terrible moral smugness competed with the year's flu epidemic for infecting the greater number of citizens. Everywhere, the watchdogs of public morality—churchmen who often lost touch with the meaning of faith and politicians who bore no resemblance to statesmen—were on the prowl, eager to imply, to indict, to condemn, to destroy. Accusations of sedition and treason were tossed about like handbills to pedestrians, and cries of outrage were heard on radio and read in newspapers whenever a celebrity divorced, was seen tipsy at a restaurant or expressed an opinion on anything more controversial than the season's fashions. The Puritan spirit that never lurks far below the surface of American life was poised for attack, and the rich and famous were always convenient targets. Had much of anything been known about the private life of Ingrid Bergman in 1947, her star would have quickly faded, and she might even have been hounded from the country.

But Puritans also need righteous folks to adore (a later generation called them "role models"), and for the time being Ingrid Bergman was thought to fill that assignment. Among many astonishing requests put to her that year, one may be regarded as typical.

A Philadelphia priest arrived in New York, tracked down Joe
Steele and asked if he could arrange for Miss Bergman to pose for
the bust of St. Joan of Arc that was to be placed at the entrance to
his parish church. Without consulting his client, Joe gently replied
that she was, after all, an actress; this request seemed—well, perhaps not entirely appropriate? When Joe told Ingrid of this, she was
more horrified than amused: suppose there was ever any public
denunciation of her, or even the whisper of a scandal! She could not
bear the thought of the bust of Joan of Arc being dragged from a
Philadelphia pedestal and smashed to pieces.

Throughout December and into January, the occasional presence of Robert Capa in the life of America's uncanonized saint
would have provided the enemy with enough ammunition to
destroy Ingrid Bergman. Several times he escorted Ingrid from the
stage door to her hotel suite, whence he slipped quietly away hours
later, just before dawn. But not all their rendezvous were ecstatic.
"He knows we are closing the chapter," Ingrid wrote to Ruth. "We
are drinking our last bottles of champagne. I am tearing a very
dear piece away from my life, but we are both learning and also
making a clean operation so that both patients will live happily
ever after."

But at least insofar as the real-life surgeon was concerned, the
procedure was not quite so neat. Not long after Capa's last amorous
night with Ingrid, he ran into Petter. The circumstances vary
according to the teller; from husband, wife and lover, there is a total
of at least eight versions of the time and place the two men came
together. The likeliest scenario was a chance encounter later that
winter in Sun Valley, where Capa and Lindstrom were by coincidence taking brief holidays. One day on the slopes, Capa offered
Lindstrom some advice on his skiing style, Lindstrom declined, and
Capa said that Ingrid really needed a vacation, too—she had
seemed to him so pale and weary in New York.

With that little slip from Capa, Petter knew just about everything, and when he rang Ingrid late that night, she calmly admitted
the truth. Now it was Petter's turn to request a divorce, which she
instantly declined, telling her husband what Capa had not: that the
affair was history. Ingrid was also unwilling to lose both lover and
husband and so every shred of emotional security—apart from the

risk to her career (since Petter would certainly claim adultery as grounds for his divorce).

Within days of her conversation with Petter, which included a promise of fidelity he had extracted from her, Ingrid opened the door to her theater dressing room and there stood Victor Fleming. She had seen him only occasionally, at parties or movie events, since the conclusion of *Dr. Jekyll and Mr. Hyde* six years earlier. Her infatuation had, of course, cooled—but not her remembrance of Fleming's talent and his take-charge attitude.

This time, the tables had turned with a vengeance. Fleming, who had seen her performance that evening, caught Ingrid in a tight embrace. She was brilliant, he said, not releasing his grip on her; she was beautiful, radiant, luminous, fragrant—his words tumbled like excerpts from a review. She was Joan, he went on, and he would make her immortal as Joan by directing a film of her performance. That would be too good to believe, replied Ingrid. Could he really make it happen?

They must make it happen—and it must be soon, Fleming said, resuming his old nickname for Ingrid, "Angel," but now speaking it with passionate intensity. David Selznick, among others, was murmuring that he was finally going to make a St. Joan epic, and there were other producers talking about the same topic; Fleming and Bergman had to be first at the starting gate. At supper that night, he spun his plans, and Ingrid felt the return of her old feelings for Victor Fleming. Their reunion recalled nothing so much as Jekyll/Hyde's overtures to Ivy at the Palace of Frivolities—a scene full of champagne and promise, of excitement and danger. Aware of how Hollywood could sabotage the simple account of a saint-in-spite-of-herself, Ingrid also longed to portray Joan on film; wary of Fleming's passionate insistence, she was also vulnerable and very much alone.

Ingrid, of course, first consulted her husband—who dashed off a cordial letter to Fleming, urging him to act quickly, for Petter had already rejected an offer from Paramount studios and was now speaking with director William Wyler about a film of *Joan*. This had the desired effect. First, Fleming made an offer Petter could not refuse: with independent producer Walter Wanger, Victor Fleming and Ingrid Bergman would work under the banner of the trio's own production company (to be called Sierra Films) and in addition to a salary of $175,000, the Lindstroms—the Lindstroms, not Ingrid Bergman—would receive a major share of the film's profits.* It had to net about $9 million before I could collect a penny," Ingrid said later, calculating her losses. "Well, it looked good on paper, and I might get a good funeral out of it!" Finally, Fleming said he was setting up shop in a suite he had taken at Hampshire House, so that he could begin preproduction with Ingrid at once. Petter offered to fly to New York for a weekend to meet with Fleming about contractual details.

And then, with all the haste of an impetuous young lover, Fleming at once sent out a press release. Before there were signed agreements, he announced a forthcoming film of *Joan of Lorraine* starring Ingrid Bergman; in fact, he had not even acquired the rights to Anderson's play. Fleming's precipitous announcement also had the desired effect: in light of Ingrid's New York success and the nationwide publicity attending it, the Hollywood competition immediately halted all plans for a rival film on the same subject.

THE FIELD OF FLEMING'S ABANDON WAS AT ONCE WIDENED, AND SOON Ingrid was spending every night with Victor, now no longer a fantasy lover but the real thing. He was sixty-four, she thirty-one, but he surrounded her with a kind of possessive ferocity and convinced her that only he—who had coaxed such a brilliant performance from her as Ivy—could immortalize Ingrid as her beloved Joan. Only he, Fleming insisted, understood the association between Ingrid and the maiden who, true to her own voices, had to isolate herself from everyone to be true to her vocation. Teaching her like a father, Fleming worshipped her like a first love.

By day, Fleming met with researchers, art directors and designers; Ingrid sometimes stopped in to observe, but often she wandered about the city, toured art galleries, strolled through museums, spent her allowance from home on an occasional addition to her

---

*Separately, for tax reasons, Ingrid formed her own corporation, which she named EN Productions (the word means "one" in Swedish), which was her idea, for she was the company's only property. Walter Wanger was nominal president; Ingrid, vice-president; Petter, secretary and, of course, treasurer; and Ingrid's pro forma lawyer, a director.

wardrobe and rehearsed for a few Sunday evening radio dramas in which she participated that season. After her performances, she returned to Suite 2606 and immediately rang Victor, eight floors higher; within moments, they were together in one place or the other, sharing a cold supper and champagne before bed.

Kay Brown, who saw a great deal of her friend, said of her, "Ingrid is changing—changing fast. She's growing away from everything she used to be. And she knows it. She said so herself." Now, as Kay recognized, Ingrid wanted much more of life than the house in Benedict Canyon and a movie or two each year. *Joan of Lorraine* had been a critical interval, but there was no guarantee of any future work in the theater.

She did not know what to put in the place of the theater and Hollywood after *Joan*. Perhaps she ought to return to work in Europe? No, the postwar economy there was appalling; abroad, how and where would she live? Like all people "changing fast," she was a bundle of contradictions: having already severed her ties to the comfortable shores she had known for a decade, she had no sure land in sight. Longing for freedom, she still needed the security and leadership of a strong man—thus the attachment to Victor Fleming.

But there was a difference in this latest intimacy, and this, too, may have been in Kay's mind. Without coldness or calculation, Ingrid was beginning to have a different attitude toward lovers. Distance from home and Hollywood had given Ingrid perspective, and her experiences with three men in less than two years had given her a confidence she had never known. Capa, Adler and Fleming were guides and mentors to fresh new aspects of creative life. With each, she felt a sense of newness, of the kind of learning that can come only by being with a man of ideas—from this time forward, she prized this quality most of all in husbands, companions and friends.

Her father had been the first man like this, of course, and his death had robbed her of the single solid, stable relationship of her life before Petter. The loss of her parents, of Aunt Ellen, of Uncle Otto, the strange character of Aunt Mutti, who was perforce separated from her with the outbreak of war—everything had conspired to make her believe that no human connection endured, that in a sense no one could be trusted. Shy and awkward, she had found her refuge in public approval of her extraordinary performances. Her romantic liaisons were like scenes in the film of her life—precious for the moment, but they could not be trusted to persevere. Perhaps, in the final analysis, she never demanded more from her romances not because she placed her art first, but rather she placed her art first because relationships had, at a crucial time of her youth, played her false. After all, from their first meeting, Petter had confirmed her in commitment to the primacy of duty.

In her intimate relations with men, Ingrid Bergman was neither Puritan nor libertine. But it was not, it seems, a desire for sex that motivated or attracted her, it was a desire for a deeper connection. All her life there was something dependent, girlish and fresh about her; always there was a sense of newness, of anticipation for the next day, the next film, the next play, the next journey. ("We must never try to recapture or recreate," says Lena Geyer in the Marcia Davenport novel. "Everything must go forward. Every experience must be a new one, a fresh start.") Sometimes, she seemed withdrawn or distant, but this was the natural reaction of someone who detested the specious adulation of starry-eyed fans who really had no idea who she was.

Ingrid was never humorless or unkind, and throughout her life she had a remarkable lack of rancor or bitterness. To be sure, her high-strung nature, her constant alertness for the means by which she could stretch her imagination and so her gifts, sometimes took her away from the people she loved.

Her conduct suggests that for her sex was fine as far as it went, but it did not go nearly far enough in creating lasting intimacy. It was, in other words, possible to make entirely too much of sex—to ask it to bear a greater burden than reason allowed. Very early, she recognized that her beauty and her outgoing personality attracted men in great profusion, and that she could have exploited her allure for just about any objective. But to do so was not in her nature. She was most of all aroused by intelligence and wit; men who offered mere pretension or the waltz of sexual posturing found a short route to her disfavor. But she was also a woman who needed to be comforted, to be cherished, and when she found a bright, sensitive and energetic man who could offer warm consolation, too—well,

that was fine. Still, from 1947, something indeed changed. Thenceforth, passion meant much more than sex: it meant the freedom to
learn, to achieve without restriction. Few lovers were willing to give
her that lead.

It would, therefore, be facile to assess her relations with Capa,
Adler and Fleming as blithe or detached tumblings of the flesh. On
the contrary, her romantic involvements invariably occurred at particularly lonely times in her life, and to them she gave herself completely.

Such was the season of the Fleming affair in 1947—until Petter,
without warning, arrived at the Hampshire House late one evening.
There was no reply when he tapped at Ingrid's door and so, acting
on instinct, he returned to the lobby and rang Fleming's suite.
"This is Petter—may I speak to Ingrid?" He could and he did. She
left Fleming's room at once. Of Ingrid's explanation to her husband, and of the reunion between them, nothing can be known.
Next afternoon, after his business meeting with Fleming, Petter
returned to Los Angeles—and so did his rival, who had to set up a
production company in California.

Aboard the Santa Fe Chief, Victor wrote to Ingrid:

Like a lover I love you—[I] cry across the miles and hours of
darkness that I love you—that you flood across my mind like
waves across the sand. If you care—or if you don't, these things
to you with love I say. I am devotedly—your foolish—ME.

And from Hollywood:

Angel—Angel—why didn't I get a chain three thousand miles
long with a good winding device on the end. Better quit now
before I start telling you I love you—telling you Angel I love
you—yes—yes—yes—it's ME.

She was indeed his angel—and sometimes, for fun, he called
her "The Witch," Joan's nickname among her enemies. For Fleming, the sobriquet was appropriate, he said, because she had
beguiled him, had cast a spell on him, and he was forever her slave.

After she telephoned him, he wrote again: "How good to hear

your voice. How tongue-tied and stupid I become. How sad for
you. Then when you put the phone down, the click is like a bullet."
He was back in New York twice more, each time for three weeks,
during the run of *Joan*. As for Ingrid, the last weeks of performance
were tiresome, and she felt she was getting stale. "I am very tired,"
she wrote to Ruth. "Too many people. Too much food and drink
lately. Maybe that's what kills the feeling. I have only three more
weeks. Then I'll go back into the cage, sit in the sun, obey Petter
and be sober and look eighteen years old."

The play, which could have continued for a year, posted a closing notice for Saturday, May 10, 1947, for Ingrid's contract had
stipulated a limited run of six months, and by that time—exhausted
and suffering chronic throat problems from backstage dust and her
new habit of excessive smoking—she was glad to offer the last of
199 performances as Joan. Petter had once again arranged excellent
terms for her ($1,000 weekly and 15 percent of the gross receipts),
and since October she had earned a total of $129,082. In a year
when $5,000 was a respectable annual salary for an American, this
sum challenged her belief.

Between the matinee and evening performances of that last day,
the usual mob of about three hundred fans gathered; for months the
"Alvin Gang," as her admirers styled themselves, had led a crowd of
devotees every Wednesday and Saturday. Wanting to cheer and
thank her for gracing New York, they hoped, yet again, for a touch,
an autograph, a smile. Instead, Ingrid sent Joe to invite them inside
the theater, where—with her hair unbrushed and wearing a maroon
dressing gown, she sat on the stage, thanking the hushed crowd and
then answering their questions. When she finally stood up and said
that she had to go and eat a little supper in her dressing room
before the final show, there was a thunderous standing ovation.

Late that night, Ingrid threw a party at the Hampshire House
for the entire cast and crew of *Joan of Lorraine*. She and the Playwrights Company shared the expense of a hundred-dollar bill for
each colleague, and to her two leading men (Sam Wanamaker and
Romney Brent) she gave engraved silver cigarette cases. No one in
the company could recall so warm and memorable a finale to a
Broadway production.

*   *   *

NEXT DAY, SHE WENT BY PLANE TO BEVERLY HILLS, WHERE PETTER told her that negotiations were well along for a project to follow *Joan of Arc*—and more to come after that.

As early as 1944, Selznick's people had got hold of a novel by Helen Simpson called *Under Capricorn*, which Ingrid told them would make a fine film and which contained a superb dramatic role for her. By early 1947, Hitchcock (also free of obligations to Selznick) had purchased the rights to the novel (and to an unproduced play based on it) from Selznick and planned it as the first production of his own company—Transatlantic Pictures, which he set up with his old friend, the English producer and media mogul Sidney Bernstein. "*Under Capricorn* I made to please Ingrid Bergman, who was a friend of mine," Hitchcock maintained. "I was looking for a subject that suited her, rather than myself." His devotion, however muted and repressed, had not diminished.

But as it turned out, the job of transforming the novel into a screenplay took rather longer than anyone expected, and Hitchcock decided first to do a film of Patrick Hamilton's play *Rope*. *Under Capricorn* would follow in 1948, to be made in England, since according to Hitchcock's arrangement with Bernstein, Transatlantic Films would have its first production in England and then, for tax reasons, make movies alternately in America and the United Kingdom.

Petter had seen to his own interests as well as Ingrid's. On May 27, they signed an agreement he had negotiated with Hitchcock's fledgling production company: he and Ingrid would jointly be paid $200,000 and 41 ⅓ percent of the film's profits. In addition, Petter was separately contracted to do publicity and public relations for the picture when it was released in Scandinavia and elsewhere in Europe; for his efforts, he was to receive one-fourth of the Swedish profits on the film—and, of course, a stipend for travel.

This was a fascinating development, for of course Petter had no intention of curtailing his medical career or entering the publicity business; that year, for the first time in America, he had an income. In addition to sharing a private practice, Petter was then joining the neurology staff at Los Angeles County General Hospital, Cedars of Lebanon and Harbor General. But as he later wrote to Pia, "until 1949 most of our income came from your mother's fees"—in fact, all the family income came from Ingrid's salary except for the small amounts then paid to interns and residents (about $65 a week). The reason for his insistence on a contract as "publicist" (which Hitchcock had to submit to if he was to have his beloved Ingrid in his film) was simple. Hitchcock would pick up the bill for Petter's travel expenses the following summer when Petter came to England to see Ingrid during production, and when he went on to visit his family in Sweden thereafter. (He also promised to visit several neurology departments in England and Scandinavia during the summer of 1948.)

As it turned out, *Joan of Arc* would not be ready for filming until September, and the quiet routine of life in Benedict Canyon was difficult for Ingrid to sustain. Her restlessness became intolerable to both of them. "I had a lovely daughter and a nice husband," Ingrid said.

> Petter and I didn't love each other any more, but many marriages are like this and they endure. I had a beautiful house and a swimming pool. I remember one day sitting at the pool, and suddenly the tears were streaming down my cheeks. Why was I so unhappy? I had success, security. But it wasn't enough. I was exploding inside.

Gradually, the reasons for her discontent became clear. "I was bored. I felt as if it was the end of growing. I was searching for something, I knew not what." In her travels to Alaska and Europe, and after her success in New York, Ingrid realized that she was "not so helpless as I was in my own home—that I could express myself freely and people would listen." She wanted, she told Petter that summer, to travel all over the world, to work in different countries and enlarge her capacities. Fine, he replied: did any husband ever give his wife more freedom than he? Yes, that was true, as she had said, but freedom had meant being away from home. That season, there was nothing for her to do but await the beginning of *Joan of Arc*.

Filming finally began on September 16, at the old Hal Roach Studios in Culver City, very near Selznick. For a picture that was planned as a spiritual testament, *Joan* had somehow grown to be an unwieldy epic that cost a million dollars more than *Gone With the Wind*.

First of all, the theatrical framing device that had supported the play's ideology had to be discarded. That done, only a straightforward historical approach was left, and so the script fashioned by Maxwell Anderson and completed by Andrew Solt was a kind of medieval Western, with the Maid of Orleans as a pious Calamity Jane, fighting the English instead of the Indians. The production, like Topsy, grew and grew until it was unrecognizable as a work based on Anderson's austere play. And Ingrid, too darkly cosmeticized in an effort to tone down her Swedish prettiness, looked rather like Maria, transplanted from *For Whom the Bell Tolls*. Arranged around her in the studio were 71 cannons, 500 crossbows, 110 horses and 150 suits of armor, but despite the historic verisimilitude, Ingrid saw the rushes with increasing alarm. "Those were very beautiful," she said after watching the last scenes in early 1948. "Let's shoot the rest of the picture over again." But no one was willing to come up with another $4.6 million.

She did not need to complete filming to know that they were all in very deep trouble indeed. Executives at RKO, contracted to release the picture, had the right to make "suggestions," and so they did, joining the many already on the film. To any viewer with a critical eye, *Joan of Arc* was turning into a very big, very expensive bore.

But Ingrid, as usual, was doing brilliant work in the role. "She is bullet-proof," said Fleming, summarizing the views of his three cinematographers. "There has never been another figure like her before a camera. You can shoot her [from] any angle, any position. It doesn't make any difference—you don't have to protect her [from unflattering photography]. You can bother about the other actors on the set, but Ingrid's like a Notre Dame quarterback. An onlooker can't take his eyes off her!"

Nor could audiences, who flocked in massive numbers to see Ingrid as Joan and were not disappointed. It would have been easy for her to offer the usual pious glances actors are tempted to substitute for inner conviction; instead, her performance had a quality of utter translucence—the lighting seems to shine through rather than on her, and that is entirely due to the deep humanity she gave the maid. This is no portrait of a plaster saint, but rather a recognizably human, confused woman who knows that God sometimes writes straight with crooked lines. And it is unlikely that anyone who saw the picture ever forgot her final scene at the stake.

INGRID WAS ANXIOUS ABOUT THE TOTAL PRODUCTION, AND THIS— combined with her unhappiness at home—led her to spend more and more time at the studio after the day's work was complete. "I must have my hands in everything," she said that season. "I can't be any other way." According to Laurence Stallings (who had co-written *What Price Glory?* with Maxwell Anderson and who wrote *Joan*'s battle scenes), "She approached her work with the deepest humility, the utmost desire to do the right thing." At the end of the day, she continued to discuss the production as she poured a glass of bourbon for herself and generous drinks for Fleming and his colleagues.

Trying to transform a battle and a trial into compelling drama, everyone worked overtime. Following the day's filming on October 31, for example, Ingrid and Fleming parted at about nine in the evening. But this time she did not drive home. Instead, she hurried off to the makeup department, where she fashioned for herself a wart-marked face painted sickly green and donned a black fright wig and a hastily fitted costume. Half an hour later, "The Witch" burst into Fleming's home in Beverly Hills, circled him on her broom and left in an echo of shrill, cackling laughter after dropping bags of candy into the laps of Fleming's startled daughters. Fleming wrote Ingrid a note next day: no matter the garb, she would always be his Angel.

But the late hours were usually more intimate, and once too often she told Petter that she was staying overnight at Ruth's apartment to rehearse her next day's lines. "But to the surprise of Ruth, I went to her apartment," Petter said years later. "At first, Ruth mentioned that Ingrid had locked herself up in a room to work there. I searched the apartment. There was no Ingrid there, and Ruth had to admit that Ingrid had gone out for the night with a boyfriend. A few days later, Fleming's wife came to me and said, 'You must help me! My husband has got to stop this relationship!'"

"I was never perfect and the marriage was anything but ideal," Petter admitted. "One of my many mistakes was that I did not proceed with the divorce I firmly proposed [after the meeting with

Fleming's wife] in 1947. She [Ingrid] pleaded with me and assured me that she was changing her life"—in witness whereof, Ingrid suggested that they would have another child immediately after the Hitchcock picture the following summer. Petter, perhaps even to her surprise, agreed. "We decided to rebuild the house," she recalled, "to make room for a new family member. I wanted to have another child, feeling that in that way my life would be filled and fulfilled. I thought that maybe in this was the true answer to my restlessness. But every time a workman hit the roof with a hammer, it was like a nail going into my head." Pia, meantime, longed for more time with her mother, and in this regard it might be argued whether Ingrid's plans for a second child were perhaps her most preposterous fantasy.

Since he could easily have sued for divorce on her admitted grounds of infidelity, why did Petter not do so? Why did he remain a complaisant husband?

He answered the question himself. "I lived with that because of her income."

Chapter Twelve

1948

This affair must be unraveled from within.

AGATHA CHRISTIE,
The Mysterious Affair at Styles

NOT LONG AFTER NEW YEAR'S DAY, ALFRED AND ALMA HITCHCOCK invited the Lindstroms to a party at their home in Bel-Air, a quiet, gated enclave between Beverly Hills and the Brentwood section of Los Angeles. Aware of Ingrid's personal unhappiness and her disappointment about *Joan*, Hitchcock commiserated, for he had problems, too. He was beginning *Rope*—with the unprecedented experiment of using only ten-minute takes for uninterrupted, continuous, real-time action—and the difficult technique was driving his crew and cast very close to armed rebellion. (The normally placid James Stewart, for example, complained that the camera was being rehearsed, not the actors.) Neither Hitchcock nor Ingrid was very happy that evening, but for him there was an added poignancy to his feigning a festive spirit: more than ever in love with Ingrid, he poured his infatuation into plans for their journey to England to make *Under Capricorn*, scheduled for the summer.

Hitchcock's restraint makes even more touching the image of

one of Hollywood's most admired stars affecting a graceful gaiety
when her personal and professional life was so unhappy, and the
corresponding image of one of Hollywood's most admired directors, affecting a jovial mood as he fixed a sad, rapturous gaze on his
unhappy beloved. Hitchcock's manner that January evening, as
other guests recalled, was pointedly melancholy, and as usual, his
deepest feelings found their way into his work in progress. "Ah, yes,
Ingrid Bergman!" he had a character say in a scene for *Rope* filmed
the following week. "She's the Virgo type—I think she's just
lovely!"

A few days later, Hitchcock invited Ingrid to lunch, outlined his
ideas for *Under Capricorn* and gave her a copy of the novel and of
Hume Cronyn's first treatment for the script. As she leafed through
the pages, Hitchcock pointed out that Ingrid would notice enormous differences between the literary version and his ideas for the
forthcoming film.

The narrative, set in 1831 in Australia, concerned Charles
Adare (portrayed in the film by Michael Wilding), cousin of the
governor of Australia, who visits "under Capricorn" and there
meets an embittered ex-convict named Sam Flusky (Joseph Cotten).
Exiled for murder to Australia (then a penal colony), Flusky long
ago married the wealthy Lady Henrietta Considine (to be played by
Ingrid), who is, for reasons that are unclear, a pathetic dipsomaniac.
Adare takes an interest in the Fluskys' strange household, which is
dominated by the swinish, jealous housekeeper, Milly (Margaret
Leighton), who is in love with Sam.

To further complicate matters, Adare, while attempting to
reform Henrietta, falls in love with her. Provoked by the Iago-like
conduct of Milly, Sam shoots Adare (who survives), and then Henrietta's neurotic guilt reaches a breaking point. She admits to Adare
that it was she—not her husband—who was responsible for the
death of her brother, and that Sam assumed guilt for the crime and
went to prison for seven years. Before Adare renounces his love for
Henrietta and returns her to the affections of Sam (whose devotion
is at last reciprocated by his wife), it is discovered that Milly has
been poisoning her. Adare exposes the housekeeper and then bids
farewell to the Fluskys, who now face a better life together.

*   *   *

As Hitchcock described his ideas, Ingrid at once saw the astonishing similarities between his vision for *Under Capricorn* and her two previous films for him. From *Spellbound* there was the motif of the secret and the transference of guilt from a childhood that infects adulthood with crippling neurosis; from *Notorious*, the theme of a woman's alcoholic intemperance and the attempted poisoning of her. In all three narratives, there was a sturdy romance, an over-arching sense of remorse and the need for confession before pun-ishment exacts a terrible price. Melodramatic though it was, the part of Henrietta Flusky had both mystery and a range of emotions that offered Ingrid several powerful scenes and an opportunity to be someone completely different from Joan of Arc.

And so, in March, she took the *Capricorn* materials with her to read during her journey to France, where she posed for pho-tographs in Rheims, Rouen and other sites of Joan's story, to be used for movie publicity later that year. When she returned to Bev-erly Hills, a gift arrived from her French host, a scholarly priest who had acted as her guide and intermediary with the press. But the parcel, containing a small, antique wooden statue of the Madonna, had been damaged in transit. A note from the customs authorities explained: "Virgin arriving Hollywood—slightly damaged—lost her head." Which prompted Ingrid's amused reaction: "Well, that's Hollywood for you!"

Between France and California, Ingrid had made two stops. In late March, she arrived in New York, where she went to plays and visited Irene Selznick, then enjoying great success as the producer of Tennessee Williams's play *A Streetcar Named Desire*. Hurrying along Broadway to the theater one evening, Ingrid spotted a familiar name on a movie marquee. Roberto Rossellini's *Paisà* had been released in America, and next afternoon, Ingrid was in line to buy a ticket. She was one of only a half-dozen in the audience that day, and when she left she was bewildered by the public's indifference.

Once again, Ingrid was captivated by Rossellini's powerful art-lessness. Produced in 1946, just after *Open City*, *Paisà* spun six tales about the heroism and dignity of common folk during and after the war. Every scene stressed beauty of character over appearance, of idealism over selfishness. The realism and simplicity of Rossellini's story was effectively, for Ingrid—trained amid the rigors of Swedish production and Hollywood's careful attention to every visual detail—both a reprimand and a summons to conversion.

Watching *Open City* two years earlier, she had been moved to tears by a scene in which Anna Magnani convinces her lover to keep faith in ideals by believing in her love for him. Ingrid also described to friends in vivid detail the later scene, in which Magnani is shot as she pursues the police van that has arrested him. It was, Ingrid said, the exact antithesis to the sanitized finale of *For Whom the Bell Tolls*— just as the courage of *Open City*'s Resistance leader and of the priest, who face torture and death rather than endangering the lives of their fellows, was in another universe from the sentimental finale in which Ingrid had faced Bing Crosby in *The Bells of St. Mary's*. She had nothing against McCarey: his story was true to its form. But Rossellini had shown her recognizable people faced with harsh dilemmas that could not be resolved by a wink or a cliché.

Now, having seen *Paisà*, Ingrid was more than ever convinced that Rossellini, who always subordinated actors to themes and never condescended to mere glamour, was the key to transforming her dissatisfaction. She had worked successfully in three national movie environments—why not a fourth? She had learned German and English—why not Italian? That cold day in New York, Ingrid ignored the languid pace of the film and the incompetence of its wooden performances (mostly by people whom the director had picked from the streets of Rome): instead, she saw straight through to the issue Rossellini stressed—honor over expedience. The character of the peasant Carmela, who becomes a misunderstood martyr, and of Harriett, the heroic nurse, deeply touched an actress devoted to Joan of Arc; she saw for the first time what a master who was free of the restraints of Hollywood's easy entertainments could accomplish.

Open City was unquestionably the greater film, but *Paisà* (again benefiting from the collaboration of Fellini) had moments of greatness whose force derived from its visual and emotional intimacy and its complex, ambiguous but always honest portraits of characters like Francesca, a once innocent girl whom harsh necessity has forced into prostitution. She is accidentally reunited with her old boyfriend, who no longer recognizes her and leaves without knowing her true identity. A story of purity lost and later longed for, it cut close to the bone for Ingrid, whom neither affairs nor marriage

had left with much security. That came only from her work. But the
impending fate of her film of *Joan of Arc* suggested that now even her
work seemed also to be on the wrong track.

HER SALVATION, INGRID TOLD IRENE SELZNICK AT DINNER THAT NIGHT,
lay only in a dramatic change of career direction. She had always
acted on intuition, like Rossellini's amateurs, and she had always
been willing to appear unglamorous for a role. Was she not just the
right one for a Rossellini film? And could not her celebrity help him
find acceptance by a wider international audience, too?

But Ingrid could not have been aware of a critical element in
Rossellini's method, which no one put more clearly than the director himself: "In order to choose my actors for *Paisà*, I began by
establishing myself with my cameraman in the middle of the district
where a particular episode was to be shot. The onlookers and
pedestrians then gathered around us, and I chose my actors from
among the crowd. We adapted ourselves to the existing circumstances and to the actors we selected." And then came the crucial
statement: "The dialogue and the intonation were determined by
our nonprofessional actors. I never finished our script before we
arrived on location."

The truth was that his story and script remained unfinished
even after the filming was: Rossellini acted on a kind of inspired
caprice in the dubbing room and at the editing table. So did his
writer, Federico Fellini, but in the masterworks he later directed, it
is arguable that Fellini worked with a sharper, more focused genius
than Rossellini, as well as a firmer commitment to storytelling and
to the idea that psychological or spiritual truth often requires flights
of visual imagination that take the audience beyond mere realism.

But there was one significant contradiction among many in
Roberto Rossellini, as Ingrid learned over dinner that evening from
Irene (whose husband had prolonged dealings with him). Although
he wanted virtually to do away with actors, Rossellini recognized
increasingly that he needed them. That very season, he was in negotiations with David Selznick to make a picture, and so he had sent a
wire to Selznick's contract player and mistress, Jennifer Jones: "Congratulations for your wonderful performance in Duel [in the Sun].
Hoping to be working with you soon." In fact, Rossellini had not

seen *Duel* and, never interested in Hollywood actresses, had no idea
who Jennifer Jones was. But he had savvy advisers, like his lawyer, a
cultured gentleman with the stately name Ercole Graziadei (Hercules
Thanks-be-to-God), and an agent with the equally colorful autograph Arabella Le Maitre. While their names suggested characters in
a nineteenth-century opera, their interests were firmly modern.

The idea Rossellini and Selznick had discussed was a neorealist
version of *Joan of Arc*, starring Jennifer Jones, who had won the
Oscar for her performance as St. Bernadette and was soon to
assume the real-life role of the second Mrs. Selznick. But in light of
Ingrid's film, the *Joan* project was jettisoned. Still, producer and
director left the door open for other projects. Before dinner was
over, Ingrid told Irene she would send Rossellini a simple letter as
soon as she could find out his address.

Irene got the address and sent it to Ingrid in Washington a few
days later. There, on April 5, President Truman gave Ingrid the
Women's National Press Club Award for outstanding achievement
in the theater. After a few words of gracious acceptance, Ingrid—
clearly inspired by Rossellini—fearlessly remarked that the production of honest films in America was being hampered by censorship
(there was terrific interference from the Motion Picture Code over
everything from *Intermezzo* onward), by government interference (J.
Edgar Hoover and his cronies had come down heavily on Hitchcock
over *Notorious*, its motif of making a bomb and its shockingly
immoral American intelligence agents) and a demand for shallow,
escapist entertainments in postwar America. This was not a climate
for serious work, she concluded to politely restrained applause.

Also in April, *Arch of Triumph* was at last released. A typical
review observed that "Miss Bergman and Mr. Boyer look lovely, but
they are just actors in a slow, expensive film [that is] all too
tedious." The picture's critical and financial failure convinced Ingrid
all the more where her artistic future lay. With that, she showed
Petter the letter she wanted to post to Rossellini:

Dear Mr. Rossellini—

    I saw your films, *Open City* and *Paisà*, and enjoyed them very much. If
you need a Swedish actress who speaks English very well, who has not for-

gotten her German, who is not very understandable in French, and who in
Italian knows only "ti amo" [her final words in *Arch of Triumph*], I am ready
to come and make a film with you.

Best regards,
Ingrid Bergman.

This seemed fine to Petter, who added that perhaps together
they could convince Rossellini to come to America, that they might
be the first to get him to Hollywood, and that surely Petter could
make a deal—perhaps even with David Selznick—for a Rossellini-
Bergman picture. He urged her to post the letter at once, which she
did, on April 30. Thus Petter Lindstrom unwittingly ignited a situation that blazed into an international scandal and finally left his
marriage in ashes.

Rossellini received the fateful letter on May 8—his forty-second
birthday—and at once, recognizing an extraordinary stroke of coincidence and good luck, cabled his reply to Ingrid. Although he had
never thought of working with her (and was only vaguely aware of
her credits), he took good advice from his staff, who convinced him
that the best way to win American financial support was by obtaining the services of a popular American star:

DEAR MRS. BERGMAN

I JUST RECEIVED WITH GREAT EMOTION YOUR LETTER
WHICH HAPPENS TO ARRIVE ON THE ANNIVERSARY OF MY
BIRTHDAY [AS] THE MOST PRECIOUS GIFT. IT IS ABSOLUTELY
TRUE THAT I DREAMED TO MAKE A FILM WITH YOU AND FROM
THIS MOMENT I WILL DO EVERYTHING THAT SUCH DREAM
BECOMES REALITY AS SOON AS POSSIBLE. I WILL WRITE YOU A
LONG LETTER TO SUBMIT TO YOU MY IDEAS. WITH MY ADMI-
RATION, PLEASE ACCEPT THE EXPRESSION OF MY GRATITUDE
TOGETHER WITH MY BEST REGARDS,

ROBERTO ROSSELLINI.

In the ironic twist such matters often have, Rossellini immediately used Ingrid's adulation to try to conclude a deal with Selznick,

who would have liked to contract Ingrid once again but was unconvinced of the vague ideas Rossellini was floating to Hollywood through his representatives. Five days after he received Ingrid's letter, Rossellini met in Milan with Jenia Reissar. Because he did not speak English and she did not know Italian, they spoke in French.

"Rossellini said he was most anxious to have Bergman," Reissar wrote to her boss,

> and that naturally it would be under the [Selznick] deal. I told him we'd had trouble with Bergman, and that she might not want to work for us. His reply was that he was going to tell her that he wanted her for a film, had a story for her, and that he had associates with whom he worked in Italy—no mention of Selznick! It was not her business who they were. If she turned the story down or wanted too much money—well, that was the end of it! . . . He wanted to know what sort of money Bergman got. I told him I didn't know, but that she was very expensive. He said she must realize that he couldn't pay her Hollywood prices, and if she did want an impossible sum, there would be no film.

Rossellini hoped for one of three eventualities: (a) that Selznick would finance the entire project; (b) that Selznick would provide only American distribution of the finished film and the money for it would be raised in Europe; or (c) that Selznick would loan him contract players. Whatever the situation, he had no intention of providing vast sums to mere actors. "Je signerai tout ce que vous voulez," Rossellini said to Reissar in parting: "I'll sign anything you want." As everyone soon learned, that was easy for him to say, for he never honored contracts in any case. "He is a temperamental and irresponsible man," Reissar wrote to Selznick. As for Ingrid, his "dream" to make a film with her came to him as he drafted the telegram.

From the start, then, it was Rossellini's aim to have American financial backing for a movie—what project and with which players he knew not. But whatever means were necessary, he would take them. And he would be pleased to make his first film a vehicle for Selznick's beloved, Jennifer Jones. Rossellini made only one stipulation: he must have the participation of his mistress, Anna Magnani, in some picture to be negotiated. She was, he added, furiously jealous that he was even discussing a Selznick contract without her presence. "But he said she was a crazy woman," Reissar reported, "that success had come to her very late in life [she was forty!] and that she understood nothing about business." The fan letter from Ingrid Bergman was a trump card he had not expected.

On May 15, Ingrid received a long letter, in which Rossellini (again with the help of a translator) outlined his idea for a screen story. In the belief that a script was too confining, he did not use one. That should have sent up the first cautionary signal to Ingrid, but she read on, fascinated.

Recently, Rossellini had been traveling outside Rome when he passed a camp for refugee women from all over Central and Eastern Europe. He managed to speak to one of them, a haunted and lonely Latvian. From this grew his idea for a film.

His concept was to tell of just such a woman he named Karin who, out of desperation, marries a fisherman from the Lipari Islands and goes with him to Stromboli, dominated by an active volcano. On this barren island of fire, ash and parched earth, the foreign woman is more isolated than ever. But Karin hopes that she has at last found her savior in this foreigner, and she decides to remain. They soon learn that they share nothing in common. "The man lives beside her and loves her with a kind of savage fury," Rossellini continued. "But even the God that the people worship seems different from hers. How could the austere Lutheran God she used to pray to, when a child, possibly stand comparison with these numerous saints of various hues?"

Karin, eventually pregnant, tries to rebel against her arid, lonely life, but there is no escape. Intending to throw herself into the fiery volcano, she climbs to the summit but collapses, crying out to God. And with that she is saved: the miracle she longed for occurs, in the sudden freedom that floods into her own soul. Abandoning herself at last to the simple new life and about to bring forth a new one, she returns to the village and accepts her life in what will be her Terra di Dio—God's Land. That was Rossellini's working title.

"With you near me," Rossellini concluded, "I could give life to a human creature who, following hard and bitter experiences, finds peace at last and complete freedom from all selfishness. Could you possibly come to Europe? I could invite you for a trip to Italy, and we could go over this thing at leisure . . . Pray believe in my enthusiasm." He signed the letter, "Your Roberto Rossellini," and in a way, from that day, he was.

Ingrid Bergman read her own story in that of Karin's struggles. She replied at once that she was going to London that summer, and she and her husband could easily meet him. Could they meet halfway, perhaps in Paris, toward the end of August? That was fine with Rossellini: that summer, he was to conclude another film on the Amalfi coast and would zoom up to her in one of his racing cars. And with that precipitously romantic image in her mind, Ingrid arrived in London on June 21 to begin work on *Under Capricorn*.

BECAUSE OF POSTWAR WILDCAT STRIKES AND PROBLEMS WITH BOTH the screenplay and the demands Hitchcock was placing on his technical crew, the first day's shooting did not begin for another month. Idleness took its toll. "I'm going to be in trouble," Ingrid wrote to Ruth Roberts. "I smoke all the time. I drink more than ever. I have put on at least ten pounds." The weight, as usual, could easily be lost, for Ingrid regularly went on a strict regime just before filming; besides, there were flattering period costumes for this picture that could hide a multitude of indiscretions.

But cigarettes and alcohol had gradually become, since 1946, another matter entirely—increasingly indulged habits that would, in time, contribute to grave illness. Remarkably, her speech was not affected: Ingrid never developed that common affliction, the "whiskey voice" that so often announces a heavy tippler and smoker. And perhaps because of her extraordinarily strong constitution, she could consume generous amounts of alcohol and still be alert; nor did she ever miss work because of a hangover.

Ingrid was never an alcoholic: she never drank from need or compulsion, never before the end of the day's work, and certainly her acting was never compromised by the effects of drinking. But just as certainly, she enjoyed the afternoon ritual of cocktails, for which she had a remarkable capacity that matched her zeal for life. It is also important to recall that only many years later, in America, were the hazardous long-term consequences of tobacco and of excessive alcohol intake known and widely proclaimed. In 1949,

virtually everywhere in the world, these were luxuries to be grate-
fully taken up by any post-adolescent. They were the props of smart
society.

After costume fittings and makeup tests were complete, Ingrid
was free to shop, to go to the theater, to socialize with her producers (Hitchcock, Bernstein and their wives) and to become better
acquainted with a new friend, the English actress Ann Todd. Ann
had also worked for Hitchcock and Selznick (in *The Paradine Case*,
made in Hollywood in 1947) and was now the wife of director
David Lean. That summer, the two women often went on excursions around greater London—to the parks and museums, to Kew
Gardens, to the Greenwich Observatory.

SEVERAL YEARS EARLIER, PRODUCER-DIRECTOR GABRIEL PASCAL, WHOM
George Bernard Shaw had entrusted to film *Pygmalion* and *Major
Barbara*, had approached Ingrid about the possibility of starring in a
movie of Shaw's *Candida*. Their schedules were not congruent, however, and so the idea was dropped. But now the playwright was
reading in the London daily newspapers about the shopping expedi-
tions and social comings-and-goings of Ingrid Bergman, and he
wanted to meet her. One very warm July afternoon, Pascal escorted
Ingrid to Shaw's country house at Ayot St. Lawrence.

Then ninety-three, Shaw was as alert, cantankerous and appreciative of female beauty as ever. An imposing figure with his full
head of white hair and long flowing beard, he greeted Ingrid at the
gate and at once asked why she had not done his play *St. Joan* in
New York. "I didn't like it," she said with a smile.

"What do you mean you don't like it? It's a masterpiece!"

"Yes, but you gave us Shaw's Joan, not the Joan of history,"
Ingrid continued as they walked up the path to the house, and with
that she proceeded to offer him a brief lecture on the subject. "You
see," Ingrid said without haughtiness, "I just happen to know much
more about her than you do."

Shaw was completely disarmed by Ingrid's frankness and
charmed by her refusal to be intimidated by him. "Nobody has ever
had the courage to tell me they don't like my work," he said, and
then asked, "What plays of mine have you done?"

"Well, Mr. Shaw, I haven't done any of your plays."

As his housekeeper brought in the tea tray, Shaw sighed and gazed mournfully at Ingrid. "Well, my dear girl, you haven't even begun yet." Years after Shaw's death in 1950, she "began."

AFTER NUMEROUS DELAYS, UNDER CAPRICORN AT LAST ROLLED ON JULY 19. There had been much discussion, up to that morning, about the problem of accents in the film: could everyone affect an Irish brogue for these transplanted characters? What about Ingrid's lilting Swedish cadence, Joseph Cotten's slight Virginia drawl, Michael Wilding's proper English rhythms? How could they all sound Irish?

Ingrid's entrance, twenty-five minutes into the picture, was shot that first day. She gave her director a brilliant, letter-perfect performance, an uninterrupted four-minute scene in which Lady Henrietta, pale and neurasthenic, walks unsteadily and barefoot into the dining room and greets her husband's dinner guests—her hair unkempt, her clothes askew, her eyes misty with drink. In her dialogue with Wilding, about their meeting as children long ago in Ireland, Ingrid managed an Irish lilt that was entirely acceptable, audible but just slightly slurred, befitting a lady's effort to cover her drinking. When Hitchcock called "Cut!" there was loud applause on the set.

But after that, the brogue was rarely heard again. Cotten could not shake his Virginia-gentleman tone, Ingrid's Irish-accent teacher fell ill, and the rest of the picture featured an international cast proudly speaking in their own speech patterns. But when Under Capricorn was released, no one seemed to mind, for there were far more serious problems.

The evening of that first day's work, Ingrid wrote to Petter, urging him to bring Pia to England by boat, so that her daughter might have the sheer fun of the voyage and learn how great was the distance between America and Europe. She wanted Pia to see the Statue of Liberty disappear, she said, and the white cliffs of Dover emerge out of the mist. The journey would also give Petter a time to relax. He must also, she begged, bring soapflakes, canned food, nylon stockings, tissues—and tinned meat, since there was virtually none available: the staples of ordinary life were desperately lacking in postwar Britain, even to film stars.

The use of the Technicolor process at the Elstree Studios, just outside London, was a great success. But the ten-minute takes with which Hitchcock was so obsessed that year had mostly to be abandoned, although there were several complicated shots that ran six, eight and even nine minutes.

This technique put a temporary strain on the Hitchcock-Bergman friendship. "He got such pleasure out of doing those camera tricks," she told a writer years later,

> but of course the continuous shots and the moving cameras were very hard on everybody. We rehearsed for days, and then at last we put on makeup and had a try at a reel. We had perhaps six minutes just fine and then suddenly something went wrong and the whole reel had to begin again. Hitch just insisted.
>
> Then the propmen had the job of moving all the furniture while the camera was rolling forward and backward, or from this side to that—and the walls were flying up into the rafters as we walked by, so that huge Technicolor camera could follow us. It just drove us all crazy! A chair or a table for an actor appeared the minute before a cue. The floor was marked with numbers and everybody and every piece of furniture had to be on the cued number at the right moment.
>
> What a nightmare! It's the only time I broke down and cried on a movie set. I think Hitch did all this to prove to himself that he could. It was a challenge only to himself, to show the movie industry that he could figure out and accomplish something so difficult.

Years later, Ingrid had to admit that sometimes Hitchcock's tortuous method worked brilliantly. "The one gorgeous scene in that movie is my long confession scene in the dining room, when the camera never left me—followed me as I rose from the chair, walked around the room, leaned over a table, sat down again." But during the rehearsal, Ingrid was not so calm.

"She got into a terrible state that day," Hitchcock remembered, "and just told me off." First he tried an old method that usually brought calm and a smile from an anxious actor: "Ingrid, it's only a movie," he said calmly—knowing that both of them believed that while in the grand scheme of life and death it was indeed "only" a movie, they also knew that of course it was a movie, which meant so much, in so many ways, to both of them. But this time Ingrid was not mollified by his placid irony, and she continued to argue that what he wanted from her was impossible. "And then," said Hitchcock, "I did what I always do when people start to argue. I just turned away and went home. Next day, Ingrid said, 'Okay, Hitch—we'll do it your way.' I told her, 'It's not my way, Ingrid—it's the right way!'"

In this case, it was. That day after the rehearsal, Ingrid delivered her nine-minute confessional monologue like a Richard Strauss aria. She began quietly, smiling as she recounted happy memories of Henrietta's youth. Then she was resolute, recalling her marriage to the stableman Sam Flusky against the wishes of her aristocratic family. From this she rose to the climax, the dramatic description of her shooting of her brother. From there she dipped to a coda, the tearful expression of grateful loyalty to her husband for his suffering and his fidelity over the years. In a film not generally regarded very highly even by Hitchcock partisans, Ingrid's scene was, years later, studied by apprentice and accomplished film actors.

PETTER AND PIA WERE LONDON TOURISTS BY MID-AUGUST, AND ON weekends Ingrid joined them for excursions; for the moment, for the child's sake, there seemed to be an uneasy truce. As for their forthcoming meeting with Rossellini, that depended on Hitchcock's shooting schedule. Ingrid told Hitchcock only that her husband wanted to take her to Paris for the weekend of her birthday, and for this he readily rearranged everything. Thus the Rossellini-Bergman-Lindstrom meeting was scheduled for luncheon at the Hôtel George V in Paris on Saturday, August 28—which augured well, Ingrid said, for her thirty-third birthday was the next day.

But Petter had misgivings: he told her that during the summer there had been calls and letters from Selznick's people about difficulties in coming to any kind of arrangement with Rossellini, who was invariably hard to deal with. To Ingrid, this was typical Hollywood business talk. She wanted to make a picture with the great director, and that was that. If Selznick could not be brought in, they would go to Samuel Goldwyn or Howard Hughes or another mogul. "My mother sometimes compared herself to a train moving down the track," Pia said years later. "Nothing and no one could stop her once her mind was made up. She had a determination of steel." Summer 1948 was one such time when that will was not to be blocked, even by Petter.

The meeting finally occurred at the George V—not over lunch, but at a long dinner in the suite of film distributor Ilya Lopert, who very courteously arranged to have a translator present. Rossellini had coached himself for this meeting more carefully than he had ever directed any amateur. His appearance was unremarkable: he wore a wrinkled dark suit at least two sizes too large, and this he explained by telling Ingrid that he was forever on a diet. She understood that, she said with a laugh. Then, as they ate heartily, Rossellini's reticence vanished: he retold the story of *Terra di Dio*, his dramatic gestures and descriptions alternating with an impressive air of philosophical gravity.

"Do we make the picture—yes or no?" he asked, affecting a sudden air of diffidence when he finished. He then drew a rose from a table arrangement and began plucking its petals: "We make it, we don't make it—we make it, we don't—"

"I shall be honored to have a part in it," Ingrid replied, ignoring a sharp glance from Petter, who began to discuss some financial matters with Lopert. Since these matters interested Rossellini and Ingrid not at all, they proceeded to speak of food and wine, of Alfred Hitchcock and Jean Renoir, of music and art and history— anything that swirled into Roberto's capacious, free-ranging mind.

She repeated her admiration for his two films she had seen and, waving his arms, he spoke passionately of the conditions under which they were made—circumstances of great humility and simplicity. He spoke with authority, he had clear and definite opinions about everything. And his life was making movies—a new kind of movies, he said, a language of visual truth. Although Ingrid had said that she "fell in love" with him earlier, when she saw his work onscreen in New York, this evening was the real moment of first fervor. The dinner meeting lasted until midnight, when Lopert opened a bottle of champagne for Ingrid's birthday. Roberto's intense, dark eyes never left her until everyone disbanded for the night; her hand shook as she accepted his good wishes and touched his glass to hers.

*   *   *

IT HAD NOT BEEN EASY FOR ROBERTO TO LEAVE AMALFI, WHERE HE WAS filming *La Macchina ammazzacattivi*. Magnani visited him on weekends, and it had been a chore slipping away from her. When the final arrangements were being made for Paris, he told the hotel porter, "I expect a cable, but do not give it to me until I ask for it—understand?" Understood. That evening, while Roberto was dining with members of his crew, the porter approached and in a perfectly clipped, dutiful voice, announced: "Signor Rossellini, if you will now ask me for the cable I am not to give you until you ask for it, I can now give it to you." Fortunately, Magnani was somehow away from the table, otherwise the dinner plates and glasses might not have survived.

Impetuous and often violent, she had the colorful habit of crowning him with a platter of steaming pasta when she was overtaken with jealousy. Roberto, known far and wide for his passion for sports car racing, was equally fast and furious with women. That summer, he was juggling at least five: Anna Magnani, his mistress since 1944; Marilyn Buferd (Miss America of 1946, who was playing in his current film); Roswita Schmidt, a German nightclub dancer, now mostly an ex-lover but still summoned for an occasional dalliance; a Hungarian blond named Ava; and, occasionally, his estranged wife Marcella de Marchis, with whom he had a relationship that was in an odd way emotionally faithful, at least. Of this harem Ingrid knew nothing when she met him.

ROBERTO ROSSELLINI WAS NINE YEARS OLDER THAN INGRID. BORN MAY 8, 1906, in Rome, he was the eldest of four sons of an architect who built the Corso and Barberini movie theaters in Rome and taught his son to tinker with gadgets, among them movie projectors and cameras. Raised in an intellectual environment, Roberto was shamelessly spoiled by his father. Arriving home one evening, for example, he asked Papa for money for the taxi driver waiting outside. "Certainly," said Signor Rossellini, reaching for his wallet and asking where his son had come from. "Naples," Roberto replied without blinking. Papa laughed and gave him the cash to cover the 150-mile trip.

Young Roberto eventually quit school and worked at odd jobs in editing; every free moment he spent at the movies. Fascinated by airplanes and racing cars, he also became known as something of a latter-day Casanova in Rome, where his fine features and charm won him entrance to circles both fashionable and doubtful. Among his early romances was a pretty French girl named Titi Michelle, whom he followed halfway across Europe before accepting her loud rejection. According to some sources, this was the only time he took no for an answer.

But something odd happened when Roberto was about twenty. For reasons that may never be clear, his parents had him committed to a lunatic asylum near Naples. The official document (rendered into English when Rossellini unsuccessfully petitioned for an American visa in 1946 and 1948) stated only that "his parents wished to detract him from what they considered at the time a dangerous juvenile passion unfavorably considered by them." This was a masterpiece of circumlocution, and it has been variously interpreted: Rossellini fell into a band of drug-taking youths; Rossellini drove his sports cars too wildly; Rossellini fell in love with an undesirable woman. Forced hospitalization would have been strong medicine for these tendencies, and nothing in his parents' character suggests they would have put their boy in a hospital were it not necessary. On the contrary, it was maintained (by, among others, Jenia Reissar, who knew him well for several years) that Roberto had suffered some kind of nervous breakdown and was subject to occasional bouts of a mild form of mental illness throughout his life. Whatever happened, he was back in Rome within a year and carrying on a torrid affair with Liliana Castagnola, a good-natured, second-rate variety show singer.

From the start, Rossellini's connection with movies was inextricably linked to his romantic exploits. In late 1931, just after the death of his father, he met a young actress named Assia Noris, a Russian-born comedienne destined for a successful career in Italian films. But Assia had old-fashioned ideas, and one of them was that marriage preceded sex. "We'll get married," he declared amiably, and in no time a church wedding was arranged with an archbishop, priests, a choir and organist—and a formal dinner afterward, after which the Rossellinis duly consummated the union and settled down to married life. Within a year, both of them realized they had made a mistake: he was already straying, and she had met a man much better suited to her temperament and ideals. When she discussed their dilemma, he merely shrugged and said, "Go and marry him!"

"But I'm already married!" she cried.

"No, you're not, my dear," Rossellini replied calmly. "That was all an act. Just actors and extras, all of them. You're quite free." Later, some took this incident as mere youthful highjinks, but it also indicates a rather capricious (not say to imprudently theatrical) approach to his own life and that of others.

With Noris now in the past, there was a brief revival of the Liliana Castagnola affair: he so lavished jewelry on her that his inheritance dried up. And then a terrible thing happened: Liliana was found dead of a drug overdose. It was perhaps no wonder that his films came, more and more closely, to concern the people and situations of everyday, for little about Rossellini's own life did. He was literally fantastic.

IN 1936, ROSSELLINI MARRIED MARCELLA DE MARCHIS, WHO WAS from an old aristocratic family; she bore him two sons, Marco and Renzo. After working as a sound technician, editor, script supervisor and assistant director, Roberto had his chance to direct. Before 1941, he produced half a dozen short films and was a collaborator on a feature supervised by Vittorio Mussolini, son of Il Duce. Prior to the liberation of Rome, he directed four features during the Fascist regime even while belonging to the Christian Democratic Party—a bit of political fence-sitting that alienated some friends and critics then and later. Of his humanistic and anti-Fascist faith there was no doubt once the world had seen *Open City*, which began filming in secret in January 1945, and which marked the birth of the movement later known as neorealism. Its release in 1946 ushered Roberto onto the world's stage.

His private life, meantime, could have provided material for a successful potboiler. *Open City* was partly financed by Roberto's wife and by Roswita Schmidt, who sold jewelry on his behalf. On August 14, 1946, his eight-year-old son Marco died suddenly of peritonitis. And at the same time, the illegitimate young son of Anna Magnani fell ill with infantile paralysis. Roberto's tempestuous affair with her had begun in 1939, and although the child was not his, Roberto was often a surrogate father. By the summer of 1948, she had placed herself firmly at the center of Roberto's life, having demanded that Roswita be exiled to the isle of Capri, where Rossellini supported her for many years in semi-comfort. Magnani's powerful performances—in *Open City*, *The Human Voice* and *The Miracle*—contributed in important ways to his exalted status among European filmmakers. Soon after, for the second time, Marcella initiated proceedings to have her marriage annulled (divorce then being illegal in Italy).

IT WOULD BE AN UNDERSTATEMENT TO SAY THAT ROBERTO'S WORKING methods were unconventional. Everything might be in place on a location, but if he had the idea to go fishing, he vanished for hours or an entire day. When he returned, his loyal crew was expected to work tirelessly for twenty hours or longer to compensate for time lost. If a nonprofessional actor could or would not follow directions precisely, Roberto often exploded violently—a reaction oddly at variance with his lifelong sensitivity and generosity. His unpredictable temper made his crew and players anxious and encouraged the rumor that indeed he had, beneath all his charm and evident creativity, an unstable mind.

Often, Roberto was prodigiously active, tossing off ideas like a Roman candle; he could also be remarkably indolent for several months, returning to work only when he needed money—which was, indeed, the only habitual condition of his life. Roberto could be all charm, and there is no question that he had good instincts in some things. But he was essentially a sluggish, disorganized soul, and this got him into trouble.

"You know that I am a good friend of Roberto," wrote his agent, Arabella Le Maitre, to Jenia Reissar that September,

> and I hate to say things against him. I have talked with people who worked with him in the last picture. Every one of them is disgusted. Imagine that he did not even finish the picture himself—he left Majori and asked [scriptwriter Sergio] Amidei to finish it! Everything was so disorganized; they hardly ever worked during the day, and only because he had to go fishing! People who

know him close and even relatives say he will never change, and I am afraid that if he signs a contract with Mr. Selznick, the one who will be in trouble will be Mr. Selznick. He may change and reorganize his life, but I thought it was my duty to tell you what I know and warn you.

The letter, drafted on September 16, when Arabella thought a Selznick-Rossellini-Bergman deal still possible, indicates how grave she felt the matter had become with her (soon to be former) client. Equally cogent as a witness to the problems with Rossellini was his attorney, Signor Graziadei, who (in a letter dated September 21), also warned Reissar about his client. "Graziadei does not consider [Roberto] a serious businessman," Reissar wrote to Selznick that same day. Away off in Culver City, Selznick might have used the lawyer's name, punning in gratitude to God for the advance warning. With that, the Selznick deal collapsed.

When Roberto met Ingrid that August, Marilyn Buferd was the lady of the moment. Their affair had begun in July, but after Roberto's visit to Paris, Marilyn grew weary of hearing so much about Ingrid Bergman and his professional plans for her. He said only that he had no doubt that he had overwhelmed her with his charm, and he was dead right. "Swedish women are the easiest in the world to impress," he told Marilyn, "because they have such cold husbands. The love they get is an analgesic balm instead of a tonic."

IN BARELY CONCEALED EXCITEMENT, INGRID RETURNED TO LONDON and the Hitchcock set on Monday morning, the day after her thirty-third birthday. She found the director awaiting her patiently, surrounded by other cast members. How was her weekend? everyone asked. "I met a director from Italy, that's all," replied Ingrid, blushing. But of course everyone knew exactly what had transpired, and no one was more concerned than Alfred Hitchcock. "When it finally happened, he resented her going off with Rossellini," according to Arthur Laurents (who had written *Rope* and still remained close to the Hitchcocks). "His resentment was not caused simply by the fact that he adored Bergman. It was also because she was leaving him for another director."

By the end of September, *Under Capricorn* was complete, and the three Lindstroms departed for a holiday in Sweden—Ingrid's return after a nine-year absence. A horde of photographers surrounded them as they descended from the airplane, and autograph seekers rushed forward. Gustaf Molander, who had directed six of her Swedish films, was on hand to greet her, along with Victor Sjöström and a committee from the film community. Flowers were presented, and she drew one from each bunch for Molander. Asked about the rumors that she would make a film with Roberto Rossellini, Ingrid replied diplomatically, "I like him. I have even written to him and said I would like to work with him. We will meet and discuss projects, but he speaks no English and I no Italian!" Of their meeting she said nothing.

The family spent a week at the Grand Hotel in Stockholm, strolling along the canal and revisiting her favorite restaurants and tearooms. The press reported her every outing, detailing the color of her shoes, the length of her hair, how long this or that stroll took. Reporters of the leading newspapers referred to Ingrid and Petter, without sarcasm, as the Queen and the Prince Consort. Things were more peaceful when they proceeded to Petter's family in Stöde on October 12; there, Ingrid took Pia on long walks in the countryside, and they all enjoyed her father-in-law's prize golden plums, a rare type for which this wizard of a gardener was widely known.

Before the end of October, the Lindstroms were back in Beverly Hills. Ingrid received a call from Walter Wanger, asking that she fly to New York, where Victor Fleming waited, for the premiere of *Joan of Arc*. She departed at once, and although she and Fleming met privately for one night, it was clear to both of them that the relationship was over. She looked forward to a lifelong friendship; he said he was not very good at that.

Amid much ballyhoo, the film began its run on November 11, and because Ingrid received superb notices, audiences stood in long lines for hours, despite an unseasonably cold autumn—and despite a generally unfavorable critical reaction to the film. "There is no resisting her goodness," ran a typical rave for Ingrid. "Hers is an uncommon gift for making virtue interesting, and there is a genuine effulgence about her." But the film was repudiated as "a masterwork of cinematic archaisms, neither real drama nor historical pageant [and] its spiritual theme is told on a Sunday school level. It should have been inspirational, but it is pretentious and hollow."

Ingrid was not pleased to have collected the only good notices. "It's true that people who stand in line at theaters don't read the critics," she told a columnist, "but I do care what they say." She had devoted more study, more care, energy and love into preparing this role than any other in her career thus far. No one recognized its production problems and its final flaws more than she, and none felt the failure more bitterly. The critics' denunciations notwithstanding, the film earned back its investment with a sturdy profit, and early in 1949 *Joan of Arc* received seven Academy Award nominations—among them was the fourth in Ingrid's career, for the best performance by an actress. (Only the picture's cinematographers and costume designers won statuettes the following spring.)

As usual, Ingrid's own success did not turn her head; quite the contrary, she was now more afraid than ever that she had become, after ten years and fourteen films in America, no longer suitable or right for Hollywood, and that it was not right for her. As 1948 drew to a close, she looked back on *Arch of Triumph*, *Joan of Arc* and *Under Capricorn*; the last, like the others, was not a critical success but earned Ingrid splendid reviews when it was released in September 1949. The three pictures were all personal disappointments, as she knew even while she was bringing so much to them. The final nagging disappointment was her inability to interest anyone in bringing *Of Lena Geyer* to the screen.

"I was scared to death that Hollywood would not like me," she had said on the eve of her departure from Sweden almost a decade earlier. Alas, she was soon to be proven right—but the dislike would eventually have to do with her private life, not her talents, and this she never anticipated.

That autumn, Ingrid was buoyed only by the thought that she might indeed go to Italy the following year to make a film with Roberto; he said that his production could easily be completed in less than two months, and in it she could speak any language she wished, since it would all be dubbed later in any case. He had also been sending Ingrid letter after letter since her return to California, spinning out more ideas for scenes in *Terra di Dio*, apologizing for his rambling and signing his letters "Yours devotedly, Roberto."

On November 20, for example, he wrote saying that he was at work, but some pages of the script were good, some bad, and next day some were good again. In fact, there was no script at all, for as usual he planned only vaguely, and with nothing on paper. On December 4, reminding him of their meeting when he plucked the flower's petals ("We make the film, we don't make it—we make it, we don't . . . "), Ingrid replied:

> Dear Mr. Rossellini,
>
> From today on, there are no more flowers for you to pluck. Now it is me saying, Good script, bad script, good script, bad—It does not matter! I am very happy.
>
> Ingrid Bergman.

As Christmas approached, she threw herself into holiday preparations. Pia, now ten, had begged for a bicycle, and Petter had given Ingrid the money to buy it. But when mother and daughter went to a department store to see the decorations and to visit Santa Claus, Pia's eyes were drawn to an enormous stuffed cow, wearing an apron and a maternal smile. It was Elsie Borden, a life-size advertisement for the milk company, and Pia at once said she wanted Elsie, not the bicycle. Nonsense, replied Petter when Ingrid told him: a stuffed cow for $75? No, that would not be right. A bicycle made more sense. Pia got the bicycle on Christmas morning and had to make do without Elsie Borden for a roommate.

At home, the holidays were the bleakest ever. Ingrid still said (although with less passion) that she would bear another child—a boy, she hoped, and perhaps they would name him Pelle. She and Petter celebrated the completion of the nursery addition to the house by a lavish dinner at Skandia, a celebrated Nordic restaurant on Sunset Boulevard.

But there was a terrible consequence to that evening, which they might have taken for an omen: a few hours after returning home, Petter became violently ill with food poisoning and suffered severe gastric distress (perhaps aggravated by stress) for almost a year thereafter. "Physical problems were thus added to my strange marital ones," he reflected years later.

But Ingrid's concern for Petter was overshadowed by a telephone call she received a few days into the new year. Just before his sixty-sixth birthday, Victor Fleming, on holiday with his wife and daughters in Arizona, dropped dead from a massive heart attack. Fleming was a hard-drinking chain-smoker with a choleric temper, and he had ignored warning signs for years. For days, Ingrid was inconsolable.

The afternoon of his burial, as if on cue, a telegram arrived at 1220 Benedict Canyon Drive. After having several requests rejected, Roberto Rossellini had at last obtained a visa and was en route to New York to receive an award. Could he not continue on to Hollywood to discuss their film?

Petter thought that was a splendid idea, and he went further, suggesting that Ingrid invite Rossellini to be their guest. Such an arrangement would certainly capture the respectful attention of producers like Samuel Goldwyn or Howard Hughes. More to the point, Rossellini's visit to their home would serve notice that Ingrid was planning her own future, talking to the most lionized foreign filmmaker of the day about a project the Lindstroms would supervise. In Hollywood, Petter added, they would never be regarded the same way again.

Chapter Thirteen

1949

HELMER: First and foremost, you are a wife and mother.

NORA: That I don't believe any more. I believe that first and
foremost I am an individual, just as much as you are.

HENRIK IBSEN,
A Doll's House

FOR A LONG TIME—LONGER PERHAPS THAN I EVER ADMITTED TO
myself—something had been dead inside me. I never knew
what it was exactly. Something was missing from my work, my life at
home—from my entire life, in fact. Yet whatever was wrong, it
wasn't wrong enough to force a change. Until Roberto."

The change in her life began at once, when he arrived in a flurry
of Hollywood hoopla. On Monday, January 17, ten days after Victor
Fleming was buried, Roberto stepped from the train in Los Angeles—the anniversary of his new life, he told waiting journalists
portentously, for this was the date on which he had begun filming
Open City. From there, it was a rush to Benedict Canyon and then to
a party at the home of director Billy Wilder.

Ingrid watched Roberto carefully that evening. She had the sudden realization that he was unimpressed with everything Hollywood represented, and this might stymie their joint efforts to raise American money. "I was uncontrollably nervous," Ingrid recalled. "I couldn't talk. I tried to light a cigarette, but my hand trembled so much that the flame died out." Despite the presence of a translator (and the fact that many of the guests were multilingual), Roberto simply nodded and smiled, ignoring the major producers, failing to compliment the big stars, and generally disregarding the complex rituals of adoration prescribed by the liturgy of Hollywood social life. "I don't need stars for my films," he said, "but I have nothing against Miss Bergman just because she is a star."

By curious irony, the result of the evening was that Wilder's guests took the impression they desired: shy Rossellini, he was just simply awed by all this attention! "The truth," according to one of his children, "was that my father always had a very strong hatred of Hollywood!"

He needed Hollywood money, in other words, but he did not like the people and felt they deserved no respect. In testimony of which he said, a week later, that he did not think Hollywood was really terrible, it was merely uninspiring: "It is a great place—like a sausage factory that turns out fine sausages. Still, I go back to Italy where I have freedom."

With the Lindstroms, Roberto was the quintessence of Latin charm. "He was so warm and outgoing," Ingrid recalled of their first weeks together, when he spoke in halting English. "When I was with him, I didn't feel shy or awkward or lonely. He was easy to talk to and interesting to listen to. Most of all, he was alive, and he made me feel alive."

And what did Roberto feel for Ingrid, besides need of her talent, besides her power to obtain American financing and to gain a wider audience for his next film? His love life never required time for passion to emerge, and so after only a week in the Lindstrom house he said he was, in his fashion, very much in love with her. "What [Roberto] was really interested in," said his friend and colleague Sergio Amidei, "was capturing Ingrid not so much to make a film but for love, because he was completely in love. There was also a little vanity involved." Doubtless more than a little: "Swedish women are the easiest in the world to impress," as he had told one of his mistresses.

Certainly it would be a harsh and unverifiable judgment on
Roberto Rossellini to label him a scheming seducer with only the
basest of motives; he had not the callousness for that. But his love
life was more than a tangle—it was a net of rather pathetic semi-
detachments. In this regard, it is difficult not to see a jumble of
motivations at work in Rossellini as he moved toward Ingrid. He
needed cash; he wanted a confirmation of his prestige; he longed to
acquire a new postwar audience worldwide. Ingrid Bergman was
without question one of the two or three great, bankable stars of the
day, and he would have been a fool not to recognize (as eventually
he must have) that she was also a great artist.

So was Anna Magnani, to be sure. But Roberto had wearied of
Magnani's transference of drama from art to life: everything, for
her, had taken on the flavor of a very bad verismo opera. All was
violence and tears, recriminations and threats, mad love duets and
hysterical outpourings of grief. And so he had, like a character in
a forgotten music drama, casually left her when he went to America to receive the New York Film Critics' Award and to see Ingrid.
He went to Magnani's home and offered to take two of her dogs
for a walk, but he handed them over to the porter of a nearby
hotel with instructions to return them to the owner. Next day,
without revisiting Anna or telling her of his plans, Rossellini left
Italy.

His exit was perhaps unworthy of him, for Rossellini had been
planning another film for Magnani, something called *Aria di Roma*,
that year. "We spent months getting everything ready to start shooting the picture," Magnani told an American writer, and her assertions are supported by Italian press clippings of the time.

> The story was prepared, the cast selected, the contract with the
> producer signed. Then, in the midst of everything, Roberto sud-
> denly left for the United States and Ingrid Bergman! I don't
> reproach him for his treatment of me as a woman. But I do
> resent his insult to me as an artist.

Unlike Petter Lindstrom, who for weal and woe was reliable and
consistent, Roberto Rossellini was a man of many personalities. And

very much in his life, and in his relationship to Ingrid Bergman, has been too blithely explained (even excused) in light of Rossellini's presumed "genius." Herein lies an arguable premise.

At a specific moment in Italian history, Rossellini made a noble virtue out of brute necessity. With very few of the resources of traditional moviemaking, he had made *Open City* and *Paisà* and so given cinema history a fashionable new word—neorealism, as if it were a method brilliantly incarnated by a rigorous theorist. (The clarion call and the basic theory had already been articulated by the writer Cesare Zavattini, the great collaborator of Vittorio de Sica.) But it is critical to note that Federico Fellini provided the story, the through-line for the characters and most of the dialogue for *Open City*. Rossellini knew what to do with his camera when blessed with artists like Magnani, Fellini and company: he did very little, as he said. The camera was to be a humble observer.

After *Open City*, there had been problems. *Paisà* had its moments of grandeur and certainly was a worthy tribute to the triumph of the human spirit. But if good intentions make for great art, all the saints would be aesthetes, and *Paisà* suffered from a surfeit of ideas and a lack of what might be called artistic economy. After that, *Germania, anno zero* (*Germany, Year Zero*) was a war-horror story, a terse and tense depiction of decadence in Berlin at the end of the war that mistook frightful gloominess for profundity.

Magnani was powerful for him again, in *Una voce humana* (*The Human Voice*), but that was a straightforward rendering of the Cocteau play. As for *Il Miracolo* (*The Miracle*), its virtues owed yet again to Magnani, to Fellini (both writer and actor in it) and to Tullio Pinelli, who cooperated with Fellini on the story. Of *La Macchina ammazzacattivi* (*The Machine That Killed Bad People*), the less said the better—as even Rossellini knew, for he abandoned it.

This, then (apart from some early short films and collaborations), was what later academics often called Roberto Rossellini's oeuvre up to the time he met Ingrid. It was a respectable output, to be sure, but even considering the admirable sum of his life's work, it is at least tenable that Rossellini lacked the soaring imagination of Fellini or the lyrical humanism of Vittorio de Sica. It is a fine thing to have given the world one or two brilliant works, but

perhaps this does not justify the hyperbolic admiration of his
fiercest partisans.*

These are important considerations in light of Rossellini's precipitous arrival in Hollywood and his suave courting of Ingrid
Bergman. Over two months, they spent most of each day together,
listening to music, jumbling their English and French while Roberto
taught Ingrid elementary Italian, driving to Malibu for lunch, dining
openly (why not?) with Roberto even when Petter's schedule prevented him joining them—and talking about *Terra di Dio*.

HUMAN MOTIVATIONS ARE RARELY UNDILUTED; FOR INGRID, TO BE
sure, Roberto offered both a passport to freedom and the promise
of new creative life. He was also (at least at the outset) an exciting
mentor, and he could be a warm, caring father—to her as well as to
his progeny. But people rarely act only from disinterested devotion.
Once that is admitted—once, in other words, one does not expect
this pair of lovers to have acted out of heroic, fairy-tale, undiluted
love for each other, with no thought of their own benefits—then
one is free to understand the ardor that linked Ingrid to Roberto, to
sympathize with their respective frailties and needs, and yet to see
that they were embarking on a road that was doomed to be twisted
and finally lead to a dead end.

There was one overarching problem from the start. She knew
absolutely nothing of his moods and whims, the utter turmoil and
battle he created to get through life with gusto. "He needed stormy
weather," said his friend Liana Ferri. "Unless there was a hurricane
blowing and he was building barricades and fighting battles, he was
bored." Roberto began a project, a friendship, an idea, was mad
with enthusiasm—and promptly forgot everything about it the next
day. "His personality was impossible to understand," Ferri continued, "since Roberto would kill someone with kindness on Monday
and kill him with coldness and disinterest on Tuesday." Of all this
Ingrid was ignorant.

But one friend, Leo McCarey, knew a great deal about

---

*Rossellini's late work in the documentary genre and for television deserves separate
consideration, and it must be admitted that these are very fine teaching tools. He was, it
should be noted, a first-rate classroom instructor in the last years of his life.

Rossellini, and he invited Ingrid for lunch one day when Roberto
was visiting a museum with the Italian cultural society. "Ingrid," he
said, "you're falling for him just because he's the opposite of Lindstrom. Go to Vienna, and you'll find guys with the flowers and the
hand-kissing bit who make Rossellini look like an amateur." She was
deaf to his advice.

Ever the amorous swain, Roberto was sometimes brilliant and
audacious, at other times wily and irresponsible. He was never
vicious and always intemperate, and he considered himself the
world's great lover, who blessed empty lives by the sheer force of his
presence. Ingrid, therefore, was both challenge and prize. She was
intense and intelligent, vivacious, intuitive and amusing. And she
belonged to Petter, a man who seemed not to appreciate the extent
of these qualities—who saw, indeed, only her failings, and who but
rarely expressed the slightest admiration for anything she accomplished.

In more than two thousand pages of letters to Ingrid, relatives,
friends and the press; of reflections written for publication and for
his own projected (but unrealized) book; of notes and personal
papers about his life with Ingrid in which he attempted to tell his
"side" of the story of 1949 and 1950, there cannot be found forthcoming from Petter Lindstrom a single word of admiration for the
sensibilities and talents of the woman he had, presumably for good
reasons, chosen for his wife a dozen years earlier. "Not bad" had
been his highest praise for her work during those years. When
Roberto Rossellini arrived, spinning a story about spiritual enlight-
enment and saying it needed Ingrid to give it life, what could she do
but spring to the moment? What could she do but link her destiny
to his? She could not see the possibility of future disappointment;
she gave herself fully to the present.

What was asked of Ingrid, she sensed at once, was loyalty and
deference to Rossellini's needs—which at the moment meant finding a generous producer. Samuel Goldwyn had for a long time been
eager to sign Ingrid for a picture, and so she arranged for a meeting
at his office with her and Roberto. Goldwyn tried to follow the outline of Terra di Dio and said he would be willing to support it if, of
course, Rossellini prepared the usual shooting script and production
schedule.

"Oh, he won't have a script, even when we start shooting," said Ingrid sweetly, forestalling a severer reply from Roberto. "But he knows precisely what he'll do and what dialogue and actors he'll use. I found that out in our talks." Putting that aside for the moment, Goldwyn asked to see one of Rossellini's earlier films. Fine idea, said Ingrid, believing that would win him over. Goldwyn threw a screening party at his home, and when the lights dimmed, there was Rossellini's choice: *Germania, anno zero*, the relentlessly bleak movie he had filmed on the streets of Berlin after *Paisà*. At the end of the evening, Goldwyn and his guests were numb with depression, and he at once withdrew his offer of support for a new production.

When word of the project reached Howard Hughes, the new owner of RKO, he quickly stepped in to make a deal. Ingrid and Petter would receive $175,000, Rossellini $150,000, and Hughes would have American rights to the picture and a share of foreign profits. He was not much excited by the austere story Ingrid described, but he was still keen on her, and he stipulated that after *Terra di Dio*, Ingrid would come back to Hollywood and do a second picture for RKO with a more sensible setting and a more appealing wardrobe—a project, in other words, better suited for his new business partner, Ingrid Bergman.

THE DEAL WAS PICKED UP BY THE INTERNATIONAL PRESS AND SO CAME to the attention of Anna Magnani, who at once swung into action and announced that she would produce and star in (of all things) a picture about a woman on a volcanic island; with no mention of *Terra di Dio* or its principals, she said that her *Volcano* would be ready for release before the end of the year. But to her great credit, the peppery Magnani—who now realized that she had been permanently supplanted by Ingrid—never uttered an unpleasant word about either her lover or her rival. Her public behavior about the situation, and about Roberto's abrupt abandonment of her, was forever impeccable. And despite the odds, Ingrid Bergman and Anna Magnani never met during all their years in Rome.

To celebrate the RKO deal and to thank Petter for his hospitality, Roberto wanted to buy presents for the family and for his own son, too—but to do so he had (as usual) to borrow cash, this time from his host, who gave him $300. Ingrid and Roberto went shopping, and he bought ties for Petter and a handbag for Ingrid before spotting what he thought was the perfect gift for Pia: a huge stuffed toy, a cow with a broad smile and an apron. Good God, no, Ingrid said—but Roberto as usual had his way, and that evening the delighted Pia welcomed Elsie as her roommate at last. Petter's reaction has not been documented.

ON FEBRUARY 28, ROBERTO DEPARTED FOR ROME TO PREPARE FOR *Terra di Dio* and Ingrid's arrival. She and Petter then took a brief ski holiday in Aspen, where they settled on plans to meet in Italy in late May, after the film's completion.

"I would say that our relationship at the time was one of affection and matrimonial bliss," he said later, at his divorce trial, perhaps causing waves of surprise among those who knew the Lindstroms. But that was the belief of the American press and public as they still worshipped at Ingrid's shrine: "Wholesome as a girl scout, happy wife and mother, she can play a saint . . . Bergman's family life is a model of connubial felicity [and] not a breath of scandal has smirched the Lindstroms." To which Ingrid replied, as if sounding a note of caution, "I cannot understand why people think I'm pure and full of nobleness. Every human being has shades of bad and good."

"Nobody could have lived up to that unreal image people had created of me," Ingrid Bergman said years later. And in a very true sense, that unreal image began with Selznick: "I wanted to keep Ingrid on a pedestal," he had said, "and I insist upon keeping her on that pedestal." Ingrid added:

And when people saw that I did not perfectly fit that image, they felt betrayed and all hell broke loose. They decided that I had planned so much deception all along, and that when I left my husband and daughter I had no intentions of ever coming back— that I wanted to go to Italy and be a star, and to hell with everything else. But why would I have gone to Italy and to Rossellini if I wanted to be a big star? That would have been the worst possible thing to do! In Hollywood, I was being offered the best scripts and the best directors in 1949—Hitchcock, Huston,

Wyler, Mankiewicz, they all wanted to work with me. But I wanted something else. I wanted to expand my talents.

On March 11—two weeks ahead of her original schedule— Ingrid departed for Rome, stopping first for a week in New York to visit Irene Selznick, in whose apartment she slipped on a freshly polished floor and bruised her head on the edge of an air-condi- tioner. "It must have been symbolic!" Ingrid wrote to Irene later. "The fallen star!" Which is how she was regarded in America soon after her arrival in Rome on March 20.

In light of the subsequent furore, it was presumed that when Ingrid departed Beverly Hills, she blithely left her husband and abandoned her ten-year-old daughter, never intending to return— or at least to return only after she had set in motion the circum- stances that would make a divorce inevitable. But nothing in her actions supports a presumption of such callousness. This was to be simply a new experience: she was going to make a film in Italy with a man she loved, and with whom she would perhaps have an affair (which may have already begun in Beverly Hills).

Would it last forever? Her growing knowledge of Roberto sug- gested it might not, but her sight line did not, in any case, extend to forever. "Do I know if this is my big chance at happiness?" she wrote in a letter to one of Petter's sisters later that year. "I take it as the big adventure, but who knows how it will end? Petter and I have grown apart. He took me as a little girl and formed me, taught me everything. But now I want to grow, and Petter doesn't want to fly where I want to fly.

"You see, I am a migratory bird," she continued.

Ever since I was a little girl, I have looked for new things—I have longed for big adventures. Whatever I had, saw and experienced was never enough. I have always tried to blast away triviality to find happiness, but I never knew what would give me happiness and peace. I sought and sought, changed and changed. And it was the same thing with my work. I tried to change the roles, change my type, move from studio to studio, find new people to work with, who could develop me and help me reach my goal of matu- rity. And Petter knew how restless I was.

Then I met Rossellini, and in him I found another migratory bird. He grew up like a wildcat, and is never completely satisfied with anything. What is said about his women is no exaggeration, either. But now he has met someone who he says understands him. And with him I have the world I wanted to see . . .

With Fleming and *Joan*, there had been not a whisper in the press. But Fleming had not lived in her home, dined with her every night, gazed adoringly at her while surrounded by Hollywood society. Already, gossips in and out of print were stirring the cauldron of rumor. At the time, she calculated nothing except the "big adventure" of Italy, Rossellini, *Terra di Dio*, the conjunction of work and love, and tutorials beside another father-with-a-camera.

"She had no idea of what would occur," her third husband, Lars Schmidt, said decades later. "Of course she and Lindstrom knew the marriage was over, but how they would deal with that was not yet clear to them. The idea that she intended to leave her daughter forever is absurd. After all, she had just made a film in London, and her husband and daughter had visited her there—she had every reason to believe that would happen again." And of course there had been similar separations before—most notably in 1939, when she left Petter and Pia for Hollywood and *Intermezzo*, and in 1946, when she was on Broadway.

In addition, Ingrid arrived in Rome with little cash and a modest wardrobe; because of Italy's uncertain weather in early spring, she had prudently brought along the fur coat she hardly ever needed in Hollywood. "She came to [Italy] with barely a change of clothes," said Art Cohn, the American writer who accompanied Rossellini when Ingrid arrived in Rome, and who worked with him on the screenplay for the picture. "She might have made some money in her day, but she showed no signs of having any now. I don't think she has any—and I won't say who has what I think she should have." Even Lindstrom admitted that Ingrid's departure suggested her eventual return: "The last thing she did before leaving was to select the wallpaper for the new nursery. We had made plans for a second child [to be conceived some time later that year.]" In other words, she believed she might be away three or four months at the most.

*   *   *

THE ITALIAN RECEPTION FOR INGRID WAS ANYTHING BUT HOSTILE: after the grave deprivations of wartime, the subsequent Allied occupation and the widespread destitution and corruption in postwar Rome, Rossellini had brought back the biggest star in the world. In no time, Ingrid was Rome's great trophy, the spoils of romantic warfare. "One had the feeling," said Federico Fellini, "that she was like a fairy godmother who had just come to Rome. One could expect anything from her. She could work miracles for us, like a Walt Disney character. This is what made her so fascinating."

Thus—alerted by Howard Hughes, who thought it good publicity for the film—a wild swarm of cameramen and journalists rushed toward Ingrid as she descended from the airplane in Rome toward midnight on March 20. Roberto elbowed their way past, punched a few photographers and whisked Ingrid into his red Cisitalia sports car. An hour later, she was introduced to Roberto's friends at a reception at the Excelsior Hotel, and it was almost dawn when she went upstairs to her suite, adjacent to his (the cost for everything paid for by RKO).

Four days later, Roberto and Ingrid were speeding south from Rome. They stopped for Ingrid to sample the bracing wine of Frascati; they stood silently near the bombed ruins of the abbey of Monte Cassino; they drove into the narrow, crowded streets of Naples and gazed over the blue waters of the gulf. Then they drove further south to Amalfi, where they took rooms at the Albergo Luna Convento, a hotel that was once a monastery. Overlooking the sea, with quiet cloister gardens and a medieval tower that had been turned into a dining room, the inn provided the only serenity the couple would know amid the coming months of frantic and uncomfortable activity. Ingrid was not the first to be seduced by both the Albergo and by Roberto's amorous attentions.

"I knew Roberto was in love again," said Marilyn Buferd a few weeks later, when she was in Amalfi. "He was offering the same dream, only with tassels and festoons of fairy lore on it. Don't get me wrong. He meant every word of it. He believed in it himself. But I could repeat, almost phrase by magic phrase, what he was saying [to Ingrid]. And believe me, it's wonderful. It's a grand experience, and even if a Rossellini romance is only a one-day butterfly, it's terrific while it lasts. Ingrid would have had to be made of stone not to be caught up and swept away by it." In this case, Ingrid would be the longest romance of his life—but it, too, had a short lease.

Marilyn was not the only visitor to Amalfi to note the cooing lovebirds. A photographer caught them in an incautious moment, holding hands (fingers intertwined) and strolling along the rampart of a ruined castle—just the right pose, in other words, that looked so good on a page of *Life* magazine at the end of April. Ingrid had not anticipated that her private life would be the leading news of the day, all over the world. But now the Italian spring of Ingrid and Roberto recalled the European summer of Edward VIII, King of England, and the American divorcée Wallis Simpson: in 1937, they had been observed walking and swimming together on holiday. Cameras, microphones, jotting pads and what was perceived as "the public's right to know" had made privacy all but obsolete.

There at the Albergo—appropriately in the room where Ibsen was said to have written *A Doll's House*—Ingrid took up a pen on April 3. On hotel stationery, she wrote a letter to her husband that was a manifesto worthy of Ibsen's Nora, who had closed the door on one life to open another.

Dear Petter,

It will be very difficult for you to read this letter and it is difficult for me to write it. But I believe it is the only way. I would like to explain everything from the beginning, but you know enough, and I would like to ask forgiveness, but that seems ridiculous. It is not all together my fault and how can you forgive that I want to stay with Roberto. I know he has also written you and told you all that there is to tell. It was not my intention to fall in love and go to Italy forever. After all our plans and dreams, you know that is true. But how can I help it or change it? You saw in Hollywood how my enthusiasm for Roberto grew and grew and you know how much alike we are with the same desire for the same kind of work and the same understanding of life. I thought maybe I could conquer the feeling I had for him when I saw him in his own milieu, so different from mine. But it turned out just the opposite. The people, the life, the country is not strange, it is what I always wanted. I had not the courage to talk more about him at home than I did with you, as it all seemed so incredible, like

an adventure, and at the time I didn't realize the depths of his feelings. My
Petter, I know how this letter falls like a bomb on our house, our Pelle, our
future, our past so filled with sacrifice and help on your part. And now you
stand alone in the ruins and I am unable to help you. Poor, dear papa, but
also poor dear

Mama.

Roberto had indeed written to Petter, insisting that it was not
their intention to hurt his feelings and asking him to agree to an
amicable divorce.

For the rest of his long and fruitful life, Petter Lindstrom never
recovered from this blow, nor did his resentment ever diminish;
alas, it became an obsession. He felt he had been, as his friend Åke
Sandler said almost half a century later, "jilted before the whole
world." The marriage had been long over, and they both knew it.
But with a finality Petter had not expected, Ingrid rose to the occasion and, perhaps for the first time, took resolute action. Petter had
lost his control at last. The measure of Rossellini's triumph was the
measure of Lindstrom's defeat.

ON APRIL 4, ROBERTO, INGRID AND A CREW LOADED MOVIE EQUIP-
ment, food and a few staples into a rickety schooner and headed
into the Tyrrhenian Sea. Four hours later, the black cone of Stromboli's two-thousand-foot-high live volcano pierced through its fetid
vapors, and then they could see the barren hillsides and the squat,
chalk-white hovels of the impoverished peasants who supported
their families with a wretched living as fishermen. Life was primitive, isolated and without any modern conveniences like plumbing,
electricity, newspapers or radios. "All this talk about authenticity is
swell," muttered Harold Lewis, production chief for Howard
Hughes, who arrived as troubleshooter, "but you sure can overdo
it." Indeed. Stromboli would have been more appropriate for a
penal colony than a movie crew. The film could only be made
because Roberto had brought along his own generator. Said Ingrid
not long after, "I wanted to flee from it, just as the heroine in the
picture did when she first saw it."

The story Rossellini wanted to tell was becoming more and
more, in his spontaneous filming of it, an emblem of his reading of

Ingrid's relationship to himself. She was Karin, a displaced person whose only hope for escape from the prison of her past life is offered by a man who takes her away to Stromboli where, after initial happiness, she thinks she has made a grievous error and is more displaced than ever. "I'm a civilized person," Karin shouts to her husband before collapsing in tears. "I'm used to a different life!" (The role of her husband was played by Mario Vitale, a darkly handsome fisherman Roberto had brought over from Salerno as they were en route to Stromboli.) Only in her attempt at flight and her subsequent mysterious epiphany does she accept that her destiny is to remain with the man who has freed her.

INGRID WAS HOUSED IN A FOUR-ROOM STUCCO HOVEL RENTED FROM the village teacher. When she wanted to bathe, she called out to an assistant, who poured a bucket of sea water down on her through a hole in the room. Food had to be shipped in from the mainland, and most of it was tinned goods or pasta, which the local ladies prepared for the cast and crew—most of whom Rossellini picked up according to his usual method, wandering around the island and tapping natives ("You will stand here and look there . . . You will carry this . . . You will take this over there," and so forth).

Ingrid felt isolated as never before. She had thrown her fortunes in with Rossellini because she wanted to do something completely different, and now she certainly was. She had been trained and prepared according to the careful procedures of traditional moviemaking, and now she was the odd woman out. Rossellini dragged in his amateurs, whom he treated like professionals, while Ingrid the professional was treated like a rank amateur. "You can have these realistic pictures!" she shouted at Rossellini a few weeks into the shooting. "To hell with them! These people don't even know what dialogue is! They don't know where to stand! They don't care what they're doing! I can't bear to work another day with you!" With that, Rossellini took her aside, worked his persuasive charm, and Ingrid returned to the set, mollified and, somehow, eager again to please the lord and master.

"He doesn't need actors to make pictures," she said more calmly later. "He just makes pictures naturally—with people." Throughout the production, Ingrid was told not to act, to tone everything down, to dress in whatever fitted her that turned up that day in someone's house.

"I thought we had trouble on 'Arch,' 'Joan' and 'Capricorn,'" Ingrid wrote Joe Steele on May 12. "But this way of making a realistic picture leaves you dead by the realistic roadside. And to have only amateurs to play with when you have as little patience as I have! But all the hardships and bad weather I take gladly when I work with somebody that is really remarkable . . . He writes the dialogue just before the scene. He chooses his people a couple of hours before the work. He is full of new ideas. His violence, if something goes wrong, can only be compared to the volcano in the background. His tenderness and humor come like a surprise immediately after. I understand well that people call him crazy. But so are all people called, if they dare to be different, and those are the people I always loved, isn't that so?"

She had, then, made a decision, and she accepted its consequences—even to the difficulties of making the picture. She had no stunt double, so she had to walk on sharp rocks in the water and climb up the side of the volcano. These she did gamely, although the sulfuric fumes burned her eyes and throat, took her breath away and nauseated her for days.

BY THE END OF APRIL, THE RUMORS OF ROMANCE HAD BEEN SUFFIciently reported for reporters to find their way to the island. "I do not choose to answer," replied Roberto matter-of-factly when one asked him if he intended to marry Ingrid. "I neither confirm nor deny. I have nothing to say as yet." His denial was very close to a loud affirmation.

And then things happened quickly.

On April 29, Petter Lindstrom arrived in Rome en route to Messina, Sicily, where Ingrid was to meet him two days later. "I have come to Italy primarily because Ingrid's letters kept telling me of the unusual beauty of this country," he said to reporters who must have wanted to laugh aloud. "Then, also, I have come to see and embrace my wife, with whom I am tied by bonds of indissoluble affection." Well, yes—but . . .

Ingrid and Petter were reunited for a discussion in a gloomy little inn during the afternoon and evening of May 1 and the morning of May 2. During the entire time of their meetings, Roberto paced and fumed in the dining room and the hallways—and for several hours, furious with jealousy, he raced his sports car under their windows. Fearing that Ingrid would be persuaded to go home with Petter, he sent them a note threatening to drive his car into a tree and kill himself if she should be reconciled to her husband, but by this time Ingrid was accustomed to his melodramatics and ignored him. Kay Brown, shipped out on orders from her boss, Lew Wasserman at MCA, arrived to find Ingrid "lost and wan and bewildered."

"There will be no divorce," Petter told newsmen at the Messina railway station as he headed back to Rome. "There is no reason for dissension between us." Nothing could have been further from the truth, of course, but Petter said he believed that this affair would pass like the others, and that Ingrid, ever dependent on him, would return humbled to where she belonged.

Ingrid had told Petter what they had both known for years: that their marriage was over. Now, she wanted a divorce, for she intended to marry Roberto; to that end, Rossellini, too, had begun the process of ending his marriage. How, she wondered, could Petter want it any other way? They both knew that their marriage had been only a legality for years. And if there was indeed anything like affection between them, why would he want them both and their Pia to be subjected to the relentless glare of unwelcome publicity? Should they not put the marriage behind them as quickly, quietly and amicably as possible and move on with their lives?

Would that not, most of all, be much better for Pia's sake? Their names were already in the world's newspapers and magazines daily: if the matter were settled with all dispatch, the press would soon lose interest and Ingrid would be able to return to Beverly Hills within a few weeks to reassure Pia that she was not losing her mother. Pia had been raised in Hollywood, after all, and knew about divorce. This need not mean she had to see rancor between her parents. Perhaps, too, Ingrid remembered herself as a child, and did not want the circumstances revisited on her own daughter: she had been raised by a father only. Yes, she would probably live in Italy with Roberto, but Pia could spend her summer vacations with her mother, and certainly there could be visits by both of them back and forth during the rest of the year. Ingrid begged Petter to be reasonable and understanding. Clearly, there was no marital bond between them any longer; clearly, too, Petter had neither religious nor philosophical objections to the formal dissolution of the marriage.

But she did not take fully into account his fierce obstinacy: on the one hand, he did not want the public opprobrium of losing Ingrid Bergman to another man. But at the same time, Petter insisted, as she swore later, that "he didn't love me and didn't want me back even if I tried. He told me it delighted him to see me cry and suffer and [it] would make me understand how much he had suffered." Of course, he eventually did agree to a divorce, but he had no intention of making things easy for her. Over all the years to come, Ingrid alone bore public vilification for breaking her marriage, for abandoning her daughter and causing her the pain of unwanted celebrity. And because Ingrid had left her daughter, the child—forlorn and confused—had no evidence to the contrary. In the final analysis, Pia was the one most wounded. The success of her later life attests to her own remarkable inner strength, and to her ability to forgive and reconcile when forgiveness was asked for and reconciliation extended to her.

IT IS LIKELY THAT MUCH OF THIS BITTERNESS COULD HAVE BEEN avoided had Petter agreed to an expeditious resolution to a situation that he protracted for another year. Before they parted, he did agree to meet Ingrid a few weeks later in London; meantime, he would visit Sweden and discuss the possibility of divorce terms with the lawyer Cyril Holm. For the present, Petter agreed to nothing; he said only that he would like the matter to be resolved outside Italy. And then nothing happened for too long. "If Mr. Lindstrom had readily consented when Ingrid first asked him for a divorce," Roberto was right to say later that year, "I am sure we would have been spared all the criticism which has been poured on us."

"I have seen nothing but bad press from all over the world," Ingrid added in her letter to Joe Steele. "Here, we have been continually hunted. The photographers have been everywhere. It makes me so terribly unhappy that Petter and Pia must suffer for my sins. And also that the people involved in 'Joan of Arc' may suffer. I can't imagine that 'Capricorn' will, because I'm not a saint in it."

As for Petter, she elaborated in a second letter to Joe on May 30: "I cannot go back home with him. Tell me if it is true [as Petter had told her] that [Joan] is falling off [in box-office business] because of my scandal. To me it seems such hypocrisy to go against your true feelings for business reasons. In the end, people would hate me even more because I was afraid the truth would hurt my career . . . Well, I don't worry about myself, but the future of Pia and Petter alone, and the work of RR. That is enough to make me afraid." As for being honest before the world, Ingrid (naively if bravely) spoke freely to one journalist who accosted her: "We have been trying to keep it quiet. There will be a statement when we are ready."

Her remark, of course, reached Hollywood within hours, and there Howard Hughes announced that he wanted the film finished as quickly as possible. Eager to cash in on all the publicity, he announced that the picture would be released under the title *Stromboli*, and he designed an advertising campaign that showed Ingrid against the background of an erupting volcano. Subtle good taste was evidently not his strong suit. Now even *Time* magazine jumped in with an essay, "Fantasy on the Black Island." Petter was quoted as saying that Italy was a beautiful country but "too full of fantasies," and the article reminded readers that the crater of Stromboli was in ancient days known as the gateway to purgatory.

AND THEN TWO THINGS HAPPENED ON THE SAME DAY—A CONFLUENCE of events that no writer would have dared to insert even into the most hackneyed romance.

On June 6, Ingrid learned that yes, she was most definitely pregnant; she expected to deliver some time in late January or early February.

And that evening, the volcano of Stromboli erupted, pouring ash and steam into the sky and onto the inhabitants and visitors below. Fortunately, the ooze of lava streamed down only the north-western slopes, away from the village.

The eruption prevented Ingrid from proceeding to London, where she had promised to meet Petter. When he returned to California, he knew only about the inconvenience of the volcano: the pregnancy was revealed to no one for an astonishingly long time, although some sniffed a hint when Art Cohn and Joe Steele floated the news that Ingrid was so tired from the production that she might indeed take a year's rest afterward—or maybe two years of rest.

Petter, meanwhile, wanted Ingrid to know the discomfort her life was causing him. "The hyenas have been hunting me from hospital to hospital, asking about your romance," he wrote from Los Angeles. And then he issued an indirect indictment of Ingrid, introduced his trump card, Pia, and revived the sting of guilt that Ingrid had felt for placing her career before everything (in the manner of Lena Geyer).

> Our girl, I think, is unaware of the issue. I have never been closer to her in my life than the last two weeks and I am going to make up for the time I have wasted in less important things. She is now in Minneapolis [for a summer holiday, with the wife of their business manager]. I shall try hard to give her a feeling of security ahead of the threatening storm ... Some time ago, you told 'Life' you could never be married to a director. Now what freedom and independence do you think you can get?

His comments hit the mark, and Ingrid, almost hysterical with remorse, ran to Roberto. Were they wrong in their actions and plans? Would she lose her daughter? Nonsense, said Roberto: no parent loses a child who does not want to be lost. In time, he said, Pia will understand.

But precisely because of the way the matter was handled over the next two years, Pia never did understand—indeed, how could she? She was first neglected, then used at home, used in letters and used in court: this once winsome and cheerful child became (her own word) "miserable—there is no other term for it." She became the chief supporting player in the regular installments of the melodrama continuing in the pages of the world's newspapers and magazines. For the rest of her life, Ingrid regretted only one aspect of the circumstances of her divorce: the prolonged estrangement from her daughter, which of course could not be foreseen in 1949. Each time

Ingrid planned to return to America, circumstances made that impossible; each time she planned to welcome Pia to Europe, obstacles made that impracticable. She did not wish to be shut out of her daughter's life for so long: she *was* shut out of her daughter's life for so long.

"I thought sensible people could get divorced and be reasonable about everything," Ingrid said later. "It never entered my head that I'd encounter such bitterness and that I'd lose Pia. I thought she'd be with me some of the time and her father the rest of the time. I thought he and I could remain friends. Was I wrong to believe it would be that way? Aren't lots of people divorced, and don't they behave decently to one another?"

By June, things were out of control—the film, her life and practically every relationship in it. She was also, by now, as completely under Roberto's dominance as she had been under Petter's.

But she did not forget her daughter. "Our life, Pia dear, will change," she wrote that summer.

> The difference is that you'll stay more with Papa, and Mama will be away like so many times before, but this time she'll be away for an even longer time [but] it doesn't mean we'll never see each other. You'll come to me for your vacation. We'll have fun and make trips together. You must never forget that I love Papa and I love you, and that cannot be changed. But sometimes people like to live with somebody else that is not their proper family. That is a separation or a divorce. I know we talked about how many of your friends had divorced parents. It is nothing unusual but it is rather sad . . . Write to me and I'll write to you, and the time will go so fast—I hope—until we meet again.

Although there was great misery in all this for several years, this was due neither to an act of cruelty on Ingrid's part nor deliberate abandonment. From the start, she expected to be able to arrange visits for herself and her daughter and expected to spend more of what would later be called "quality time" with Pia than she ever had. But there were terrible miscalculations in that expectation. Years later, other actresses conceived or gave birth out of wedlock. But Catherine Deneuve, Vanessa Redgrave, Susan Sarandon,

Madonna and many others were rightly allowed to be the sole judges of their private lives and did not suffer public opprobrium—nor, it must be admitted, did they leave other children to have new ones. In 1949, Ingrid's situation was very different; and, alas, things would get worse for her in 1950.

"I should have handled the entire situation with Roberto Rossellini with more discretion," she said years later, assuming the entire responsibility, which he shared. "But I didn't know that I belonged to the American people, and that everybody had a right to tell me what to do and how to behave in my private life. A movie star is a ridiculous commercial product. People said that once I was the perfect model of a wife and mother. They saw me in *Joan of Arc* and thought I was a saint. I'm not. I'm just a human being. And the result was that I always felt guilty—my entire life." Nor did she deny the appropriateness of some of that guilt.

Joan of Arc was branded a witch and burned at the stake in one quick miscarriage of justice. Ingrid of Hollywood was branded a whore and unjustly burned in the fires of public castigation for years. Only she could assess the extent of what depth of remorse was just, what level neurotic. But the court of public opinion decided for her, and the punishment was very nearly capital.

The judgment began during the early days of production on *Stromboli*, when Ingrid received a letter from Joseph I. Breen, director of the Motion Picture Production Code administration—the self-appointed watchdog for the moral purity of America. "In recent days," he began

> the American newspapers have carried, rather widely, a story to the effect that you are about to divorce your husband, forsake your child, and marry Roberto Rossellini.
>
> It goes without saying that these reports are the cause of great consternation among large numbers of our people who have come to look upon you as the first lady of the screen—both individually and artistically. On all hands, I hear nothing but expressions of profound shock that you have any such plans . . .
>
> Such stories will not only not react favorably to your picture, but may very well *destroy your career as a motion picture artist.* They may result in the American public becoming so thoroughly

enraged that your pictures will be ignored, and your box-office value ruined.

Even Walter Wanger climbed aboard the moralistic bandwagon in a singularly high-toned telegram. Fearful that the success of *Joan of Arc* would be endangered, that there would be a boycott by church and educational groups, he complained:

> I have made a huge investment endangering my future and that of my family which you are jeopardizing if you do not behave . . . We both have a responsibility to Victor Fleming's memory [!!!] and to all the people that believe in us . . . Do not fool yourself by thinking that what you are doing is of such courageous proportions or so artistic as to excuse [yourself].

Later, Ingrid may have found grim amusement in Wanger's hypocrisy. He found his wife, actress Joan Bennett, in bed with her lover and agent Jennings Lang—and reacted by grabbing a loaded revolver and wounding Lang in the groin. The trio then realized that once this news was broadcast, their careers might also suffer a serious injury, and so Bennett and Wanger trundled the bleeding Lang into their car and took him to a parking lot in Beverly Hills, where Lang had put his own car. There, the three staged an elaborate scene that, when police were summoned, made it seem as if Lang, mistaking his own car for Wanger's, had tried to enter it and had been caught in the act by Wanger—who understandably pulled a revolver to protect his property from a "thief." Lang recovered, and the Wanger family's investment was for the moment secure. Hurray for Hollywood.

LETTERS OF CONDEMNATION FOR INGRID POURED IN BY THE THOU-sands and tens of thousands. She had been known as a loyal wife and a good mother, people cried. How could she remotely consider such a change? "So if I had been a bad wife and mother, this would be all right?" she asked cogently. "Am I being punished for having been a good wife?" But it was no time for logic or restraint, much less kindness. The lines were drawn, and no quarter was to be given.

And then something occurred that Breen might have regarded

as a caution from heaven. On the final two days of shooting the film, August 1 and 2, Roberto directed Ingrid to climb the side of the volcano. But she was so overcome by the fumes that she slipped, sliding several hundred feet down a rocky incline until her legs and arms were badly scraped and bleeding. Indeed, she was fortunate to have avoided a miscarriage. Still, she fared better than a production engineer named Ludovici Muratori, who was so exhausted by his task at the crater's edge that he collapsed and died of a heart attack. *Stromboli* was certainly not, as Hitchcock said of the craft, "only a movie"—it was a series of discomforts and disasters. And however much its finale was recut by RKO before its release, the picture has no rhythm, pacing, emotional conviction or philosophical clarity.

Rossellini's method, so successful in *Open City*, when he had a firm script by Fellini, had fatally tripped him up. *Stromboli* was not controversial, it was merely monumentally tedious. Of the director's good intentions there can be no doubt, but noble struggles—men against nature, displaced persons trying to find identity, lonely souls crying to God—do not necessarily make for compelling drama. And because Rossellini was entirely the master of *Stromboli*, because there was so little collaboration, the singular vision became myopic.

As for their finances once the picture was completed in August, life did not improve much simply because they quit *Stromboli* for Rome. There were a few more comforts in Rossellini's sprawling, ten-room apartment at 49 via Bruno Buozzi, but not much cash for luxuries.

The first portions of Ingrid's salary for *Stromboli* had been paid jointly to her and Petter in California, and she readily gave up her share of that for Pia's support. In addition, the Internal Revenue Service had a lien on her income, since there had been a substantial tax bill for 1946 to 1948; their business manager, an odd character named John Vernon, when accused of embezzlement, conveniently settled the matter (for himself) by committing suicide. The IRS gave the Lindstroms no leniency for this. The disposition of Rossellini's RKO salary was a matter of some mystery: he was, he claimed, supporting his mother, a sister, a niece, one son, several animals, an indeterminate number of ex-mistresses and a platoon of auto mechanics always working on his sports cars.

Nevertheless, once the film was complete, Ingrid found her

strength returning—doubtless supported by Rossellini's insistence.
Breaking her silence on August 5, she told the press (through Joe
Steele) that she had decided to retire from films and to lead a private life, and that she had instructed her lawyer to begin divorce
proceedings immediately. That day, the *Los Angeles Times* ran an inch-
high, stop-the-presses headline above the page one masthead:
INGRID TO DIVORCE MATE, QUIT FILMS. The story filled several
columns below. Newspapers around the world were not so familiar,
but the story was not suppressed anywhere. In Hollywood, columnists Louella Parsons and Hedda Hopper were livid that they did
not receive exclusive advance news from Ingrid herself.

As for Roberto, his wife Marcella agreed to cooperate in his
effort to find grounds for an annulment. "Ingrid Bergman is the
ideal wife for him—sweet, restful, an oasis of charm. Miss Bergman
and Roberto will marry just as soon as they can." Indeed, Marcella
seemed quite content to end the mere formality of her own long-
dead marriage. She cheerfully agreed to sign a document claiming
that she was not of sound mind when she had married Roberto in
the first place, and this was enough to obtain an annulment of her
marriage before an assizes court in Austria; thanks to some personal
influence, this was then accepted in Italy. Their eleven-year-old son
remained with her.

Thus on August 29, her thirty-fourth birthday, Ingrid celebrated
the removal of another obstacle to her marriage to Roberto. They
dined out in Rome, and were spontaneously mobbed by an enthusiastic crowd of well-wishers. Romans evidently adored the lovers,
and a throng accompanied them back to their neighborhood,
applauding, singing old Italian love songs and showing their
approval in every way except by throwing three coins in the foun-
tain.

THAT AUTUMN, INGRID BEGAN THE LONG PROCESS OF OBTAINING A
divorce by long distance.

First, she and Roberto selected Monroe MacDonald, an American lawyer living in Rome who was highly recommended by friends;
his task was to select a California attorney with whom to work. In
late September, MacDonald—a plain, timid man who seemed pub-
licity-shy—proceeded to Los Angeles with a long statement Ingrid

282

- 282

.2828

282 88282

.8 8888888.8888888888888.

had dictated and signed, detailing her life story and the reasons for the gradual erosion of her marriage. Taking care neither to offend nor to misrepresent Petter's conduct, she did, nonetheless, clarify that he had too severely managed her life and career, and that only apart from him, in Alaska, Europe and New York, did she come to appreciate her strengths and learn how deeply the distance between them had widened. Devoid of rancor and free of indictments, Ingrid's statement nevertheless indicated that her creative and affective life was now once again in Europe.

So armed, MacDonald proceeded to Los Angeles. En route, he had to stop in New York, and there MacDonald did something completely unexpected and outrageous. Wrongly believing that it would be advantageous for Ingrid to have the American press and public on her side, he foolishly handed her confidential statement to the syndicated columnist "Cholly Knickerbocker" (pen name of socialite Igor Cassini), who broke a long story under the banner headline INGRID'S LAWYER IN U.S. TO TALK WITH LINDSTROM, which appeared in the pages of hundreds of American newspapers on September 21. Said MacDonald: "Her first and last words to me before I left [Rome] were, 'Don't do anything to hurt Petter'"— who was predictably furious not only with the charges leveled in public by MacDonald but also with this intolerable way of announcing a private suit for divorce.

The situation was aggravated when MacDonald, showing his true personality and evidently relishing his fame by association, ran for a publicity touchdown and took a call from gossip reporter Louella Parsons. Her headline two days later was the absurd assertion, INGRID OFFERING FORTUNE TO GAIN MARITAL FREEDOM, and the accompanying story quoted MacDonald, who madly reported details of private conversations and correspondence between Ingrid and Petter. By this time, MacDonald was so far beyond his competence that he began to theorize openly about Ingrid's past, her psychological history, Lindstrom's emotional makeup and possibilities for their future lives.

With this offensive, flamboyant and thoroughly unprofessional conduct, MacDonald effectively short-circuited smoother litigation: Lindstrom, rightly livid, virtually halted negotiations as he read more and more colorful accounts of how he had ruined his wife by dominating her. Some tales, ravenous for readers' attention, vaguely hinted at physical abuse, which was of course utterly without foundation. Thus began the feeding frenzy of the American media, which, from autumn 1949 to the end of 1950, churned out a total of more than 38,000 newspaper and magazine articles, editorials, essays and homilies about the Bergman-Lindstrom-Rossellini case.

WHEN INGRID LEARNED OF MACDONALD'S DISGRACEFUL ACTIVITIES, she was frantic. But by this time, MacDonald had landed the services of Hollywood attorney Gregson Bautzer, a tall, tanned and athletic crackerjack whose clients included Howard Hughes and Louella Parsons, and who counted Joan Crawford, Lana Turner and Ginger Rogers among the many stars he had escorted. Bautzer was charged with the dismissal of MacDonald, who limped home protesting that he had acted in his client's best interests.

Petter, meantime, had secured an advantage by the simple act of taking his oath of citizenship on October 28. Ingrid was now a nonresident alien suing an American husband and daughter. He eventually began negotiating through his own attorneys, who demanded (a) that Ingrid be permitted to visit her daughter only in the United States; (b) that Lindstrom be granted 50 percent of the salary and profits for *Stromboli*; and (c) that in a settlement, Ingrid be assigned only one-third the total value of the Benedict Canyon house and their joint assets—which share Petter reckoned as $50,000.

When this was conveyed to Rome, Rossellini reacted first, and with one of his operatic tantrums. He was, as usual, sunk in debt; Ingrid had no money and no prospect of any; their living and professional expenses were enormous; and a baby was due in three months—an event of which the world knew nothing. Any announcement of a forthcoming birth would have torpedoed the picture's box-office success by inviting a massive boycott. Such was the power of the forces of moral vigilantism in postwar America.

RUMORS OF INGRID'S PREGNANCY BEGAN INEVITABLY TO FLY, AND AT the end of November she had once again to take someone into her confidence. Naturally she turned to Joe Steele, now back in Hollywood and as loyal as ever. Some people had counseled an abortion, she wrote to Joe in November, but she had at once rejected that as "a poor, miserable way out" of her dilemma. In fact, a number of nonjudgmental clergymen in Rossellini's social circle had offered Ingrid friendship and sympathy. "I have left all in God's hands, as they advise," she told Joe. "No storm will be strong enough to wash us away."

She was, however, continually assaulted by tempests—none more terrifying than one unleashed by Petter, who was obviously coaching his daughter. Pia wrote to Ingrid saying that she could not look at a world map in school because she did not want to see Italy. She then asked why Ingrid was going to dub the film's dialogue in Rome and not in Hollywood: "No picture has ever taken so long. Something very funny going on over there!" Ingrid of course recognized the source at once; it was impossible for the child to have come up with these ideas on her own.

Friends always admired Ingrid's courage in the face of this unnecessary contest for the child's loyalty. Her humor, too, buoyed her. "Roberto is going to make a film about St. Francis," she wrote to Joe on December 5, "and the Vatican has been most helpful and very enthusiastic about it. All these holy men seem to have adopted Roberto as their favorite sinner. We have priests coming and going all the time and joining us for dinner. My reputation as a Lutheran is shot to pieces!" And relative to "Cholly Knickerbocker," who had wired his love and admiration—and then begged for exclusive details and a telephone interview!—Ingrid said she was going to "beg [him] to drop dead."

As Christmas approached, Ingrid, now seven months along, was seen in public less and less. With their salaries for *Stromboli* blocked in Hollywood, she and Roberto were desperate for cash, and so Steele went directly to Howard Hughes. Begging for his confidence, Steele told him of Ingrid's pregnancy and urged Hughes to rush the picture into release before the baby's birth ("before anybody starts banning it"). Hughes nodded.

Next morning, December 12, a Beverly Hills bookseller telephoned Joe Steele to inform him that the *Los Angeles Examiner* had a two-inch headline announcing the imminent birth of Ingrid Bergman's illegitimate baby. Howard Hughes, thinking that a scandal could only help the publicity for *Stromboli*, had at once called

Louella Parsons, who ran the story, thus sealing a lifelong symbiotic relationship with Hughes.

And so, at the precise season when merchants were cashing in on the hardy commercialism of Christmastide, an outcast woman with child was vilified from coast to coast. Roberto fumed and swore, but Ingrid was remarkably calm. "I am not afraid," she wrote to Joe on December 13. "I am glad that all those other women, in small and big towns all over the world, who suffer because of their 'sins,' will take on a little more courage because of me." She could even banter about Parsons, who said she cried over her typewriter when she had to write the news of the pregnancy: "I think they were tears of joy," Ingrid said.

There were a few lone voices of affectionate support.

"Why do they talk about a scandal," asked an elderly Italian priest who had no patience with human judgments, "when God has been so good and blessed their union with a child?"

"Ingrid dearest," wrote Cary Grant, "It would not be possible in a single cablegram to tell you of all your friends who send you love and affection."

And Alfred Hitchcock sent warm holiday greetings, too, urging Ingrid to keep everything in proper perspective: "After all, nothing is permanent and people soon forget."

But people did not forget soon at all.

"Having been so loved, I was now deeply hated," Ingrid said of this time. During the last decade, she had gradually grown in the public's estimation until she was all but identified with Sister Benedict and St. Joan. But the halo had become a noose, and now—horrors!—she had fallen in love with a man not her husband and was about to bear a child by him. This was not, it was felt, just her own business. Vast numbers of so-called ordinary Americans had fallen in love with her as an emblem of moral security, and they now felt both deceived and uncertain of themselves and their own destinies.

In 1939, Ingrid Bergman had been hailed as a fresh-faced girl, "dignified, gracious, unpretentious and spiritual," who represented everything good that America loved and needed. She was married and a mother then, but the word most often used to describe her was "innocent," by which was meant, in some magical way, "virginal."

But in 1949, she made it clear that she was nothing like a nun and did not want to be a martyr for the myth of the movies. And so she was regarded as the foulest of sinners, a renegade whose "powerful influence for evil" was soon to be condemned not only in churches and schools, but even on the floor of the United States Senate.

Chapter Fourteen

1950

Nor is the people's judgment always true:
The most may err as grossly as the few.

JOHN DRYDEN,
Absalom and Achitophel

FROM NOVEMBER 1949, INGRID WAS VIRTUALLY A PRISONER OF HER apartment, for day and night the via Bruno Buozzi was thick with Italian reporters and photographers ravenous for a word or an image they could sell around the world. After December 12, when Louella Parsons announced Ingrid's pregnancy, these journalists were joined by an influx of their international colleagues. On the twenty-third, she was whisked away after midnight to record some last-minute dialogue of *Stromboli* at a nearby recording studio. But on January 22, her third time out in three months, her attempt to climb into a car with Roberto for a drive in the country was subverted when a photographer jumped out at her and snapped a shot seen round the world within hours. IS SHE OR ISN'T SHE? screamed the headlines in America, rhetorically asking readers to assess the meaning of Ingrid's voluminous dark overcoat.

By some stroke of good fortune, the photographers were absent, perhaps taking a prolonged lunch, on the afternoon of Thursday, February 2. Ingrid had not been seen, even at a window, for days, and there was some speculation that she had left Rome—perhaps for America, since the Lindstrom divorce was getting more and more thorny and delay followed delay.

At three o'clock that afternoon, she went into labor and at four was bundled into a car by her physician, Dr. Pier Luigi Guidotti, and taken to the Villa Margherita clinic, a block behind Mussolini's former home in the northeast quarter of Rome; remarkably, the journey went unnoticed. Roberto met them at the clinic, and at seven o'clock, with Dr. Guidotti and Dr. Giuseppe Sannicandro in attendance, Ingrid delivered a healthy baby they named Renato Roberto Giusto Giuseppe, familiarly called Robertino in childhood and later Robin.* The Roman press did not pick up the scent of news for another hour, since most reporters had converged on the Fiamma Cinema for the premiere of William Dieterle's *Volcano*— Anna Magnani's competition against *Stromboli*.

The evening was something from the pages of a farce—or more accurately, a fantasy sequence from a Fellini movie. First, the photographers, eager for a shot of Magnani, lit up the night with flash after flash directed at every woman with black hair who arrived at the theater: the star was here—no, she was over there—no, she had just climbed out of a car over *there*. But La Magnani, who had somehow been tipped off about Ingrid's trip to the clinic, had in fact stayed away from her own premiere, cursing Rossellini for going so far as to upstage her picture by somehow arranging the coincidence. The screening of *Volcano*, which began just about the time of Robertino's first wail, was then suddenly interrupted—as if on cue, Magnani might have said—when a projector bulb blew out. A messenger was sent across town for a replacement.

With that, a man named Renzo Avanzo, who had written the story basis for *Volcano* (and who was, of all things, Rossellini's cousin), stepped before the Fiamma audience and entertained them during the awkward interval by launching into a tap dance. But the

*Italian law forbade using the same first name of a living parent, so Renato was chosen after one of Roberto's favorite cousins. Giusto is the Italian form of Justus, Ingrid's father, and Giuseppe was the name of Roberto's father.

press wearied of this, and some of them decided to race across town, where there was a private preview of *Stromboli*. They might be able to get some comments from the departing audience, composed of a dozen bishops and about four hundred priests, invited to see that the picture had an edifyingly religious conclusion (the cry, conversion and final prayer of Karin).

But the circus had only begun. At nine o'clock, the baby's birth was announced by ANSA, the Italian news agency, and all hell broke loose. For the next two weeks, the news of the world (including that of the development of the hydrogen bomb) took second place to the hysteria outside the Villa Margherita, and Rome seemed more like a Hollywood set. Sometimes the madness infiltrated the clinic, too— not least of all in the two hundred letters poured daily onto Ingrid's bed. About half were from movie fans around the world, who told her how courageous she was. The other half was divided into the obscene, the threatening and the accusatory. This was nothing compared to the forty thousand she had received since she had left America.

The iron garden gate to the clinic was forthwith locked against the newsmen by one of the nuns, who was bluntly asked by a member of the Associated Press if she would swear on a Bible to the truth of what they had earlier been told on telephoning the clinic— that there was no patient registered as Miss Bergman. The little sister, who was either very ignorant or very smart (and decided to take the question literally) replied no, there was no Signorina Bergman within. There was a Borghese, the Principessa Borghese, and she had delivered twins earlier in the day, but no, no one by the name of Miss Bergman—which was indeed the case, for Ingrid had of course been permitted to register under a pseudonym.

For several hours, therefore, the news remained unconfirmed by the hospital administration, the Rossellini family, their friends, the discreet nuns—*e tutti quanti*. Weighing their odds, the American syndicated press ran stories about Ingrid's tears of joy, or her laughter of delight, when the baby was brought to her. As a matter of fact, she had been somewhat dazed by the strong anesthetic, and when she heard her baby's first cry, she bestirred herself only to ask, "What's the matter? What time is it?" before drifting into exhausted sleep.

At midnight, the reporters and photographers started to climb over the gate and the stone wall surrounding the clinic. Riot police were summoned to stop that invasion, but the press did not budge from the outer precincts. Next morning, the superintendent of the clinic, which had just recently opened for business and needed some good free publicity, went out (with Roberto's permission) to announce the time of the birth, and the gender and weight of the newborn. And that was supposed to be that.

BUT THE ADMINISTRATOR THEN DECIDED TO PERMIT A HANDFUL OF reporters—no cameras, please—to inspect a few public rooms and the chapel. But cameras were indeed smuggled in capacious winter overcoats, and suddenly the atmosphere turned decidedly Keystone Kop-ish. Angry aides and outraged nuns were running after cameramen who were making a mad dash through corridors, around corners, poking into private rooms and popping flashbulbs like fireworks. But no one got access to Suite 34, guarded by police to assure the privacy of the notorious mother and child.

By noon, the curtain had been rung down on this scene of the farce, but the play was not over. Journalists were authorized by their home offices to rent rooms in a hotel across the street, training their cameras on the clinic's entrances and sweeping the facade for any sign of a tall, Nordic female patient who might be gazing from her window. But Ingrid's imprisonment continued, secured by the iron blinds of her room, which were kept lowered throughout her stay.

Meanwhile, all sorts of coy tricks were attempted. Nuns, immune to the temptation, were offered bribes to take pictures. A newsman brought his pregnant wife to the clinic for admission, but they were both booted down the stairs when it was determined that she was at least seven weeks away from delivering. A photographer gingerly climbed up a drainpipe to the balcony of Ingrid's room. Another managed to pay a midwife to weigh another newborn, and that picture managed to fly around the world with the caption, "Is This Ingrid's Little Roberto?" Alongside it was a publicity still from *Stromboli*, with Ingrid, sad-faced and wearing the tatty striped robe for one scene: "In the Villa Margherita, Ingrid is not smiling now!"

Some newspapers dug out stills from *Notorious*, with Ingrid in bed, acting sick from poisoning ("Ingrid, resting after her ordeal!"). Others went to their more recent files, where photos of Ingrid arriving at Rome Airport a year ago, eyes wide with alarm as she confronted the crush of the press, were recaptioned "Frightened Ingrid en route to hospital!" The only photographs actually connected to the real event were of Roberto, who punched one of the cameramen in the nose; and of his older son, who on leaving the hospital mouthed obscenities at the cameras.

The Swedish press contented itself with photo-less articles, none the less vicious for all that. Never especially laudatory about Ingrid over the last ten years, they now claimed that she was a great, great actress who had been ruined by a demented Italian. One Stockholm newspaper went so far as to call her "a blot on the Swedish flag." But there was a strong response from the influential Stockholm newspaper *Expressen*, which decried "the forms of hypocrisy in this matter. Here in Sweden, general opinion is that Ingrid honestly took the consequences of her emotions. This is to be preferred to the reactions of the puritans, who demand official spotlessness in accordance with a hypocritical moral code." And so it went, day in day out, as Ingrid Bergman tried to lead her so-called private life.

The final comic indignity occurred in mid-February, when Roberto registered the baby's birth and arranged for the baptism to be performed by his friend, the monk then playing Francis of Assisi in his new film. The child was identified as the son of Roberto Rossellini—"mother temporarily unknown." This hilarious assertion covered an Italian law that specified that the child of every married woman is presumed to be the child of her husband; since the Lindstroms were still not divorced, Petter would be named the father, and technically the question of paternity could arise. "Isn't it funny," Ingrid said, appreciating the irony, "infamous though I was, I was suddenly unknown! No—temporarily unknown. I suppose that meant that when we got married we could tell them who the real mother was!"

She retained only one happy memory of the entire clinic experience: "I'll never forget how wonderful the nuns and the priests were at the time of the birth of Robertino in Villa Margherita. They protected me and helped me. It was a wonderful consolation for me to know that the truly religious people were understanding and sympathetic when the storm of public opinion was mostly against me." Indeed, she never felt judged or rejected by any of the sisters or clerics at the Villa Margherita, all of whom treated her with affection and respect—and some of whom were publicly excoriated for even attending to the physical needs of the sinner. In America, the response of the religious establishment could not have been more different.

AMID ALL THIS PALAVER, *STROMBOLI* WAS ABOUT TO BE RELEASED IN America—but not everywhere. At the instigation of Senator Frank Lunsford of Georgia, a resolution was passed in that state's senate banning the public screening of all films made by Rossellini or starring Ingrid Bergman on the grounds that this couple "glamorized free love" and so were a danger to American society. So much for Senator Lunsford's belief in the strength of Americans' moral fiber.

"The actions of Ingrid Bergman are a stench in the nostrils of decent people and a disgrace to the finer sensibilities of womenhood [sic]," blasted a Los Angeles minister in an explosion worthy of the volcano. Another, in Philadelphia, excoriated Ingrid for leaving behind her "the dirt and muck of immoral behavior." And Dr. Norman Vincent Peale, admired by so many as the soul of genial, American, easygoing devotion, thundered that Ingrid had "disqualified herself from her profession and should be purged from the screen."

And so it went. In Indiana, where the film was never shown, a powerful clergyman said that Ingrid's conduct was "a symptom of a decline in morals." The Federal Council of Churches, with headquarters in Cleveland, condemned the Rossellini-Bergman affair as the sort of "sex exhibitionism which is a symptom of the moral decay of the West," which not only failed to understand the nature of the relationship but also gave it a universal influence far beyond its capacities. And the Salvation Army, which for a moment lost touch with the deepest meaning of its own name, withdrew all the recordings Ingrid had made in early 1949 on behalf of its annual charity appeal.

Alas, one of the two most concerted efforts against Ingrid Bergman in 1950 was orchestrated by the Roman Catholic Church in America. Unlike European Catholic clergy and laity, who considered this a private matter of conscience—and who had far more pressing problems after the war—the American wing of the Church was her most vicious attacker. "The Devil himself is at work," proclaimed the *Boston Pilot*, speaking as the official organ of that diocese in an editorial typical of many that proliferated in Catholic communities. "Some people have tried to make 'romance' out of a cheap, sordid, immoral affair." Ingrid had "openly and brazenly flouted the laws of God," and "decent, moral Americans should stay away from these practitioners of moral filth." The essay concluded with a ringing endorsement of the civic actions in Georgia, Washington and elsewhere, banning *Stromboli*.

The record is clear, too, on another matter: to the end of her life, Ingrid never fired back at her critics—much less did she harbor anti-Catholic or anti-religious sentiments. One might indeed ask who better expressed the spirit of Christianity. That year, very few people seemed to recognize that condemnation was itself profoundly indecent—and was, indeed, a far more egregious symptom of America's corrupt religious sensibility. Those who took a higher road generally kept quiet, for it was not a time in American life to defend the unconventional victims of moral smugness.*

At the same time, the Council of Churches in Bellingham, Washington, and in Memphis, Tennessee, successfully petitioned their city councils to ban *Stromboli* in those cities. In Chicago, Federal Judge Michael L. Igoe upheld a recent law that limited the run of successful films in the downtown area to two weeks, so that they might be shipped to the suburbs. This he did with specific reference to *Stromboli*, at the same time excepting Walt Disney's *Cinderella*, which, said the judge, could be screened forever if it continued to draw crowds. In all, a total of 5.5 million American clubwomen voted to boycott Ingrid Bergman's films. And in a rush to curry favor with America, the Women's Club of Manila was pressed by the country's government to issue a condemnation of all Ingrid's pictures in the Philippines.

But it is worth noting that in Rome, *Il Popolo*—the newspaper of

---

*Marion Davies, herself the victim of moral censure when she was the lover of William Randolph Hearst, was one of the first to send Ingrid a message of support.

the Catholic Party—considered the American condemnations "a
pre-ordained plan of cannibalistic aggression against Miss
Bergman," and the Vatican newspaper printed no critical denunciation of *Stromboli*. Still, one tough old cleric named Monsignor Dino
Staffa continued to hammer away at the immorality of Roberto and
Ingrid, and his censure was quite wrongly taken to be the official
position of the institutional Church worldwide. The fact is that in
Europe, but not in the United States, the clergy minded their own
business. And even in America, the Catholic-sponsored National
Legion of Decency, which wielded such extraordinary power that it
could ruin a film's financial success by condemning it, issued an
astonishing statement: "It is our policy to judge the film itself, not
the actors in it." And with that—would wonders never cease?—
they rated *Stromboli* an acceptable motion picture for public viewing.

ON FEBRUARY 15, RKO RELEASED THE PICTURE. DESPITE AN ADVER-
tising campaign that tried to cash in on the presumed dolce vita of
its director and star, it was resoundingly damned—not as immoral,
but as artistically "feeble, inarticulate, uninspiring and painfully
banal," a judgment with which it is hard to disagree. For the first
time in her life, Ingrid had bad notices: her performance had "no
depth," her expressions were "vacant."

Years later, *Stromboli*, available only in its Hughes-edited version,
seems poorly conceived and markedly tedious; and Rossellini's original notes for the final cut, if followed, may not have improved it.
Regarding Ingrid's acting, it is clear that her image was being
reviewed, not her art: she portrayed Karin with a controlled panic
that was a textbook on how to convey implications of longing and
imprecations against an inhospitable society.

The film drew crowds in nineteen cities for the first few days,
then quickly faded into oblivion in all but the major art houses. But
there was a terrible double standard behind the decision to withdraw it. Where the picture failed to charm at the box office,
exhibitors canceled its run on the grounds that Ingrid was an
immoral person whose work ought not to be shown. But where it
made money, it was shown as an act of defiance on behalf of artistic
freedom. "How can they openly and without shame express such
hypocrisy?" Ingrid fumed. "And they call me a person of low

morals! My baby Robertino joins me in a big scream against human stupidity." In a matter of weeks, *Stromboli* was no longer news.

But Ingrid was. Because Petter temporized about the terms to dissolve their marriage, she and Roberto went ahead with a Mexican divorce, for which she applied on grounds of incompatibility, mental cruelty and nonsupport. She added, against her will at first, the true statement that she had not seen any of the final payments of her *Stromboli* salary, kept by Lindstrom in California on grounds that funds were needed for Pia. Ingrid had, after all, willingly given up the first payment for that purpose, but now Petter, too, was a wage earner. Her divorce was granted in absentia on February 9, while she was still resting at the clinic. Informed of this, Petter, perhaps predictably, announced that he considered the divorce invalid and would file his own suit in due course. That took more time than anyone had anticipated.

And then entered the politicians.

On March 14, 1950, Senator Edwin C. Johnson of Colorado took the floor of the Senate:

> Mr. President, now that the stupid film about a pregnant woman and a volcano has exploited America with the usual finesse, to the mutual delight of RKO and the debased Rossellini, are we merely to yawn wearily, greatly relieved that this hideous thing is finished and then forget it? I hope not. A way must be found to protect the people in the future.

And then he moved in for the kill, accomplishing it with an unintentionally funny mixed metaphor in which he confused pirates with Indians:

> When Rossellini the love pirate returned to Rome smirking over his conquest, it was not Mrs. Lindstrom's scalp which hung from the conquering hero's belt; it was her very soul. Now what is left of her has brought two children into the world—one has no mother; the other is illegitimate. Even in this modern age of surprise, it is upsetting to have our most popular but pregnant movie queen, her condition the result of an illicit affair, play the

part of a cheap chiseling female to add spice to a silly story which lacks appeal. To bolster the box-office take, *Stromboli* simply has to have a private scandal on the part of the leading lady . . . [and] the vile and unspeakable Rossellini sets an all-time low in shameless exploitation and disregard for good public morals.

As for Ingrid, Johnson diagnosed her as a schizophrenic or under a hypnotic influence; either way, she certainly was "a free-love cultist [and] an apostle of degradation." Nathaniel Hawthorne could not have done better with his characters' diction. Johnson then arrived at the point of his diatribe, which was to use Ingrid and Roberto as a launching pad for a bill aimed to please an America steeped in a skewed sense of moral superiority: he wanted to see the Department of Commerce officially license actresses, producers and films according to their moral decency. Ingrid Bergman had perpetrated an "assault on the institution of marriage. She is one of the most powerful women on earth today—and, I regret to say, a powerful influence for evil." Two weeks later, Johnson said the same of Rossellini, claiming (without a shred of evidence) that Roberto was a narcotic addict, a Nazi collaborator and a black market operator. At least he did not accuse him of being a politician.

Johnson concluded that every decent American must recognize that "under our law no alien guilty of turpitude can set foot on American soil. Mrs. Petter Lindstrom has deliberately exiled herself from a country which was so good to her. If out of the degradation associated with *Stromboli*, decency and common sense can be established in Hollywood, then Ingrid Bergman will not have destroyed her career for naught. Out of her ashes may come a better Hollywood."

And then the dramatic coda: "Since both of these alien characters are guilty of moral turpitude, they cannot set foot on American soil under our immigration laws."

The bill never went to a vote, but the damage to Ingrid Bergman's freedom was considerable. The Immigration and Naturalization Service, asked its opinion on the matter of disbarring Ingrid Bergman for reasons of "moral turpitude" (pursuant to alien and immigration laws of 1907), replied that indeed it was a matter of fact that Miss Bergman was not a United States citizen.

More than this the Service did not say, but the challenge was issued. If she came to America, Ingrid might indeed be detained on reentry (her visa had expired the previous year). She could also be led away to detention on Ellis Island. Such action may have been unlikely—and several experts said so at the time—but in 1950, as witch hunts swept the land, no extreme measures were impossible to imagine. And for Pia, who would have seen news photographs of her mother (perhaps in handcuffs) led away as if she were a common criminal, the detention of her mother, as Roberto and even Petter admitted, would have been far more traumatic. The press, to be sure, would have relished this as the story of the century. "The worst part of the whole business," Ingrid saw, "was in having to hurt my daughter. To do that to her, knowing it wasn't her fault—I was sick over it. Nothing that has ever happened in my whole life has made me feel half so rotten."

THAT YEAR, HOLLYWOOD FOLKS WERE ALREADY UNDER THE WORST cloud of suspicion in the history of the business. The House Committee on Un-American Activities (HUAC) was on the rampage, tearing up the lives of filmmakers, writers, actors and even arts professors in a search to root out the specter of Communism among "dangerous" artists and intellectuals. If traitorous Americans were not exposed (so ran the conventional wisdom), then Russians would creep into the house while decent Americans slept, and suddenly the country would be under the control of the Soviets. The traitors were probably already embarking on a plan to atomize the minds of innocent Americans: according to a very active (and misguided) citizens' group, the numbing of America was to be achieved when Communists got their way and put fluoride in the nation's water supply.

The paranoia that gripped postwar America had several causes. First of all, China had fallen to a Communist regime in 1949. That same year, Moscow announced the detonation of an atomic bomb. Communist troops were preparing for a war (beginning in 1950) against American-supported armies in Korea. And there were, alas, some authentic cases of treason and espionage on the home front. All these fueled a terrible suspicion among ordinary people.

The triumph over Fascism in Europe and the hitherto unimaginable display of power demonstrated by America's atomic bombs at the end of World War II bestowed, in their wake, an unspoken presumption that there was something like a divine mandate to protect everything "pure" about American values and American success. In June 1949, peace and prosperity were proofs of that. A certain moral smugness often occurs in such circumstances, the odd but unspoken hunch that God is an American. Thus the coagulation of pride and paranoia.

It all began in October 1947, when the HUAC, which had developed unchecked from a congressional committee to investigate suspicious activities among American intellectuals, acted more and more like medieval Crusaders. Nineteen prominent men in Hollywood were ordered to testify about their involvement in Communist activities. The first group (who came to be known as the "Hollywood Ten") at first refused to testify and at once lost their jobs, were sentenced to prison and fined for contempt of Congress.* Studio executives initially condemned the witch hunt, but when threatened with the loss of financial backing from East Coast banks, they became friends of the HUAC. The deepest loyalties of moguls are always to the cashier. Hence, too, the hypocrisy over the box-office receipts of *Stromboli*.

In short order, those suspected of having Communist associations—or who might even have belonged to intellectual groups critical of society in the 1930s—were blacklisted unless they cooperated with HUAC. The result was that those who did not, who included some of Hollywood's finest talents, never worked there again or were forced to take a long leave of absence. At the same time, during a writers' strike, studios fired all employees who refused to toe the mark by cooperating with the HUAC.

All this reached critical mass with the rise of the disreputable Senator Joseph McCarthy, a forty-year-old Wisconsin Republican who was about to launch one of the worst assaults against American constitutional rights in the nation's history. Almost single-handedly, McCarthy—with the loud support of millions—expanded the Hol-

---

*The Hollywood Ten: screenwriters Alvah Bessie, Lester Cole, Ring Lardner, Jr., John Howard Lawson, Albert Maltz, Samuel Ornitz, Adrian Scott and Dalton Trumbo; and directors Herbert Biberman and Edward Dmytryk.

lywood witch hunt, claiming he had the names of known Communists who were working in the highest government offices. The
"lists" of these names he never produced, nor could he ever provide
a convincing case against a single individual. Nevertheless, capitaliz-
ing on the country's anxieties about Korea and Eastern Europe,
McCarthy raged on, trampling civil liberties in the name of patriotism.

McCarthy was finally disgraced in 1954 after his lunacy led him
to attack (of all people) President Eisenhower as tainted with Communist sympathies. But by the time the Senate finally censured him,
McCarthy's fantasies had ruined countless lives and helped to can-
onize a dangerous ideal of extreme right-wing conformity—a
notion that was itself anomalous in a nation born in revolution,
raised on healthy dissent and encouraged on a diet of rugged indi-
vidualism.

Senators McCarthy and Johnson and their species had talked a
lot about God blessing their undertakings, and they were mighty
sure where those undertakings led and where they were being corrupted. In the entertainment industry, one of their staunchest sup-
porters was Walter Winchell, whose reports to "Mr. and Mrs.
America" approved the blacklisting of actors, writers, and technicians in radio and television.

Thus the country was hot with both rage and fear regarding
Hollywood people. No writer, producer or actor who wanted to
work dared to submit a story that was even vaguely critical of something gone wrong in the nation, nor would he or she dare to imply
that the culture was increasingly blanketed by paranoid delusions.
An appallingly narrow, conservative smog darkened the entire landscape of the entertainment industry just when Ingrid Bergman fell
in love and became pregnant.

For many Americans, movie actors were strange, immoral, no-
account scoundrels. Newspapers had recounted the antics of Lana
Turner, Charles Chaplin, Mickey Rooney and Errol Flynn. Movie
stars, as Louella Parsons and Walter Winchell implied on the radio,
were not always nice people. Sometimes they drank too much and
got arrested; they had extravagant homes and wild parties; worst of
all, they seemed to get divorced and remarried as often as normal
folks have birthdays. Ingrid Bergman was held above all that—until

now. "People saw me in *Joan of Arc* and declared me a saint," Ingrid said. "I'm not. I'm just a woman, another human being." Well, that was no excuse. The Puritan public disgrace heaped upon her was so virulent that it is remarkable that she was not close to a nervous breakdown.

ON MAY 24, INGRID BERGMAN AND ROBERTO ROSSELLINI WERE MAR-ried by proxy. In Juarez, Mexico, two gentlemen—Javier Alvarez and Arturo Trevino—stood before Judge Raul Orozco and took the oath of marriage on their behalf.

Only Mexico would acknowledge the divorce it had granted Ingrid, and because neither she nor Roberto wanted to travel and risk the presence of American newsmen, the oddity of a proxy mar-riage—valid but weird—was chosen. (There was a precedent: in 1945, actress Merle Oberon had married cinematographer Lucien Ballard in the same sort of ceremony.) "Of course, we were very sorry not to be present at our own wedding," Ingrid said with her usual good humor, "but that doesn't make it count any the less for us!" At that same hour as the proxy marriage was being sealed, the real happy couple knelt in a quiet, dark Roman church that had been kept open for them throughout the evening; they exchanged gold bands, pronounced their vows only to each other without wit-nesses and joined a few friends back home for champagne.

A few days later, the Rossellinis drove to a seaside house Roberto had bought—Santa Marinella, about forty miles north of Rome. The money for this, as for maintaining the Rome apartment, the servants and the cars, came from Roberto's sale of foreign rights to this or that earlier picture, by borrowing against his St. Francis film, by wheedling cash from prospective producers, and by pro-ducing his magnificent wife, who did nothing but smile graciously and in short order—*ecco!*—Roberto had a gift from this tycoon or an unrestricted loan from that one. He also kept cash in his pockets by simply ignoring bills, which may have evoked wonder from mer-chants who heard his little speeches about concern for the humble and the poor. "Roberto lived and worked in creative chaos," according to Ingrid. "Nothing was ever organized."

Santa Marinella hung picturesquely over the sea on a small coastal inlet just south of the old Roman port of Civitavecchia. That first

With Bing Crosby, in
The Bells of St. Mary's (1945).
(*Museum of Modern Art/Film Stills Archive*)

Above, rehearsing script revisions with Hitchcock
and, below, with Cary Grant and the director,
Notorious (1945). (*National Film Archive*)

With Mal (Mrs. Ray) Milland, Jack (son of Ernest) Hemingway, Gary Cooper, and Clark Gable in Sun Valley (1948). (*IMS Bildbyra*)

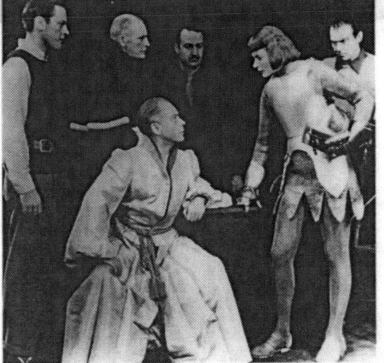

With Broadway cast members in *Joan of Lorraine* (1946). (*Museum of Modern Art/Film Stills Archive*)

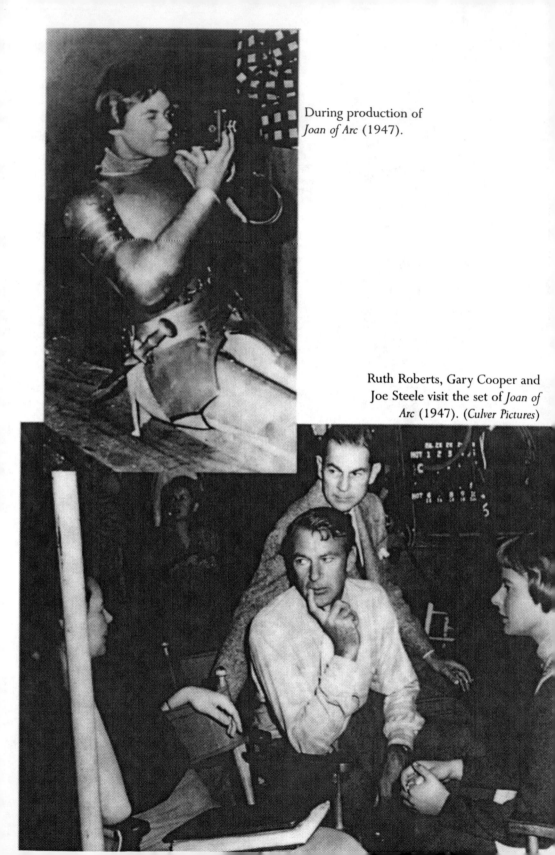

During production of
Joan of Arc (1947).

Ruth Roberts, Gary Cooper and
Joe Steele visit the set of *Joan of
Arc* (1947). (*Culver Pictures*)

With Victor Fleming at the New York premiere of *Joan of Arc* (1948). (*Culver Pictures*)

With Hitchcock in London, during production of
Under Capricorn (1948). (*National Film Archive/Stills Library*)

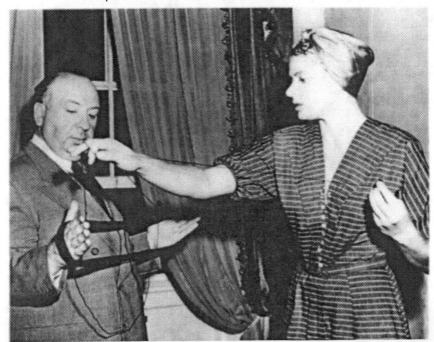

Returning to Sweden,
October 1948.

With Mario Vitale,
on location for
Stromboli (1949).
*(Museum of Modern
Art/Film Stills Archive)*

Robert Capa in 1951.
(© *Ruth Orkin, 1951*)

With Roberto Rossellini in Rome (1951).

With Ettore Giannini,
in *Europa '51* (1951).
(*Museum of Modern
Art/Film Archives*)

Petter and Pia
Lindstrom, en route
to visit Ingrid (1951).
(*IMS Bildbyra*)

OPPOSITE: With her three
Rossellini children in Italy,
about 1955. (*Museum of
Modern Art/Film Stills Archive*)

With George Sanders, in
Viaggio in Italia (1953).
*(Museum of Modern
Art/Film Archives)*

With Helen Hayes,
in *Anastasia* (1956).
(*Culver Pictures*)

With Jean-Loup Philippe,
in *Tea and Sympathy* (Paris,
1956). (*From the collection
of Robert Anderson*)

Robert Anderson, 1956.

With Pia,
in Paris
(1957).

With her children, at
Santa Marinella
(1957). (*IMS Bildbyra*)

With Lars Schmidt (1958).
(*IMS Bildbyra*)

In *The Inn of the Sixth
Happiness* (1958).
(*IMS Bildbyra*)

As Hedda Gabler (1963). (*Courtesy of the Academy of Motion Picture Arts and Sciences*)

With Alfred Hitchcock, at opening night of *More Stately Mansions*, Los Angeles (1967). (*Courtesy of the Academy of Motion Picture Arts and Sciences*)

With director Guy Green
and Anthony Quinn, during
A Walk in the Spring Rain (1969).
(*From the collection of Guy Green*)

As Greta Ohlsson, in
*Murder on the Orient
Express* (1974). (*Courtesy
of the Academy of Motion
Picture Arts and Sciences*)

With Ingmar Bergman
and Liv Ullman, in
Autumn Sonata (1977).
(*Courtesy of the Academy
of Motion Picture Arts
and Sciences*)

As Golda Meir (1981).
(*Movie Star News*)

Not long before her death (1982).
(Kip Rano/Sipa/IMS Bildbyra)

summer, Ingrid supervised the workmen landscaping flower beds and completing the vast garages for Roberto's fleet of automobiles. The eight-room house itself, on seven acres, was white, cool and casually designed. A fireplace dominated the cozy living room, which gave onto a wide veranda overlooking the sea. The place had its own beach and a vast garden with palms, pines and flowers everywhere. Beginning in the summer of 1950, the Rossellinis divided their seasons equally between the two homes, and Roberto set up an editing studio at Santa Marinella to be near his family all summer long.

In both residences, servants attended to heavy housework, but Ingrid, who always claimed her Swedish eye found more dirt and dust, could often be found scrubbing and polishing. "Save some dust and some cobwebs—Mother's coming," was a family joke about Ingrid's passion for tidiness in later years. She also loved to shop and to argue with the fishmonger over the best catch and the fairest prices. Concerned about their finances, Ingrid was ever the thrifty Swede, counterpoising Roberto's role as the lavish, grand signore. That summer, Ingrid told her husband that she wanted to return to work, that they needed money and she needed to do something with her life. Of course, he replied, but certainly she must be only in a Rossellini film. "He knew that Fellini and other Italian directors, like Visconti, wanted me to work for them. But Roberto always refused to allow this . . . He was very jealous, and so many of us lived in the shadow of his moods. If Roberto was worried or burdened by things, we were." But when her husband was cheerful, the sun shone brilliantly on everyone.

In late summer, the Rossellinis made an attractive couple—she slim and bronze in a long, strapless formal gown, he elegant in a white dinner jacket—at the Venice Film Festival, where *Stromboli* and *The Flowers of St. Francis* were cheered loudly by an overflow crowd, and where Ingrid was something of a popular cause. There was not a single word of censure, or anything but applause and encouragement for her. Roberto's films took no prizes, but he was everywhere hailed as a great maestro of the cinema. The Italians loved them, reported Tennessee Williams, back from a visit, "but Ingrid doesn't want to return to the United States. American tourists flock around them in Rome and make insulting remarks. But they are a happy couple over there."

*   *   *

AT LAST, AFTER PROTRACTED BATTLES OVER FINANCES AND THE CUS-
tody of Pia, Petter Lindstrom won his divorce, on grounds of cruelty and desertion, on November 1 in Los Angeles. Some of his
statements before Judge Thurmond Clarke may have astonished
Ingrid when she read them in the newspapers:

The Lindstrom home had been a happy one, Petter said, and the
marriage apparently solid before she left precipitously to "take up a
certain relationship with that Italian motion picture director." This
came as a great shock to him, he said, but when he went to meet
her in Sicily, she had changed her mind about the man and was
going to break off the affair and return home. Did he feel bitterness
toward his wife? "I feel only sympathy for the awkward predicament
she has placed herself in. I think she has many good qualities
besides being very beautiful, and she is a very fine actress." But that
was all her own doing, he said—and then he made a shocking statement. Ingrid had worked, he said, "certainly without any interference from her husband."

Ingrid acceded to virtually every one of Petter's demands,
mostly to have the case done with and to schedule her first visit to
her daughter. According to terms of the settlement, Petter received
the house in Benedict Canyon (bought entirely by Ingrid's earnings)
and physical custody of Pia. She was to remain with him in America,
and Ingrid would have only the right to half the girl's summer vacation—and Petter would never be required to bring her to Italy.
Ingrid also gave up her guardianship of moneys that she had earned
and that had been put in trust for Pia. The divorce was uncontested,
and Judge Clarke granted an interlocutory decree by default.

As Christmas approached, Roberto said he had a special gift for
Ingrid—a wonderful idea for a new picture, and he was working
with at least ten writers on trying to get a narrative settled. The idea
for it had come to him while he was filming *The Flowers of St. Francis*:
If a woman like Francis returned to earth in the twentieth century
and attempted to live in his spirit, how would she be treated? As
mad, no doubt. But Roberto also wanted to make a film of social
conscience, about contemporary European problems, and this was
getting him into trouble as he worked on the outline.

Eventually, he and his writers had something to show Ingrid.

Europa '51, as it was to be called, was the story of a wealthy American lady (Ingrid) living in Rome, whose twelve-year-old son, believing she has lost interest in him, throws himself down a flight of stairs and dies a few days later. Advised by an ardent Communist to overcome her grief by working for the poor, she at first works in a factory and then turns to offering spiritual counsel to the needy. After caring for a woebegone prostitute who dies of tuberculosis and an unwed mother with a troop of children, she helps a young delinquent to escape from detention and so is committed to a lunatic asylum by her husband, who is embarrassed by his wife's activities. She will be confined there for the rest of her life.

Now, Roberto asked as he gave his wife the outline, isn't this a wonderful, meaningful, compelling story? Merry Christmas, Ingrid!

Chapter Fifteen

1951–1956

How many cares one loses when one decides not to do something
but to be someone!

COCO CHANEL

IN ROME, INGRID SHOPPED CAREFULLY FOR PIA'S CHRISTMAS GIFTS, which were posted by air to arrive in Beverly Hills well before the holidays. She was especially proud of a delicate wristwatch she bought for Pia, which she had given to a friend to deliver personally. But when she telephoned Pia after the New Year, she learned that the watch was nowhere to be found. Ingrid then discovered that the deliverer had found no one at home and left the package in the dog-house—"so the dogs know what time it is," as Ingrid said, "but no one knows where the watch is!" Ingrid replaced it for Pia at considerable expense, saving money from her household budget for several months.

Roberto, meanwhile, continued to be completely ignorant of the value of money, spending lavishly on his family as on his friends and himself, despite Ingrid's appeals for economy. He had the habit, Ingrid often said, of not only giving away the shirt off his back, but in the process giving away everyone else's shirts, too. Still, he entertained on the grand scale at the apartment and the summer house, and he never had fewer than four expensive racing cars. "Why don't we sell one of them?" he asked his secretary one day. "Fine," came the reply, "then we can make payments on the others!"

Life was never dull. "Unlike my big empty house in Holly-wood," said Ingrid, "my apartment in Rome was always filled with people from all walks of life—monks, writers, racing-car drivers, beggars. I learned so much of warmth and love, things I'd never have learned beside my swimming pool in Hollywood. Oh, there were difficulties in Italy, too, but difficulties in Italy are so much more interesting."

Of Ingrid's devotion to Roberto, her admiration of his wide inter-ests and her delight in the amusements he invented for her and Robertino, there was never any doubt; nevertheless, her husband did indeed present "difficulties." In addition to his casual lack of concern for finances and a chronic inability to focus his attention or to disci-pline himself for work, Roberto took almost adolescent risks. Sluggish and disorganized at work, he thought little of racing his Ferrari at 150 miles per hour, no matter who was with him. And his blithe uncon-cern for politeness sometimes caused his wife considerable aggrava-tion: he often invited ten or a dozen people for dinner and then failed to appear, leaving Ingrid as hostess for a room full of strangers. "He was so Italian and disorganized, and I was so Nordic and precise!"

She, on the other hand, was methodical, prepared at work and at home, had impeccable, discreet manners without a drop of arti-fice and, for her leisure time, liked to wander slowly through a grove or along a beach. "I relax with my family," Ingrid said. "Roberto relaxes by racing about in fast cars. That is his way. I just wait for him to come home."

"Roberto was not easy to live with," she added quietly. But she was in earnest about this marriage. It was going to work. And Rossellini, who could be maddeningly vague and self-centered, knew how to win back Ingrid's good graces after he had committed a particularly annoying gaffe: he performed an impromptu skit, he made her laugh, he told her stories of his family's colorful past; he took over the kitchen and cooked a lavish pasta for her, then ran to the garden and returned with an armful of flowers. He was in every way the antithesis of dependable Petter.

*   *   *

RELIABLE AS EVER, LINDSTROM FULFILLED HIS AGREEMENT TO ALLOW Pia to spend part of her vacation with Ingrid in the summer of 1951. Fearful that somehow the Rossellinis would go so far as to kidnap the child, he brought her to London, and Ingrid had to come from Rome to meet them at the end of July. Pia was shuttled between the country house of Sidney Bernstein (Hitchcock's partner on *Under Capricorn*), Ann Todd and David Lean's London townhouse, and a London hotel. Petter was always present during their visits except for one afternoon.

The reason for his constant presence was clarified at the beginning of the reunion, when the Leans invited the Lindstroms to dinner at their home in Ilchester Place, Kensington. They had arranged a guest bedroom for Ingrid and Pia for a few nights, but they did not have another for Petter, who told Lean he feared "that if he left the house he might not be admitted again." Furthermore, he suspected that Ingrid would whisk the child away and initiate litigation in England to prolong her visit with her daughter.

Now this was very close to frank paranoia. David Lean asked Petter if he would be willing to leave if Lean gave him a key to the front door. That offer was accepted, and Petter returned to his hotel. But very early next morning, the Leans' housemaid found him sitting in a chair outside Ingrid and Pia's room, keeping watch against possible abduction. He would not come to breakfast until he was satisfied that Ingrid and Pia were back in sight. That afternoon, when Ingrid asked to take her daughter to a West End screening of Disney's *Alice in Wonderland*, Petter flatly denied the request—until Ann Todd intervened, saying she would guarantee their return, and that she, her daughter and her secretary would accompany them. Kay Brown's daughter Kate, a bright and energetic teen, had been invited to come from America as a companion for Pia. The girls tried to put a good face on things and to enjoy the journey. Inevitably, Pia could later recall only a terrific strain and stress during the entire journey. Almost thirteen, mature, bright and well mannered, she was subjected to a doubly impossible task: pleasing her father while trying to reacquaint with her mother.

The glacial atmosphere among the adults did not improve when they proceeded to the Bernstein country home in Kent two days later. If Ingrid and Pia went for a walk, Petter trailed fifty paces behind, never letting them out of his sight. When Ingrid and Pia sat watching television, Petter sat in an adjacent hallway, as if they might bolt from the house—as if there were a private plane on a nearby field, to spirit them away to God knew where.

Finally, after a mere three-day visit, Petter announced that he was forthwith taking Pia to visit her relatives in Sweden. Ingrid begged for more time, but Petter was obdurate. She had ruined his life, he said coldly; he would have had a university professorship long ago, but his career had been stymied by international gossip. He had done everything for her, he insisted, and she had been only an ingrate. According to Petter, he knew she was capable of infinite perversity and was unworthy of trust—hence his vigilance over Pia and his cancellation of a longer visit. According to Ingrid and her hosts, she was reduced to tears, and her farewell to Pia was perfunctory.

"The child was wonderful," Ingrid wrote to Irene Selznick from Rome. "So calm about it all. So serene. She talks about Roberto and the baby without any strain. It all seems so natural and simple when you listen to her. She loves me (I pray) but she loves maybe her father more because she has to take care of him . . . She has nothing against coming here, in fact she would love to, but she understands that it hurts Petter, so she has asked me to be patient!"

JUST AS INGRID HERSELF HAD TO BE PATIENT WITH ROBERTO, WHO could not come up with the financing for *Europa '51* until October. At last Carlo Ponti and Dino de Laurentiis came aboard as producers, and in a very hot October, filming began in Rome. Memorable only as a study of Ingrid's face—subtly but expressively beautiful, wistful, sad, determined, amused, frightened—the picture otherwise suffered from abrupt transitions, unclear motivations and an odd mix of religious conviction, social conscience, political outrage and frank sermonizing.

Rossellini never seemed certain whether he was telling a story of a female St. Francis, whom tragedy converts to selfless sainthood, or whether he intended a meditation on the virtues of social revolution ("If you must blame someone for your son's suicide, blame postwar society!" cries a sympathetic Communist in the story). Most of all,

the picture seems to urge Italians to have babies by the score: Giuli-
etta Masina plays a penniless woman living in a state of delirious
happiness because (without a husband) she cares for a hutful of
adorable children and constantly urges everyone else to propagate
to the point of exhaustion.

On its release the following year, Italian audiences loved *Europa
'51* and it was a great success. But elsewhere the picture was all but
ignored, and it is not hard to see the reason. In any case, the
Rossellinis saw not a lira of profit, for Roberto had sold out his
interest to pay bills. This was sadly ironic, for some of Roberto's
closest associates believed that he cast Ingrid in his pictures only
because he had one eye on the box office. When it was finally
released in America as *The Greatest Love*, in 1954, it was the first
Ingrid Bergman picture to be seen there in four years (since *Stromboli*). Audiences then and later noticed that the picture, filmed when
she was thirty-six, showed a strength and mature beauty in Ingrid
that would endure for years to come.

The making of *Europa '51* was a nightmare. Instructed by
Roberto to invent her dialogue as the scene was shot, Ingrid was at a
loss. She tried, but good actors need good writers, and she was
given none. To aggravate the situation, Rome was in the grip of a
terrific heat wave, so Roberto decided to film at night and sent his
cast to bed by day—even though Ingrid wanted to be with
Robertino during daylight hours. In addition, she came down with a
heavy cold she could not lose for weeks. And not least of all, the
filming had to be rushed that autumn before Ingrid's appearance
changed dramatically: she was pregnant again. As she told friends,
bearing and raising her children by Rossellini provided the happiest
experiences of her time in Italy. The films did not.

INGRID HAD HIGH HOPES FOR A NEW STAGE IN HER CAREER WHEN SHE
left Hollywood, but from the start it was clear that she had terribly
miscalculated her suitability for Rossellini's method of filmmaking.
The production of *Stromboli* had been an awful disappointment—
but by then she was pregnant, relying on Roberto as her only source
of strength and moral support. The films she subsequently made
with him were equally disappointing, and she quietly accepted that,
well before forty, she seemed to have lost the direction of her career.

There she was—her career blocked, her talents underused and unappreciated, her relationship with her daughter imperiled, her worldwide popularity dimmed, her sole occupation the household duties of any bourgeois mother. Perhaps worst of all, the marriage for which she had abandoned so much was quickly going stale, and however much they needed a financial success, Roberto would not allow her to work with another director, nor would she endanger their relationship by opposing him. Her situation was, in other words, a variant of her marriage to Petter.

Ingrid had been an artist always eager for work—or for travel if she had no project. Those close to her in the early 1950s worried that the sudden stasis in her career would drive her away from her husband. But even though professionally she was miserable and the tasks of motherhood were insufficiently rewarding, something in her attitude had shifted. She was intent, almost fiercely so, on making this marriage work—and was resolute, too, that she would prove herself a good mother. And so, without a whisper of complaint, she assumed the most unexpected role of her life, that of Signora Rossellini, and she acquitted herself brilliantly.

Trained in the austere Swedish film tradition of the 1930s, she had been crowned with success in the exacting routine of Hollywood in the 1940s. Nothing had prepared her for Rossellini—except her first marriage. Subordinate to a commanding husband for a dozen years, she now found herself in a similar situation. Earlier, her reaction had been flight, but now she remained where her fortunes had led her—and Ingrid Bergman may have been, of all people, the most astonished at herself. Of her deep frustration during her years in Italy, she said only that she once again began to overeat, but that "all the troubles and anguish kept me thin; the spaghetti didn't touch me—I got thinner and thinner." But only, of course, before and after her pregnancies. As the winter days of 1952 became longer and spring approached, Ingrid was unusually large—a condition that caused her some alarm until her doctor confirmed that she was bearing twins.

The babies were due in June, and so in April Ingrid petitioned a Los Angeles court to send her Pia for the summer, against Petter's insistence that he would never allow their daughter in Italy for fear of Rossellini's influence. It would be impossible and undesirable for her to leave her newborn children at home to come to California, Ingrid wrote; in addition, the publicity attendant on her return to America would be unpleasant for Pia.

Among other friends and colleagues, David Selznick spoke most eloquently to the court on Ingrid's behalf. He and Irene had visited the Rossellinis several times in Rome and at Santa Marinella, and he drafted a typically lengthy and forceful letter to the appointed judge in the case. Ingrid and Roberto were the most devoted parents, he insisted, while Lindstrom remained "obviously and bitterly vindictive [and] a revengeful father" intent on destroying Pia's relationship with her mother. Selznick asked rhetorically how much she ought to suffer, how much longer cast in the role of an unforgiven Magdalene.

There was an even more surprising witness to Ingrid's character and to the loving home Roberto provided—Judge Thurmond Clarke, who had granted Lindstrom's divorce in 1950. He had once visited the Rossellinis at Santa Marinella and testified that Pia would be visiting a secure and loving environment: "I would say that the Rossellinis' conduct toward their children [Robertino and Renzo, who was visiting] is one of kindness and devotion. It was what you would call a happy home life." And, he might have added, a somewhat cheerfully chaotic one, as befitted Roberto. In addition to the house staff, there were, at Santa Marinella, six dogs, a score of chickens roaming freely around the grounds, a team of doves and whatever creature dropped in from the surrounding neighborhood and decided to stay for a long visit.

Petter, meantime, submitted a twenty-one-page affidavit rejecting his wife's claim to spend time with their daughter—and in support of his moral outrage, he included Ingrid's letter to him of April 3, 1949, from the Albergo Luna Convento ("Dear Petter: It will be very difficult for you to read this . . . ").

Ingrid's support from Selznick, Clarke and others was unavailing, and her request was denied, for Lindstrom had armed himself with testimony from a psychiatrist named Charles Sturdevant, who stated that a trip to Italy would be emotionally harmful to Pia. He did not add that Petter had told a colleague that "if Pia is asked, he [Lindstrom] would see to it that she would say she did not want to go to Italy."

Which is exactly what Pia, then almost fourteen, said when summoned to court on June 13. "I don't love my mother," she said stoically. "I like her . . . I don't want to go to Italy . . . I would rather live with my father . . . I don't think my mother cares about me too much." Years later, Pia elaborated on the background to that sad day: "My father won custody of me—with my cooperation. He was desperate, and I felt that I was all he had." The judge denied Ingrid's request for a summertime visit with her daughter, who did not see her mother until 1957.*

This latest stage of unpleasantness concluded, Petter and Pia Lindstrom returned to their new home in Pittsburgh, where he assumed the position of chief of neurosurgery at Aspinwall Veterans Hospital and directed a research project on brain disorders at the University of Pittsburgh. His career then flourished for many years. In 1954, at forty-seven, he married Dr. Agnes Rovnanek, a gifted physician twenty-one years his junior. A skilled and devoted pediatrician, she was later a clinical professor of public health. Dr. Rovnanek bore Petter four children, and more than forty years later they were still a devoted couple, delighting in the next two generations of their family.

ON JUNE 18, 1952, IN ROME, INGRID BORE ISABELLA FIORELLA ELETTRA Giovanna and Isotta Ingrid Frieda Giuliana, who was always called Ingrid. That summer, Signe Hasso visited. "I could never understand all that nonsense about Ingrid being a bad mother," she recalled years later. "She was a wonderful mother to her children and always saw that they were well looked after and provided for. Some people might say that in our profession as actors we shouldn't have children—that we're always too busy—and of course there may be some truth to that. But the claim that she was negligent is just ridiculous."

Ingrid's failure to return to America to see her daughter—if only for a brief visit during the next several years—was due not only to her fear of an embarrassing situation on reentry (an excuse ever less likely with each season), or only to a dread of adverse publicity for herself and Pia.

---

*When Pia became a U.S. citizen, she decided to be known as Jenny Ann. But eventually she made peace with her given name and resumed it.

The singular element preventing her reunion with her daughter was Roberto, who was as stern and dominating a mate as Petter. "No one will really understand the force and the fury of Roberto's will," she said later, "[and] I wasn't capable of leaving against Roberto's wishes." Had she gone, there would have been a violent scene on her return, for Roberto said he regarded any such visit as an act of betrayal that would irreparably damage their marriage. And so she stayed, torn between one loyalty and another—and dealt with her anxiety by lavishing time and attention on her three young ones.

Ingrid would not risk this, and so she bowed to Roberto's jealousy the way she had accepted Petter's benevolent autocracy. And on at least a few occasions over the seven years they were together, Roberto's temper turned violent. He had seizures of rage, she said later, episodes that terrified her. Once, at the height of his frenzy, she raced over and threw her arms around him to calm him with a display of devotion—"and bang! he threw me against the wall so hard I almost broke in pieces. I couldn't do anything. Even to get near him was to risk your life."

There was a bitter and ever deepening irony that in Hollywood she had considered Pia something of a burden and an intrusion on her successful career, while Ingrid's children by Rossellini were a refuge and a source of joyous responsibility in Italy, where her career was such a disappointment. In this regard, a telling moment was recorded by the journalist William Safire, then an army corporal with the American Forces Network. She was, he recalled in detail years later, animated and articulate about her work and her life—until Rossellini entered the room, at which time she "underwent an immediate transformation, [becoming] submissive [and] deferring to him on all questions, fearful of expressing herself" in her husband's presence.

FOR THE SECOND HALF OF 1952, INGRID WAS A FULL-TIME MOTHER, while Roberto prepared to direct a production of Verdi's *Otello* at the San Carlo Opera, Naples, in December. Traveling there for the first night, the Rossellinis happened to meet the poet Paul Claudel and the composer Arthur Honegger. Ingrid owned a recording of their religious oratorio *Joan of Arc at the Stake*, which had first been performed in 1938, and when she expressed her admiration, the authors suggested that she perform it on tour across Europe. The role of Joan did not call for singing: the chorus and orchestra provided the music while Joan meditated in verse on her life and trial. Roberto realized that this was a perfect vehicle for his wife and plans were made for them to stage it later that year. Ingrid, to no one's surprise, was delighted with the idea. "There she was, my favorite saint, once again coming to my aid."

While that deal was negotiated, Ingrid swam in the sea and played Ping-Pong with her niece Fiorella, then seventeen and like a daughter to her. By this time, Ingrid spoke superb Italian and was avidly working on her French, for Roberto insisted that one day they would have an apartment in Paris and make films there. Meantime, eager though she was for good work, she accepted that she was under Roberto's control.

DESPERATE AS EVER FOR CASH, ROSSELLINI BEGAN A NEW PICTURE IN Naples on February 5, 1953; the money came from a Milanese industrialist who had worshipped *Open City*. Roberto started, as Ingrid recalled, "without a script, not even an outline, just an idea with no ending!" George Sanders, her co-star in *Rage In Heaven* a dozen years earlier, was imported to play opposite her, and very soon he was close to a nervous breakdown. Even more than Ingrid, he was driven to distraction by Roberto's methods, which included morning levées in the Rossellini hotel suites in Naples, in the countryside and on Capri (which Roberto chose for a few scenes because he needed an excuse for spear-fishing). Everyone scurried around doing very little—a producer and a writer, two assistants and the three children scampering under foot—and Ingrid tried to keep the peace. Sanders hoped in vain, after two weeks, that the film would finally begin in earnest. This period stretched to three months, most of it spent idling as Roberto overslept, played cards and generally temporized.

Scenes scheduled for Sanders's character at two in the afternoon were delayed until three next morning, Roberto having not the remotest idea what he wanted; scenes set for another day and delayed again and again were finally canceled, Roberto having suddenly decided to take off in his Ferrari for a Naples-Rome trial race.

Eventually Sanders was so upset by the lack of work, the nonexistent
script and any real direction that he demanded his wife by his side,
and so the chaotic activity reached a new fever pitch with the arrival
of Zsa Zsa Gabor. But no one was very consoled—except Ingrid,
who took refuge in her children. Her old flame Larry Adler visited
for a few days that spring: "I could see that Rossellini didn't care a
bit about Ingrid's fame, much less how she felt," according to Adler.
"But she went gamely on, making the picture and looking after her
children."

Viaggio in Italia (*Voyage in Italy*), as the film was eventually titled,
was never widely released in the 1950s. The story of an English
couple on holiday in Italy, where they have to confront the emptiness of a dead marriage, it was mostly a travelogue in search of dialogue. The husband decides on a divorce, but at a religious festival
he and his wife are swept along by a crowd crying "Miracle! Miracle!" as the couple realize (why is never explained) their need for
each other. End of so-called story. One indication of its confusion
was that Ingrid always believed the final miracle was the couple's
discovery of love, "and the marriage is going to be good." Roberto,
on the other hand, insisted for the rest of his life that "they come
face to face and realize they do not love each other."

Critics excoriated the film as pointless and dull, poorly written,
incompetently directed and atrociously edited. Ingrid looked nervous and statuesque, which was appropriate enough for a character
shown, for the most part, wandering through museum halls and
empty villas. *Voyage in Italy*, later inexplicably canonized by the
French New Wave, is a triumph of mind-numbing, elegant emptiness. "We never knew one day what we'd be doing the next,"
exclaimed Roberto proudly. "Things came together on the spot!"
No, they did not.

A briefer and lighter episode in the Bergman-Rossellini collaboration occurred before the year was out. Roberto was invited to
contribute a brief comic sketch to the anthology movie *Siamo Donne*
(*We, the Women*), and he decided, as usual, to make things easy for
himself. He set up his camera at Santa Marinella and documented
an afternoon of his wife in the kitchen, coping with a chicken that
kept munching at her favorite roses. This was, as it turned out, a
delicious bit of fun for Ingrid, who delivered, with deadpan gravity,

her invectives against the chicken; this time, her husband's command to make up the dialogue as she proceeded was successful. Adept at spontaneous humor, Ingrid muttered and scolded, and with a malicious grin turned to the camera, to which she confided that her only recourse was to turn the dog loose on the annoying bird. Even three-year-old Robertino made a cameo appearance.

In November 1953, Rossellini's staging of *Joan of Arc at the Stake* opened at his "lucky theater," the Teatro San Carlo in Naples. This was a huge popular success in Italy, and because Ingrid loved it and Roberto needed money, they booked it in Palermo, Milan, Paris, Barcelona, London and Stockholm—and Ingrid very quickly learned the text in five languages. "You read it so simply," said Honegger in appreciation. "Everyone who has done this part usually goes in for exaggerated dramatics and follows the music," Claudel added, smiling, "but you don't." This was the highlight of their lives, said these frail old men; both died in 1955, and Ingrid became very attached to their families.

But the reviews outside Italy were unenthusiastic, for Rossellini missed the point of an oratorio that gave most of the story to singers and required little more of Ingrid than a still, almost mystic calm. She was never more impressive than in the scenes at the stake, but as the company went from city to city a flatness crept into the performances, and it became something less than a dramatic evening under Rossellini's direction. Intrigued by the use of background slides and perhaps thinking of neorealist cinema, he lost the oratorio's intimate, meditative subtext.

Critics were dubious about the production, which was awkward and static, but for Ingrid there was considerable praise. In the middle of the tour, Roberto arranged to film it; later, he said tersely that it was "a total failure, and no one has ever wanted to see it. That is all." Ingrid elaborated: "The language had to go with the music, and [Rossellini] wasn't too careful about that. He played it as background music. In the opera house, it was perfect, but something went wrong with the movie. The music was prerecorded, and that was part of the problem."

As for their income, Ingrid mentioned in letters to friends that with all their traveling expenses (they took their three children and a nanny with them) there was not much cash. "If a good picture comes up, it might be better to do that so as to buy the children new shoes!" There were, perhaps predictably, sneers from columnists who scolded the Rossellinis for wandering around Europe with three small children whom they subjected to such rigors. "I heard that kind of advice before," Ingrid replied. "I never took Pia with me anywhere. This time, I want my children with me!"

Roberto, as usual, would not hear of Ingrid working for another director—although, also as usual, Ingrid and Kay Brown were receiving calls and letters weekly from European directors, and for the first time Ingrid was answering them. The first offers were coming from Hollywood, too, whence George Cukor wrote to ask her interest in a film version of the Hawthorne novel *The Marble Faun*. Ingrid had to reply that her husband read the script and pronounced the treatment of the Italian setting completely unbelievable and impossible. Never mind that it could readily be corrected to conform to accurate style and history: Rossellini had put his foot down, and that was that. This, as her old friend Joe Steele knew, made clear the first fissures in the Rossellini idyll.

Meantime, Roberto came up with a Stefan Zweig story called *Fear*, which they filmed quickly in Munich (home of the producers) in 1954, during an interval in the *Joan* tour. Seen years later, *Fear* is a movie that almost succeeds. Ingrid (again named Irene, as she was in *Europa '51*) portrays the wife of a successful scientist and factory owner. She has taken a lover and is blackmailed by the lover's former mistress—until she learns that her husband is behind the blackmailing. Separated from her children—whom the husband has forced to live in the country—and now without lover or husband, she is about to take her life when her husband stops her. "I love you!" she says improbably as they embrace. End of story.

With a bit more attention to the script and a more complex finale, *Fear* might have been a kind of renaissance for Rossellini. It has better pacing than any film since *Open City* (except for the little homemade documentary in *We, the Women*), and Ingrid's performance is well matched by those of her co-stars. Especially effective is the central telephone scene: her voice quivers as she expresses her love for her children even as she implies her imminent suicide. As so often, she focused a conflict of feelings with minimal expression—a talent recognized at the time by the few critics who saw the film, which disappeared quickly without a trace. After ten days of work on it, Ingrid was convinced she would never make another picture with her husband, whose self-confidence was by this time completely broken. His creative energy shut down.

BOB CAPA'S SUDDEN DEATH IN MAY 1954, WHEN HE WAS KILLED BY A land mine in Indochina, brought a long haze of grief to Ingrid, whose unhappiness was relieved only by her children. She and Capa had not met in several years, but her fondness for him was quietly tucked away in a corner of her heart, as she wrote to Ruth and Kay. There was no use unburdening to Roberto, who was jealous of all those who preceded him.

On October 2, Ingrid, Roberto, the children and a small staff of retainers arrived in London, and three weeks later *Joan of Arc at the Stake* opened for twenty-nine performances at the Stoll Theatre. The production was generally regarded by critics as a synthesis of styles, fussily elaborate and static. Ingrid was respectfully (but not ardently) praised, although several critics found her inaudible and ill at ease onstage.

BUT THE REACTION OF STOCKHOLM'S CRITICS EARLY THE FOLLOWING year was far chillier. *Joan*, which began its run at the Konserthus on February 17, 1955, was demolished by the press, whose leading critic used the opportunity to savage the character and personality of their own native daughter. "She travels around and is exhibited for money," wrote Stig Ahlgren in *Vecko-Journalen*. "The ringmaster is Rossellini, with whom she has three children and one Rolls-Royce. She is paid very well and deserves nothing, for she is not even an actress, let alone an artist." There was worse, and invariably the remarks were directed at her private life; Ahlgren, for example, went so far as to mock Ingrid's low-heeled shoes and her children's clothes.

After consulting Edvin Adolphson, with whom she had a friendly reunion, Ingrid decided to strike back. After a benefit matinee to aid victims of the infantile paralysis scourge that had so badly affected Sweden, Ingrid was invited to draw some winning tickets in a charity raffle. Then, as planned, Adolphson turned to the audience: "Ingrid Bergman would like to address the audience." There was a rustle of uncertain discomfiture in the house. "Would you like to tell us your impressions about your return to Sweden?" he asked.

Pale but fearless, she stepped to the footlights:

I am very happy to be home again, and to speak Swedish again. But a group of brave knights from the press came forward and have tried to cut me down. Yesterday, I read Stig Ahlgren's article. And everywhere I am accused of doing nothing but seeking publicity. But it is not I who ask for publicity! I am not sending the photographers to hound me at the theater and at my hotel. They condemn me for not allowing them to take photos of my children, and they condemn me because I finally relented and allowed a few to be published. I feel like Indra's daughter in Strindberg's 'Dream Play,' of whom it is said, "Beat her if she answers and beat her if she refuses to!"

But of course I am not the only one treated this way in my own country—it was the same with Garbo and others. I am afraid Swedes do not want anyone to be different—like the situation in Hans Christian Andersen's fairy tale in which anyone taller than the crowd is decapitated so all will be alike.

I wanted to take this opportunity to speak to you directly, not through the press, who would of course only distort my words. For the past six years, others have constantly been slandering me, condemning me, passing judgment without knowing anything at all of my life. I wanted you good people who have supported our oratorio, to know the truth, at least.

With that, she stepped back and bowed to the audience, who at once stomped their feet, clapped, shouted and rose in approval. Her triumph was greater than in the performance. Still, unpleasant letters poured in to her suite at the Grand Hotel. "They have driven me to the point of desperation," she said of the ugly words. "I cannot sleep for the mental torture I am subjected to by my fellow countrymen."

EARLY THAT SUMMER, THE TOUR WAS FINISHED AND THE ROSSELLINIS returned to Rome, where there was a message waiting from the Romanian-French actress Elvire Popesco, now a theatrical producer at the Théâtre de Paris. Tennessee Williams's play *Cat on a Hot Tin Roof* and Robert Anderson's *Tea and Sympathy* would soon be produced in Paris: would she consider returning to the theater in one of them? It was obvious that Ingrid, who marked her fortieth birthday in August, was certainly much too old to play Maggie in *Cat*. But the role of Laura, the headmaster's wife who offers tea and sympathy, and, it is implied in a scene of exquisite delicacy at the final curtain, also offers herself to a shy young man, was tailor-made for her, and she wanted very much to do it. Deborah Kerr had had a huge success with the play in New York, and Ingrid would make it her own in Paris.

At first, as Robert Anderson recalled years later, Popesco sensed some doubts among critics and the public when Ingrid was mentioned for the part, and so the producer asked Anderson (whose wife was gravely ill at the time) to meet the Rossellinis in Rome.

"She wanted very much to do it," recalled Robert Anderson years later, "and of course I approved of her immediately. When I went to Rome, Roberto didn't know the play at all, and he withdrew to another room of their apartment while we spoke." Directly Anderson departed, Roberto gave his opinion of *Tea and Sympathy*: "Ingrid, it is trash, and if *you* do it, it will fail after a week!" So much for spousal encouragement.

Nor would Rossellini condescend to direct *Tea and Sympathy*, as Popesco and Anderson had initially suggested, to assure Ingrid's participation. Besides, Roberto was preparing to go to India to make a documentary: she would have to look after the children. "Roberto prefers a wife who sits at home and waits for him," Ingrid said at the time. "In his terms, I am his property." But I just can't stand our insecure, hand-to-mouth existence. Maybe if we'd had one successful picture together, it might be different. I have to go back to work, and he'll just have to get used to it. I've got to do something—for myself as well as to buy the children shoes. Our increasing debts worry me enormously."

The silences between Ingrid and Roberto grew more obvious and more tense throughout 1955. He became more anxious about the evident collapse of his own career, and more anxious still that his wife might have a renaissance once she was free of his direction. "He liked to fight," according to Ingrid, who was first advised to end her marriage by Mathias Wiemann, her co-star in *Fear.* That was out of the question, she replied. What would become of him—and what of her children, whom any court would assign to his custody? She did not, it must be noted, add that she still loved Roberto; indeed, one could say that the Bergman-Rossellini marriage failed because the art failed. His promise to her was unfulfilled, therefore the bond vanished—just as her marriage to Lindstrom failed when his "support" became empty business, without reference to her art.

LATER THAT SUMMER, THERE WAS A CALL AND THEN A VISIT FROM HER old friend Jean Renoir, who was creating a story and screenplay specifically for her—a comedy with music. At Santa Marinella, Ingrid sat at the seaside and read an actual shooting script for a film with period costumes, a musical score, characters, professional actors—a *movie*, prepared meticulously, something she had not read in seven years! Each time she put the script aside to think about the part, she gazed over the calm waters, smiling in anticipation.

To be called *Elena et les Hommes* (*Elena and Her Men,* eventually released in America as *Paris Does Strange Things*), the film was a Gallic farce about Princess Elena Sorokowska (Ingrid) who dallies with men and brings them considerable professional success: a general (Jean Marais) who plans to become a benevolent dicatator after a coup d'état; a young count (Mel Ferrer) who really loves her; and a rich, older bourgeois (Pierre Bertin). The story was messy, needlessly convoluted and gossamer thin—a fancy burlesque of chauvinism, French country life and shallow amours—but it had a lively affability, and the humor was exactly what she wanted at the time. It was, in other words, entirely different from the fare created for her by Rossellini—who, as it happened, reluctantly agreed to let her do it. His journey to India was postponed, and he accompanied her to Paris with the children.

Ingrid took a small suite at the Raphael Hotel, which would be her occasional home for much of the next several years, especially when she worked on the Paris stage. Did she miss Rome and Santa Marinella? Had she ever really missed her homes in Stockholm and Beverly Hills? Well, she always said when such a discussion arose, she felt no such nostalgia for past residences. Home was where she was at the moment; of her it could be said—as Marcia Davenport had written of Lena Geyer—"She was indeed sentimental, but only in the matter of her personal feelings, not where she could be fixed in a literal attachment to a place or to things."

CLEARLY, INGRID WAS BACK IN HER ELEMENT AT THE JOINVILLE STUDIOS six miles outside Paris. With her usual industrious alacrity, she learned the role in French as well as in English for the foreign market. Dressed in magnificent gowns and photographed in crisp, lush Technicolor, she was more beautiful than ever. Time and trouble had stamped strength and maturity on her face—but not hardness—and her vivacity was highlighted by a warm elegance. Renoir wisely made her character a Polish princess to cover her accented French, which thus seemed charming and not gauche.

Production lasted from November 1955 to early March 1956, and of course the news of Ingrid working without Rossellini was very quickly trumpeted by the world's press. And with that, Kay Brown took action. Twentieth Century-Fox had bought film rights to a British play that had a healthy run in New York in 1954— *Anastasia*, the story of Anna Anderson's claim to be the Grand Duchess, daughter of Czar Nicholas II, who had survived the 1918 massacre of the Romanovs. Ingrid read the script adapted by Arthur Laurents from Guy Bolton's play: the role had a marvelous range, from her scenes as a grimy, suicidal wanderer to her training as a credible Grand Duchess to the final triumph of acceptance by international society.

This was not only a glamorous, exotic story with a highly desirable leading role: it could also become virtually an analogue of her image in the eyes of America (from royal princess to outcast Cinderella and back again); at least it was a fine script with a deeply sympathetic and serious character. (In this regard, the character of Anastasia was not at all consistent with the truth that most suspected and was later firmly established—namely, that the real Grand Duchess had indeed been slaughtered with her family, and that Anna Anderson was a third-class fraud.) Such a marvelous character would surely not hurt the cause of Ingrid's restoration to the graces of censorious America.

To play Anastasia, Jennifer Jones was the first choice of Spyros Skouras, Fox's president. But he was challenged by production chief

Darryl Zanuck, who agreed with Kay that this was the perfect time
to reintroduce Ingrid Bergman. She would not only draw the curious, insisted Zanuck: the hysteria of seven years earlier had surely
been inflated, she would again be accepted as the great actress she
was, and Fox ought to spare no expense in the production to back
their corporate assertions with confidence. But Skouras countered
that Bergman would be a curse on any project, and to support this
he submitted the results of a poll. "So long as I am censor here,"
replied a civil servant from Tennessee, "I will never permit any picture with Ingrid Bergman on Memphis screens." That, Skouras said,
was evidence enough.

But Zanuck held firm, Tennessee or no Tennessee, and eventually he had the support of Buddy Adler, who was to produce the
picture in London and Paris, and of Anatole Litvak, a Russian-born
immigrant to Hollywood who had a strong feeling for the Romanov
culture. Rather than risk revolt by these talents, Skouras relented,
his board nervously agreed, and Ingrid, in December 1955, signed a
contract to appear in *Anastasia* the following summer. The picture
will be a total failure, said Roberto, who walked out of the room as
Ingrid was putting pen to her agreement. "But I had decided the
time had come to face up to him," she said later. "I had been in
professional exile for more than seven years and that was long
enough." That evening they quarreled violently, and Roberto threatened, yet again, to kill himself by crashing his Ferrari into a tree.
Ingrid made herself a cup of tea.

SHE WENT DIRECTLY FROM THE DUBBING OF *ELENA ET LES HOMMES*, IN
March, to wardrobe and makeup tests for *Anastasia*, to be made in
Technicolor and CinemaScope from May to August 1956. Roberto's
trip to India was again postponed, this time until the end of the year
because of a money shortage and seasonal monsoons. While he
waited, he accepted an offer to direct a movie called *Sea Wife*, a
drama about a shipwreck, starring Richard Burton and Joan Collins.
But after a week's work in Jamaica, he had so alienated the cast and
crew that producer Andre Hakim threatened to take him off the
picture.

Demanding a meeting with Hakim in London, Roberto arrived
and was greeted by the director of MCA's London office, Laurence

Evans, the dean of London agents and a man who exercised his considerable influence with a rare combination of keen intelligence, graceful wit and impeccable ethics. He had looked after Ingrid during the production of *Under Capricorn*, had quickly become a good friend as well as a wise counselor, and now had been contacted by her with the request for help in deflecting adverse publicity from her husband. With his usual skill, Evans simply ordered Roberto to say not a single word to the press and escorted him to the Savoy Hotel, where Ingrid was also lodged.

The meeting with Hakim changed nothing, and Roberto was dismissed from *Sea Wife*. Now he began to regard with irrational suspicion and resentment his wife's revived career. Just as 1950 through 1955 had been a *rallentando* in her own life, so now there was in one year a flurry of rewarding activity. Roberto, during that visit, had the odd idea that Ingrid's business would endanger the family life, and so he threatened to take the children away with him to Italy and then to India: they were his children as she was his property.

Roberto's possessiveness, which frequently became verbally angry and abusive, "has gone on for so long I don't know what to believe any more," as Ingrid wrote to a friend. Now he suddenly demanded a separation—with full custody of their children. Threats and tirades followed in rapid succession, and Ingrid was terrified. "I am afraid of losing my children again. I am not afraid of being alone, but of having made four children and all taken away from me." And with that, Roberto took Robertino, Isabella and little Ingrid and went at once to Santa Marinella, his refuge where he could be alone with the children.

Anastasia was, as it turned out, made entirely in London's Borehamwood Studios but for a few exteriors in Paris at night, and Zanuck and Adler were true to their promise: the film had the unusually high budget of $3.5 million, and no expense was spared to assure a first-class production. "I am," said Ingrid the first day of shooting, "so excited to be back working on a set." Some bystanders may have appreciated the implication.

Yul Brynner was in the cast as the intense Bounine, who trains and tutors Anna Anderson until he, too, is disturbed by her awareness of things only a Romanov could know; and Helen Hayes was playing the Dowager Empress Marie, Anastasia's grandmother.* In their recognition scene—beginning with the rejection of Bergman by the suspicious Hayes—both actresses prepared privately, with great respect for one another's strength in the scene. Laurents greatly improved the play's dialogue throughout, and in this sequence especially, the players rose gradually from remorse to querulousness to pleading and finally to love born of desperation.

Litvak, Hayes, Brynner and the entire international cast knew very early on that Ingrid's performance was nothing short of marvelous. She portrayed a woman steeped in the pain of rejection who is, quite against her will, used by people eager for fame and cash. But the game goes so far that she offers evidence that she might be the real Anastasia—and from a disturbed wanderer she emerges out of a chrysalis of confusion to become the most royal of princesses. Perhaps no one in her time could be so convincing in this as Ingrid Bergman; surely very few would have brought the sense of inner struggle, the ambiguous feeling of resentful, pained longing that Ingrid projected in every scene.

Zanuck's delegates, murmuring about the strong likelihood of an Academy Award, dropped none too subtle hints with the press— especially the popular television variety-show host Ed Sullivan, who negotiated to bring a crew from New York to London to film a brief interview and some documentary footage of the production in progress. This he planned to broadcast, with the hearty approval of Fox, that August. But first he decided to poll his nationwide network audience. "It's your decision," he announced on July 29, 1956. "Drop me a note if you want her on the show—and if you don't—well, tell me that, too. I'd like to get your verdict." Overconfident that she had, as he said, "suffered enough for her sins and done enough penance [!]" and that the public would welcome Ingrid, he was shocked by the mail: 5,826 letters were in favor of her interview on the show, but 6,433 were not. A humorless man of his word, Sullivan reluctantly abided by the verdict. Ingrid was any-

---

*The role of the Dowager Empress had been played to great effect on the London stage by Helen Haye, a classical English actress and a renowned teacher. Accordingly, the cable to Litvak from Fox's New York offices read SIGN HELEN HAYE. But this was read as a typographical error, and Helen Hayes was contracted and signed.

thing but home free in the eyes of America, although these may have been only the eyes of those who watched Ed Sullivan and were parochial enough to send letters of their undiminished disapproval.

PRINCIPAL PHOTOGRAPHY OF *ANASTASIA* WAS COMPLETE BY LATE AUGUST 1956, and it was hurried through editing and scoring for a December release. Then, for readings and rehearsals of *Tea and Sympathy* with director Jean Mercure and co-stars Yves Vincent and Jean-Loup Philippe, Ingrid rushed back to Paris. There she found Roberto chilly, withdrawn and moodily preparing for his long delayed journey to India. Everything seemed to go against him, he said, when Ingrid pressed for an explanation of his dark spirits. At the same time, she knew her marriage was deeply troubled when she insisted on going ahead with *Tea and Sympathy*. "It was for the children's sake that Roberto and I stayed together as long as we did," she said not long after. "He does not want me to do this, he does not want me to do that. But I am assuming my own responsibility for a change."

Rehearsals proceeded slowly, for Ingrid stumbled on some of the French translation by Roger Ferdinand. Then, on Saturday, November 10, she felt ill but insisted her trouble was mere indigestion. Three days later, she could no longer ignore the abdominal pain, then complicated by other nasty symptoms. On November 14, Ingrid underwent an appendectomy at the American Hospital at Neuilly, where she remained for a week—memorizing her role as Laura.

Meantime, in America, the long ordeal of Robert Anderson's wife Phyllis was soon over: she died of cancer on November 28, after a bitter, five-year struggle during which he somehow balanced dedication to his work with devoted care of her. Then thirty-nine, Anderson was coping not only with the necessary postmortem details but also with a profound grief that left him close to nervous collapse save for the attention of his family and friends. Christmas was a short time away, and Kay Brown called Ingrid, who at once telephoned Anderson: "I think you belong over here during this difficult period," she told him. "It's Christmas, and the play will supply you with a family." And so a room was booked for him at the Raphael Hotel.

Tea and Sympathy was a resounding triumph for both playwright and actress. The audience of twelve hundred brought Ingrid back for fifteen curtain calls, and she received superb notices. That night, crowds surrounded the theater for hours afterward, straining for a glimpse of a woman who had never fallen from grace in the City of Lights. The critics were adoring, even to the point of ignoring her heavily accented French, which sometimes led to such hilarious gaffes as referring to the boy Tom as a "mushroom": instead of correctly saying the French word *champion*, she tripped and turned him into a *champignon*. Both the audience and her co-stars were mute, shaking with laughter and pressing handkerchiefs to their faces. Ingrid stepped forward, held her hand high to the audience, faced them and corrected herself: "Il est le champion de l'école!" That won over the crowd and they stood and cheered for three minutes. How could Paris not fall in love with such a performer?

But one spectator was far from benevolent. Roberto sat backstage during the entire performance, refusing to join the audience, denying his wife a word of encouragement or congratulations. After the first act, he asked his wife, "Is anybody still there? Hasn't the whole audience left by now?" After the second, he said, "Have they started throwing things yet?" And after the third, the roar of applause was like a slap in Roberto's face. "He was red with fury," recalled actress Simone Paris, also in the play. "At the end," Ingrid told Bob Anderson (who arrived a few days after the first performance), "I had a fourteen-minute ovation. But when I looked over and saw Roberto in the wings, I knew my marriage was over."

The audience's wild enthusiasm, the rush of admirers backstage and the crush of the press were too much for Rossellini, and that night he sped from Paris to Rome, whence he finally departed for India. His last words to Ingrid: "It won't last a week, you will kill this terrible show." This ominous prediction—wide of the mark, indeed, for she had a nine-month sold-out run of the play in Paris—was like a dagger to her heart. She would so have appreciated a kind word from a man whose talent she held in such high regard.

ON HIS ARRIVAL IN PARIS ON DECEMBER 10, BOB ANDERSON, STILL enveloped in a haze of mourning, was immediately warmed by the performance of the actress who, he reckoned, had blessed his play with her own particular grace and style. Together, they shared their separate hurts: she spoke of what was happening in India, he of his great loss. It is not surprising, then, that these two people found a deep and abiding comfort with each other, nor that during his time in Paris they were the most devoted lovers, caring for one another and rejoicing in the success of his play and her performance in it. "One critic," recalled Anderson, "liked Ingrid more than *Tea and Sympathy*, and he wrote 'Ingrid Bergman saves the play.'" The playwright would, soon after, use those words well.

Every evening, Anderson attended the performance or came backstage to meet her afterward, and they returned to the Raphael together. By day, they spent quiet time together, lunched in a cafe of the Bois de Boulogne, accepted invitations to parties given in her honor, huddled in the December chill and quickened their steps as they browsed along the Rue de Rivoli. "She really dedicated her time to me," Anderson reflected forty years later. "And she didn't make any plans for after her performances unless she knew I was taken care of."

And so it went that winter. One of them was enduring the terrible wound of a beloved's death, the other had just faced the awful truth that her marriage was dead. "He was very close to me in those days," wrote Ingrid of this precious time in their lives. "Maybe I was in need, too. I knew it was important perhaps to both of us." That season was, as Anderson may have realized, very like the situation of his play: a sensitive man near to heartbreak was loved by a woman who was also in a state of needy confusion because she had at last broken with her husband. Onstage, Laura approached Tom, in Anderson's classic, touching final scene, with a delicacy that has entered the iconography of the modern theater. Offstage, Ingrid Bergman and Robert Anderson brought to one another the gentleness, the compassion and consolation that blunted the keen edge of their grief. She would not, for example, allow him to spend hours weeping over the mass of condolence letters he felt obliged to answer. "Come along, Bob!" she said, sweeping the letters aside. "Now let's go out and do something!"

One of their errands was to find for Ingrid a copy of a new, highly praised novel, *The Nun's Story*, which Bob had read. Based on the true-life account of a Belgian woman who entered and years later left the institutional religious life, it was quite a success that year, and film rights had been sold to Warner Bros., where producer Henry Blanke sought the ideal writer and cast for the project. Phyllis Anderson had thought Bob would be the right screenwriter, and Kay Brown had recommended it to Ingrid. But when Ingrid read it, she realized at once that (quite apart from her earlier role as Sister Benedict) she was really too old for the part; she agreed, however, that Bob ought to do the script. The rest, as the saying goes, is history. Robert Anderson's subsequent screenplay for Fred Zinnemann's film of *The Nun's Story* was a masterpiece of writing for the screen. It was also arguably Audrey Hepburn's finest performance. No one was happier for their success than Ingrid.

THEIR VARIETY OF ACTIVITIES THAT WINTER, WAS, BOB KNEW, NOT ONLY Ingrid's way of distracting him: she was also diverting herself, for with the speed of the racer, Roberto Rossellini had, within days of his arrival in India, stirred up a terrific scandal. He was photographed day and night, at work and at dinner, hand in hand with an exotic beauty named Sonali Senroy Das Gupta, his co-writer on the film and the wife of his Indian producer. The press was immediately at Ingrid's door, they were at the theater, they rang her room and left her notes. Had she any comment on the rumors of her husband's affair? With great dignity, she mocked their temerity; privately, she confided to Bob that she was not at all surprised. Bemused, and with a sense of irony, she saw the situation as the reverse of her own, seven years earlier. Now it was her spouse who had gone off to another country and had taken a collaborator for a lover.

Whatever unhappiness or humiliation she felt Ingrid kept to herself. Christmas was upon them, and with it a bittersweetness both she and Bob blanketed with generosity. She took considerable time and enormous care shopping for presents for him and for her children, who were brought up from Rome for the holiday, while he brought a tree to her suite and carefully decorated it.

And very unlike the case of Roberto and *Tea and Sympathy*, Bob was delighted with the marvelous news Ingrid then received from America. *Anastasia* had opened with gala premieres in New York and

Los Angeles, and Ingrid's critical and popular praise was undilutedly brilliant. One had to go back more than a decade to read such riotous acclaim for her acting. She was "nothing short of superb in a beautifully molded performance worthy of an Academy Award," wrote Bosley Crowther in the *New York Times*. His colleagues were just as laudatory. Tracing the passage of a woman from emotional collapse and confusion through doubt to the acceptance of a new identity—as the celebrated "discovery" Anastasia and as an ordinary woman capable of love—Ingrid gave moviegoers a double blessing. She was a haunting, pathetic figure, lost in delusion, and then she was resplendent in her nobility.

It was perhaps this once lost but ever indomitable and finally triumphant Anastasia, so like Ingrid Bergman herself, that audiences and critics recognized when they fell in love with her all over again at the end of 1956, for America liked nothing so much as the grand gesture of forgiving a sinner who had, it was felt, done time enough in penitential garb. It was time for her to be restored to glory.

Chapter Sixteen

1957–1964

I am gradually approaching the period in my life
when work comes first.

KÄTHE KOLLWITZ,
Diary

L ATE ONE AFTERNOON, INGRID RUSHED BACK TO HER SUITE AT THE
Raphael after a shopping expedition. "Look what I bought!" she
said excitedly to Bob Anderson. She unwrapped a parcel slightly
larger than a postcard, and there was a miniature oil painting by
Auguste Renoir, the father of her recent director. "This," she said
significantly to Bob, "is the first time in my life I have had the
chance to handle my own money. So I surprised myself, went out
and bought something for me!" It was, as they both knew, a marker
of a new freedom in her life, although that would come at a price
dearer than that of the Renoir. And as for handling her own money,
it was clear that Ingrid was living modestly. She had to: there had
been no income from her Rossellini films, and everything she had
prior to 1950 was spent in her divorce from Lindstrom.

That same season in early 1957, after her performance in *Tea
and Sympathy*, Ingrid and Bob were sharing supper in her suite at the

Raphael when a telephone call came through from Cary Grant in Hollywood. He and director Stanley Donen had just formed a production company, and they wanted Ingrid to join them in their first venture, a movie of Norman Krasna's 1953 comedy *Kind Sir*, which had failed on Broadway but for which they predicted great success as a movie. Ingrid asked Cary to wait while she consulted an expert.

"*Kind Sir?*" she asked, turning to Bob.

"A terrible disaster," he whispered. "Don't do it."

"My adviser here says it's awful," Ingrid told Cary, who asked if she would meet with Donen, perhaps that summer? She would.

Another evening, *Tea and and Sympathy* was dark (a Paris tradition, so that all working actors might have the opportunity to see colleagues in other plays) and Bob and Ingrid attended a performance of *Cat on a Hot Tin Roof*. During a party backstage, Bob introduced Ingrid to a tall, blond, handsome man—a gracious waiter, thought Ingrid, who was momentarily distracted during the introduction. But no, as she learned later from Bob: the "waiter" was the play's European producer, a successful impresario named Lars Schmidt—who also happened to be Bob's Scandinavian agent.

Sometime after that, at the suggestion of Kay Brown, who thought that two Swedes in Paris ought to meet, Lars rang to ask Ingrid to lunch. She was sorry, Ingrid replied, adding (so as not to complicate the matter) that she "needed to play with her children in the Bois de Boulogne." Hours later, after she and Bob had dined and were strolling in the park, none other than Lars Schmidt happened by. "I saw a couple who looked so romantic," Lars recalled, "and it turned out to be Ingrid and Bob. I passed them and said, 'Well, so this is how one plays with the children in the Bois!'" Ingrid blushed and asked me to call her, we had dinner that night, and were never really separated for very long again."

Before his return to New York, Bob went to Cartier's, where he bought a silver plate for Ingrid. On it he had engraved a quote from one of the critics: "Ingrid Bergman saves the play," and to this he added "—and a playwright."

Soon there was good reason for a temporary shuttering of *Tea and Sympathy* that month. Ingrid had won the New York Film Critics' Circle Award as best actress for *Anastasia*, and producer Buddy Adler wanted her to come to Manhattan to collect the award. After all, the Oscar nominations were coming up on the calendar, and the publicity could not hurt either that chance or the box-office for *Anastasia*. In fact, later that winter Ingrid indeed received her fifth best actress nomination.

She was, understandably, very nervous about such a return, having resigned herself perhaps never to return to America and certainly not to submit to the press, which was the point of this journey. But her contract specified publicity appearances on behalf of *Anastasia*, and so she honored the clause. Twentieth Century-Fox paid Madame Popesco to shut down her theater for the one night Ingrid would be away: she would be back on the stage of the Théâtre de Paris immediately after. And so on Saturday morning, January 19, Ingrid stepped from an airplane to greet a crowd of fans and a squad of newsmen awaiting her at Idlewild Airport, New York.

This was her first visit to America since her departure eight years earlier, and every moment of her schedule, up to her departure Sunday evening, was booked by Fox's publicity staff (who had agreed to allow her three hours to see a Saturday theater matinee). They had, first of all, arranged for a press conference at the airport—an event Ingrid got through with remarkable calm and good humor. Journalists were not shy: did she have any regrets about her life? If she had it to do all over again, would she do things differently? How did she think of herself?

"I have had a wonderful life," she said calmly, smiling at each reporter in turn. "I have never regretted what I did. I regret the things I *didn't* do. My life has been rich and full of interesting things. All my life, I've done exactly what I wanted to, often at a moment's notice. Well, I was given courage, a sense of adventure and a little bit of humor . . . It was pretty tough in those days [in 1949 and 1950], but time takes care of everything. I don't think anyone has the right to intrude in your private life, but they do." She would not be trapped, and she might have seemed, to anyone who knew her literary forebear, to be taking again a page from Lena Geyer, who said, "I never have regrets for anything. I feel everything—but I must look ahead!"

That afternoon, she was whisked unnoticed past the stage door into the Mark Hellinger Theater, where she saw *My Fair Lady*. Word rustled through the house, and after the final curtain, the audience gave Ingrid a standing ovation. From there, she was rushed to the

Roxy Theater, where Joan Crawford presented her with an award from *Look* magazine for *Anastasia*. That evening she accepted the Film Critics' award at a dinner-reception at Sardi's, the legendary theater restaurant, where she was interviewed by Steve Allen for television broadcast. On Sunday morning, after giving several interviews in Swedish, German, Italian and French, she prepared to depart, having pocketed the heart of the city and staked a claim to that of the country as well. "No one could be happier over Miss Bergman's comeback than I," said ex-Senator Edwin C. Johnson, who seven years earlier had asked the country to join him in barring her from its pure shores.

These details of Ingrid's itinerary would not otherwise be necessary but for an ugly rumor that circulated for decades—namely, that Ingrid refused to see Pia, then a student at the University of Colorado.

Ingrid knew very well that if she brought her daughter to New York, the press would have overwhelmed both of them on her arrival and that she (perhaps not Pia) could not refrain from breaking down. She would have been fortunate to have a few moments alone with her daughter during the entire thirty-hour sojourn, and that would have been inevitably misreported by journalists, who would have taken their brief meeting as either trivial or a sign of a rupture between them. Ingrid and Pia spoke by phone, which did little to bridge the six-year gap between them.

NOR COULD INGRID FIND PRIVATE TIME FOR ROBERT ANDERSON, WHO by now had fallen deeply in love with her. They did meet, however briefly, at a reception given by Irene Selznick before the award dinner. In a letter Ingrid wrote on a page of a small pocket notebook as she departed New York (a letter subsequently posted from Paris), she explained her feelings about their relationship, why she urged him to move on with his life, and why she thought that a certain realism—no matter how hard it may sound—ought to determine the course of their lives.

Dear Bob,
I can't wait to write! The plane has just taken off. I cried. I turned my face outside the window so no one would see it. I am so tired, Bob, but I

was also moved by all the people who were there to wave and stayed on and on in the cold until we took off. I have so much to be grateful for. I had to go through television, radio and photos, almost as bad as when I arrived. I was just on the verge of breaking down and crying in front of them.

It was too tough. That's why I thought it better you didn't come to the airport. You've asked me so many times [when you could return to me in Paris], and I said, "Wait." It is not that I don't want you to. I want you to get hold of yourself alone. I can't help you. Right now, you must fight it out alone. To be in Paris again would just be to hide away with one person. But you know it would only be worse for you afterwards. There will always come the time when you have to face the loneliness. I'll be thinking of you tomorrow as the curtain goes up and I count the house.

Goodnight,
Ingrid

Anderson was touched by and grateful for her honesty. Yes, he was in love with her. But that had happened very quickly, and however deep the attachment and genuine the mutual devotion, it sprang from a critical, *ad hoc* moment of profound need in their lives. She could easily have encouraged the affair, but after all she was still both Mrs. Rossellini and Ingrid Bergman, a woman whose life was again changing dramatically, both personally and professionally. Life with her would have meant geographic chaos and disarticulation for Anderson, who was an important voice in the American theater and had been contracted for major screenwriting assignments.

Without their life together, his talent would increase and multiply; but if they threw in their fortunes with one another—well, she, at least, sensed dragons, and she was right. He was still a grieving widower, and this was no time to make a commitment. Ingrid and Bob were, in the final analysis, two good and decent people who cared deeply for one another, and she wanted their love to endure beyond passion and into friendship. That it did was a testament to their maturity, their dignity and the deep, affectionate respect they always kept for one another.

*   *   *

INGRID RETURNED TO THE TAXING SCHEDULE OF PERFORMANCES onstage in *Tea and Sympathy*, a routine that occupied her into the summer of 1957. And very soon she was called on by Lars Schmidt.

Born June 11, 1917, Lars Schmidt was the son of Hugo Schmidt, a career lieutenant in the Swedish army, and his wife, Sigrid. Lars had at first prepared to enter the shipbuilding business, but he was always intrigued by the theater, and by 1941 was producing plays—mostly in Gothenburg but then elsewhere in Sweden and on the Continent, where he introduced works by Arthur Miller and Tennessee Williams, among many others. In 1954, he moved to Paris and later established himself as a major producer with the success of *Cat on a Hot Tin Roof*. That spring of 1957, he was negotiating for the European rights to *My Fair Lady*. Intelligent, perceptive, witty and unaffectedly charming, he had good friends and admirers all over the world. A previous marriage had been dissolved, and he had suffered the tragedy of his only child's accidental death. That spring, Ingrid and Lars enjoyed each other's company enormously—but for the present, Ingrid did not encourage anything other than friendship.

That quality was very much evident on March 27, when Ingrid received her second best actress Oscar and Cary Grant accepted on her behalf: "Dear Ingrid, if you can hear me now or will see this televised film later, I want you to know that each of the other nominees and all the people with whom you worked on *Anastasia*, and Hitch, and Leo McCarey, and indeed everyone here tonight, send you congratulations and love and admiration and every affectionate thought." Two days later, Ingrid wrote to Cary:

> I got the news about the Award in the morning at six o'clock. I said on the phone, "I got it?" The answer was "yes," and I fell asleep again. This seems a very indifferent way of accepting an Oscar . . . Several hours later, when I was in the bathtub, Robertino rushed in with a portable radio and I heard my name and heard you say [in a recorded news item on the radio], "If you can hear me now," and I said, "I am here, Cary, in the bathroom!" That was the moment I really received the Oscar and I felt tears coming to my eyes . . . I got it in the bathroom. What a place to get an Oscar.

That season, Lars and Ingrid spent more and more time together, and he came to know her as a remarkably honest person who, in spite of her problems, retained an admirable passion for life and work. In the early stages of their life together, Lars felt that the physical and emotional connection with Ingrid "was based on complete abandonment and boundless generosity on her part. I gave her the security she lacked, and she gave me the passion and the confidence to complete the union."

They had met after their respective ruptured relations—she after two failed marriages, he after one and the death of his son. And although their constant companions for the first two years of their life together were lawyers in Rome, Paris, London and Stockholm (negotiating the Rossellini separation), Ingrid never ceased to be present to Lars—indeed, to depend on him even more than she ever did on Petter and Roberto.

But not everything that spring of 1957 was so pleasant. In the middle of the night of May 17, Ingrid received a telephone call from Bombay, India, in her suite at the Raphael. Roberto warned her that a scandal was about to break, but that she must not believe a word of it—which of course had precisely the opposite effect. Two days later, the press broke the story of fifty-one-year-old Rossellini's affair with twenty-seven-year-old Sonali Das Gupta, who had two children. Ingrid turned aside reporters' questions with a wave of her hand and a laugh of denial, but it was an unconvincing performance. From India, the principals issued flat denials for the next several months.

THAT SUMMER, INGRID HAD A VERY WELCOME DIVERSION FROM thoughts of marital discord and, it seemed ever more likely, imminent separation. On July 8, Pia arrived alone in Paris after visiting Sweden with her father. The first reunion of mother and daughter since the difficult few days in London six years earlier was naturally awkward at first; Ingrid was particularly exhausted since she had rushed down to Paris the day before, when five-year-old Isabella required an emergency appendectomy. Pia had grown from a pert child of twelve to a very attractive young woman of eighteen. There was a great deal they had to learn of each other, but their meeting and Paris excursions were not facilitated by photographers who swarmed around them like summer bees. Ingrid was afraid this would place on Pia an insupportable strain, but she perhaps did not take into account that her daughter had inherited her own strength and tenacity.

"I found that Paris meeting and all that attention very exciting," Pia said years later. "There were hundreds and hundreds of people at the airport just to see my mother and me. I mean, it was really a combination of being excited and being, I suppose, a little embarrassed and ill at ease." A few days later, they left for Santa Marinella, where Pia spent the summer with Robertino, Isabella and Ingrid. "Sometimes I said [to myself], this is ridiculous!" Pia added. "'What am I doing here? What would my father think? I'm sure my father did not think well of it—he must have thought it was a terrible thing for me to go to Italy and live with those three children. Anyway, I did it and it did strike me sometimes as very peculiar."

Everyone made an enormous effort that summer, but the easy, loving bond between Ingrid and Pia, so gushingly reported by the press, was, alas, another fiction. Pia was quick to help with chores, learned Italian with remarkable facility, accepted that she had to share Mama's attention with her half-siblings and behaved with a maturity beyond her years. "I was, I suppose, looking for a family," Pia said years later, "and in a real sense I found it there for the first time that summer." But the sensitivity of both mother and daughter made their reunion as delicate to manage as it was full of longing and inchoate love.

Pia returned to college in America on August 18, and within days after she had waved farewell to her at the airport, Ingrid returned to meet another traveler—director Stanley Donen, who had come to persuade her to appear with Cary Grant in a film of *Kind Sir*. But he had no difficult task. "I want to put you at ease," Ingrid said when they arrived back at the Rossellini apartment, "I'm going to do the picture. I've read an article about you that said you were very gifted . . . and Cary obviously wants to work with you. That's enough for me. Only please—if you'd be kind enough to tell me, what is the picture about?"

That was easy—it was really about nothing except Ingrid Bergman and Cary Grant looking stunning in Technicolor. But Donen did not, of course, say any such thing. The story concerned a man (Cary) who, to remain a bachelor, tells any woman—before he proposes a love affair—that he is already married. He then meets a successful actress (Ingrid) who bedazzles him and who on learning the truth plays a similar game to entrap him. At the fade-out, it is certain they will marry. Much ado about nothing, and the censors would be satisfied. Once Donen had spun the story out in his own charming way, Ingrid reiterated her willingness to under-take the role of Anna Kalman.

She did not add, while offering her quick acceptance, that she needed money badly. Having known nothing of tax planning during the Lindstrom and Rossellini years, she had suddenly been notified that French authorities had attached an enormous lien on her the-ater salary, and that the Italians were staking a partial claim, too. Roberto, nearly as poor as a beggar in India, provided nothing but tender affection for his children that year; for his wife, he sent only more bills to pay. Ingrid was to receive $125,000 for the picture, and because she was a nonresident alien, the American production company withheld no taxes—but France and Italy took a hefty bite from this salary. Over the next several years, Ingrid set herself back on an even financial keel, and by 1961 she had deposited several hundred thousand dollars in a Swiss account.

As for the title of the Donen picture—well, *Kind Sir* had been a resounding failure on Broadway, so that was rejected, and for obvi-ous reasons (once Ingrid had signed), they had to turn down the suggestions of *Mister and Mistress* or *As Good as Married* or *They're Not Married*. Not long before filming began in London that autumn, the title was fixed as *Indiscreet*.

At this news, Ingrid could only smile ruefully, for it aptly reflected the situation of her own past—and her husband's present. He did not yet appreciate how easy it would be for him to obtain a separation from her, for although she hated the thought of a custody battle for the children and a revival of adverse publicity, she had determined to end the marriage. That decision was confirmed on October 1, when Ingrid opened the door of her suite at the Raphael to find none other than Sonali Das Gupta, all tan and exotic and lovely, extending one hand and holding a baby in the other. She quickly calculated the time of her husband's absence and was within moments reassured by Sonali: the baby was not Roberto's. But Sonali was now pregnant with Roberto's child, and there was another child back home in India.

And so there was Ingrid, in a situation very like that of Anna Magnani eight years earlier. Now she was the woman whom Roberto had left for another; and here was Sonali—"Isn't it strange," Ingrid said later, "that she had left a child behind, exactly as I did." Of the meeting with Sonali nothing can be known for certain except that she said she intended to marry her beloved Roberto, and that Ingrid promised to place no obstacles in their path.

Five days later, Roberto arrived in Paris, ten months after he had stormed out of Ingrid's Paris premiere. They affected a loving reunion for the omnipresent photographers and then went immediately to the Raphael to discuss a separation. He did not earn points by asking about the play, "You are still doing this junk?"

On November 7, they signed a separation agreement in Rome. For the present, Ingrid had custody of her children but Roberto had full visitation rights. But he did not have custody of the film he had completed in India, for he had incurred such a debt that the government refused to allow the negative to be taken out of the country. Without a moment's hesitation, Ingrid made an overnight trip to London, sought out Prime Minister Nehru (then visiting his emigrant sister), and charmed him for the sake of her husband's art. The film was released to Roberto within twenty-four hours.

THERE NOW BEGAN ANOTHER TIME OF LEGAL ENTANGLEMENTS TO DISsolve the Bergman-Rossellini union. A separation was only a temporary measure, and now the real problems emerged.

First, there was in 1957 no divorce in Italy. The only recourse was to establish that serious conditions had prevented the contraction of a lawful marriage in the first place, and thus an annulment would be pronounced. Second, the three Rossellini children were Italian citizens. Third, Ingrid had no wish to deprive Roberto of her children's loyalty and presence. Fourth, he commanded her never to remarry, or he would pronounce her an unfit mother and remove all her visitation rights with their children. Fifth, if Ingrid contracted a marriage outside Italy after obtaining a foreign divorce, Italy would consider her a bigamist.

Eventually, after much argument and academic hair-splitting, Ingrid's attorney, the shrewd Ercole Graziadei, came up with a solution. Ingrid, a Swedish citizen, had not registered her proxy divorce in Sweden before her proxy marriage to Rossellini. Hence, according to an obscure Italian law, Ingrid the Swede was still considered the wife of Dr. Lindstrom when she married Roberto—and was still so considered by Roman courts. And so Graziadei filed for an annulment of the Bergman-Rossellini marriage: it had simply never existed. Happily, Italian law also provided for the dignified status of the children: no Italian baby was illegitimate as long as the father acknowledged paternity. The entire plea entered by Graziadei was so ingenious (not to say unprecedented) that the Roman judge listening to the case simply nodded his approval and went off to lunch. This did not solve one last hurdle: the fact that Sweden regarded Ingrid as no longer a citizen when she contracted her Italian proxy marriage in an undivorced state in 1950. That, too, required adroit attorney skills throughout 1958; eventually, her Swedish citizenship was duly restored.

"I was not really crushed," Ingrid said later of the end of her marriage.

> I was unhappy, certainly. You think something is going to work and it doesn't. Well, that's life. But I have one strength not all women have, and that is my work. Nobody can take that away from me. If I were just a woman who depended on her husband, on his money, on his protecting me, it would be an entirely different story.

She might have added that during the Rossellini years she had learned a great deal indeed about life, love and failure—and, not least of all, how to relax a little from time to time, to bend so that she would not break under the strain of the constant impulse to keep on working. And she grew because of hardships, too, as friends like Kay Brown realized. "She never felt the years with Roberto were a waste of time. I think she knew that in important ways she had grown up."

AND SO ON NOVEMBER 10, INGRID ARRIVED IN LONDON FOR *INDISCREET*, her unhappiness temporarily banished by the presence of her old friend Cary Grant, who met her at the airport and shielded her from the usual assault of the killer photographers. Three days later, filming began, interrupted only by Ingrid's insistence on returning to her children in Rome for the winter holiday: "She felt the family should be together at Christmastime," noted the production's publicist, Phil Gersdorf, in a memorandum, "and she's taking with her lots of gifts for the children."

Ingrid was, as Signe Hasso said of those years, more of a concerned mother than ever—but it was often concern from a distance, and thus her brand of maternity had what some people considered its limitations. From 1958, Ingrid was the successful professional once again, and she felt she could be a devoted mother even if she was not constantly with her children. Having become more herself through her art, she believed she had more to bring them of that self—a radiant joy in work and in life, most of all.

She was certainly nothing like a bad mother, and her children, before and after Ingrid's death, always insisted on the secure love they received from her. But Ingrid Bergman—incomparable as a wife, friend, lover and artist—was also a different kind of mother, more in the tradition of the English or French than the American. "I don't relish being at home and being a mother all the time," she admitted with her usual candor. "It's fine during the periods I don't work—and that's often!"

Isabella spoke for herself and her siblings when she said, "It didn't hurt me that my mother wasn't there every day. We had two months with her in the summer, one month at Christmas, two weeks at Easter—and she always managed to be with us at least one week every month. So we really saw each other a lot . . . And when Mamma came, she had nothing to do but look after us. She went to our school to see that everything was all right. She never went out to dinner. She never even had a friend come to dinner to distract her from us. She was all ours."

Regarding Ingrid's feeling of inadequacy about her untraditional style of mothering, Isabella added:

> The guilt over us four children wasn't so much that she was an actress. It was over how she could have avoided fighting with [Lindstrom] and my father—and how the fighting had become

so incredibly violent. She wondered if there was anything she could have done to keep at peace the rage of the fathers.

On February 6, 1958, *Indiscreet* was completed and readied for a June release. Despite her almost daily conversations with lawyers and her unfailing patience with an increasingly intrusive press, Ingrid was, for the first time in her English-speaking career, a hilarious, emotionally pitch-perfect comedienne in this picture. Her subtle reactions, ideally timed and matched with Grant's debonair grace, offered audiences a new aspect of her range as an actress. "How dare he make love to me and not be a married man!" she cried, and that old chestnut of a switch never sounded funnier. She also looked spectacular in the dresses and gowns designed for her by Dior, Balmain and Lanvin.

She wore one of them to a farewell dinner in her honor given by Cary Grant, who had put at Ingrid's place a small, neatly wrapped packet with a gift card from him. She opened it and recognized at once the wine cellar key from *Notorious*, the prop he had purloined in the hope that it would open a new door in his career. Well, he said, the talisman had done its work in the last dozen years. Now it was to be hers, and he offered it with the loving hope that she, too, would find an auspicious new door. Ingrid kept the key for twenty-one years before turning it over to yet another worthy recipient.

In a way, another door was already opening in Ingrid's life, and not only professionally. Her friendship with Lars Schmidt was becoming both more trusting and more intimate. She admired his self-confidence, his understanding of the actor's temperament and his lack of desire to control her: he had, after all, his own demanding career, and was entirely supportive of Ingrid's wish to maintain her own. She found that he knew her feelings before she expressed them, and that a glance communicated their thoughts. "One reason I liked him is that we started off joking about our fellow Swedes," Ingrid added. "Besides, it was such fun to surprise the press. Here they were, writing about poor jilted Ingrid—and then I turned up with Lars! With him, I am starting on my third life."

For his part, Lars was attracted not only to the beautiful, gifted movie star but to the warm, honest woman who knew how to please and honor a man she liked. "I admire her intuition, her will power and her sense of humor," he said at the time. "Best of all, we speak the same language." As the friendship became a romance, they began to speak quite openly of marrying—"when everything is legally possible," as Ingrid said. But that did not occur until December 1958, for as soon as Rossellini learned that Ingrid intended to remarry, he made good his promise, branded her an unfit mother and fought for complete custody of their three children—which the Italian courts awarded him, and with which Ingrid, much later, ultimately complied, unwilling to subject them to a publicity onslaught such as had been endured by Pia.

ADLER, SKOURAS AND COMPANY AT FOX WERE NOW BESIEGING KAY Brown with offers to secure Ingrid's services for several pictures— at the unprecedented salary of $1 million (a price the same studio later paid to Elizabeth Taylor for *Cleopatra*). But to everyone's astonishment, Ingrid refused the offer, replying that she did not want to return to the status of a contract player, and that if she could earn enough independently to provide a comfortable life for herself and a good education for her children, she required nothing more. Her one desire that winter: "I want to live with you," she wrote to Lars on January 21, "and I want to have peace and quiet, and work when it amuses me." If Petter Lindstrom had been the producer in charge of finances and contracts, and Roberto Rossellini the errant storyteller who rewrote her destiny, then Lars Schmidt was surely the editor, allowing order to emerge at last, enabling the polish of the finished product to shine forth in all its radiance.

Her letters to Lars that year reveal a passionate woman, not the cool Nordic soul so often portrayed by the press; indeed, at forty-two she knew the rapture of a young bride. On February 13, en route from London to Rome for more meetings with attorneys, Ingrid wrote:

> I love you more than everything on earth … I keep thinking of us, of all the beauty that we have, with God's help … I imagine you here, I kiss you … My beloved, I thank you for your love, but most of all for your understanding. I haven't even been gone from you an hour and a half, and already I long for you. There has never been anything better than we two. Thank God for you,

and that you came my way. Here I am—your old lady, your troll and your misfortune—I am all your burdens, and will hang around your neck forever.

Soon after, Ingrid and Lars traveled to Sweden for two weeks, where he had several business meetings. That year, Lars produced a number of plays in Europe, among them *The Diary of Anne Frank* and *Twelve Angry Men*; he was also preparing the Stockholm premiere of *My Fair Lady*. Just as important was his desire to show Ingrid his most prized possession—the two-acre island of Dannholmen, a few miles off the western coast of Sweden; he had purchased it several years earlier.

A condition for their marriage, Lars made plain, was that Ingrid be willing to spend the summers with him there. And so they climbed into a little launch docked at Fjällbacka, a sleepy fishing village, and set forth—shades of her first visit to Stromboli—to a barren rock in a windswept archipelago of the North Sea. But as they approached, Ingrid saw that this was nothing like the volcanic isle, nor was there a difficult project awaiting her. A blue-white sea crashed endlessly against the colored rocks of Dannholmen, and despite the bite of March winds, there was something pure that appealed to Ingrid's own spiritual austerity—not for Lars's sake, he soon realized, but because the island satisfied her long repressed need for times of isolation, quiet and simplicity.

Perched on a slight promontory was a modest saltbox of a cottage with a small kitchen, a bedroom and a cozy living-dining area. A special device purified seawater, but there was no electricity, plumbing or telephone. Eventually, Ingrid and Lars added modern conveniences and furnished a guest and work space. "And with Ingrid came the telephone, since of course she wanted to stay in touch with the children." Still, Dannholmen retained its antique, almost timeless atmosphere. Ingrid never had a home she loved more than this place, where she found a stillness and peace that soothed so much of the dither of her celebrity. To the end of her life, she loved to clamber along the rough rocks, where she found a smooth slab of granite, sat down with her script or a book, memorized her lines and found a fresh serenity at the water's edge—just as she had in childhood, when she sat on the benches along Strandvägen and Djurgården, and later, at Santa Monica, Malibu and Santa Marinella, always her places of refuge.

TIME HAD SEALED HER HANDSOME FEATURES WITH CHARACTER LINES around her mouth and eyes, and the contours of her face were henceforth ever more tanned and rugged, yet somehow more radiant for all that. Even later, with devastating illness, that radiance could not be extinguished.

In early March, Lars introduced Ingrid to his family and to his old friend, Baron Göran von Essen and his wife, Marianne. All were as surprised at her lack of affectation as they were by the sight of Ingrid, after a late-night party and much champagne, looking (thus the von Essens) like a newly opened rose early next morning: there was simply no sign of the extravagantly bubbly vigil and so little sleep. "It isn't fair!" said Marianne, echoing countless women. Even the Swedish press, which tracked Lars and Ingrid down at the home of Lars's parents, was newly won over, perhaps because her new partner was a native.

In mid-March, immediately after a visit with the children, Ingrid returned to London for a second picture with Fox producer Buddy Adler—about, of all things, a woman who adopts one hundred children. "I swore that I wouldn't play any more saints or nuns, so now I'm playing a missionary!" she said of *The Inn of the Sixth Happiness*, which began shooting in London and in Wales (doubling for China) in March 1958. The film was based on the true story of Gladys Aylward, a domestic who quits England for religious work in China, where the Sino-Japanese War and social hardships very nearly sabotage her good work. The finale, in which she leads scores of children on an arduous journey over mountains to safety, remains memorable for its choral repetition of the song "This Old Man."

Despite *Anastasia* and the general sympathy for Ingrid during the current state of the Rossellini débacle, Adler and his colleagues at Fox were a trifle nervous about attaching Ingrid to a particular denomination—and so she is never seen teaching religion, much less entering a chapel. Despite the many script inconsistencies she pointed out to Adler and to director Mark Robson (most of which were suggestions at once incorporated), she could not win a clarification of just what Miss Aylward believed. She even had to say that she was "not an accredited missionary," a phrase so meaningless as to imply the doubtful condition of a freelancer, proselytizing without creed and preaching without anything so disturbing as the mystery of faith.

Just so, this attenuated movie (over two-and-a-half hours in its released version) came alive only in the final saving of the Chinese children, a long sequence given enormous power by Ingrid's refusal to substitute bathos for tenderness. Otherwise, this inn is overcrowded with a cast of more than two thousand—and seemed, as one wag said, nothing so much as Cecil B. DeMille's version of "Now I Lay Me Down to Sleep."

Whatever its handicaps, *The Inn of the Sixth Happiness* certainly did not hurt the rehabilitation of its star, for it capitalized on a fancy for inspirational pictures in the late 1950s—perhaps partly because the Cold War had become so heated and the sounds of international saber-rattling could be heard everywhere. Among other movies, Deborah Kerr had just been a very effective nun in *Heaven Knows, Mr. Allison*, Audrey Hepburn was filming *The Nun's Story*, and *Ben-Hur* was being prepared. As for Ingrid, she had by this time been so completely restored to public favor that the matter of her accent was ignored as readily as her past notoriety: she was blithely presented as British, just as her co-star, the German Curt Jurgens, was cast as a Chinese army officer and the Englishman Robert Donat played a mandarin.

BUT THERE WAS ANOTHER KIND OF RESTORATION TO UNDERTAKE after the picture was finished that summer. Together, Ingrid and Lars had found a place in the French countryside where they set to work supervising the modernization and decoration of a three-hundred-year-old building that might have come straight from the pages of a fairy story. An hour from Paris and two miles from the tiny village of Choisel, in the Chevreuse Valley, was a lush setting thick with ancient cedars, cypresses, poplars, chestnuts and pines. Deep within lay "La Grange aux Moines"—the monks' barn, a house of quarried stone, dormer windows and pastel tiles. For years, Ingrid had wanted a parcel of French soil, because of her deep affinity for Joan of Arc. Now she would have it—a place for relaxation near and yet far from the hubbub of Paris, and a place for her children.

In the Register Office of Caxton Hall, London, on Sunday morning, December 21, 1958, Ingrid and Lars exchanged vows in the presence of a few friends. They then slipped quietly over to the Swedish Church for a blessing, sipped champagne at a luncheon at the Connaught Hotel, and—before the flashbulbs blinded them— boarded a plane for Choisel. The matter of her annulment or separation or divorce from Roberto Rossellini had not yet been resolved by Graziadei's ingenuity, but the precedent of English law—bless its unwritten, tolerant heart—regarded the Lindstrom divorce as definitive and the Rossellini marriage illicit because it was contracted before that divorce. And so Lars and Ingrid were truly married.

Throughout every month of the new year 1959, the custody battle for the children continued with unabated bitterness on the part of Roberto—uncharacteristically, Ingrid said, insisting that the real losers would be the boy and the girls. But Roberto battled along, unwilling to have his children so much as visitors to Choisel or Dannholmen until the Italian courts eventually required him to allow the children their own say—but that took several years indeed. "I am from the south, where we are warm," he said venomously to a reporter, "but she is from the frigid north. I am more of a mother to the children than she is." And to Ingrid he wrote in a tone that recalled nothing so much as that adopted by his predecessor, Petter Lindstrom: "Try not to make mistakes. You have to be very careful. You are always making mistakes. In the beginning of our lawsuit, I could have arranged that you see the children as often as you wished, but now you are making things very difficult."

This kind of statement did not, of course, endear him to the very children he wished to keep permanently. Nor did Ingrid respond in kind. "He is a great director and the father of three of my children," she said when a journalist repeated such outbursts. "I can't nourish hatred and vengeance. These are unlikable qualities in other people and even less likable in myself! Maybe I gave him a hard time, too."

"For two years the fight for the children went on," she said later, "and then I saw that my children, when the telephone rang, would stiffen and say, 'Is that the lawyer?' So I gave up, and they moved to Italy, and since then everything has been peaceful." Well, not entirely, but from the late 1960s Roberto and Ingrid were, thanks entirely to her insistence, able to meet in a less incendiary (and even sometimes cordial) atmosphere.

A very friendly ambience indeed surrounded Ingrid when she arrived in Los Angeles on April 3. This marked her first return to Hollywood in ten years and a month, and she and Lars made the trip at the invitation of the Motion Picture Academy. There was a reunion with Pia, who skipped a day of classes to fly down from Mills College in Oakland; and there were parties tendered by Buddy Adler and by Alfred Hitchcock, who had especially missed Ingrid. On April 6, at the Pantages Theater, Cary Grant introduced Ingrid. She came onstage to announce the best picture award (to the makers of *Gigi*), but was delayed by a prolonged standing ovation. "It is so heart-warming to receive such a welcome," she finally said—and then there was more applause before she could continue. "I feel that I am home. I am so deeply grateful."

UNTIL AUTUMN, INGRID'S TIME WAS OCCUPIED WITH THE RESTORA-tion of the house in France, the endless legal battles regarding her children and the status of her marriage to Rossellini, and a careful search—with Lars's guidance—for the right properties for film or even for television, which she was willing to try for the first time that year. She was also kept busy selecting a few pieces of furniture for a small Paris apartment she and Lars took adjacent to his office on the Avenue Vélasquez, with a view over the Parc Monceau. As she turned forty-four in August, Ingrid was pleased to be considered now for a character role—thus she undertook the part of the name-less governess in a much condensed version, for television, of Henry James's classic novella *The Turn of the Screw*. This was taped for broadcast by NBC on October 20, and for her performance Ingrid was awarded the Emmy (American television's equivalent of the Oscar) as the year's best actress in a dramatic performance.

This she achieved with no little difficulty, for James Costigan's script, hammered out to fit a ninety-minute television format (with time for commercial interruptions), discarded completely the bril-liant ambiguity of the original work and became simply a languorous and ineffective tale of some not very terrifying spirits and two irritating children. But her performance was full of nervous tension and fluttery agitation—a style, she later confided, that derived mostly from her dissatisfaction with the young director John Frankenheimer—"a crazy man, a man who was just not in control of himself." That seemed clear from his displays of temper barked from the control room. "If you're going to yell at me," Ingrid replied into the boom microphone, "then I'm going to yell back!"

"I'm not yelling!" cried Frankenheimer, his voice rising higher.

"It sounds like that out here!" Ingrid shot back. And so it went, until the final taping was complete after more than two weeks of rehearsals. "She's the greatest actress in the world," said one cameraman as the NBC crew applauded Ingrid after the final take. "No," corrected a colleague, "she's the greatest woman in the world." Variations on this kind of spontaneous praise were heard from film technicians and stagehands (groups not easily impressed by stars) for the rest of her career.

Christmas found her more happily engaged in the rituals of shopping. Laurence Evans recalled that Ingrid somehow seemed to remember everyone's special preferences at holiday time. He recalled her coming to the MCA offices one Christmas carrying a tray overflowing with delicately wrapped little parcels for him and his staff, an errand she repeated in the years to come. Once, Ingrid brought Laurence and Mary Evans a silver tree populated by white ceramic doves. Ingrid became a frequent guest at the Evanses' homes in London and Sussex in later years, and Mary's confidence and help were especially valuable years later, when Ingrid moved to London.

THERE WERE ALSO GIFTS TO SHIP TO AMERICA EARLY IN 1960, WHEN Ingrid received the surprising news that Pia, then twenty-one and in her senior year in college, had eloped on February 21 to marry a man with the impressive name of Fuller E. Callaway III. The wedding was so hastily executed in Elko, Nevada, that the bride and groom brought along no witnesses, and a befuddled justice of the peace had to dragoon the town jailer to stand as best man. Eight years older than Pia, tall and strikingly handsome, Callaway was a business manager for an electronic company in Palo Alto, and he had a marriage and divorce already behind him. But for that single detail, Pia might have been repeating her mother's choice of a first husband: a financially stable, handsome mate with a solid career. Then an ominously prophetic moment occurred when Callaway reached into his pocket for Pia's ring that evening in Nevada: the jailer's dog objected to the gesture and lunged for the bridegroom.

That, alas, set the tone for a marriage that quickly turned sour. The first six months of the union, the Callaways traveled together, and in so doing learned that they had made a mistake. They separated the following year and were divorced in December 1961, after Pia charged extreme cruelty, claiming her husband had struck her and pushed her down a flight of stairs. "By marrying, I naively believed I was solving all my problems," she admitted, referring perhaps to her uncertain relations with her parents. "Neither Fuller nor I was ready for marriage. Fuller was intelligent, hypersensitive and a complex genius. I was a young girl who looked forward to candlelight dinners for two and playing house. Our marriage lasted one year and a half." Eventually, Callaway's personal problems completely overwhelmed him, and he took his life.

THE SAME MONTH OF THE ILL-FATED MARRIAGE, FEBRUARY 1960, Buddy Adler and Twentieth Century-Fox secured film rights to Friederich Dürrenmatt's play The Visit, which had been performed on Broadway by the Lunts in 1958. The studio had not the remotest idea how to handle this grim fable of human venality: their first thought was to turn it into a Western, à la Nicholas Ray's Freudian cowboy movie Johnny Guitar. But Ingrid had begged Adler to buy it for her: it was, she said, so different from the usual gentlewomen she played. The Visit told the story of the world's richest woman, who hatches a diabolical plan to avenge herself on her former lover. Adler's death soon after this announcement delayed the production almost three years.

Meantime, Ingrid was pleased to be the mistress of Choisel and the summer hostess for friends who managed the journey to Dannholmen—among them a handsome and highly intelligent young man named Stephen Weiss, who dated Pia and subsequently became a close friend to Lars and Ingrid—and, later, an invaluable financial adviser. Weiss soon learned, as did all her friends, that her career was, as he put it, "ninety percent of her life, and the other ten percent had to fit around it." She loved Choisel and Dannhol-men, to be sure, "but then she tired of them, became restless, and had to be off and busy again at her profession."

Ordinarily, because Lars asked it, Ingrid refused to work during the summer, her inviolable time with him on Dannholmen. "There she lived in a completely different world from the one she worked in," said their friend Lasse Lundberg, long a resident of Fjällbacka. He recalled that Ingrid mingled easily with villagers and visitors alike, deflecting the conversation from herself, serving coffee for women learning to sail during the annual "Ladies' Week" and even volunteering to leap in a dinghy and tip it over for an important part of the course. "We offered her private sailing lessons, but she would have no special treatment and insisted on being part of the group. Ingrid was always suspicious of Sweden and the attitudes of the Swedes towards her, but for her, Sweden meant Fjällbacka and Dannholmen."

In the autumn of 1960, Ingrid accepted an offer from Anatole Litvak, the director of *Anastasia*, to undertake her first movie role in over two years—that of the unhappy Paula Tessier in *Goodbye Again*. Samuel Taylor's bittersweet, provocative script from Françoise Sagan's novel (*Aimez-vous Brahms?*) offered her an opportunity to find just the right notes of passion, hope, disappointment and grim acceptance in the role of a forty-year-old woman. Paula, miserable with a faithless lover (Yves Montand), yields briefly to the blandish-ments of a young man fifteen years her junior (Anthony Perkins).

Loneliness and romantic despair were never attributes associ-ated with Ingrid's screen image, which was precisely the reason she signed the contract—she longed for something different, although Ingrid at forty-five was simply too attractive to be entirely credible as a woman desperate for attention. Indeed, her makeup artist, John O'Gorman, had to reverse his usual task: "We had to put shadows under her eyes and wrinkles on her neck to give her the required maturity!"

Her character in *Goodbye Again* might quickly have been reduced to caricature by a less instinctive artist, but Ingrid gave Paula a wist-fulness counterpoised with strength. The final shot—in which she gazes at herself in the mirror—made a monologue unnecessary and remains a deeply affecting image of loss; Ingrid had found the spirit of unhysterical resignation that recalled, for example, the elegant nobility of the Marschallin in Richard Strauss's *Der Rosenkavalier*.

The picture, filmed that autumn in Paris, at once spawned rumors apposite to the script. Ingrid was having an affair with Yves Montand, it was whispered in some Paris salons; no, she had tried to seduce Anthony Perkins; on the contrary, my dear, she did corrupt young Mr. Perkins. Actually, nothing happened during the production of *Goodbye Again* except hard work.

This sort of gossip was fueled by Perkins's later account of an incident during production: Miss Bergman had invited him to her dressing room, he said after her death, where (blush!) she said they ought to practice their kissing scenes. But she went too far, said Perkins, striking his best Norman Bates/*Psycho* grin, and after a few moments he just barely escaped with his honor intact.

The story certainly revealed how seriously the young man— then twenty-eight and surprised to find himself playing Ingrid Bergman's lover—had taken his part in the picture. But the truth of the incident was very different. Perkins, as was well known, routinely hopped from the bed of this man in Hollywood to the couch of that boy in New York, and that season, he had extended his list of affairs to Paris. Ingrid, ever tolerant, believed his private life was none of her business or anyone else's. Nevertheless, she and Litvak were quite concerned about his evident difficulty with the first love scenes he had with her. She decided, therefore, to discuss these with him privately, and to create a relaxed atmosphere of friendliness between them so that Perkins would not appear onscreen, as he was in life, frozen with terror at the touch of a woman. She thought his discomfort sadly unnecessary, and the conversation and gestures in her dressing room were strictly professional. Ingrid Bergman had no interest in trying to seduce a young gay man.

Perkins's remarks indicated either a hyperactive imagination or his desire to transfer into life the role of Tom in *Tea and Sympathy*, which he had taken over on Broadway: perhaps Ingrid, he may have reasoned, would live out her role in that play, too, and release him to the heterosexual life for which he longed but from which he was very distant. Perkins was in a pathetic state, frightened (like so many others) that the revelation of his private life would mean the end of his career. To exploit the celebrated final line of Robert Anderson's play: When he spoke of this years later—and he did—he was not kind.

Whatever the reason for Perkins's little fiction, he hurt himself more than Ingrid, who always said that if she really wanted an affair with someone in the cast of *Goodbye Again*, Yves Montand had made it abundantly clear that he was available. But, *honi soit*, Ingrid Bergman was very happily married, had no desire to take a lover and may not have been intimate with anyone other than Lars Schmidt for the rest of her life. And therein, of course, lies the problem: in the absence of facts for the gossips, fantasy often suffices.

Goodbye Again was not a commercial success, for the style of international films was changing greatly in the early 1960s—and with those alterations there was an egregious lack of good leading roles for women in their early forties. She would be very glad to leap from forty-five to fifty and beyond, Ingrid said then and ever after, for then she would have a crack at the good character roles. Always frank about her age and amused at any suggestion that she alter her appearance beyond a different hairstyle or a little lip rouge, she let it be known that she looked forward most of all to resuming serious work in the theater.

After she completed the film in Paris, there came another offer from American television—this time from executives at CBS. "We never thought we should work together," said Lars, "but then we found this story and decided we'd both like to be a part of it." He signed on as producer for John Mortimer's ninety-minute adaptation of a Stefan Zweig story. They had fully expected permission to film in Monte Carlo's grand casino, where most of the action was set, but negotiations collapsed and the entire production was moved to New York. "Ingrid had no comment," according to Lars, "but for her the program could never be lifted to the same level as she had hoped for, in the natural setting."

Directed by Silvio Narizzano, *Twenty-Four Hours in a Woman's Life*—taped in New York in February 1961 and broadcast a month later—was a study in tedium. But it gave Ingrid the chance to add a startling new character role to her repertoire—that of an aged woman who, in an extended flashback, is seen in a youthful escapade with a dashing but suicidally irresponsible roué (played by Rip Torn).

Ingrid had to carry the entire burden of a windy, undramatic story overlaid with a bogus moral; this she did more than ably, as usual, but her keen reading and lovely appearance in long period gowns could not compensate for the uncompelling script and clumsy staging. "I'm at a very difficult stage in my career," she said after this broadcast. "And now, if I can't find something important, I'll just sit and wait for the right play or movie." A wise decision, said Lars. She had earned the right to be selective. Still, as he said, "her pace was fast, and she was easily bored."

It was not hard to see when restlessness evoked a higher level of zeal in Ingrid: she had a deeper level of anxiety, and she smoked more than ever. The summer of 1961 on Dannholmen was one of her most relaxed, for she had all four children for several weeks. The playwright Pierre Barillet, who had worked with Lars on several productions, was invited for a visit that established a lifelong friendship. He recalled the sunny, long days when the whole family swam, sunbathed, fished, read, sailed and luxuriated in an elementally simple life.

The only darkness that season was brought by the deaths of Ingrid's two old friends, Gary Cooper and Ernest Hemingway, who died within six weeks of each other in May and July 1961. "It hurts so," she wrote to Ruth Roberts. "It's strange how they went together [Cooper died of cancer, then Hemingway killed himself]. I think they had planned it. I heard from a mutual friend that the two used to telephone each other all the time through their sickness and laugh, 'I'll race you to the grave.'"

That same season, as Barillet recalled years later, Ingrid spoke with the director Ingmar Bergman; he had for a long time been dangling before her the possibility of a collaboration. Working with Ingrid would have been unusual for him, for he generally avoided international stars and employed, as often as possible, the same small circle of actors he knew, liked and trusted—all of them, apart from the Norwegian Liv Ullman, fellow Swedes such as Ingrid Thulin, Gunnel Lindblom, Max von Sydow, Bibi Andersson and Gunnar Björnstrand. Ingmar had come up with a vague idea of a character for Ingrid, but he had no story or plot, and all his projects sprang from original ideas. Now even his good intention had to be postponed, for he had accepted the directorship of the Royal Dramatic Theatre in Stockholm.

Meantime, a script for *The Visit* finally reached her that summer on the island, but there were serious problems: the producers did not want to present Ingrid as a woman who would bribe townsfolk to kill her ex-lover. They also wanted someone stronger than William Holden, who very much wanted to work with Ingrid and was willing to defer his salary to do so. She had no dispute with either of these points, but when Anthony Quinn picked up the expired film rights and became co-producer, he substituted himself for Holden and agreed to his backers' demands for a distinctly less grim ending than in the play. Years later, Quinn stoutly maintained that Ingrid herself repudiated the original, harsher plot, insisted on softening the finale and demanded that he be her co-star, but production files indicate that memory failed him in this regard. Doubtless he wished, however benignly, to find an excuse for the utter failure of *The Visit* when it was at last filmed in Rome in 1963 and released the following year.

"WELL, HERE I AM," INGRID TOLD PIERRE BARILLET THAT SUMMER OF 1961, "too old for the younger parts and too young for the older! What am I to do? One film a year is enough to keep me happy, but it must be something just right. And I am not like these young actors, all eager to become directors!" Nor did she wish merely to trot around the world being honored at retrospectives, indicating there was no present. Perhaps no era canonized youth more than the 1960s, and Ingrid, not yet fifty, knew that for many moviegoers she was simply a reminder of the past.

That autumn, she and Lars decided that the past was good enough. She was the only Scandinavian actress living in Paris, and he the only Scandinavian producer—thus they settled on a stage production, in French, of Ibsen's *Hedda Gabler*, the first Scandinavian classic that Ingrid undertook. Precisely because famous actresses (among them, Duse, Nazimova and Le Gallienne) had played the familiar and horrifyingly sadistic Hedda, Ingrid's choice was a far riskier project for her than *Tea and Sympathy* had been. This time she had not only the French to master but also the nuances of one of the most antipathetic characters in dramatic literature. The entire spring and summer of 1962 she dedicated to a careful study of the text, its interpretation, and the subtleties of Gilbert Sigaux's translation. Raymond Rouleau, the director, praised her industry. Well, Ingrid replied, she wanted to become a serious stage actress, and the classics would be her means to that end.

Also of great help was her preparation while taping a much abbreviated (seventy-five-minute) version of *Hedda Gabler* in London, where her co-stars included Michael Redgrave, Ralph Richardson and Trevor Howard—a performance eventually broadcast by CBS in America and preserved in television archives. Even in this radical abridgment, Ingrid found Hedda's poisonous elegance and somehow altered the usual effect of her warm smile by projecting a glacial severity.

The stage production had its premiere on December 10, 1962, at the Théâtre Montparnasse, where there were, alas, opening night problems. Despite all her efforts, Ingrid had difficulty with the complete French text, over which she stumbled repeatedly and even jostled her colleagues into confusion. But after several nights she was calmer, and critics much admired her study in amoral malignity; the play had a healthy run into 1963, and Ingrid was far more successful as Hedda than as the vindictive woman of the Dürrenmatt story. "One loves almost everything Ingrid Bergman does," wrote the critic for *Le Figaro*, praising "the special voice, her artistic presentation—it's an experience to see and hear her." *France-Soir* noted her "dreamlike pride—never has Ibsen been played so magnificently."

When the run was complete, Lars and Ingrid went off on a long and exotic expedition to the East. Katmandu's so-called Royal Palace Hotel was not (water ran from faucets only between four and six in the morning and the food was inedible, but the Schmidts coped with this); they climbed the mountains and happily exhausted themselves visiting Patan and Bhatgaon. From there, they traveled to Darjeeling and Sikkim, and thence to Laos, Cambodia and Malaysia. In Djakarta, President Sukarno was host at a dinner in their honor.

IN 1964, LARS ENJOYED ONE OF HIS BUSIEST AND MOST PROSPEROUS years with his productions of *How to Succeed in Business Without*

Really Trying, *My Fair Lady*, *Annie Get Your Gun*, *Who's Afraid of Virginia
Woolf?* and *Barefoot in the Park* attracting audiences all over Europe.
With her houses now in order, Ingrid was eager to work, too, and
so—after welcoming Alfred Hitchcock to Paris for a brief visit—
Ingrid in May went to London, where she appeared in an anthol-
ogy film, in the visually stunning final sequence of *The Yellow Rolls-
Royce*.

As an ornery, wealthy American on holiday in Europe at the
outbreak of World War II, she meets a Slavic patriot (Omar Sharif)
who is fighting the Nazis. At first annoyed by his politics and the
interruption of her luxurious travels in the eponymous car, she is
soon forced to realize the truth of the world situation—and having
done so, she is transformed by love, in a trice, from a lazy bigot to a
passionate Florence Nightingale. Shifting easily from comedy (feeding her dog while bombs crash through a hotel dining room) to
tragedy (nursing the wounded), Ingrid made everything credible.
When she said of her brief affair in the story, "Hearts are never broken—they just sometimes get a bit bruised but they always, always
mend," the words had a wistful ring of truth.

Even more congenial was her reunion with her old friend and
director, Gustav Molander, for whom she appeared in another
anthology film made in Stockholm that autumn—her first film in
Sweden in over twenty-five years. Then seventy-six and nearly deaf,
Molander simply returned to the quiet, mimed direction he had
used with Ingrid three decades earlier. Her performance as a foolish
and greedy social climber in a short film of Guy de Maupassant's
story "The Necklace" was tinged with nostalgic regret, and for once
the Swedish critics were unanimous in their praise of the aging
mentor and his famous protégée.

SHE WANTED TO PROLONG HER TIME IN STOCKHOLM, BUT INGRID
hopped over to Rome, when an early winter influenza brought
down the entire Rossellini household and sent Roberto into near
hysteria. By Christmas, Ingrid was nursing in life as she had in
The Yellow Rolls-Royce—but now with the help, it must be said, of
Pia.

After college graduation, a failed marriage and a brief term
working at UNESCO, Pia at twenty-six was (her words) "at loose

ends—I couldn't figure out a profession that I was capable of doing." A few stabs at film acting were unsuccessful (mostly because her small roles were edited out, not because she lacked talent), and so she was welcomed by Ingrid and Lars in Paris, and by Roberto in Rome, where she became a kind of house manager for the children. They soon came to love and confide in her as a devoted older sister.

Perhaps because her own childhood had been isolated, she relished the ordinary business of family life and adjusted to the constant anxiety about money that plagued Rossellini and to the chaos of a household that included, at various times, a brigade of children (including two by Sonali Das Gupta) from Rossellini's past and present marriages. Coping with disorder and an array of personalities, and making swift, sensible judgments may well have contributed to Pia's eventual success as a television journalist and arts critic—a profession she later mastered in San Francisco and New York.

By year's end, Ingrid was tired, but she accompanied Lars to several of his premieres and prepared a holiday for the entire family. "Ingrid was the perfect wife," said Lars. "As perfect as you could want. She was a man's woman and would do anything to please her husband. But she was also a migratory bird who passionately pursued the best outlets for her talent. Her love for acting had no boundaries, ever, and she was always ready for a new adventure."

Michael Redgrave, her co-star in the British television version of *Hedda Gabler*, provided the incentive for the new adventure when he telephoned Ingrid just as 1964 drew to a close. He was to direct Turgenev's elegiac play *A Month in the Country* in Guildford the following spring and wanted her for the role of Natalia. But of course, she said at once—wasn't it logical, after Molnár, O'Neill, the two Andersons, and Ibsen, to undertake a Russian classic? It had been almost twenty years since she had worked onstage in English.

On New Year's Day 1965, she sipped champagne and read the history of the Russian theater. Ingrid Bergman was becoming, as she always longed to be, a serious stage actress, not just a movie star—

and not just by default, at the time, of good movie roles for women over nineteen. But her achievement was coming at an enormous price. "I knew, no matter how intense our happiness was," said Lars, "that Ingrid was the artist, a star—and that her public and her work were her life."

Chapter Seventeen

1965–1970

I share no man's opinions; I have my own.
TURGENEV,
Fathers and Sons

INGRID'S OLD FRIEND ALFRED HITCHCOCK OFTEN SAID THAT THE BEST actors were never caught acting; that the real craft, in other words, was making the craft itself and the actor's methods vanish. "What should I do?" was a question often put to him by players eager to please. "Nothing at all," he replied. Which was simultaneously not much help and the best advice in the world.

In this regard, it is noteworthy how very few actors can achieve real excellence in both stage and screen acting—perhaps because the technique for each varies so greatly. For a movie, one has to "bring everything down" (also Hitchcock's frequent advice to an actor), to minimize reactions, to allow the slightest turn of the head, lowering of a gaze or the modulation of voice to indicate profound emotions. But in the theater the tools have to be altered—spectators in the second balcony must somehow be informed of a character's feelings. So it was perhaps indeed remarkable that Ingrid Bergman perfected her theatrical abilities after such a long apprenticeship with the system of making movie scenes, which are built from little bits and pieces.

She had no "technique" she could elaborate, no "method" she could claim as her own, and in any case such discussions invariably bored her. But there was no question that when she stepped onto the stage, a kind of inner switch was turned, and a character was illuminated through the complex filters of understanding and the light of intuition. This became abundantly clear when she appeared, from June 1965 to March 1966, in *A Month in the Country*: she played the bored, forlorn Natalia, who finds herself suddenly in love with her son's tutor, but is left, through unfortunate machinations largely her own, even more deserted, dissatisfied and lonely at the conclusion.

But as with *Hedda Gabler*, things did not, at first, go smoothly, as critics hastily pointed out when the play opened at Guildford in June. "I wasn't ready," she admitted with typical candor. "We had four weeks of rehearsal and it wasn't time enough for me. English is not my language, so that—though I think I know my lines—I probably don't know them profoundly." She required several weeks early that summer before she was comfortable with the words and so with the character.

There was only a short holiday at the end of the summer season before the transfer of the play to London in September, and Ingrid managed but a brief visit to Dannholmen. She knew that she had promised Lars the summers, she said apologetically, and of course he replied that he understood. But her devotion to the stage sowed the first seeds of a clear rift in the marriage—not one born of rancor, unkindness or infidelity, but one arising from her passion for her career. Of course Lars had his professional life, too. When he was in Paris, she was in London; when he traveled to the Orient, she was in Rome; when she was in New York, he was in Copenhagen.

Hence there was a kind of vicious cycle: Ingrid pitched herself into her art because her husband was occupied. As for the children, Robertino was fifteen, the twins thirteen; they were, by now, accustomed to occasional visits from Mama. This is not a rare family situation: a performer (or diplomat or other professional) gives nothing less than everything to a career requiring much travel—and pays an extraordinary price in the bargain. As do loved ones.

Ingrid's brief time on the island that August coincided with her fiftieth birthday, an event she at first begged Lars to ignore and then decided what the hell, it was a good excuse for a party. "A few people were invited," he recalled, "but somehow everything changed, and international society arrived en masse!" She had a wonderful life, Ingrid said in reply to the toasts, and as long as she enjoyed good health and a poor memory of unhappy past moments, she intended to continue to have a wonderful life. "I do not know why I am not gray," she said with a laugh. "I do nothing to stay young and I do all the things to age—I drink, I smoke, I eat dessert. Perhaps one day my face will collapse like a piece of *Lost Horizon!*"

When *A Month in the Country* reopened at the Cambridge Theatre, London, on September 23, the character of Natalia was hers completely, although Michael Redgrave felt "she was not at the top of her form, but in most people's opinion and in mine it simply didn't matter." Gowned in a haze of pastels, she commanded the stage with a radiant presence. Her great monologue held the audience almost breathless with wonder: "Am I in love with him, or what?" she asked, projecting the character's depth of confusion by a kind of motionlessness. "How did it all happen?" she continued with the slightest movement to stage right. "Have I been poisoned? Suddenly everything is broken, scattered and carried away."

The tragic folly of human self-absorption could be heard in her affectless tone and almost empty gaze over the audience: "I have only one apology to make," she said to her young love, "and that is that it was beyond my control." The silence that followed was not awkward, it was loud with her repressed sentiment. Ingrid gave the impression that when she was offstage she retired not to her dressing room but to some other part of the character's house, there to resume a life from which she was momentarily plucked.

There was a deep layer of ruefulness in this performance, and the London critics, no pushovers, responded ardently. "Miss Bergman's performance now has a comic edge which throws the overwritten pathos of her part into more proportionate relief . . . " "A most skilfully integrated and convincing portrait . . . " "It is by her Natalia that she will live in my mind from now on . . . " "Ingrid Bergman has softened and deepened her interpretation, giving a brilliant delineation of a woman's mind caught in the turmoils of love." When the production finally closed in early March 1966, Ingrid departed London almost as sadly as Natalia in her final scene. As usual, she left an exquisitely wrapped gift for each cast member on closing night.

SHE THEN HURRIED TO ROME, WHERE THERE WAS ALARMING NEWS about the health of Isabella, who was not yet fourteen. For about a year, the family had noticed her faulty posture—she seemed to walk with a slight stoop, like a girl afraid of growing too tall too rapidly. One of the nuns at school, with the approval of a family physician, urged a series of exercises, but then Isabella began to complain of severe pain. Roberto was summoned at once. By February, the girl could walk only with the greatest difficulty, and she wept with pain from the effort. And then, almost overnight, she was unable to straighten her back.

Oscar Scaglietti, a leading orthopedic surgeon, diagnosed severe crippling scoliosis, a curvature that causes the spine to twist into an almost serpentine shape. Without dramatic and immediate intervention, Isabella might never be able to stand straight—or even to walk. On the morning of April 21, Ingrid took Isabella to the Trauma Center in Careggi, in the Tuscan hills outside Florence, one of Italy's most advanced clinics. The costs for this, and for the expensive and difficult procedures to follow in the next year and a half, were borne entirely by Ingrid; Roberto shared the emotional burden. (During the eighteen months after *Indiscreet*, Ingrid had voluntarily given him 75 percent of her $125,000 salary for the care of their three children.)

But the protocol was far from simple or painless. Before surgery could be performed, Isabella had to be placed in a plaster cast from neck to pelvis and subjected to a series of appallingly painful stretching exercises: her head had to be pulled sharply backward so that she would not become deformed within the prison of the cast. This was a hideous torture for the girl, and it had to be performed without anaesthetic for three reasons: so that the doctors would know when the appropriate reversion of torsion had been effected along the spine, so that her head would not shrink down into the cast from the curvature, and so that Isabella—who would have to endure these maneuvers for two years—would not become addicted to narcotics.

And so, from the spring of 1966 until summer 1967, Ingrid
Bergman devoted her entire life (save for a two-week trip to London to fulfill a contractual assignment) to the care of her daughter.
It seemed as if she was determined to avoid a repetition of the guilt
she had felt regarding Pia seventeen years earlier. She would not
allow Isabella to endure the agony of the stretching exercises alone,
and so she was present every day, her own tears mingling with the
girl's as Isabella was tied with ropes to a large table while a nurse,
with Ingrid's help, pulled on her neck until she nearly fainted from
pain. The attending doctors were guided by Isabella's cries, for if
she were sedated she might be stretched to the point of irreparable
damage. "I tried to be brave," Ingrid said of this time, "but each
time I cried, because she wept with pain. I couldn't help her or
myself." But she did indeed help—as did Lars, who visited often to
offer moral support (and who somehow managed to avoid meeting
Rossellini).

Isabella was in the Careggi clinic four times for these awful
"pullings," and finally the day was set for the difficult and delicate
six-hour surgery on her spine, a procedure performed by Dr.
Alberto Ponte and supervised by Scaglietti. That day, Ingrid and
Roberto paced nervously in a visitors' lounge, smoking endless
cigarettes, muttering distractedly about politics, the weather and the
movies. At one point, Ingrid stepped down a corridor, and after a
twenty-minute absence, Roberto followed, to find her in a small
laboratory where she had requisitioned a sink and was washing her
hair. What in hell was she doing? Roberto wanted to know. He
could see what she was doing, she replied from beneath the spray
and shampoo. But why? She had to do something, Ingrid replied:
she was going mad with anxiety and had already puffed her way
through three packs of cigarettes.

The operation was complicated. First, bone from Isabella's leg
was removed and cut into pieces thin as matchsticks. Then sur-
geons opened the spine—at last stretched straight—and proceeded to insert the pieces of tibia at appropriate points. For three
weeks after surgery, Isabella Rossellini was in intractable torment;
for the next year, she was in severe discomfort. From 1966 to
1968, when she was confined in hospitals and at home to a plaster
harness, her mother was at her side virtually every day, trying to

soothe, to comfort, to bathe her face and feet with eau de cologne, to help her eat and drink and cope with all the other traumas of adolescence.

"Mama stopped work completely for me," Isabella said years later, "and I was very touched by that because I know how much she loves her work and I love her working. She didn't work for that whole eighteen months—except for one two-week period when she was contracted to do a television film of Jean Cocteau's *The Human Voice*."

IRONICALLY, INGRID APPROPRIATELY BROUGHT THE DISTRESS ABOUT Isabella to her London taping of the Cocteau piece, a one-woman tour de force: in December 1966, *The Human Voice* (which Ingrid had earlier read for commercial recording release) was produced by David Susskind in collaboration with Lars Schmidt. Cocteau's play (filmed in Italian by Rossellini with Anna Magnani in 1948) is actually a fifty-minute monologue about a woman and a telephone. She waits, she lights a cigarette, she listens, she rages, she puffs furiously, she flirts, she tries to accept the inevitable, she stubs out the cigarette and smokes a fresh one, she is resigned—and all of this over her loss of her lover to another woman. Anguish is at the center of the piece, and anguish had been her constant companion for eight months.

Her director, Ted Kotcheff, at once noticed Ingrid's anxiety and insecurity during the two weeks of rehearsal, when she attacked the new translation by David Exton. At every third line, she stopped the reading, complaining that this line was inappropriate, that line unreadable, this phrase incomprehensible, that one awkward. Kotcheff, a patient young director who understood actors' sometimes fragile temperaments, urged Ingrid to proceed calmly, and he promised that he would attend to any of the script difficulties before taping. But the more he pampered her, the tenser and edgier she became, until Kotcheff, his voice rising with each breath, shouted, "Ingrid, stop this hysteria immediately! Just go ahead with the rehearsal and read the text as I've asked you—nothing is written in stone! This is only for timing—I promise you we will resolve these things and we will—so please go on with the reading!"

With that, certain he had sabotaged their relationship, the

director telephoned Susskind to announce his withdrawal. But next
morning, Susskind contacted Kotcheff to say that any talk of resignation was nonsense, that he had spoken to Ingrid, who liked and
admired her director, did not want him to leave, and would do anything to cooperate. Thenceforth, rehearsals and taping continued
amiably—and Kotcheff insisted on proceeding without any visitors
or crew. He and Ingrid would work as a pair.

And then the director hit on a brilliant device: dialogue was created for the hypothetical lover at the other end, and to these lines
Ingrid reacted when they were read during rehearsals. From that
time, director and actress were fast friends. "Had you allowed her
to get away with that behavior," Lars told Ted, "she would never
have trusted you again. When you shouted at her, she realized, 'Aha!
This is a man who knows exactly what he wants and what he's
doing—and I am safe in his hands.'"

Ever since the end of the Rossellini era, beginning with Jean
Renoir and Anatole Litvak on *Eléna* and *Anastasia*, Ingrid had to be
confident in her director's strengths, and the only way she could
test that was to question and complain, badger and disagree—not
always, and not for long. She was not the stereotype of the moody,
volatile star who puts herself at the center of the universe. But she
had a healthy respect for her own experience and talent, and she
needed to reassure herself that the director could evoke the best
from her.

Her manner was not calculated to wield power, much less was
she personal in her attacks. Kotcheff described her as the ultimate
romantic actress, kept free of sentimentality by the depth of her
feeling, her candor, "her great humor and enormous generosity of
spirit—not only in giving everything to the role but everything to
the production." If she did not know her director, she had to dis-
cern ways of knowing him, and in this regard her tactics were anything but "romantic."

Insecurity is a trait common among even the most talented
artists. Actors, especially—dependent on voice, appearance, memory and imagination as well as on the variables of popular and critical assessment and the estimation of often jealous associates—are
among the most prone to such anxieties. Laurence Olivier, to mention only one master of the craft, so suffered from anxiety and stage

fright during a ten-year period late in his career that he was very nearly psychologically disabled; only sheer willpower saved him from complete collapse. Still, his agony was constant. In her case, Ingrid's return to work after so long an interval was, after all, in a one-woman piece: attention was never deflected from her. And her trepidation was not much alleviated by the appearance of several production financiers, who had arrived to see the great lady at work in a solo piece. She was intimidated by that, as Kotcheff recalled, and it threw her.

"Anything I don't mention is fine," he told her reassuringly once taping began in the third week. At one point, he suggested she was overacting just a bit, and Ingrid agreed. "Remember, Ted, it's because I think I'm back in the theater and I'm playing to the third balcony. But the moment I see the camera—." Yes, replied Kotcheff, "I know, you'll scale down." And so she did. Ingrid judged every movement, pause, hesitation and silence, and at the final rehearsal she delivered the entire monologue in only thirty-five seconds beyond the required fifty minutes.

These she trimmed easily, and when the piece was broadcast in the spring of 1967 (her first appearance on color television), critics and viewers found this a virtuoso performance of what is often an annoying nonplay. She acted with a fierce intensity and a tragic despair that was almost impossible to watch without flinching. "We should always do plays with a cast this size," Susskind told Lars. "It's economical." Replied Lars, with deadpan humor, "But she's heavy on cigarettes. Maybe we could cut down on the budget there." There was a dark portent in his observation that Ingrid was "heavy on cigarettes."

AFTER MORE TIME IN FLORENCE AND ROME HOSPITALS, ISABELLA WAS at last released to the care of her family in the summer of 1967, after the body cast was removed on July 3. Ingrid and the other children accompanied her to the seaside villa of Roberto's sister Marcella, and there she was surrounded by the most loving attention. Finally, her body still encased in a shorter plaster harness for another year, she returned to Rome, to school and eventually to the normal routine of a healthy teenager. By this time, Roberto had made peace with Ingrid's marriage, and there was even an occasional invitation to Lars. And with Isabella settled for the season, Ingrid planned for work. Eventually, of course, Isabella recovered completely, and matured to become a tall, lithe, ramrod-straight beauty who enjoyed a successful career as a model and actress.

Before Ingrid resumed her own career, there was a bit of benign revenge to be indulged. The previous year, Ingrid had succumbed to Lars's offer of a fiftieth birthday party. Now, she prepared in secret for his, telling her husband only that yes, she had invited a few friends and relatives to join them for lunch at Choisel.

But Ingrid had planned another spectacle for that same evening. Lars wanted to show his mother his theater in Paris, and so they drove from the country—only to find the auditorium dark despite his instructions to his house manager. Mama, Ingrid and Lars stood awkwardly for a moment, and then he shouted for an assistant. With that, the stage curtain was raised, and a chorus of 150 friends and colleagues sang the traditional birthday melody. At Ingrid's invitation, they had come from all over the world. She had designed a lavish dinner for the occasion, complete with Franco-Swedish decor and an enormous cake.

INGRID'S NEXT PROJECT HAD BEEN CHOSEN DURING EARLY SPRING. AT first, she and Lars had discussed the possibility of a Paris stage production of *Anna Karenina*. But she was still uncertain about this: it had been one of Garbo's great successes, and her fellow Swede was still living, however eccentrically remote from the world. Ingrid was eager to return to work onstage after so long an interval, but at fifty-two she saw herself at an awkward, almost uncastable age. She had been too old for Natalia, but no one had minded. Now what?

And just then, as if on cue, Kay Brown telephoned from New York in March. She had an inquiry from theater producer Elliot Martin, who was working on the unfinished text of Eugene O'Neill's last play, *More Stately Mansions*. The playwright had ordered all incomplete manuscripts destroyed after his death, but this one turned up in a library at Yale University and had, with his widow's approval, been given a provisional production in Stockholm in 1962. Now José Quintero, who had directed *The Iceman Cometh* in 1946 and *Long Day's Journey into Night* a decade later, was burrowing into the text with Martin, cutting and rearranging the sprawling tale of a neurotic family in nineteenth-century Boston. "The unfinished manuscript was about an inch and a quarter thick as O'Neill wrote it, and as such it would have been a five-hour play," Elliot Martin recalled. "Incomplete and imperfect, it also had pages and pages of O'Neill's notes, written in his very tiny handwriting."

That September, Martin was going to open the new, two-thousand-seat Ahmanson Theater at the Los Angeles Music Center with the American premiere of *More Stately Mansions*, and he very much wanted Ingrid to join two gifted actors, Colleen Dewhurst and Arthur Hill. She would undertake the role of Deborah Harford, a wife and mother so greedy for possessions and the souls of others that she retreats into a world of power-mad delusions. Very like Christine Mannon in *Mourning Becomes Electra* (a character Ingrid was also considering that same year), Deborah plots and connives for control of her introverted and idealistic son, against his equally determined wife. Lost in an incestuous fantasy yet grounded by vengeance, she is at the center of a vortex of materialistic avarice that infects not only a family but also, by implication, an entire derailed society.

More Stately Mansions was a sequel to *A Touch of the Poet* and followed the fortunes of the Melody family; it was also one of O'Neill's planned cycle of nine plays on the theme of the intersection of American social and family history. More than twenty years earlier, when Ingrid played *Anna Christie*, the playwright himself had invited her to commit to the entire forthcoming series. Thus when Martin and Quintero arrived at Choisel on April 2 to discuss the script with her, she saw the matter as a fulfillment of her theatrical destiny. With Lars's approval, Ingrid accepted at once to play this profoundly unsympathetic role.

In July, she went to Dannholmen, where she read and made notes on the play-in-progress, sitting on the sun-drenched rocks each day, the sounds of the sea accompanying her study. Meantime, there were murmurs of discontent from some board members of the Ahmanson: Ingrid Bergman's name would not sell tickets, they insisted—wouldn't Jessica Tandy be a safer choice? Martin and Quintero stood firm, the board reluctantly relented, and everyone awaited Ingrid Bergman's return to the American stage for the first time in over twenty years.

*   *   *

ON AUGUST 3, SHE ARRIVED IN LOS ANGELES TO FACE 175 MEMBERS
of the world's press corps. Because she was sensitive to the fact that
Isabella had received such attention and that her twin deserved
some time with her mother, she brought young Ingrid to California
for a long visit.

"At the airport, reporters asked some rude questions about the
events of eighteen years earlier," according to Elliot Martin, "but
Ingrid had a backbone of steel and handled the boys well that day.
Yet at the same time she was a very gentle, soft creature." His cast,
he added, collaborated brilliantly and amiably. Ingrid, Dewhurst and
Hill became fast friends.

"Everyone in the company adored her," Arthur Hill recalled
years later. "Ingrid worked from instinct, not from intellect, and in
this regard she might have made a mistake in taking on the role—
not because she couldn't do it, but because the play was such a
shambles! And of course she was a bit frightened of making a stage
appearance in America after more than twenty years. Ingrid relied
on Ruth Roberts for help with diction and on José to give her
notes."

"My God!" cried Colleen Dewhurst after working a few days
with Ingrid. "I knew she'd look good, but this was ridiculous! She
looks better now [at fifty-two] than I did when I was thirty! She has
her Scotches, she stays up late, she tells jokes and she still looks glo-
rious! Everything you get from her is right in the face—nothing
phoney."

As Ingrid herself admitted to Lars, she had as many notes for
Quintero—more than he for her—and the atmosphere was far
thicker with tension than it had been with John Frankenheimer or
Ted Kotcheff. For a time, Quintero did not indeed much "adore"
her at all. "I drove poor José crazy, I confess that. You know how
sure I am of myself." But the truth is that she was far from sure of
herself—and so the pitched battles. During rehearsals, she cried,
"Oh, you're wrong!" aloud to Quintero, and then she ventured
comments about his direction of the other players, too. This sort of
conduct occurred so often that finally the director "blew his top
and bawled me out and told me off"—and later she knew he was
right to do so.

A combination of deep anxiety about the play and an equally profound confidence in her own talent had led Ingrid to a state of nervous tension, and for a time this ran like a virus through the production. Ingrid seemed to have realized, too late, what Hill and Dewhurst knew: that some things in this work could not be resolved easily (if at all), but that an imperfectly realized O'Neill play was superior to very much else that passed for theater in 1967. Elliot Martin and José Quintero had bravely undertaken to offer the last work by a great writer, and so their cast went gamely ahead.

Opening night in Los Angeles, on September 12, was at first disastrous. Prolonged applause attended her first entrance, and at once Ingrid froze: she simply forgot the dialogue. After an awkward moment, the stage manager threw her the first line, and everything improved. No matter the problems, the three principals won the admiration of Los Angeles critics. As for Ingrid's performance as the formidable Deborah, her first act soliloquy was delivered in a metallic voice, full of wonder at the character's own malevolence: "Really, Deborah," she said to "herself" aloud, as if there were another in the room, "I begin to believe that truly you must be a little mad!" Her eyes gleamed, a slight smile curled on her lips.

> You had better take care. One day you may lose yourself so deeply in that romantic evil, you will not find your way back. Well, let that happen! I would welcome losing myself. But how stupid. These insane, interminable dialogues with self!

She paused, then shifted her posture and her tone to indicate an inner resolve:

> I must find someone outside myself in whom I can confide, and so escape myself—someone strong and healthy and sane, who dares to love and live life greedily instead of reading and dreaming about it. Ah—[her son] Simon—Simon that was, your Simon!

Ingrid made Deborah her own by first understanding the calm callousness of the character's approach to people and then discarding her rational comprehension and finding an emotion of cold disdain.

DESPITE HER APPREHENSIONS AT THE FIRST PERFORMANCE, INGRID DID something Elliot Martin described as typical: she sent him a bouquet of flowers with the note: "I'm a producer's wife, so I know the one person who is forgotten on opening night is the producer!" The press gathered for the premiere party after the performance, and every Hollywood personality with the slightest twinkle to his star was present; it seemed everyone wanted to touch Ingrid as if she were royalty returned. Lars and Pia came to town for the performance and party.

Among all the adorers, Alfred Hitchcock was perhaps the most ardent. "Best wishes for a faulty stocking!" he said to Ingrid. She looked at him blankly, and he asked, "Know what that is?" She shook her head. "A long run!" answered Hitch, beaming like a smitten schoolboy before his beloved teacher. Soon after, a quiet dinner at the Hitchcock home gave Ingrid the opportunity to reminisce and to bring him into the circle of her present life.

Hitch had come to a difficult time in his long career: his most recent film, Torn Curtain, had been savaged by critics; and he was still nursing, after more than three years, a very deep wound—a self-destructive passion he had harbored for the actress Tippi Hedren, whom he had starred in his two previous pictures, The Birds and Marnie. These were the actress's first two films after a successful modeling career, she was the most willing actress, and her two performances had been solid achievements.

Like Ingrid, Tippi Hedren had at first successfully managed to maintain a friendly rapprochement with her director. But during the production of Marnie in late 1963, it had become clear that Hitchcock wanted much more than an amiable professional relationship, and to his demands Tippi Hedren would not submit. The repressions of decades had finally erupted, and Hitchcock responded to polite but firm rejection with fierce anger and unquenchable bitterness; in the end, alas, he hurt himself far more deeply than he hurt Tippi Hedren. The visit with Ingrid, whose wit and intuition matched his, much lightened his spirits, for she brought him back to a time when he was far more discreet.

*   *   *

AFTER SIX WEEKS IN CALIFORNIA, *MORE STATELY MANSIONS* MOVED TO New York for an opening at the Broadhurst Theater on October 31. "Swedes will sit through anything as long as it's O'Neill," Ingrid said at the time, "but Americans come to the theater with a couple of martinis under their belts and they just want to be entertained." But in this case, neither critics nor audiences were. "It does O'Neill's memory a disservice," wrote the critic of the *Times*, adding that while Ingrid was "a woman so beautiful that she is herself a work of art . . . she seemed strangely gauche. She trades heavily on her natural charm [but] makes less of the character than you might have hoped." His colleagues found the play murky, tedious and soporific, but most were kinder to Ingrid. She did not, she insisted when she read her unenthusiastic notices, need kindness—but the savagery toward the efforts of Quintero, Martin and O'Neill made her livid.

Never mind: the play ran sixteen weeks, until March 1968, which in that season meant a profit. Neither she nor her colleagues regretted the experience. "She had no star attitude at all," Arthur Hill continued, adding that at Christmastime everyone arrived to find that Ingrid had stayed late one night, decorating the backstage area, the staircases and dressing rooms with colorful designs and merry little Swedish trolls.

Christmas 1967 coincided with Kay Brown's sixty-fifth birthday, for which Ingrid wrote "An Ode to Kay," which revealed not only Ingrid's warmest side but also her astonishing facility for English light verse:

> *I sat up one night rather late,*
> *Thinking up rhymes for my Kate—*
> *But could find only "holy"*
> *To rhyme with "Stromboli"*
> *So I quickly called in Mrs. Haight.* *
>
> *I first met this lady named Brown*
> *When she flew into my dark, frozen town*

---

*A neighbor of Kay Brown.

With a contract to sign
On the cold, dotted line
And a smile I couldn't turn down.

In New York, as Mrs. James Barrett,
She said, to meet all, I must dare it.
Both you and your Jim
Took me into the swim
With you at my side I could bear it.

With the flick crowd your girl was soon in
So you warned her of whiskey and gin.
You advised how to dress her,
Was her mother confessor,
And taught her the wages of sin.

But on Stromboli, that glamorous isle,
Where you came at the height of your style
In a lovely mink coat
And a small fishing boat—
But you failed, Kay, in spite of your guile.

You continued your Ingrid to sell
Though things didn't go very well.
Life just didn't fit
Work wasn't it
My luck seemed to quit.
Love was—oh, well!
So instead of a hit
You found me Lars Schmidt
With his island, his dogs and Choisel.

With "Mansions" you found me a part in
A drama I lost my whole heart in.
When I accepted, you cried,
Saying, "It's so dignified."
Then you sent me Quintero and Martin.

After opening, we all went to dine
And to greet me you headed the line.
And the picture will show
What I already know:
I'm safest when your hand's holding mine.

In your capable hands I am still,
And God help me, I always will.
Men have tried to replace you
They still push and race you—
As you also can see in the still.

Now these silly verses must end.
As you hear them you must comprehend
That what these verses say
Is "I love you, dear Kay,
My matchmaker, angel and friend."

INGRID HAD GOOD WORDS FOR ANOTHER CLOSE FRIEND THAT WINTER. On January 25, 1968, she dashed from her performance to the opening night party at Sardi's for *I Never Sang For My Father*, by Robert Anderson. Since Paris that winter of 1957, he had indeed taken Ingrid's advice and moved on with his life: several months after their parting, he met Teresa Wright, and they were married in 1959. Adding fresh distinction to an eminent and award-winning career on stage, screen and television, Teresa was now co-starring in Bob's new play, with Hal Holbrook and Lillian Gish.

When Ingrid arrived at Sardi's, everyone was anxiously awaiting the play's early newspaper reviews. As it happened, all of them raved except the *New York Times*. "Oh, Bob," Ingrid said, referring to her own recent experience with the same paper. "Read your ads—don't read your reviews!" *I Never Sang For My Father* had a healthy Broadway run, was successfully transferred to the screen, and later was often revived.

Ever alert for the right projects for Ingrid, Kay Brown sifted carefully through the latest novels sent to MCA's literary department each week. Among the submissions was one from the writer-producer Stirling Silliphant, who had prepared a treatment based on Rachel Maddux's novella *A Walk in the Spring Rain*. This was the story of a middle-aged professor's wife who accompanies him to rural Tennessee during his academic leave for a writing sabbatical. There, she has a brief romance with a very different kind of man— a primitive sort to be played, appropriately, by Anthony Quinn. But at the finale, she resumes her less independent but more realistic life back in the city.

Ingrid read the treatment with some misgivings. This movie would be made in America, and she really had had little prolonged time with Lars in Europe during the last several years. "Our professional lives had kept us apart, leading us to different places in the world," he said. "And even if we did everything we could to keep in close contact, there were many lengthy periods when we were alone." Ingrid had tried to become the country French matron that spring after *More Stately Mansions* closed, but as usual life in Choisel was not enough. She and Lars had been married almost ten years, and while there was neither rancor nor suspicion on either side, "it wasn't really a married existence," as she admitted.

Her second hesitation about accepting the role had to do with the first draft of Silliphant's screenplay, which she returned to him with copious critical notes. That, she believed, would effectively end the negotiations.

But exactly the opposite occurred, and rumors of Ingrid Bergman's return to American movies after twenty-one years caused a flurry of interest among other producers—Mike Frankovich, for one, who had bought film rights to the successful comedy *Cactus Flower*, performed all over the world and recently a huge New York success. While Silliphant toiled on the problem of walking in the spring rain, Frankovich and director Gene Saks rushed to Choisel with I.A.L. Diamond's screenplay for *Cactus Flower*. Her role—that of an apparently sexless dentist's nurse who blossoms like the title—could be shot very quickly in Hollywood the following spring, they said, offering a fee so high ($800,000 for a few weeks of work) that she could not refuse.

But, Ingrid said, she was almost fifty-three and the part called for a woman in her thirties. "I am rather proud of my wrinkles, after all, and have never tried to hide my age." Wouldn't Frankovich and Saks like to do a screen test first, to see if she could play opposite Walter Matthau (five years her junior)? Also, she had never been to a discothèque and knew nothing about the wild new nightclub dancing indicated in the script—wouldn't this be a problem, too? The men looked at each other. A now legendary actress asking for a test? The result confirmed their fervor, and the deal was made.

The announcement of Ingrid's participation—and the Oscar Stirling Silliphant received in April for writing *In the Heat of the Night*—was exactly the incentive he needed. That summer, he went to Dannholmen with the second draft—much improved, she said. Well, replied Silliphant, he was going to produce the picture as well, and if she was going to be in America for *Cactus Flower*, he could arrange an equally expeditious schedule for *A Walk in the Spring Rain* later that spring. Two films in succession with high salaries, a triumphant return to Hollywood, and she would be back in Europe with Lars by summertime. Ingrid accepted.

AND SO, IN EARLY 1969, SHE ARRIVED IN LOS ANGELES, WHERE SHE was installed at the Beverly Hills Hotel and met Matthau and twenty-three-year-old Goldie Hawn. Unsure of how she would be welcomed on a Hollywood set, Ingrid arrived nervously at Columbia Studios, so Matthau suggested they lunch together on the first day. She downed three martinis before returning, cold sober, to work. "I remarked how well she held her liquor," Matthau recalled, and she said, 'Ya, isn't it terrible?'"

Goldie Hawn was afraid of feeling "so awfully inhibited by her that I wouldn't be able to function. But it wasn't that way at all. I didn't feel I had to try to compete. I just felt privileged to be in the same picture with her. She took me on very lovingly and taught me a great deal in my first picture" (for which Hawn won the supporting actress Oscar).

After a few weeks on the set, word got around Hollywood that a former star was (as the saying went) a hot new star, and so Ingrid was invited to present the Oscar for best actress at the rites of spring. She opened the envelope and announced the award with a lilting giggle that had the audience laughing with her even before she announced that there were two winners (Katharine Hepburn and Barbra Streisand).

*   *   *

JUST AS WITH JOSÉ QUINTERO, INGRID HAD SERIOUS IDEAS AND WAS unafraid to speak her mind to Gene Saks. She might have hesitated about the role, but on the set her steely intelligence bore into every aspect of the production. Ingrid was very much in command of herself, according to Saks—and sometimes she was in command of him, too. High-strung and sure of her experience, she could sometimes go too far, and diplomacy was often not her strong suit in this third phase of her career.

"I think Gene Saks is very thankful for all the good advice I'm giving him," she wrote to Lars in March. "As usual, I interfere with his direction!" In fact, Saks found her "a sensational combination of irritation and charm" as she indicated small points in script or direction which he thought settled. "But then she laughed, often at herself, and frankly I was charmed all over again." Her suggestions, never trivial, smoothed some rough moments in the script, which, alas, had lost much of the sparkle of the brilliant French original— *Fleur de cactus*, by Ingrid's friend Pierre Barillet and Jean-Pierre Grédy.

To no one's surprise, Ingrid looked lovely—whether in nurse's white or in a sequined gown. She danced the wild flings of the late 1960s with appropriately feverish style and showed, by her typical understatement, a delicious flair for comedy not seen since her Swedish films more than thirty years earlier—thus her transformation in *Cactus Flower* from apparent Nordic iceberg to passionate mistress is neither unrefined nor incredible.

JUST AS DURING THE SELZNICK YEARS, INGRID SPRINTED DIRECTLY from one picture to another. Despite many difficulties with the script and casting, *A Walk in the Spring Rain* was ready for production, and a week after presenting the Oscar, Ingrid was in the Smoky Mountains with Anthony Quinn, Fritz Weaver and director Guy Green, best known for his successful and sensitive films *The Mark* and *A Patch of Blue*. Green had, years before, brought his keen artist's eye to the cinematography of several David Lean pictures, and, though a last-minute replacement on *Spring Rain*, he gave the picture much of its visual appeal and narrative economy. Ingrid worked on the film in Tennessee, New York and Hollywood from April 21 to June 13, 1969.

More than any other actress in his career, Green said, he found Ingrid "cooperative, modest, always pleasant and never a problem. She was a remarkable person to everyone in the cast and on the crew—always as concerned for anyone's troubles as she was, for example, about the squeaky wheels on a camera dolly. She was completely absorbed in the production."

Sometimes, perhaps too absorbed, for although Ingrid never had pretensions to be a director, she was now effectively acting like one, and this wore out Anthony Quinn's patience. Shooting an exterior scene one day in Tennessee, the crew had perfect sunlight and all was ready. But after a brief rehearsal for the scene, Ingrid turned to Quinn and asked, "You are not going to play it that way, are you?"

Quinn's Mexican-Irish temper flared: "Who is directing this movie, anyway—you or Guy?" At once, he threatened to leave the picture: they could bring in Burt Lancaster to replace him, he said. Quinn then huddled with Green, while Ingrid sat with Ruth Roberts. "The sun is going down," she said to Ruth. "God, we might lose a whole day's shooting, and it will be my fault!" And with that, her professional spirit took over. "I am so terribly sorry," she said, approaching Quinn and Green. "I shall never open my mouth again about how you should play a scene. Let's just go on shooting, because we want this picture in the can."

IN HER WORK FROM THE EARLY 1960s, INGRID COULD INDEED BE, AS she admitted in a letter to Lars that spring, "very tiresome, [and] both Tony Quinn and Guy Green say it and have helped me understand what was wrong. I never listen and I talk about something else right in the middle of somebody else's conversation; you know that well. That Tony Quinn has taken out of me. He looks at me without saying a word until I've asked his forgiveness. I'm much kinder now, you wait and see." She certainly was kinder at the end of filming, when Ingrid presented gifts to Tony Quinn and Guy Green—artist's tools to her co-star (who had taken up painting) and an elegant cache box for her director. On the lid was engraved the motto

Within you see
what pleases me

—and Green opened to see his own reflection in a small mirror. Whatever the circumstances, Ingrid was never ungrateful and always mindful of what she owed patient colleagues.

But she was also more agitated about each project in her late career—partly because of the lack of really good new scripts; and partly, too, because she knew that her marriage was being eroded by the slow attenuation of time and distance. She smoked more, occasionally drank a little too much (though never to frank insobriety) and often seemed edgy and confused. Simultaneously, she sometimes felt vaguely ill, but in the absence of identifiable symptoms and in the presence of so many other clear concerns, she simply ignored her discomfort and got on with her life.

Still, the obsession with youth culture annoyed her: "There are no movie scripts being written for a woman my age! Here I am, considered an old lady in my fifties," she told a writer. "Well, maybe I can play one of the witches in *Macbeth* some day!" And then the irrepressible laughter bubbled up. Still, she was not always in good humor.

A Walk in the Spring Rain had lovely moments, but 1970, the year of the film's release, was not a good time for romances about adults. Ingrid promoted the picture across America, but it was not well received, and she received compliments only on her looks—very nice as far as such words went, but they did not go far enough. That was the way movie stars were reviewed, she said: but she was something different—a serious actress still working at a difficult and demanding craft.

INGRID RETURNED TO PARIS, WHERE LARS AWAITED. SHE TALKED ANImatedly about the state of the new Hollywood, which had exchanged the traditional studio system and long-term contracts with an aimless, youth-oriented and youth-controlled business. Technically, she said, America had the best facilities in the world, but these were at the service of some of the silliest, most emptyheaded stories one could imagine. *Casablanca*, hardly Ingrid's favorite picture, could never have been made in 1970, she said, and she was right: it had no explicit sex, no overt violence, no auto chases, no rock music soundtrack. And *Notorious*? Hitch could never have sold so subtle and adult an idea in this brave new world.

But it was not only her profession that had changed, as Ingrid learned the evening of her arrival. Her life was altering swiftly, too. As gently as he could, Lars told her that he had fallen in love with a young woman named Kristina Belfrage, who lived and worked in Paris. Their relationship, he said, had become more serious and important than he had expected. Twenty years had passed since the death of his only child, and his longing for another was deep and persistent.

Ingrid did not take the news calmly. She knew that she had been an absentee wife, and that this made such a development perhaps inevitable. They discussed divorce, but neither of them was ready for that. Suddenly it seemed to Ingrid that this was a repetition of the end of her marriage to Roberto, and that Kristina was the new Sonali Das Gupta. Was her entire life to be an act of penitence for 1949?

Ingrid gave the marriage one last, long try, and while Lars divided his time between her and Kristina, she waited at Choisel virtually every evening for over eight months—trying to read scripts, welcoming her children and a few friends for visits, contacting friends, and feeling, for the first time in her life, useless and unwanted. "Part of her said, 'Oh, let life go on,'" recalled Stephen Weiss, "because this business with Lars and Kristina was so close to her own past. But for all her strength, she was timid and frightened and needed him—although she needed her career first."

"Even in this situation, Ingrid showed her greatness," said Lars. "She was a rare artist and a beautiful woman with an exceptional inner strength. She had the courage to speak up in her work, in her family life and in her human relationships. She was looking for love, she gave love and she was loved. She was happy and she laughed easily." But the laughter was muted that season.

And then one evening, Ingrid had a telephone call from the London theatrical producer Hugh ("Binkie") Beaumont. He was planning a revival of a minor Shaw comedy, *Captain Brassbound's Conversion*. Written in 1899 for Ellen Terry, this was a somewhat windy play, but at its center was a brilliantly contrived role, Lady Cicely Waynflete. After Miss Terry, major stage actresses (among them Gladys Cooper, Sybil Thorndike and Edna Best) had enjoyed enormous success as Lady Cicely.

Ingrid read the play and yes, Binkie was right: it was not very good. But what a part for her—the only woman in a cast of twenty-five, and she had all the sparkling lines. Ingrid accepted, Laurence Evans negotiated a deal for her to receive 10 percent of the gross weekly box-office receipts, and, after Christmas 1970, she prepared to depart for rehearsals in London. Whether Lars would or would not continue his life with Kristina was, Ingrid felt, entirely up to him; in any case, she could not wait anxiously for the other shoe to drop.

Chapter Eighteen

1971–1975

Strange to see how a good dinner reconciles everybody.

SAMUEL PEPYS,
Diary

"THE TEARS YOU HAVE SHED MAKE YOU INTO A HUMAN BEING AND that is much to be grateful for," Ingrid told a reporter, without elaboration, on arriving in London in January 1971. For several years, no one had any idea that she was speaking of her third marriage. Whatever her private anguish as she moved into the Connaught Hotel that winter, she wore the mask of her usual casual, gay elegance. Her role in *Captain Brassbound's Conversion* helped.

So charming that she can easily manipulate all the men around her, Lacy Cicely Waynflete is one of Shaw's most intriguing creations, despite her presence in a play that has been generally bewailed since its premiere as "pretty tiresome." She and her brother-in-law are in Morocco, when they encounter his nephew, the notorious brigand "Black Paquito," alias Captain Brassbound, who has an ancient score to settle. With humor and logic, she disabuses the title character of his desire for revenge and angles for justice. Wily, candid, suspicious of romance and sly about the foibles of men, Lady Cicely disposes of masculine malevolence and by her strongly maternal direction moves her world toward a better course.

Rehearsals during January 1971 proceeded astonishingly smoothly, perhaps because Ingrid had no illusions and knew how much she required Frith Banbury's direction regarding the subtleties of Shaw. Still, she had her own will. "You can't do that because people must look at him while he's speaking," Banbury told Ingrid at one rehearsal when she moved during another player's line. "But it is my reaction that is important," she countered. "Not his words, but my reaction. After all, in life it's often the person who is not talking who is worth watching." This was a lesson learned from Hitchcock, and in this instance it happened that Ingrid was right.

The premiere at the Cambridge Theatre on February 18, after a two-week tryout in Brighton, baffled a few critics: why a revival of minor Shaw, and why a Swede in the role of a British aristocrat? And why was Ingrid (in her own words) "stumbling around as usual with my dialogue" for the first few performances? They were on the mark, for this was far from Shaw's best play, Ingrid did not understand much of it, and it was not a role ideally suited to her. Nevertheless, Beaumont knew his public—which eventually supported the play for nine months—and as for the dialogue, well, this was always a bit dicey for Ingrid during the first week.

In repose, she could be quite marvelous in this play, and her multivalent reading of several lines evoked just the right sophisticated humor. When it was remarked of a certain villain that he has become a reasonable man, she replied with a mildly acerbic lilt, "Oh, you think he's as changed as all that?"

INGRID HAD SEVERAL QUIET DINNERS WITH HITCHCOCK THAT SUMMER; he was in London filming *Frenzy*, and they gossiped, drained a bottle of champagne, mourned the new style of moviemaking and celebrated an affection that had endured over twenty-seven years. Two new friendships also came with the run of *Brassbound*—that of her co-star Joss Ackland, who played the title character, and of the company and stage manager for the show, Griffith James. On Sundays, Ingrid frequently came to Ackland's home and went bicycling with his children in Richmond Park.

As for Griff James, he greeted Ingrid at her first rehearsal, for which she was a quarter-hour late, by gently reprimanding her: his professionalism and candor appealed to her, and very quickly a close alliance was formed. For the rest of her life, Griff was a faithful friend, involved in all her shows in England and America.

By mid-summer, Ingrid was grateful for the peace of Dannholmen, where she brought her children. "You know," she confided to a friend, "being a mother is more a question of quality than quantity. I mean, isn't it about the kind of time you spend with your children rather than how much time? I don't see my children too often, but when I do, I'm totally devoted to them."

Such was her philosophy of motherhood, although she admitted it was unconventional. "I wanted success, a big success as an actress, and a home and children. I have them all, so I am happy. If the price I paid was too high, I only wish I had paid it alone. My children paid for it, too. Their paths were strewn with broken homes." And for this she felt a lifelong guilt—which may help to understand why, late in her life, she often reached out with maternal tenderness to those who were lonely, whether friends or colleagues.

That summer, Lars engaged a young Finnish university graduate with a genius for assisting with the logistics of managing the household and with the talents of a world-class chef. In the years to come, Paavo Turtiainen became a close friend to Lars and Ingrid, and it was he who helped her with the complicated task of sifting through her scrapbooks and files when she at last began to work with a collaborator on her memoirs. Paavo's discretion and his deep attachment to both Lars and Ingrid helped them both in the next dozen years, and he continued to be a trusted confidant in Lars's family long after Ingrid's death.

There was a family celebration that December, when Ingrid went to New York for Pia's second marriage, to financial broker Joseph Daly. Mama was escorted to the church wedding by Sidney Bernstein, and there were polite words with Petter, who gave away his daughter. The following year, the Dalys gave Ingrid her first grandchild. According to Pia, Ingrid was "probably the most doting, involved and devoted grandmother the world has ever seen!"

IN EARLY 1972, SHE BEGAN THE AMERICAN AND CANADIAN TOUR OF *Captain Brassbound's Conversion*—a few weeks in each of several cities until summertime. During the play's run at the Kennedy Center, she accepted an invitation to a question and answer forum with the National Press Association. There was the usual round of clichés—Did she find comedy harder than drama? What did she think of the Kennedy Center? How did she manage to look so young? Should actors be involved in politics? And then a reporter asked how Ingrid Bergman studied for a role. Her answer was straightforward and instructive at a time when there was much prolix, self-important academic discourse in the air about the actor's art:

> I haven't read many of those books about acting. I think instinctively, and even the first time I read a script I know exactly how the woman is. That is why I turn down many things I don't understand. I must understand the character completely; I mean, there must be something inside me that is that person, and then immediately I feel it. It is more a feeling than a technique.

She then sent the journalists away laughing after her response to a final question: Since she had spent so much time in Italy, what did she have to say about Italians and contemporary theater? "The Italians don't care so much for the theater—because after all, what they see on the stage is so much better done at home!"

BUT THE HIGHLIGHT OF THE TOUR OCCURRED AFTER SHE HAD OPENED to good notices in New York (where *Captain Brassbound's Conversion* was the only one of fifty-six plays that season to turn a profit). On April 19, Senator Charles Percy of Illinois read a national apology to Ingrid Bergman for the injustice done to her by Senator Johnson twenty-two years earlier. Percy's statement, to which he appended several important reviews and essays about Ingrid that spring, was included in the *Congressional Record* for that date:

"Mr. President," the senator began,

> one of the world's loveliest, most gracious and most talented women was made the victim of bitter attack in this Chamber 22 years ago. Today I would like to pay long overdue tribute to Ingrid Bergman, a true star in every sense of the word.

After summarizing the events of her journey in Washington and outlining the highlights of her stage, screen and television career, he continued that it was obvious that Ingrid had

> the overwhelming admiration and affection of the American people—both for her brilliance and sensitivity as an actress and for her courage, poise and warmth as an individual . . . Our culture would be poorer indeed without her artistry . . . [She is] one of the greatest performing artists of our time.

And then came the reason for the encomium:

> I know that across the land, millions of Americans would wish to join me in expressing their regrets for the personal and professional persecution that caused Ingrid Bergman to leave this country at the height of her career . . . Miss Bergman is not only welcome in America; we are deeply honored by her visits here.

Eleven essays about Ingrid were appended to his entry in the *Congressional Record* for that day.

"Dear Senator Percy," Ingrid wrote from New York, "My war with America was over long ago. The wounds, however, remained. Now, because of your gallant gesture with your generous and understanding address to the Senate, they are healed forever."

While in New York, she appeared briefly in a picture of no great consequence, as an eccentric, wealthy old lady who befriends two lonely children in *From the Mixed-Up Files of Mrs. Basil E. Frankweiler*. This she undertook, as she told friends, not only because she was offered too much money to turn it down, but also because she saw the character role—that of a bewigged and powdered recluse—as a marvelous opportunity to satirize the only roles offered to women in their fifties: women in their eighties, arid and acrid crones finally revealed to be old dears.

BACK ON DANNHOLMEN AND OCCASIONALLY IN CHOISEL DURING THE summer and autumn of 1972, she interrupted her holiday for several journeys to London to discuss plays, but for the moment nothing was certain—in art or life. Her frequent appearances at airports and the inevitably public lives of Ingrid and Lars alerted the press, who began to sniff trouble in marital paradise. "People keep asking me about Lars," she told a reporter. "We are still married and I hope we'll sort things out and stay married. That is all I can say at the moment. I read in the papers, 'A friend says . . . Friends of Miss Bergman tell me'. . . and I wonder who are all these friends? I don't think my friends are saying anything about my marriage because, like me, they don't know yet what to say." Nor did Lars, who did not marry Kristina Belfrage.

But Ingrid knew very well what to say when Binkie Beaumont again rang from London with an idea for another revival—this time of Somerset Maugham's 1927 comedy *The Constant Wife*.

The central role was Constance, an elegant and savvy woman, married fifteen years to John Middleton, an eminent physician who is having an affair with her best friend. Badgered by her friends to bolt and told by her mother to accept the inevitable philandering male, Constance takes a different course: she tries to preserve both her self-esteem and her financial security and announces to John that she, too, has fallen out of love and is going to work so that she may pay him for living expenses: "There is only one freedom that is really important, and that is economic freedom."

A year later, solvent and available, she tells John, to his outrage, that she is about to go on a romantic holiday with an old flame. "I took the precaution to marry a gentleman," she says, "and I know that you could never bring yourself to divorce me for doing no more than you did yourself." After her adventure, she promises to return to her husband, who will accept her because, as he admits, she is "the most maddening, willful, capricious, wrong-headed, delightful and enchanting woman a man was ever cursed with having for a wife. Yes, damn you, come back!"

A half-century old, this was a play that seemed well suited to the new vocalism about women's liberation in the 1970s. During late autumn, Ingrid read the play, discussed it with Lars, surveyed its history and learned that the role had been shrewdly created by Ethel Barrymore and later elegantly revived by Katharine Cornell. Like Lady Cicely, Constance was a superb role, and Ingrid would have, Beaumont guaranteed, an exquisite wardrobe. The crowning argument that secured her participation was that Sir John Gielgud had agreed to direct.

Of course she would have preferred to do new, modern plays instead of revivals, but no one was writing roles for middle-aged women and "it's hard to find good scripts nowadays. Most authors seem to write unpleasant plays about unattractive people addicted to foul language. I will not appear in sordid plays. I want audiences to enjoy themselves, not feel uncomfortable."

And so on March 20, 1973, Ingrid and Gielgud went to London for discussions at Beaumont's home. "We found him lying in bed," Sir John recalled, "suffering from a bad back. He was getting ready to drive to [his doctor in] Harley Street for a checkup. Ingrid and I spent half an hour sitting on either side of his bed. Then his car came, and she and I were left talking over tea in his drawing room." Two days later, Beaumont was dead of heart failure at age sixty-four.

AT THE END OF MAY, INGRID WAS INVITED TO BE PRESIDENT OF THE jury at the Cannes Film Festival, at which Ingmar Bergman's *Cries and Whispers* was shown out of competition. Just before she departed from Choisel for the Riviera, she found the director's written promise—now over a decade old—to make a film with her. To this she attached a note ("Time marches on!") and slipped both it and his letter into Bergman's pocket amid the crush of photographers at the festival.

The production of *The Constant Wife* proceeded, with rehearsals late that summer for a premiere on September 29 at the Albery Theatre. "I found her enchantingly willing and responsive to direction," Gielgud added. Precisely because Ingrid herself understood both the sudden announcements of infidelity and the concomitant necessity of a wife's self-reliance, she brought to the role a sly worldliness and an irony that enabled her to catch the pebbles of marital discord in her shoe without limping toward mere crowd-pleasing sentimentality. "The first night, I was so nervous I stuttered and was a mess," Ingrid admitted soon after. "I'm so scared in a theater, but never in front of a camera. I've always felt the camera was my friend, and in any case you can do it again [if there is a mistake]. You can't in the theater."

As before, she needed a week after opening to be comfortable in the role, but still there were hilarious gaffes that seemed only to increase the audience's delight. At one point, urging that her husband depend on their cook to devise the menus, Ingrid was to say the line, "Give cook her head." Instead, she said with ringing eloquence, "Give cook your head!" She wondered, for a moment, why her co-players were shaking with laughter. "What's she going to pull on us tonight?" was the affectionate password among the cast.

GIELGUD RECALLED INGRID MAKING A VIRTUE OF NECESSITY ONE EVENING when she was talking spiritedly backstage with Griff James just before her entrance. Her cue came, but she failed to notice it. Griff, of course, did, opening the door and pushing her onstage. Breathless and almost losing her footing, Ingrid recovered, turned to the other players and announced, as if it were part of the script, "Oh, I'm so sorry—I was talking to Griff!"

The biggest hit of the season, The Constant Wife sold out every performance at the Albery, thus making Ingrid a very rich woman: again thanks to Laurence Evans, she now took home 12½ percent of the gross receipts. Despite some carping notices from critics—who, even more vocally than in the case of Shaw, deeply resented a Swede playing an Englishwoman—The Constant Wife had an eight-month run in London, until May 1974.

But never mind the critics: Ingrid was far more upset when she returned to her leased flat on Mount Street after the performance of Monday, October 29. She found the door broken, the place ransacked, and a theft of $25,000 worth of jewelry, her mink coat and several family items of sentimental value. Insurance covered the monetary loss, but for several weeks Ingrid felt a profound insecurity on returning home each night.

BUT THEN THERE WERE GRAVER REASONS FOR ANXIETY. ON SEPTEMBER 26, 1973, Anna Magnani had died at age sixty-five of cancer. Ingrid, who was now in friendly contact with Rossellini, had followed the ravaging course of Magnani's illness. The eccentric, freewheeling actress was quite alone in her final days—except for Roberto, who visited, brought flowers and held her hands through the haze of pain and narcotics until she died.

Magnani's old rancors, the misadventures, tantrums and jeal-
ousies with Roberto had faded in the last months, and forever after
Ingrid spoke proudly and generously of her former husband's loving
attention to Magnani in those dreadful final weeks. All the bells of
Rome tolled at her funeral, thousands surrounded the church, and
when her coffin was brought out, the square was silent—and then
suddenly a wave of applause began, the only way a grateful people
could honor one of their most loved artists. When it was subsequently learned that no provision had been made for Magnani's
burial, Roberto insisted she be interred in his family grave.

Magnani's death from cancer may have been in Ingrid's mind a
few weeks later.

At home in bed after a performance in late November, she read
a letter to a newspaper editor from a grateful reader who wrote that
an article instructing women about breast self-examination had
saved her life. As she read, Ingrid automatically began to move her
hand slowly over the contours of her right breast. No lumps, nothing abnormal. Good. She read on, and her fingertips moved to the
underside of her left breast. There was a small, hard nodule she had
never before noticed. No, she told herself, this could not be anything serious.

But at once she reached for the telephone and rang Lars at
Choisel, awakening him well after midnight. Ordinarily they spoke
every day, and Ingrid had routine questions about the realities of life
she could never master—how to find a good hotel or a decent
apartment, how much to tip a porter, what to do about a leaking
faucet, when to discuss a problem with a producer, how to book an
airline reservation.

Throughout her life, she had relied on her husbands or lovers to
attend to practical matters, while she devoted herself to her art.
"She was really not a very worldly person—in fact, she was very
much like a child in many ways," as Stephen Weiss said. "It may
seem surprising, but Ingrid was a very dependent person offstage.
She felt very comfortable at work, but not in other places." And
when it came to matters of health—well, she had a remarkable constitution, endless stamina, and very few days of illness in her entire
life. There had been a bout of pneumonia in 1943, an appendectomy in 1956 and a brief stay in hospital a few years after that to

remedy a minor gynecological complaint; otherwise, an occasional cold was her worst malady.

Lars heard the controlled anxiety in her voice when she asked his advice that November evening. She must see a doctor the very next day, he advised. But Ingrid did not see a doctor the next day. Instead, while putting on her makeup at the theater, she casually asked Griff if she and the play were insured in case she could not go on. Her tone and attitude, he recalled, were calm and without drama, as if she were discussing plans for a forthcoming journey. "Insured?" Griff asked, astonished. "Why do you ask? Are you sick? You don't look sick to me!" With that, Ingrid had her answer: she was not insured, and the play—London's biggest hit that season— would be closed if she withdrew. No Ingrid Bergman, no Constance Middleton, no play.

A few days later, she appeared in the offices of a specialist named Dr. David Handley. His counsel was simple: many such tiny masses were benign, but only a needle biopsy could confirm a certain diagnosis, and that he recommended at once. But Ingrid had her life in the theater to consider—her art was 90 percent of her life, after all, as Lars, Stephen, Pia and so many others realized. Everything else had to fit within that dedication.

Hence, for the present, Ingrid, always optimistic and never self-dramatizing, chose to count herself among those whose little physical problem was no cause for concern. She declined to have the biopsy. "You simply could not push her," said Laurence Evans. "She was an intelligent woman and she knew the lump might be malignant, but she would not even consider leaving *The Constant Wife* and abandoning the other actors and the production company."

Perhaps she was whistling in the dark, perhaps enacting a common defense mechanism: whatever the reason, when Ingrid was invited by Sidney Lumet to augment her schedule by assuming a role in his all-star cast of the film *Murder on the Orient Express*, she accepted. Lumet, who had directed many superb films (*Long Day's Journey into Night* and *The Pawnbroker* among them), had no trouble at all in getting Ingrid to sign on—although originally he wanted her for the role of the aged Russian Princess Dragomiroff. No, said Ingrid, I want to do the funny old Swedish missionary, Greta Ohlsson. And so she did, receiving $100,000 for a few days of work.

Filming of the lushly entertaining, droll and suspenseful picture proceeded remarkably smoothly at Elstree in early spring 1974, despite the fact that most members of the prestigious cast, like Ingrid, dashed from the day's shooting to their evening jobs in the theater. The impressive assemblage included Albert Finney, Lauren Bacall, Martin Balsam, Jacqueline Bisset, Sean Connery, George Coulouris, John Gielgud, Wendy Hiller (wondrous as the wizened old princess), Anthony Perkins (who had no scenes with Ingrid), Vanessa Redgrave, Rachel Roberts, Richard Widmark and Michael York. Ingrid was particularly delighted that, because she had only a few very minor moments and reaction shots in the picture (less than a minute), Lumet decided to film her single longer scene in one uninterrupted take.

"She gave a very pure performance," Lumet reflected years later. "She made no attempt to look beautiful, nor to glamorize the part." The single, four-and-a-half-minute-long take—during which Ingrid ran the gamut from annoyance to sorrow to fear to the kind of nervy sweetness of a maiden lady missionary—was praised by critics and audiences alike. This was a delicious bit of comedy and pathos (and nearly over-the-top mugging) but audiences adored it, and Ingrid was surprised to receive one of the picture's five Oscar nominations.

AFTER THE COMPLETION OF HER DOUBLE DUTY ON THE SOUNDSTAGE and in the West End in May 1974, Ingrid noticed that the lump in her breast seemed larger, and she revisited Dr. Handley. Well, yes, she said, she would go to have the test—but first she must visit Pia and her grandson in New York, where she would seek a second medical opinion.

The American physician agreed with his British colleague: a biopsy must be performed, since the lump seemed very suspicious indeed. She agreed to see to it when she returned to London—but first there was Lars's birthday in Europe, on June 11, and then . . . "Which is more important to you?" interrupted the doctor testily. "Your husband's birthday party or your life?" The answer came quickly and defiantly, "My husband's birthday party, of course!" Next day, camouflaging her anxiety, she bicycled in Central Park and then dined with friends.

On June 11, she did host Lars's party in Paris, and next day she departed for London. Four days later, doctors at the London Clinic removed tissue from the lump in her left breast and the biopsy confirmed everyone's worst fears. A radical mastectomy was performed on the spot.

"I didn't take it as badly as I expected," Ingrid said, although Lars, her son and daughters, who raced to her bedside, were quietly anxious. For the remaining six months of 1974, Ingrid submitted to the painful exhaustion of physical therapy and a debilitating course of radiation. Only her family, Griff James and Laurence Evans knew about her illness and the reason for her long withdrawal from public life. Whatever fear she had was hidden beneath her will to recover.

Weeks after surgery, Ingrid was swimming, shopping, taking her children to theater and acting as if she had endured nothing more serious than a bout of flu. Nor did she ever mention what was on everyone's mind: that her father had died of cancer at age fifty-eight, and that in recent years medical science had established the clear connection between smoking and cancer.

WITH THE NEW YEAR 1975, INGRID INSISTED ON HONORING HER commitment to the American tour of *The Constant Wife*, despite the rigors of traveling to Los Angeles, Denver, Washington, Boston and New York from January to mid-May; in every city, the play broke all existing house records. No one in the company had any idea of her recent surgery. On the contrary, her mood was merry and fun-loving, and she exhibited not a trace of that attitude sometimes known as "star complex."

In the Shubert Theatre in Century City, Los Angeles, there was a particularly awkward moment with an antique stage sofa that threatened to collapse after long years of inner struggle. Thinking it had been repaired on schedule, Ingrid took her cue and sank onto the piece, but the springs objected and she was tossed onto the floor. There was a collective gasp, but when Ingrid burst out laughing the audience joined her. After a moment, everything proceeded calmly. But ten minutes later, she had another cue for the same gesture and, clearly forgetting the incident, blithely sat on the recalcitrant sofa. More laughter. "The audience had the best time of their lives," Griff James recalled, adding that he could have collected the price of admission for a second time at the exit doors. It is easy to imagine other stars of the so-called golden age—other celebrities taking their fame with the utmost gravity—releasing a torrent of abuse on the crew and requiring their dismissal.

There was more ad-libbing in Los Angeles on another occasion, but this time the result was more painful. Dashing back to the theater with Griff and a few players after a light supper between the Saturday matinee and evening performances, Ingrid twisted her foot badly. By the time she limped to her dressing room, there was considerable swelling, and the house doctor said there were two small broken bones in her foot: a cast would have to be applied immediately. The theater manager panicked, the cast was anxious, and the producers huddled as if for war plans, since the performance was sold out and there was not enough cash for refunds. Only Ingrid remained calm. Don't be foolish, she said. Just tell the audience what has happened, urge them to have a drink at the bar, let them put the cast on my foot, and we'll bring up the curtain late.

"She simply refused to disappoint the customers," said Gielgud. "Instead, she sent for a wheelchair and quickly rearranged everyone's moves. And she acted gallantly under this handicap for several weeks." When the performance finally began that night (just after nine-thirty), there were no empty seats. Spectators had the time of their lives with this zanily improvised performance, no one more than the redoubtable Ingrid. She swiveled and spoke to each actor in turn, but inevitably players were bumping into one another, and more than once Ingrid crashed into the scenery or got caught on the carpet. The audience, as Griff recalled, watched a kind of play-within-a-play, and it is just possible that the impromptu antics were more amusing than Maugham's play. The show's managing director cabled her from London: "You've got the whole world at your foot"—to which Ingrid replied, "There's no business like toe business."

BECAUSE INGRID WAS NOMINATED FOR BEST SUPPORTING ACTRESS AS the nervous missionary in *Murder on the Orient Express*, it was deemed good publicity for her tour to close down a few of the Boston performances of *The Constant Wife* and send her to Hollywood for the Oscar ceremony. Lars met her at the Boston airport, and together they proceeded to Los Angeles, where she presented a lifetime award to her old friend Jean Renoir, ailing and confined to his home.

She was then astonished when she was awarded her third Academy Award—and as usual she was as frank as she was grateful. Like many people that year and later, Ingrid could not understand why François Truffaut's film, *La nuit américaine* (*Day for Night*), which had won the Oscar as best foreign film the previous year, was now nominated again, this time for its screenplay. In addition, Ingrid's old friend Valentina Cortese (who had co-starred with her in *The Visit* and whom she had known since her early days in Rome) had now been nominated for best supporting actress in *Day for Night*. As she came to receive her statuette, Ingrid surprised everyone:

> Thank you very much indeed. It's always nice to get an Oscar, but in the past he has shown he is very forgetful and has poor timing—because last year, when *Day for Night* won, I couldn't believe that Valentina Cortese was not nominated, because she gave the most beautiful performance. And now, here I am, her rival, and I don't like it at all. Where are you? [She then spotted her friend in the audience, and Cortese rose and blew Ingrid a kiss:] Ah, there you are! Please forgive me, Valentina, I didn't mean to!

The audience went wild with applause, and around the world viewers saw a gracious winner share her award with a friend she genuinely considered more deserving. "Really, it was very nice," she said a month later of her third Academy Award, "but I didn't think I deserved it. People were so impressed because I did a long dialogue in a single take—but that was not nearly so long or as demanding as my big nine-minute monologue for Hitch in *Under Capricorn!*"

Lars was with Ingrid at every celebratory moment and in every difficult situation for the rest of her life, and he invariably rearranged his schedule to attend to her inquiries about the logistics of daily life as well as to graver needs. But the marriage was over, and soon they agreed to divorce quietly; none of her friends knew of it for several years. Ingrid's priority in life was her career: "that always came first," as Lars said, "and then came her children, then her husband." This was an assessment she herself could not deny: "My whole life has been acting. I have had my different husbands, my families. I am fond of them all and I visit them all, but deep inside me there is the feeling that I belong to show business."

BY THE TIME *THE CONSTANT WIFE* ARRIVED IN NEW YORK ON APRIL 14, Ingrid was exhausted and still limping; but she had been relieved of the plaster cast and graduated from the wheelchair. As usual, the critics grumbled about her appearance in a revival of what they considered a third-rate play. But her performance was, *pace* the carping, a small gem of restrained, adult comedy. Without scene-stealing or milking any moment beyond its meaning, Ingrid found the right timing and the proper pauses to give each small moment the illumination of its context. During a scene with Brenda Forbes (playing Constance's mother), there was a casual bit of dialogue:

"After all," said Forbes, "what is fidelity?"

Ingrid rose from the sofa: "Mother, do you mind if I open the window?"

"It is open."

"In that case, do you mind if I shut it?" She does so. "I feel that when a woman of your age asks such a question, I should make some sort of symbolic gesture."

This kind of conversation would not otherwise have been memorable for an audience in 1975, but Ingrid's stage business—standing, starting, hesitating, gesturing and speaking with lilting irony—brought a knowing ripple of laughter from her audiences.

DESPITE THE CRUSH OF INTERVIEWS, PRESS CONFERENCES, PARTIES AND appointments during her five-week run in New York, Ingrid found time to oblige a request from Robert Anderson. He had taken a friendly and professional interest in a writer then working on his first book, a lengthy, chapter-by-chapter critical appreciation of each of Alfred Hitchcock's films. Through Bob's intercession (and in those days before answering machines), Ingrid had tried for several days to reach the writer, but he was dashing about interviewing other Hitchcock actors then in New York (Hume Cronyn, Jessica Tandy and Anne Baxter among them) and there was no reply at his home. Finally, she rang again and this time found him at his desk.

"Oh, good!" Ingrid cried when she got through at last. "Bob Anderson tells me you are writing a book on Hitchcock and that I should definitely speak with you. Would you like to come to the matinee next Wednesday? We can have supper at Sardi's before the evening performance, yes? Bring your notebook or your tape recorder and we will talk about Hitchcock. And why not come to the performance first, then meet me backstage after . . . "

Their meeting and dinner conversation, spiced not only with Ingrid's clear recollections of working with Hitchcock but also with remarkably frank accounts of her work with Rossellini and other directors, was the beginning of a fond acquaintance that endured until Ingrid's final illness.

"I am still working at my craft and on my concentration," Ingrid said of her appearance in *The Constant Wife*. "I was not perfect at the London opening, I'll tell you that. The critics were after me because I stuttered and mixed up the lines." She also delineated the differences between stage and screen acting: she found the nightly repetition of a role difficult and sometimes resented the daytime vigilance necessary. "Be careful—not too much wine at lunch," she told herself. She loved the contact with a live audience, but she loved the camera, too—one eye instead of a thousand—and yes, she had very few plays as good as the great pictures, like *Notorious*. Without referring to her illness, she added that when the curtain went up, she was taking the world's best medicine. Something wonderful happened then, no matter life's troubles. "If you're not feeling well, it goes away, because you have to pay attention to the job and think about something other than yourself. How lucky I am to have such a life!"

DURING THE AUTUMN OF 1975, INGRID WAS IN ROME, WHERE SHE again played a white-haired ancient—this time a senile contessa, once a gorgeous and famous courtesan, now lost in reverie and reduced to scratching out a paltry life in a seedy hotel. The film was Vincente Minnelli's last, *A Matter of Time*, in which he starred his daughter Liza, who for no reason of plot occasionally bursts into song. Ingrid, who took the role for its sheer mad character (and a fee of $250,000), had her twins on the picture as well—Isabella in her first small part (as a nursing nun named, quite deliberately, Sister Pia), and young Ingrid, who helped with Mama's complicated makeup. For the third time, Ingrid worked with her old friend Charles Boyer, although this time in only one brief scene. Since the death of his only child in 1965, Boyer was imprisoned in a haze of depression now complicated by the mortal illness of his wife. (Two years later, he took his own life after she died.)

For everyone's sake, she tried to leaven the atmosphere of a production that seemed doomed from day one, and shortly after its release it disappeared almost without a trace. Ingrid, with little to do in the movie except act imperiously unaware of the passage of time and encourage Liza to become a kind of Italian Gigi, was shamelessly wasted: the picture was mostly Liza's travelogue around Rome and a showcase for her voice and wardrobe.

By this time, Ingrid had not had a really first-rate movie role in twenty years, since *Anastasia*. But as she said that season, she was nothing like the movie's contessa: "She is just the opposite of myself, because she is destroying herself by dreams of her youth. I don't dream about my past. I accept my age and make the best of it."

REGARDING HER OWN PAST WITH PETTER, ROBERTO AND LARS, INGRID had never publicly said a harsh word against them—and such comments were all but impossible to hear from her in private. Göran von Essen, Stephen Weiss, Pierre Barillet and a legion of others recalled that even when she discussed unpleasant moments of her life, a husband was not singled out for blame or resentment. "She didn't have an ounce of bad will in her," as Lars said. "The past was the past, it was over, and then she went ahead."

Ingrid had never presented herself to the world as anything but a woman who had made her way, sometimes tripped in bad judgment, and was always willing to assume culpability for however she had caused pain by selfishness, that ubiquitous danger to which no human life is immune. "I love all my husbands" was the antiphon that recurred throughout the last decade of her life. "All my marriages were good and what follows love—or should—is deep friendship. If you marry for the right reasons, for trust and understanding and love, then you cannot hate your husbands or call them idiots when the marriages are over." As Lars said, she never bore a grudge, never nursed old wounds, was quick to forget unhappy episodes and believed that there was no unpleasantness that could not be rectified with goodwill.

WITH ROBERTO AND LARS, INGRID ESTABLISHED AN ACCOMMODATION and indeed friendships based on the respect that had once underwritten married love. But with Petter things were more difficult. To be sure, he never publicly vilified her, and during her illness he wrote at least two letters offering to put her in contact with specialists he knew. But after Ingrid published her memoirs (*My Story*) in 1980, he lost all perspective. From that time, Petter increasingly regarded Ingrid as frankly beneath contempt; so much is clear from his letters to writers, journalists and friends. Indeed, his view of her was so undilutedly negative that he made Senator Johnson's attack look like a proclamation of sainthood.

Ingrid's book treated their history gently, justly and, according to the testimony of virtually everyone who knew them, truthfully. But Ingrid forever so haunted Petter that in his senior years, she became his obsession, and he nursed an exquisitely sensitive wound of lamented, lost love masquerading as bitterness. Even Pia, surely the most innocently bruised of all, had accepted her mother's hand of friendship after all the bitterness of the early years; alas, her father was intransigent.

No such problem attended Ingrid's rapprochement with Roberto during the production of *A Matter of Time*. Over the last several years, Ingrid and he had established a truce that had now become friendship. He had not enjoyed much professional success in recent years, although some of his television documentaries had been praised. Students on American campuses queued up to hear the master of neorealism as visiting professor, and time had decorated him as an éminence grise.

But in many ways, Roberto was a director regarded as once significant but no longer relevant, and this he considered a betrayal of the world's common sense. Ingrid was just the right companion for a man who felt out of place. They shared an occasional dinner, they laughed, they spoke of their children and they mocked the excesses of their earlier life together. For once, Rome's paparazzi made nothing of their sightings of the once controversial couple, now sipping wine like old friends in a quiet corner of a family-style restaurant.

1976–1979

A little still she strove, and much repented.

BYRON,
Don Juan

AFTER *A MATTER OF TIME*, INGRID SET TO WORK ON A TASK NEGOTI-
ated the previous season. Kay Brown, among others, had for
several years been urging Ingrid to write a memoir or autobiography, but she had resolutely refused. But when assured she could
have complete control over a book written about her by someone
else, she reconsidered. So it happened that Alan Burgess presented
himself as the candidate for the job and was accepted; he had written *The Small Woman*, on which was based *The Inn of the Sixth Happiness*. In short order, the idea of the book was sold worldwide, and
Ingrid worked on it for most of 1976.

But what began as a straightforward, authorized and supervised
biography was very soon altered. She found some old day-books and
diaries; friends, eager to help, sent copies of letters they had
received from her; and a team of researchers in New York scoured
newspaper archives and libraries. Most important of all in the process, Ingrid worked with Paavo, an invaluable assistant in the task of

arranging, synthesizing and organizing mountains of cuttings and scrapbook clippings. When Burgess got hold of this material, he decided to assume Ingrid's voice—hence the third-person narrative was forthwith altered to first, and the book was to be an autobiography "as told to" Burgess.

But as she read through the first sample chapters he submitted, Ingrid was dismayed. Burgess, neither biographer nor memoirist, had apparently panicked; in any case, the manuscript was messy, disarrayed, vague as to dates and full of factual errors. To make matters worse, he was often incapacitated by the effects of alcohol. Thus Ingrid Bergman's book, whether to appear as biography or autobiography, stalled hopelessly. By the time her American publisher, Delacorte Press, demanded something for the presses (three years after the contracted due date), Ingrid was in deep distress: "I am worried sick about this," she told a friend. "It is too long, it is neither my book nor his, it is impossible to read, and I fear it will be a big flop." When it finally saw the light, in 1980, it was not a failure (it bore her name, after all), but she was correct in her critical assessment: passages written in Ingrid's voice alternate with narrative passages written about her—each printed in a different typeface—material was confusingly rearranged, there was an egregious absence of specificity, and some facts were just plain wrong.*

To make matters worse, Ingrid's book outraged Petter, who thought (without justification) that it portrayed him as a villain— even though Ingrid submitted the relevant sections of the manuscript for his approval and removed from the text everything to which he objected.

On May 1, 1976, Ingrid interrupted her work on the book to

---

*A few examples among far too many: *Adam Had Four Sons* was made at Columbia Studios, not (thus the book) at MGM. Howard Hughes, it is claimed, lived in 1949 in a Beverly Hills Hotel bungalow next door to Arthur Miller and his wife Marilyn Monroe. But Miller and Monroe never met until long after, did not wed until 1956, and first visited that hotel in 1959. Again, in the crucial wine-cellar sequence of *Notorious*, Ingrid was never shown (as Burgess claimed) dancing with Cary Grant. And *Under Capricorn* was made in England not because she prevailed on Alfred Hitchcock to film there, but because his deal with co-producer Sidney Bernstein (under their banner Transatlantic Pictures) specifically required that their pictures be alternately produced in Hollywood and London. Their previous film, *Rope*, was produced in America, and so *Under Capricorn* had to be made in England.

go to Rome: Roberto's seventieth birthday was a week later. They
dined on the fifth with the twins, and then, on the seventh, Ingrid
came to his apartment to say farewell, which disappointed him:
didn't she know that the next day, May 8, was his seventieth birthday? Yes, she said, but duties summoned her elsewhere, and off she
went. In fact, she had secretly arranged everything with her son and
daughters, and the next evening, when the children took Roberto to
his favorite restaurant, he was astonished to find Ingrid, who had
gathered many friends and everyone in his family for a gala surprise
celebration. Even his first and third wives were there, along with
cousins, nieces and grandchildren. "Ah, you did this!" said Roberto
with a wide grin, his eyes brimming with tears as he embraced
Ingrid.

By early 1977, Ingrid needed respite from her grueling and
increasingly unsatisfying work with Burgess. She visited friends and
her daughters in New York and then returned to Choisel. By this
time, Kristina was pregnant with Lars's child, and so, with no melodramatic scene or display of temper, Ingrid simply moved into the
Raphael Hotel in Paris, where, quite coincidentally, Roberto was
another guest. Sensing her unhappiness, he invited her to dinner.
"Ingrid, my dear," he said, "you're a nervous wreck trying to figure
out what to do about the past. To hell with the past! Look ahead—
go forward, as you always have."

As she tried to do just that, the timing was good. She accepted
an invitation from the Chichester Theatre Festival in England,
where John Clements was going to direct a revival of N.C. Hunter's
1951 play *Waters of the Moon*, which had run for 835 performances
starring three great ladies of the English stage—Edith Evans, Sybil
Thorndike and, as the ingenue, Wendy Hiller (who was now going
to play the Thorndike role). The play was slight, but had a certain
wistful tenderness; additionally, the roles begged for seasoned performers, and Wendy Hiller, one of her co-stars in *Murder on the Orient Express* and so fine an actress in everything she undertook, was a
major attraction for Ingrid to do the play.

Set in a small residence hotel in the English countryside,
Waters of the Moon described the lives of a group of bored seniors
whose routine is suddenly upset when, stranded by a snowstorm,
the wealthy Helen Lancaster (Ingrid), her husband and their

young daughter descend on them. The play contrasts the routine lives of simple elderly folk with the frivolous and freewheeling Helen, who flirts, upsets emotional apple carts and then blithely leaves.

"It's not kind," as a young girl in the play says, "to make us dream of the waters of the moon, of all kinds of happiness that are out of reach." However, "the thing is never to give up hoping . . . The only sin in life is to be unhappy." It is just such hope and a fundamental zest for life that Ingrid's character, in her vain and clumsy way, represents. This is neither an original nor a compelling theme, but there was in the role of forty-five-year-old Helen Lancaster a fine opportunity for Ingrid to counterpoise comedy with a nervous anxiety about time's passing. The play opened on May 10 and charmed audiences during the summer festival.

There was much that Ingrid knew in her role, and she took the full measure of it. "I'm restless," admits Helen, "always grasping after some new experience, some new pleasure. I'm incapable of enjoying tranquillity and contemplation and all the rest of it. If I don't go charging through the day like a train through a tunnel, I feel depressed, I feel bored." That certainly was Ingrid herself, said her daughters, laughing, when they came for the premiere. But Ingrid also found in the text the spiritual torpor of the woman, not merely her nervous anxiety. As so often in her best films, she seemed to think the words, even to allow them sometimes to play on her lips before speaking them aloud.

She commanded the stage, for example, when she gazed out over her audience—ignoring the playwright's stage direction to pace back and forth—and said in her uneasiness: "Life must be a perpetual adventure or it's worth nothing. One must constantly renew oneself with fresh experiences, fresh scenes, new friends. The only thing in the world that appalls me is the threat of stagnation, boredom, dreariness. That—never! Never!" And, defending unrequited love as better than no love at all, she said with great poignancy, "I've wept for love a dozen times. We all have. That's life." Her delivery was neither proud nor vague. The flat frankness of her assertion enriched it with feeling—as did the admixture of hope and remorse that tinged her New Year's Eve toast in the second act:

Midnight! Hail and farewell! The world is turning, and below the horizon, in the darkness, the first day of the New Year is moving upwards, towards the light. You mustn't mind me being senti- mental and silly—I can't help it on New Year's Eve. Besides, I feel I'm among good friends. May the New Year bring you all nearer to your heart's desires. May those who have much to hope for not be disappointed, and may those who have little find con- tentment and serenity . . .

The audiences who had expected light comedy that season were perhaps surprised to hear a gently serious philosophy of acceptance in this nearly forgotten play, whose core was so movingly revealed in one of Wendy Hiller's great moments. Responding to the complaint that life can be unfair, she says with unsentimental compassion, "Life isn't fair or unfair, or tragic or comic or anything else. Life is life—that's all. One must accept it."

As Dame Wendy later recalled, Ingrid not only had her usual trouble with lines in the first few performances: "Also, we had to get her to understand that she couldn't do a whole lot of business while somebody else was going through a long speech. She couldn't take up her hat and fluff out her hair and distract the audience's attention—she had to be discreetly alive but not intruding, and I think that was a hard and special discipline for her, not to be con- stantly at work in her role. Once she understood that, she was per- fection. And of course we all adored working with her, because she loved to learn."

LATE IN MAY, INGRID RECEIVED A TELEPHONE CALL FROM ROBERTO, who had been invited to serve as president of the festival jury at Cannes. "Can you imagine," he asked, "I have to see all those movies?" Well, she replied—who better than he? But she thought he sounded weary and anxious to return to Rome. They looked for- ward to a reunion with the children that autumn. Then, just over a week later, on June 4, Ingrid received another call—this time from Roberto's niece, Fiorella Mariani. Back home in Rome, he had dropped dead of a massive heart attack; he was seventy-one. Ingrid had to perform that evening, but afterward, back in her rented cot- tage in Chichester, she was on the telephone all night to Robertino,

Isabella and Ingrid, weeping with them. "He was a great film-maker," she told the press. "He was also a wonderful father and my very good friend."

Just as Wendy Hiller had said in the play, life was life and she had to accept it—as she did within several days of Roberto's death, when she had another distracting call, this time from Lars. Kristina had delivered their son, whom they named Kristian. According to Lars, Ingrid was genuinely happy at this news, as if she had been an aunt or grandma awaiting the arrival of a beloved addition to her own family. But as he well may have suspected, she was in a way giving a magnificent performance when she heard the news—just as she was onstage. *Waters of the Moon* was so successful that it was to be transferred to Brighton for two weeks the following January, and then into the Haymarket Theatre, London.

AT LAST, IN THE SUMMER OF 1977, INGMAR BERGMAN HAD A STORY and screenplay ready for her. Would it trouble Ingrid, he asked during a long telephone call, to play the mother of Liv Ullman, who was thirty-seven? Not at all, she replied: Pia was even older. (There was some irony here, for Liv Ullman and Ingmar Bergman, who never married, had a daughter during their five years together.) What was the story of the film, she asked? It was, Ingmar continued, the story of the reunion between Ingrid, as a concert pianist who has traveled the world for years, and Liv, as the daughter who has always felt abandoned by her. Ingmar knew whereof he was creating, he said: after all, his second wife had been a concert pianist. But of course it sounded more like Ingrid's life than his.

While she was in New York visiting her daughters that summer, Ingrid felt a lump beneath her right arm. This was not an immediate problem, said a physician: it seemed to be only a swollen gland. Nevertheless, since she was soon to return to Europe, she ought to have further tests. This she did at once in London (the tests indicated no malignancy) and then she proceeded to Ingmar's island retreat to discuss his script. Of one thing she was particularly glad: the opportunity to make a film in Swedish. By 1977, she had memorized plays and scripts in no less than five languages—an achievement, it must be emphasized, that is rare if not unique in the history of acting.

Autumn Sonata, as Bergman had already titled his picture, was filmed during September and October in Norway, for Ingmar's problems with tax authorities had soured his business base in Sweden. But the great collaboration so long desired by director and star did not, at first, fulfill their expectations. Ingrid read the script and was frankly horrified: the role of Charlotte was a monster, she told the director. The character talked too much, she seemed loveless, her motivations were cloudy; and the daughter, Eva—well, she was just a complainer, so immature. No, the script was quite impossible, dear Ingmar, and so we will have to work on this scene, and that one, and . . .

The film was very nearly canceled, as Lars recalled. "There was trouble from the start. Ingrid's natural frankness didn't suit Ingmar's authoritative ways of constructing his films. Besides, Ingrid looked at life differently. She respected him enormously, but he did not appreciate her creative artistry, nor that she dared to be herself on the set and off. He was not accustomed to objections, he said— and so, to put it briefly, he did not like her and said so flatly and ungraciously."

Liv Ullman burst into tears during the first readings, Ingmar was white with anger and consternation, and Ingrid seemed adamant. She could not play a woman she could not understand, and that was that. The script's long night of confrontation between Charlotte and Eva—the sequence that formed the emotional climax of *Autumn Sonata*—was so bitter, such a tirade of anguish and resentment, that it simply seemed unreal to Ingrid. She had disputes with her own children, to be sure, she said—"many nights of truth between mother and daughter, but none filled with such hatred as in the film! I've been very fortunate with my children. They've been very understanding, really." And so they had been. But Ingrid, her director replied sternly, this woman has characteristics that . . . well, that you yourself should comprehend. She asked for a weekend alone, to reconsider her participation.

AND THEN AN EXTRAORDINARY THING OCCURRED.

As she read the script and Ingmar's notes to it, she realized with a terrible shock that this woman was indeed herself. "There's a lot of me in *Autumn Sonata*," she said later, "and I was terribly nervous when my daughter Pia said she was going to see the film." Here was a concert pianist—like Ingrid in *Intermezzo*—who could not deny her talent even if it meant sacrificing her life at home; here in the film would be the history of Ingrid Bergman's relationship to Pia Lindstrom, as Pia herself indeed recognized as soon as she saw the finished film.

Over that late summer weekend, Ingrid knew she had to make perhaps the most critical decision of her career. Charlotte was so clearly Ingrid: was the actress ready to make the identification even sharper—to place on film, for all the world to see, so naked a confession of the guilt she had carried for twenty-eight years? And was she willing to highlight Ingmar's story, to give it precisely the personal focus that would make the characters credible? Ingmar may have had her history in mind, and there were universal issues here, as usual in his films: theological issues, social concerns, spiritual reflections. All these seemed to her to weaken the script. Its central drama must focus on the story of mother and daughter—and this was a story she knew well.

Apologies, efforts, joint vacations, attempts at reconciliations with Pia—these had all been effective in establishing a kind of truce, yes. But Ingrid and Pia were too smart and too sensitive to think that everything was all right by 1977, that history could be easily canceled. Very deep resentments remained. Over the years, Ingrid had tried to unburden herself, tried to redress the past—but the pain was still there, gnawing and bothersome for both of them.

Here, then, was the opportunity Ingrid Bergman had sought. In her art, which was the only way she knew, she would confront, confess, seek forgiveness. The deepest wound of her spirit would be forever clear to the world. She would, at long last—after forty-three years in films—not merely perform a role but be that role. As she had often said, the world was full of unresolved guilt: could she not do something to alleviate her own, which was caused by the pain she had caused another, not from malice but from selfishness?

She could do nothing else. All over the world, people were shouting about women's liberation—but in the final analysis, was not the only liberation that counted one that sprang from within? She was coming to know the truth at last, through her art. "I always felt guilty—my whole life I have felt guilty about my absence when my daughter was growing up. For me, the most important thing was to work. That is maybe selfish. My children and I are together now that they are grown up, but I'm sure that through the years they have many times resented that I wasn't at home." She may have exaggerated the effect of her absence and the resentment of her children. But it was her feeling of remorse that went so deeply, after all. She would not die with that burden.

THUS IT HAPPENED, WHEN SHE RETURNED TO THE PRODUCTION THE following week, that Ingrid said she had some suggestions to make. Ingmar breathed deeply and sat down, ready for an impossible conversation that would lead to the collapse of the project. Ingrid had sharpened some of her own dialogue, she said; had looked into her own soul to bring forth the heart of the dark night in the script. She asked, gently but firmly, if Ingmar might consider her emendations.

He did, and was astonished.

Charlotte was now more Charlotte because she was more Ingrid. The time of separation between mother and daughter must be seven years, Ingrid said (she had been separated from Pia from 1949 to 1951, and again from 1951 to 1957). As for Charlotte's career: that must be forty-five years, yes (Ingrid considered her own to have begun in 1933, and *Autumn Sonata* would be released in 1978). And instead of multiple, long, sometimes unfocused monologues, there must be searing, terrible admissions from Charlotte: "A guilty conscience—always a guilty conscience?" she muses to herself, and later (to Eva), "I had a guilty conscience always being away from you and Papa." Here, at this point in the script, Ingrid said, there must be a mention of concerts in Los Angeles; and at that point, why could Eva not be a journalist (like Pia)? And Charlotte must jabber nervously—about her clothes, her hair, her concert dates—and be the center of a whirlwind. "If she slept more," says Eva, "she would crush everyone—insomnia is nature's way of using up her surplus energy!" It was indeed Ingrid Bergman herself.

At Ingrid's request, Ingmar gave Liv a terribly painful speech that could have come straight from the lips of Ingrid's own daughter: "I don't know which I hated most—when you were at home, or when you were on tour. I realize now that you made life hell for Papa and me. You were unfaithful to him. I was a doll you played with when you had time. You were always kind, but your mind was elsewhere."

But the great contribution to the film was not a particular bit of dialogue or any single reshaped scene. It was Ingrid Bergman's complete dedication to this role, to the portrait of herself. And this, in the finished picture, is most evident in the wordless sequence when Eva plays the Chopin A-minor prelude. As Ingrid listens, the camera moves in relentlessly for long close-ups, and we read the history of a troubled relationship. Ingrid's eyes, her lips, the tilt of her head move and change almost imperceptibly; there is a wash of memories here—the sweet recollections of her baby, the guilt of a mother's apparent indifference, the remorse of subsequent absence, the defensiveness, the incomprehension of self, the astonishment only self-knowledge can bring, the attempt to mask pain. This scene alone was worth a dozen of Ingrid's earlier films. At last the gap was closed between personal history and dramatic content: the pretense of feeling so necessary for a good performance had become the presence of feeling that made for a great one.

"I feel so shut out," Charlotte/Ingrid says to her agent Paul (who utters not a word in the picture). "I'm always homesick. But when I get home, I find it's something else I'm longing for." This naked emotion was her ultimate self-disclosure.

"A MOTHER AND A DAUGHTER—WHAT A TERRIBLE COMBINATION OF feelings and confusion and destruction," says Liv Ullman near the end of the film—an end that is not a conclusion, but that contains a clear indication, in Eva's letter to Charlotte after her departure, that the healing of memories is indeed possible, that there may well be a future for this unhappy pair.

The ending of Autumn Sonata, with a light of hope so uncharacteristic of much of Ingmar Bergman's work, was inserted at Ingrid's insistence. "He had originally wanted to end the film with the mother leaving the daughter's house sans espoir [without hope]," Ingrid said. "But I begged him to leave them some hope. So we added the letter that Liv sends. He did it for me."

"Dear Mama," the daughter writes to her mother after Charlotte has so abjectly humbled herself and begged forgiveness, "There is a kind of mercy after all. I will never let you vanish out of my life

again. I am going to persist. I won't give up even if it is too late. I
don't think it is too late. It must not be too late." The film con-
cludes with a very long close-up of Ingrid, facing the audience
directly, her gaze full of frank pain, her eyes longing for "a kind of
mercy."

Confession had begun the process of regeneration in the artist,
and later audiences would see for themselves one of the great performances ever put on film. This was her last picture, Ingrid said at
the time: she was sure she would never find another part as good.
Here was also the first hint to the public of the illness that had been
rumored but not confirmed.

As it happened, she was in considerable discomfort and anxiety
during the filming of Autumn Sonata, and there was a graver reason
than the demands of her role. A week into the shooting, she went
for two days to London, where Dr. Edward MacLellan, her physician there, found that the lump beneath her arm now indicated a
spread of the cancer once thought to have been arrested in 1974.

"She intended to finish the film," Ingmar recalled, "and then
asked matter-of-factly whether we could compress her contribution
by a few days—but if that proved impossible, she would stay for the
agreed time. She went on working as if nothing had happened. She
faced her illness with anger and impatience at first, but then her
strong body was broken, her senses eroded. Still, she was extremely
disciplined in the studio."

But then, late one afternoon while Ingrid and Ingmar awaited a
lighting adjustment during a scene, he noticed that she ran her hand
over her face several times, then drew in a deep breath. There was a
sudden flash of her cheerful smile before she said quietly, "You
know, I'm living on borrowed time." And as she heard herself say
the words, the smile faded and—only for a moment—there was a
look of panic in her clear, blue-gray eyes. Then the shot was ready,
and she leaped to her task. "Her conduct was extraordinarily professional," Ingmar concluded. "Even with her obvious frailties,
Ingrid Bergman was a remarkable person—generous, grand and
highly talented."

Liv Ullman was deeply touched by Ingrid's courage, too. "The
superficial part of her was her greatness as an actress and the fact

that she opened the door for other Scandinavian actresses like myself—but that is nothing compared to her true beauty. Her true beauty came as a person whose courage in the face of that awful cancer, and her honesty and directness while working, are possible for all of us. Best of all, she never told me what I should do. She inspired through example." *Autumn Sonata* earned for Ingrid Bergman her seventh Oscar nomination for best performance by an actress.

IMMEDIATELY AFTER THE COMPLETION OF THE PICTURE, INGRID returned to London, where Mary Evans helped her find a comfortable apartment in a terrace house at 9 Cheyne Gardens, Chelsea, a few steps from a small park and very near the Thames. The environment was like that in Stockholm, along Strandvägen: when the weather was fine, Ingrid could stroll along the riverbank, sit on a bench and watch the boats, reread the script of *Waters of the Moon* for its imminent reopening, and enjoy quiet time. Ingrid had rooms on two floors—a kitchen, dining and drawing rooms on the first, and two bedrooms and baths and a terrace on the second. She furnished the place in earth colors, écru and soft browns, and selected for her bedroom a paper designed with intertwined green leaves and branches—"a woodland setting," she called it. "When the time comes, I shall be sitting here among the leaves when my friends come to visit me."

First, there was the matter of her health. The growth beneath her right arm, a malignancy in a lymph node, was removed, and Ingrid submitted once again to a fatiguing course of radiation therapy. At nine o'clock every morning, Griff James came for her at Cheyne Gardens, drove her to the hospital and watched as Ingrid walked alone down a long corridor to the doors marked Nuclear Medicine. An hour and a half later, she was onstage for rehearsals. No one in the cast had the remotest idea of the gravity of her illness, although everyone noticed that Ingrid was uncharacteristically exhausted by mid-afternoon, that sometimes she needed to sit for a while and that she seemed preoccupied. "She really was much, much to be admired that season," said Wendy Hiller, in whom Ingrid soon confided. "When she told me, there was not the slightest hint of a plea for sympathy."

After two weeks in Brighton, *Waters of the Moon* opened at the Haymarket on January 26, 1978. "Ingrid Bergman captures the heart of the play and makes it entirely her own," ran a typical review. "Her effervescence, her inconsequential prattling, her impatience with pessimism, her faith in the virtues of affluence make her irresistible." Another observed that she was "more assured and shines more brightly than ever." The press was still unaware of her failing health, and so they remained during the 180 performances of the play.

In June, Ingrid received the news that the cancer had spread to her right breast. She agreed to have surgery after the final performance in July, although she became progressively weaker and more ill from the radiation treatments. Her face was often puffy from cortisone injections, her knee became swollen after she banged it on a table, and fluid had to be drained; she suffered ominous back and shoulder pain; and sometimes she moved slowly, as if each step were uncertain. "It became an increasing struggle for her to continue," Wendy Hiller recalled, "but she did go on." In fact, Ingrid missed only two performances during six months. "She battled on, unwilling to burden any of us, even though she was going through absolute hell."

Patrick Garland, director of the Brighton and London productions of *Waters*, remembered that an American producer came to the Haymarket and after the performance told him how much they admired the lighting on Ingrid—especially the pinpoint spotlight that always followed her onstage, like a small halo of radiance. Garland looked at them blankly: "There's no pin-spot on Ingrid—no special light on her at all!" But they had seen it, insisted the producer and his wife. No, Garland said with a smile: what they "saw" was an invisible quality—a woman "with a sort of magic light potent enough to fool two very experienced theater people into believing that it had been artificially created."

Nor did she lose her sense of humor: once, while giving the New Year's Eve speech, she moved slowly downstage and, suddenly dizzy, fell onto the lap of co-star Paul Hardwick, whose prop glass of champagne spilled all over his trousers. At once Ingrid giggled and improvised: "Closer, my dear—but not that close!" The audience thought it was a wonderful burlesque moment in the play. And backstage, everyone was astonished, for there she was, turning her own confusion and fear into a moment that served the play.

AFTER THE LAST PERFORMANCE, ON JULY 1, INGRID AWAITED A HIRED car to take her home. But it was delayed, and she went back inside the Haymarket. Don't worry, she told Griff, who waited to escort her to Cheyne Gardens; she was just going to sit quietly in the auditorium and look at the theater. There she watched, alone, as the last piece of scenery was dismantled, the last prop and piece of furniture removed. She did not wish to leave, for she knew that if she ever entered a theater again, it would be only as a spectator. And then slowly the house lights were darkened, and Griff drove her home.

In July, Ingrid entered the hospital (under the name Mrs. Schmidt), where Dr. William Slack performed a right radical mastectomy. On the twenty-fourth, Ingrid rang Margaret Johnstone, a nurse and masseuse who had regularly helped her with massages and relaxation exercises. "Well, I've had it done," Ingrid said brightly. "Now, when are you coming to see me?" Margaret and Griff did, and still the matter was kept from the public. But then, when Ingrid was forced to agree with her physicians that she must cancel the American tour of *Waters of the Moon*, the press had to be told—but only that an unnamed illness prevented business as usual. Because it was unimaginable for Ingrid Bergman to renege on a tour, and because suddenly she began to look beyond her sixty-three years, the news soon circulated, and at last she could not deny the gravity of her illness—nor did she any longer wish to do so. "Of course I don't want to die," she said flatly. "But I have no fear of it." And nothing in her manner, with friends or the public, indicated otherwise.

By October, she felt strong enough to go to New York to visit her children and to dub the English-language version of *Autumn Sonata*. Taking an abiding interest in every aspect of the lives of her children and grandchildren, she was full of questions and good advice. Pia, who now had two children, was working in New York as a television journalist and arts critic; Robertino (who remained unmarried into his late forties) worked in Monte Carlo in real estate; Isabella, model and actress, had three children after several marriages; and Isotta Ingrid, scholar and teacher, twice married, had two children.

Autumn Sonata was released late in the year, and Ingrid received the most sensational reviews of her career; there was no debate now, no carping about the materials. Critics ransacked their vocabularies for the kinds of superlatives usually employed for Nobel laureates: Ingrid Bergman had been "exalted" to the ranks of the finest actresses in history; she "had never done anything remotely comparable"; her acting was something "of perfect eloquence." As for the moviegoing public, it was hard to find any viewer unmoved.

INGRID SPENT CHRISTMAS QUIETLY IN NEW YORK, AND EARLY IN 1979 she returned to London to rest and to continue radiation therapy. Never in her life, she told Lars, had she felt so constantly exhausted.

But that did not prevent her from accepting an invitation to be mistress of ceremonies at the American Film Institute's Lifetime Achievement Award to Alfred Hitchcock, held in Beverly Hills on March 7. Fifteen hundred people attended the banquet and watched the film clips honoring the director, whose arthritis made even a few steps terribly painful. Wearing a magnificently layered, royal blue chiffon gown that disguised her surgeries, Ingrid rose to the occasion with enormous grace.

But at the end of the evening—instead of thanking the guests, praising Hitch one last time and ending the event as the script had indicated—Ingrid had one last touch that no one present could ever forget, a gesture that brought to fulfillment the meaning of a certain sentimental object.

"Now there is just one little thing I want to add before we finish this evening. Hitch, do you remember that agonizing shot in *Notorious*, when you had built some kind of elevator, a crane with you and your cameraman, and you were shooting this vast party and you came zooming down all the way to my hand, where, in close-up, there was the key to the wine cellar? Well, do you know what? Cary stole that key! Yes, and he kept it for about ten years—and then one day he put it in my hand, and he said, 'I've kept this long enough—now it's for you, for good luck.' I have kept it for twenty years, dear Hitch, and now—here in my hand—is this very same key. It has given me good luck and quite a few good movies, too, and now I'm going to give it to you, with the prayer that it will open some very good doors for you. God bless you, dear Hitch—I'm coming down now to give you the key."

Ingrid made her way through the crowd toward the center table, toward Hitch and Cary Grant, who was seated at Hitch's left, beaming with surprise and pleasure. With great difficulty, Hitch rose from his seat and turned to Ingrid, who handed him the key from *Notorious*. And then Alfred Hitchcock, a man never given to anything like a public display of affection, reached up and put his arms around Ingrid's neck, drew her close, held her tightly and kissed her on both cheeks. "Hitch struggled so gallantly to stand up for me," she said later that evening, "and I tried to keep the tears from coming—but I couldn't, and he couldn't, either."

While the room echoed with applause, they stood there hugging, these two old, ill friends who had so valiantly finessed a tangled and difficult love, had turned it into a trusting devotion and had given each other and the world (especially in the great *Notorious*) so very much that was good and deep and true. Ingrid took Hitch's face in both hands, leaned down slightly to gaze lovingly into his eyes, and then drew Cary into the circle of their embrace for this extraordinary moment. Rarely has television captured a moment of such profound emotion, springing without artifice from the deepest private feelings of public people.

IN NOVEMBER, INGRID RETURNED TO LOS ANGELES TO BE HONORED AT a Variety Club gala raising money for a children's hospital. The tribute was held on Stage 9 at Warner Bros. Burbank studio—the precise location where *Casablanca*'s interiors were photographed thirty-seven years earlier. Resplendent in a formal white gown, Ingrid was cheerful but looked far more ill than she had the previous March. For more than two hours, she accepted the accolades of many colleagues (Paul Henreid, Joseph Cotten, Cary Grant, Helen Hayes, Goldie Hawn) and of even more who scarcely knew her at all (James Stewart, Peter Falk and Jack Albertson, for example).

But just as at the Hitchcock tribute, Ingrid had prepared a surprise. Ingrid and her family had restored all the old silent movie bits her father had made in her childhood, and in a strong, proud voice she provided a moving narrative as the little compilation film was presented.

The evening was important, for it provided, very like *Autumn Sonata*, a résumé of Ingrid's life she wished to share with her public. "When my father had discovered that something new had happened—motion pictures—he was so enthusiastic that he went on my birthdays and special days and rented a camera that he cranked by hand," she began, describing the images as they flickered onscreen.

That is me sitting on my mother's lap, my grandfather and grandmother are behind me. That was my first appearance on the screen, when I was one year old, in the year 1916.—Now here, I am two years old, and there is my mother who pushed me around with my little wheelbarrow—that was my first prop. Now there is my mother—and how happy that makes me, since there I can see her move and smile. I didn't know what to do in the scenes—nobody gave me much direction, but here I am, I am three years old, and I am coming to my mother's grave. I am putting flowers on her grave. You can understand why I am so happy to have those earlier shots, where I can see her move and smile and hold me up—how lovely that was.

You see, I had at least learned to wave at the audience—and there are my cousins and aunts and uncles from Germany. Now you see, my father thought I should have a governess, so here she is, waving eagerly to the audience just as I am doing, too.

My father adored the opera, so here he is at the piano, giving me a lesson. He didn't play the piano, but after all this is a silent movie, so everything is okay. And as you know, nothing came from this opera career that he wanted so very badly for me!

Now here I am at twelve, in the garden, and by now my father had fallen in love with my governess so he focused on her! I don't blame him—look at how pretty she is!

This last little strip of film shows me coming off a quite small boat, back to Stockholm after spending a summer in Germany. And ten years after that, I came off a much bigger boat in the harbor of New York. And so here I am!

There had, of course, never been any shadow of resentment or remorse in Ingrid's relationships with colleagues. But after *Autumn Sonata*, Ingrid was desperate to resolve the only old bitterness that remained. Earlier that year, she had sent Petter a photo of Pia, adding, "I am so glad she is wearing the pendant you gave me at her birth." By that autumn, as she became more gravely ill, Ingrid longed for a reconciliation with Petter and a cordial meeting with his second wife, and to this end she devoted herself even as she continued medical treatments and read the proofs of her memoir. At Thanksgiving, ill and exhausted, she visited Petter and Agnes at their home near San Diego.

"What was my reaction to her in 1979?" he wrote later.

> I surely had no emotional feelings for her one way or another except for my response to anyone who has a serious cancer problem. As to my personal reactions, it can be well described by the old Swedish proverb I learned as a child—"The more you see of human beings, the better you like dogs."
>
> She herself behaved rather emotionally, but how much was acting or true reaction remains uncertain. I did wonder what she expected to get out of the meeting she had so urgently requested. She might have been curious about my looks [but] my reaction was flat and noncommittal.

As for Agnes, she was put in an awkward situation which she handled with consummate, courteous dignity, just as she always maintained warm and friendly relations with all Ingrid's children.

From that unsatisfying reunion with Petter, Ingrid went to Los Angeles for a visit with Hitchcock, who had marked his eightieth birthday in August—two weeks before Ingrid's sixty-fourth—and whose health was failing rapidly. "He took both my hands," she recalled, "and tears streamed down his face as he said, 'Ingrid, I'm going to die.' And I said, 'But of course you are going to die sometime, Hitch—we are all going to die!' And then I told him that I, too, had recently been very ill, and that I had thought about dying, too. He was so sweet—he told me he didn't want me to suffer. And so we just sat for a moment, and somehow the logic of it—that we were both facing what was really inevitable—seemed to calm him a bit."

When she returned to London for Christmas 1979, Lars was at Heathrow to meet her and accompany her to Cheyne Gardens, where he had everything ready for a holiday reunion with her children.

"Time is shortening, isn't it?" she asked her friend Ann Todd on New Year's Eve as they sipped champagne. "But do you know, dear Ann, every day that I challenge this cancer and survive it—well, that is a little victory for me."

Chapter Twenty

1980–1982

Best and brightest, come away!

SHELLEY,
To Jane: The Invitation

ELF-PITY WAS NOT ONE OF MY MOTHER'S CHARACTERISTICS," SAID
Pia. "She did not feel sorry for herself. She was very brave about
it all. She just said, 'Well, we go on—we just go on.' And so she did."

The early months of 1980 were spent quietly in the darkness of
London's winter, where Lars visited often, accompanied Ingrid to
her physicians, saw to the practical necessities of life (at which she
was no more qualified now than ever) and took her to dinner. Larry
Adler had been living in England for almost thirty years by this time,
and he dined several times with them. "I liked Lars enormously,"
Adler said. "He was the right man for Ingrid because he was a success on his own. He didn't need to be recognized, and he could take
pride in Ingrid's work instead of being jealous of it. So far as I could
see, he was a generous, open gentleman, and she relied on him
enormously."

In March, Ingrid was invited to return to the Royal Dramatic
Theater in Stockholm in any play of her choice, but her primary

physician, Edward MacLellan, forbade her acceptance; her health was quite simply too precarious. At the same time, Ingrid relied more and more on Margaret Johnstone, who became not only a private nurse but also an expert cook and devoted companion. By this time, as Ingrid remarked to several friends, she heard almost daily news of the deaths of old friends and former colleagues—among them, in the last fifteen years, Edvin Adolphson, David Selznick, Spencer Tracy, George Sanders, Charles Boyer, Bing Crosby and Gustav Molander.

Then, on April 29, came the news of Alfred Hitchcock's death. He was eighty and had been in poor health for several years. "Now dear Hitch is gone, too," she told a new friend the next day. "But he was so unhappy and so ill when I saw him last November—I suppose in some way it is a relief. His suffering was really terrible to behold."

Hitchcock's death brought Ingrid a curious dilemma. At that time, she was in New York, working with her editors on the final emendations of her memoirs. A number of telephone calls came to her at Irene Selznick's apartment in the Pierre Hotel: would she be attending Hitchcock's funeral in Beverly Hills? Ingrid had three problems with this issue: first, she was put under enormous pressure by her publisher to finish the task of her manuscript; second, she was on an experimental protocol of medication that caused spells of dizziness and nausea; third, she knew quite well that her presence at the funeral would turn the event into a celebrity circus.

"I don't know what to do," she said on April 30. "If I go, they will descend on me outside the church with all sorts of questions about our films, and how did I feel now that Hitch is dead, and is it the end of an era, and all that rubbish. And the whole dignity of the funeral will be ruined. And if I do not go, they will think I had a falling out with Hitch or something like that! Really, I am in a terrible quandary." Robert Anderson advised her not to make the trip and to forget about any criticism, and another friend concurred: she ought to make it easy on herself—which was exactly what Hitch would wish and what she did. Alas, even without her presence, the area around Good Shepherd Church in Beverly Hills resembled a wild crowd scene from one of his pictures; Ingrid would have been very dismayed indeed had she attended.

To honor her friendship with Hitch, Ingrid selected *Notorious* to be screened on October 15, when the Museum of Modern Art honored her. Robert Anderson attended with the writer of the Hitchcock book to whom he had introduced Ingrid in 1975, and they chatted with her before and after the screening. "It holds up rather well, doesn't it?" Ingrid said of the picture. "Maybe I will hold up rather well, too!"

FINISHING THE MEMOIRS WAS A TERRIFICALLY EXHAUSTING TASK, SHE wrote to Joe Steele—especially because she insisted on supervising every change and approving every word of the Swedish translation. Her life had been long and rich, she added, which was why the cutting of the final draft was such a job. So were the arduous duties of promoting the book later in the year, when she somehow summoned the energy to meet the press, to appear on television and to sign books in England, America, Sweden, France and Italy.

Yes, she admitted when asked: she had undergone operations for cancer, but no, she was not dying and hoped to go on for quite some time. "I must be a little bit of a fatalist, because I accept the things I can do nothing about. What I can do is just try to be cheerful about it and don't feel sorry for myself and don't talk too much about it!" Perhaps, she added, there was even a producer listening who needed an actress to play an old witch—a role for which no one ever thought Ingrid well suited. "She wanted to do her job," as Göran von Essen (among many others) said. "Her health came second."

As it happened, there was an American producer listening. Gene Corman had made four films in Israel and had for some time been keen to do a picture about Golda Meir, who had emigrated from Russia to America at the age of eight. After teaching school, she settled in Palestine in 1921, where she served as minister of labor and of foreign affairs, and finally won the office of prime minister in 1969. Criticized for the country's lack of preparation for the 1973 Arab-Israeli war, she resigned in 1974. A strong (sometimes headstrong) woman whose entire life was devoted to Israel, she had put her career before her husband and family and, in 1978, died of cancer at age eighty. "Pessimism," she once said, "is a luxury that a Jew can never allow himself." That statement may best sum up her complex but unequivocally forceful belief in herself and her mission to Israel.

Corman had a deal with Paramount Pictures and was able to convince the studio to back a four-hour television drama about Golda—if he could obtain the services of the right actress. From the start, there was no doubt in Corman's mind about Ingrid, and so he contacted Laurence Evans, who told him that because of her illness, Ingrid could not be insured for the production (hence there was an enormous financial risk from the start). But Corman and Paramount were willing to assume the responsibility, and so Evans rang Ingrid. Her first reaction was a hearty laugh: she was a big Swede, she said, and Golda was a little Jewish dumpling. She neither looked like Golda nor sounded like her, she said, and she certainly did not understand the politics of her life. The answer was no—which, Evans rightly suspected, meant maybe.

Then, after concluding her book tour, Ingrid slipped away quietly for a brief holiday in Israel with her cousin Britt Engstrom (one of Uncle Otto's daughters)—"I wanted to follow in Jesus' footsteps," Ingrid said. She loved the country, she told Evans on her return in early 1981, but again she asked him to please reject Paramount's repeated offer, and again he suspected the door was not entirely closed. But he was a friend respectful of her precarious health, and so he would not counsel Ingrid against her will.

By coincidence, Ingrid had been tracked down at the King David Hotel in Jerusalem by Gene Corman, who was completing another project in Israel before tackling A Woman Called Golda. They had a very cordial meeting, but Ingrid insisted she was not the right physical type—to which Corman replied gently, "Ingrid, it's Golda's style we're looking for—what she brought to the world. It's the same with you. Nobody equals Ingrid Bergman in stature." He would send her some books, he said, and he hoped they would talk soon again.

BACK IN LONDON, INGRID AGREED TO MEET WITH ALAN GIBSON, THE forty-two-year-old Canadian director assigned to the project. To his pleasant surprise, he learned that she had been listening to recordings of Meir's voice and making cassettes of her imitations in an attempt to lower her register, to erase the Swedish accent, to assume Golda's tone as much as possible. By this time, Gibson saw, the single element that seemed most to bother Ingrid—her height compared to Meir's—had been resolved. "Oh, but she was such a tall person!" several people in Israel had said. Ordinary people regarded Meir as great, and therefore she seemed a tall woman. Gibson, like Corman, at once earned Ingrid's confidence.

And then she began to speak of her growing affinity for Golda: both fought cancer (Golda battled malignant lymphoma for years before it killed her) and both, in Ingrid's words, "loved our children but were separated from them periodically because we were not willing to put them before our work. As a result, we had enormous guilt about them . . . I understand Golda's guilt about leaving her husband and children. I've lived with that guilt my whole life." Both women were obsessed with their vocations and were never satisfied with the traditional roles of housewife and mother, and both had left their native countries, had moved from place to place and worked in a variety of languages.

But there was a much more important reason that she wanted to do the role. "I was very stubborn in 1938 when I was in Germany," Ingrid said during the production of *Golda*. "I have to say honestly that I had no reason for objecting to Hitler then." Feeling so guilty for so long, she would celebrate Israel and the Jewish people now, by portraying Golda—thus the healing of memories, the need to make amends, lit her spirit during the entire time she prepared for this difficult and demanding role.

Finally, in the spring of 1981, Ingrid telephoned Corman and Gibson and asked for a screen test: if she could look the part of Golda, she said, she would do it. It was four years since she had faced the movie camera, and her appearance had altered dramatically. She arrived for the test and was clearly, as Corman recalled, "very, very nervous—actually shaking—and she admitted it to me." He tried to calm her: "Ingrid, there's a lot of excitement, a lot of tension here, a lot of energy. This whole crew is excited about you. The idea that Ingrid Bergman has asked for a test is quite remarkable. They all love you and want you here."

And then, as he spoke, Ingrid's gaze went beyond him, over his shoulder. He turned around to see the camera on a dolly, coming toward them, and Ingrid began to smile: "Gene, I see an old friend here." She stood up, walked toward the camera, and was ready for the test. Ingrid did three short scenes letter-perfect, and after watching the results with Corman and Gibson next day, she said that if they still wanted her, she would do the role. The contract was signed, and on September 4, Ingrid and Margaret departed London for Tel Aviv and Jerusalem and the production of *A Woman Called Golda*. "Work is wonderful when you're sick," she told a journalist. "It gives you strength." And somehow she found the strength to offer her last great surprise to audiences. She would look and sound so different from Ingrid Bergman that she longed to see the viewers' astonishment; she remembered *A Woman's Face*, she told a few friends, and the appearance of hideous disfigurement that shocked audiences more than forty years earlier.

DURING THE NINE-WEEK PRODUCTION THAT AUTUMN (IN AND AROUND Jerusalem, Tel Aviv, Jaffa, Lydda, Natanya and Jericho), Ingrid Bergman grew more and more desperately ill; cancer was spreading through her entire body, she was rapidly losing weight and strength, and her right arm was grotesquely swollen. This unfortunate condition was the result of the removal of lymph nodes at the time of her mastectomy (and the additional consequence of radiation therapy), which caused the accumulation of lymphatic fluid in the arm. Her puppy dog, she called her swollen arm, a pet she could not get rid of and had to take with her everywhere. The task of writing a two-line note to a friend was a chore requiring fifteen minutes, but she kept up her contact with friends new and old. Ingrid was now in virtually constant pain.

As everyone recalled, Ingrid sought no special considerations from her director and crew, and she worked every day she was needed, arriving promptly at six in the morning to endure two hours of makeup, working for twelve- and fifteen-hour sessions, sitting up late at night with Margaret to ensure she would not miss a line of dialogue, recording her voice to keep it at Golda's pitch and continuing to read everything she could about the subject. She consulted dozens of prominent Israeli figures during the shooting, including former foreign minister Abba Eban and American ambassador Simcha Dinitz. She watched documentaries about Golda and Israel's history, and she spent several afternoons with Golda's confidante and secretary, Lou Kaddar.

As makeup artist Wally Schneiderman recalled, Ingrid became Golda as soon as she put on the padded clothes, the thickened stockings to hide her thin legs, the homely wigs, the heavy cosmetics. She played Golda from the ages of fifty-five to seventy-nine (with scenes, as usual, filmed out of chronological sequence), and the wardrobe was awkward and uncomfortable. Very often, the weather turned intensely hot, and Ingrid had many exterior scenes in daytime temperatures over a hundred degrees. No one could recall a complaint or a request to stop the shooting, but one day she toppled over in a faint. "We're walking along a precipice here," said the doctor who attended her and watched, amazed, as she went back to work half an hour later. "But I am afraid that Ingrid could fall off this precipice at any moment."

But she did not. Ever her attentive friend, Lars visited frequently, dispatching the usual practical and financial matters and allaying her anxiety by the simple gift of his presence. As her arm remained swollen, it was necessary to design dresses for camouflage, but several scenes, in which Golda signed letters and polished a tea kettle, required close-ups of her hands. When Gibson, Corman and cinematographer Adam Greenberg gently suggested that they could easily use a double for her hands, she said no, she would do something to correct the problem.

The evenings before those scenes, she ordered in a metal pole, the type used in hospitals for blood transfusions or hanging intravenous fluids. She asked that her edematous right arm be suspended from it all night long, so that the fluid would drain. Next morning, she raced to the studio, the swelling temporarily reduced. "Look!" she cried to her producer and director with a smile of triumph. "Quick! Let's do the scene!" They did, and she was enormously pleased—but because the problem recurred, she had to endure many more nights with her arm suspended.

The performance was a small miracle, for Ingrid vanished into the role with a fierce intensity. Her Golda was a feisty combination of charm and bravado, of dignity and insecurity. Like the prime minister, she chain-smoked her way through Israel's kitchens and back rooms, and her mind's wheels spun constantly. Her voice, as one viewer said, was like "gravel grounded in authority." Three weeks after Ingrid's death, the Academy of Television Arts and Sci-

ences awarded Ingrid Bergman the Emmy for outstanding leading
actress in a limited series or special; *A Woman Called Golda* was also
cited as the best dramatic special of the season.

One day during production stood out above all the others—the
shooting of the scene in which Golda is told by her doctor that she
has a malignant illness. Ingrid had just marked her sixty-sixth birthday in August, and the director and his crew were understandably
anxious about the scene, which bore so close a resemblance to the
star's life. She read through the dialogue and in one take completed
it, word-perfect: "Well, I'm sixty-six. How long can I expect to live,
anyway? The question is—those few years—will they really be
good? . . . What about my mind? I don't want to live one more
minute after my mind isn't clear . . . And if anything about this is
ever to be told to anyone, I will choose who and when. Otherwise,
it is a strict secret . . . "

When she finished the scene, Ingrid asked for a glass of water
and a cigarette, and she went off to lie down. There were more than
a few tears shed by the crew that morning.

FREQUENTLY THAT SEASON, INGRID SAW TABLOID STORIES ABOUT HER
own imminent death: INGRID BERGMAN HAS ONE FOOT IN THE GRAVE
read a typical headline. "It's true I had one foot in the grave," she
said, her humor intact. "But the soil was too damp and cold for me
and I suffer from rheumatism, so I stepped out again and went back
to work in Israel, where it is warm and dry!" When her old
acquaintance, journalist Oriana Fallaci, made a quick visit and could
not conceal her alarm, Ingrid said quietly, "Well, my dear, it's been
a very beautiful life, a very interesting life and a lucky one, too. We
all must die, but in some way I do not feel I am getting old, because
I don't know indifference and I ignore bitterness."

On the eve of the last day of filming—inside a London studio
early in November—Ingrid gave a dinner party for the cast and
crew. After the meal, she tapped her wine glass and rose, in great
pain, to offer a speech of thanks. As her producer, director, cameraman, makeup director, wardrobe designer and hairdresser turned
toward her, she smiled and offered a personal message of gratitude
to each. She had, as they all recalled, the right words for everyone.
It was the same with Gene Corman's son, then a law student, who

sent a message to Ingrid that he had a monumental crush on her for years. Ingrid sent him an autographed photo from *Casablanca*, as he had requested: "Thank you for the monumental crush," she wrote in her frail hand, "and here's looking at you, kid!" And at the end of filming, she gave Margaret Johnstone a little silver bulldog with a note: "To my darling watchdog and protector, with much love."

During the final shot next day, everything seemed to go wrong. There were problems with the camera, a crucial light, with a piece of the set and a missing prop. "See, the camera doesn't want to say good-bye to me either," Ingrid said with a smile as she wiped perspiration from her brow and sat down, trying to ignore a wave of nausea caused by her medication. After a brief rest, the last scene of her career was completed. "It has been a wonderful experience," she told the crew, "both as an actress and as a human being who is getting more out of life than I had ever expected." That evening, Gene Corman was host for a farewell dinner for the cast and crew. As she went around to thank everyone and then quietly departed with Margaret, Ingrid was the only one not weeping.

THAT GRIEVING SHE RESERVED FOR HER PRIVACY LATER THAT SAME night, as she confided to a friend. "I came back here to this quiet, empty apartment, and I suddenly realized, this is my reality now, this is how it is—and I felt drained and very sad. The ending of the film, I thought, was like a death in the family." She stepped over to the window and looked out as the autumn fog came up from the river and blanketed the quiet street below, and then she began to weep—just a few gentle tears, at first, and then she could not stop crying. Wasn't it strange, she thought: she had made so many movies—why wasn't she accustomed to endings at last? There had been so much life and vitality during the production—"and there I was, weeping my heart out. All those wonderful people who have been so close to me, whom I will likely never see again. And who knows, this may be the last time I face my dear old friend, the camera."

"GOOD-BYE," INGRID TOLD REPORTERS IN A PRESS CONFERENCE FOR *Golda* just before Christmas. "I'm leaving, and I will not return to the movies or to the theater. I have finished with acting. Now I'll travel around the world and play with my grandchildren." Which is exactly what she did in the last weeks of 1981, which she spent with Lars and her family at Choisel.

But Ingrid was weakening—by the day, it now seemed—and the simplest tasks required assistance. Before she returned to London in January, Lars spoke with Margaret Johnstone, who immediately agreed to move into the second bedroom at Cheyne Gardens as Ingrid's nurse, cook and full-time companion. But however ill she was, Ingrid was not, as Margaret saw, a patient to stay at home and stare at the walls if she could at all manage to go out. Instead, she invited one or two friends for casual suppers, she went to a movie or a play once or twice a week, she strolled in the little park along the river.

As a last, desperate attempt to destroy the malignancy that was ravaging her body, Ingrid submitted to a ferocious course of chemotherapy. She spent a week each month between February and May 1982 at St. Thomas Hospital, on the south bank of the Thames, and the results were not only futile, the side effects were dreadful. For two days after each course of treatment, she vomited violently, and for three days after that she could not touch the hospital fare. Margaret offered to prepare homemade soups and pureed foods she knew Ingrid liked and that would be easy to digest, but Ingrid refused: "They are all so kind to me here, I wouldn't like to hurt their feelings about the food."

Her right arm was now completely useless, and she forced herself to use her left to write notes of thanks to concerned friends. Feeling so rotten, it was not easy to keep her humor, she told Griff—but in fact that remained unimpaired. As she gazed from her room across the river toward the Houses of Parliament, she smiled and said, "Well, now that I've played Golda Meir, I can sit here and study Mrs. Thatcher for my next role!"

Back home, she begged Griff and Margaret to book theater seats, and either one of them or Ann Todd accompanied her. "She survived far longer than her doctors or any of us expected," Ann said later, "but really, her life was wretched. Only once was there anything remotely like a complaint. One day I sat with her in her bedroom, and I was knitting while she turned the pages of one of her scrapbooks. Then I noticed she was looking at my hands, and

I remembered that of course this had been one of her favorite things to do—all her life, she was always knitting things for herself and those she loved. And very quietly, she said, 'Sometimes, Ann, I think it would be better to go than to struggle on like this. I really don't think I'm any good to anyone now. I'm overstaying my welcome.'"

But her will of steel did not desert her. She and Ann arrived at the theater one evening in late April to find a platoon of reporters and photographers in the foyer. Ingrid, who looked very frail and haggard indeed, was furious and demanded to see the manager: "Who told the press I was coming?" she asked. The poor man was at a loss and replied sympathetically, "No one told them, Miss Bergman. They are waiting for the arrival of Princess Margaret." And with that, Ingrid burst out laughing, and for the duration of the play she frequently turned to Ann and the two women had to stifle their recurring giggles.

With her family she did not discuss what she now knew was more or less imminent. But with friends like Ann, Margaret and Griff she was more frank. Never grim or melodramatic, she spoke of "the great theater in the sky," and although she denied any fixed ideas about the nature of an after-life, she often said she was "longing to find out." She was also thinking very much of her parents: Isabella noticed that small framed pictures of Justus and Frieda were on Ingrid's bedside table and there were, as she said, "traces of my mother's lips on the photos—it looked like she had been kissing them."

Stephen Weiss visited in May, too, and she spoke frankly of her doctor's grim prognosis. She saw to some important financial matters, revising her will to leave generous bequests to her cousin Britt and Britt's daughter Agneta; to Griff and Margaret; to her goddaughter, Kate Barrett; to Roberto's niece, Fiorella Mariani, who had been so loyal and helpful; and to her old maid in Rome. The bulk of her estate (valued at just under $4 million) was divided evenly among her four children.

IN APRIL, *A WOMAN CALLED GOLDA* WAS SHOWN ON AMERICAN TELEVISion, and—could it have been otherwise?—the reviews were staggering. "A truly remarkable performance," wrote a senior critic for the *New York Times*. "Miss Bergman creates a woman of unwavering strength and sudden spurts of totally captivating warmth. A superb actress has taken full advantage of a splendid opportunity." Another wrote, "For Ingrid Bergman, a woman with many dramatic jewels in her golden crown, this is the final gem"—for by this time, the press knew that there would indeed be no more performances.

But there was one, of a sort—a display of gaiety that astounded everyone. Ingrid could not be dissuaded from giving a party in New York to celebrate the thirtieth birthday of her twin daughters on June 18, and so she traveled there with Margaret. But despite her heroic efforts and her cheerful manner, her children saw in Ingrid's eyes (as Isabella said) "great pain and great anxiety." Still, Pia added, "She was fun to be with. She laughed and joked. Somehow, she managed to turn her tragedy into an act of great courage. She was a brave and gallant woman and she had a good heart—and that, after all, is the most endearing quality of all."

Ingrid saw old friends—Kay Brown and Robert Anderson, among others—and the day after the birthday celebration, she and Bob met for lunch at the Oak Room of the Plaza, just across the street from the Wyndham Hotel, where she and Margaret had rooms. Ingrid was weak and perspiring, and clearly the luncheon was an effort, but she said she simply must keep an appointment to have her hair done at Bergdorf's, a few steps away. Bob escorted her to the salon.

"I have a three o'clock appointment," Ingrid said at the reception desk.

But her appearance had so altered that the attendant, who had met her on previous occasions, did not recognize Ingrid and asked the name.

"Bergman," Ingrid replied patiently.

"What's the first name, please?"

ON JULY 3, INGRID AND MARGARET RETURNED TO LONDON. JOSS ACK-land, her co-star in *Captain Brassbound's Conversion*, brought her some books and tapes—among them a copy of Antoine de Saint-Exupéry's novella *The Little Prince*, a classic fable celebrating the eternity of imagination and the endurance of friendship.

It was a lovely summer in London, and Ingrid liked to spend

much of the long days outside, but her strength failed rapidly now. She sat quietly in her sitting room until weakness forced her to bed, and there she asked Margaret or Griff to bring her albums and scrapbooks, so diligently maintained over the decades. There was the amazing chronicle of her life, and indeed it was, as she had said so often, a wonderful life, a life full of achievement and of so many interesting people and experiences—and none of them were ever simply extinguished from her life. Her copy of the novel *Of Lena Geyer*, still in her small library of cherished books, held, once again, a mirror to herself: "She went through so many different phases in her life and really became part of each one, then when the next came along you thought she'd dropped all the others and after a while you found out you were mistaken."

Ingrid seemed to shine with gratitude and even rallied with occasional flashes of her irrepressible humor as she saw the pictures and read some of the articles and reviews.

There she was, the shy little blond-haired girl in a winter coat and hat, gazing straight into her father's camera lens. There, too, were images of Ingrid as the apple-cheeked Elsa in a striped dress, in *The Count of Monk's Bridge*; as the wistful Anita in both versions of *Intermezzo*; and as the angry, disfigured Anna of *A Woman's Face*, who finally learns the meaning of pity and love.

She lingered over her favorite roles. There she was as Ivy in *Dr. Jekyll and Mr. Hyde*, sassy at first, then ashen from torture; and of course there was the classic role of Ilsa in *Casablanca*—Ingrid laughed aloud over that, for she never understood what all the fuss was about, even though the glow of love shone so brightly on her face when, for a higher cause, she was sent away by Bogart. "Here's looking at you, kid," she said aloud as she turned the page.

And there she was as Maria, in *For Whom the Bell Tolls*—and how wonderful Gary Cooper looked, his fine features captured forever by Paramount's cameras. There was a photo of her with courtly Charles Boyer, her co-star in three pictures. *Gaslight* was certainly the best of them, and her Oscar for it, like those for *Anastasia* and *Murder on the Orient Express*, stood on a bookcase nearby.

Many pages of the albums marked America's wartime movie history as well as her own. She had to agree that she made Sister Benedict believable, and although she never really knew Bing

Crosby, she made that work for the emotional honesty that rang through *The Bells of St. Mary's.*

There were family photos, too—her devoted father and mother, the stern but loving Aunt Ellen, the whimsical Uncle Otto and the dutiful Aunt Mutti. She had kept all her favorite images of Petter Lindstrom—always ascetically handsome and clear-eyed—and of course there were scores of photos of Pia, from her infancy to the present. Pia, who matured as a wise and compassionate woman of whom her mother was greatly proud, recognized in the latter years that reconciliation was Ingrid's great goal. Just as Pia had learned to accept and forgive, so her mother had to learn to accept that forgiveness. Reconciliation was the work of a lifetime.

There were many photos of Ingrid with her friend Alfred Hitchcock, of course. *Spellbound* had been great fun, and *Under Capricorn* seemed more amusing to her now than annoying—but *Notorious*, so full of their autobiographies, remained her favorite. When she spoke proudly of her own performances, her rendering of the love-struck Alicia Huberman was invariably mentioned.

Others smiled from the pages, too: the faces of Edvin Adolphson, Victor Fleming, Larry Adler, Bob Capa, Robert Anderson. Love altered in its expression, but it did not die. She had never ceased to cherish them all.

And there were so many images of Ingrid as her beloved Joan of Arc! She never forgot her final lines from Maxwell Anderson's play, for they might well have been applied to herself: "Nobody can use her for an alien purpose. Her own meaning will always come through." And moments later, Joan's last words: "It cannot take long to die. There will be a little pain and then it will end. No, the pain will not be little, but it will end. And if it were to do over, I would do it again. I would follow my faith, even to the fire." Along with a small library of books about Joan, there was a precious memento she had kept for years and that was still with her now: a little packet of French soil from Orléans.

Ingrid's favorite pictures of Roberto Rossellini shone from the pages, images of him nuzzling her cheek with his aquiline nose as their three children scampered around them; photos of him directing her on the harsh rocks of Stromboli; and all the stages of their children's lives were documented on the pages, too. That marriage and the collaboration with Roberto had been another huge challenge, but she never regretted a day of it. And there was, of course, a lively sampling of photos of herself with Lars Schmidt—at Choisel, on Dannholmen, at premieres. The camera was indeed her best friend: it not only adored her, it left her mementos of all those she loved and of the career she cherished.

Yes, it had been a good life: in seven countries and in five languages, Ingrid had appeared in forty-six movies, had made eleven stage and five television appearances, and had won every kind of prize her craft bestows. From the golden girl of Stockholm's stage and screen to the ill and wizened Golda Meir—how could anyone ever explain the sheer radiance of Ingrid Bergman, or her profound artistry?

LARS VISITED OFTEN THAT SUMMER, AND ON AUGUST 10, INGRID insisted that he take her to Stockholm and Dannholmen. In her hometown, she took Lars's arm and walked slowly past the Royal Dramatic Theater, the scene of such exciting days fifty years earlier. She sat on the same benches along Strandvägen and on Djurgården where she had gone to memorize lines as a student, she dropped some flower petals in the water in memory of her parents, and she watched the ferries in the bay.

On arriving at Dannholmen, Ingrid had to be carried from the dock to the house, and for several days she had no strength to leave her bed. "But her love for the island was so intense," recalled Lars, "that somehow she conquered her weakness." One morning, she asked him to help her to the doorway, so that she might inhale the fresh sea air and feel the sunlight. The next day, she managed a few steps outside, and the following afternoon a few more. Over the course of two weeks, she forced herself to walk farther each day— farther and farther around the small island, until she reached the flat boulder where she had so often gone, alone, with her scripts and her books. There she gazed calmly over the sea and asked Lars to have her ashes strewn in these waters, a promise he duly fulfilled. Hands clasped, they then walked slowly back over the rocks to the house.

Ingrid and Lars returned to London on Friday, August 27, her cousin Britt accompanying them. That evening, Ingrid spoke on the telephone with Ann Todd: "Oh, I am so tired," she told Ann. "I just want to sleep." But she could not: a real agony set in on Saturday, and Dr. MacLellan prescribed generous painkillers. "By this time," according to Lars, "she felt she had overstayed her welcome, and she longed to die." Still, Ingrid remained calm, courageous and alert. Cards and bouquets began to arrive, for Sunday would be her birthday. Lars had brought in her favorite flowers, some currants and blackberries from their garden at Choisel, and there was champagne chilling.

After a restless Saturday night, Ingrid rose early Sunday morning—exactly sixty-seven years since her birth, even to the day of the week—and she insisted on dressing and putting a bit of color on her face. "There—you see?" she said brightly, her voice thin and weak but her eyes shining and a smile burnishing her face. "I've made another year!" Lars, Britt, Griff and Margaret spent the afternoon with her, chatting quietly or reading as she occasionally drifted off in sleep. In mid-afternoon, she rallied. All the children called, and Ingrid spoke briefly with each.

AT SIX O'CLOCK ON THAT EVENING OF HER BIRTHDAY, AUGUST 29, 1982, she insisted that the champagne be opened, and everyone drank a toast. The moment was very like one that Ingrid had played as Ivy, who bravely confronted the deadly Mr. Hyde: "Well, I'll just take a sip of champagne—of course, I shouldn't stay too long." By eight o'clock, she was exhausted and asked to go to bed.

At her bedside was *The Little Prince*, opened to a passage she had marked near the end, when he dies: "I cannot carry this body with me. It is too heavy . . . But it will be like an old abandoned shell. There is nothing sad about old shells . . . I shall look as if I were dead, but that will not be true . . . "

Ingrid Bergman was born as late summer sunshine illumined Stockholm and glistened over the bay—when everyone, for a time, could forget that in winter the darkness seemed never to end. It was the same now in London, as daylight reflected angularly over the Thames and dappled the treetops in Cheyne Gardens. A mild breeze drifted up from the river, stirring the curtains and the new flowers in her room. Her lips moved silently, and there was one long, gentle sigh. The quiet evening was radiant, and then starlight shone all through the brief, cloudless night.

Notes

For brevity, details of interviews conducted for this book are supplied only at the first citation; unless otherwise stated, subsequent quotations from the same source derive from the identical interview with that source. All translations from the Swedish are by Gunvor Dollis unless otherwise noted.

Chapter One

PAGE

6   **typically German:** Joseph Henry Steele, *Ingrid Bergman—An Intimate Portrait* (New York: David McKay, 1959), p. 15.

6   **many regrets:** "An Interview with Ingrid Bergman," *Redbook*, February 1964.

6   **a dreamer:** Bill Davidson, *The Real and the Unreal* (New York: Harper & Bros., 1961), p. 150.

6   **a well-known figure:** Ibid.

7   **We were not rich:** Frank Law, "Life and Ingrid Bergman," *Star* (London), Dec. 4, 1957.

8   **I don't remember:** Ingrid Bergman and Alan Burgess, *Ingrid Bergman—My Story* (New York: Delacorte Press, 1980), p. 20; hereinafter, this volume is designated IB.

9   **As I grew older:** "Ingrid Bergman, in Her Own Words," *McCall's*, November 1958.

11   **concrete factors:** Ingmar Bergman, *The Magic Lantern: An Autobiography*, trans. Joan Tate (New York: Viking, 1987), p. 7.

12   **From the time I was:** "Why Ingrid Bergman Broke Her Long Silence," *Collier's*, Oct. 26, 1956.

12   **I put her in:** On *The David Frost Show*, Metromedia Television (New York), April 30, 1971; exec. prod. David Frost; dir., Royston Mayoh.

12   **She became the character:** E.g., in "Why Ingrid Bergman Broke Her Long Silence."

13   **The Lyceum's main mission:** *Lyceum för Flicker*, Katalog 1922–23 (Stockholm: Centraltryckeriet, 1923), p. 13.

14 **I remember so well:** Steele, p. 14.

15 **How can you:** "Why Ingrid Bergman Broke Her Long Silence."

15 **He never had any steady:** From notes prepared by Petter Lindstrom in 1980.

15 **with such pathos:** Quoted in *Dagens Nyheter* (Stockholm), March 5, 1939.

16 **Miss Bergman will surely:** Ibid.

16 **It was my first touch:** Steele, p. 15.

16 **He took me to:** On *The David Frost Show*.

17 **My eyes popped out:** IB, p. 22.

18 **I remember that Ingrid:** "Härligt att vara hemma igen," *Expressen* (Stockholm), Oct. 6, 1948.

18 **It had a strong appeal:** Steele, p. 17.

18 **I hated school:** Lincoln Barnett, "Ingrid of Lorraine," *Life*, March 24, 1947.

20 **I don't want Ingrid:** IB, p. 23.

20 **She has the right:** Ibid., p. 24.

21 **Peacefully and quietly:** *Dagens Nyheter* (Stockholm), July 30 and 31, 1929.

21 **I didn't see how:** "After Stardom and Scandal, Ingrid Bergman Tells 'My Story,'" *People*, Dec. 1, 1980.

21 **As a child:** Pia Lindstrom, in Jenny Shields, "Bergman Musical Farewell," *Daily Telegraph* (London), Oct. 15, 1982.

Chapter Two

PAGE

22 The account of Ellen Bergman's death is recalled in IB, p. 24.

23 **aloof, cold even:** James Green, "Ingrid Bergman: Why the Permissive Society Shocks the Woman Shunned in 1950," *Evening News* (London), Jan. 6, 1971.

24 **absolutely to the theater:** IB, pp. 26–27.

24 **I thought only about:** Zoe Farmar, "Ingrid Bergman's Escape to Happiness," *Picture Post* (London), May 30, 1953.

24 **The theater was a kind of hiding place:** *Christian Science Monitor*, March 17, 1977.

24 **ten whole kronor:** IB, p. 29.

26 **While she has too much:** Quoted in Irving Wallace, "Smörgåsbord Circuit," *Collier's*, Dec. 21, 1946.

27 **The streets were just full:** W. H. Dietrich to DS, Oct. 23, 1995.

28 **methodical energy:** Bill Davidson, *The Real and the Unreal*, p. 154.

28 **She had a great natural:** Wallace, "Smörgåsbord Circuit."

28 **Perhaps she wasn't:** Bill Davidson, *The Real and the Unreal*, p. 153.

29 **Ingrid was a beauty:** Ingrid Lutekort to DS, June 13, 1996.

30 **At that time:** Steele, p. 19.

31 **I felt very flattered:** Igor Cassini, "Ingrid's Love Story Ranks Among Great [sic]," *Los Angeles Examiner*, Feb. 5, 1950.

31 **I like your hair:** IB, p. 32.
32 **For an orphan girl:** Quoted in Bill Davidson, *The Real and the Unreal*, p. 155.
32 **very feared:** Steele, p. 21.
32 **It was not love:** Ibid.
32 **I have never been able:** Quoted to DS by Petter Lindstrom, Dec. 27, 1995.
32 **It took:** IB, p. 32.
34 **In her film debut:** *Stockholms-Tidingen*, Jan. 22, 1935.
34 **a refreshing and:** *Social-Demokraten*, Jan. 22, 1935.
35 **That surely took:** From unpublished notes of Petter Lindstrom, reproduced here with his kind permission.
35 **What a pity!:** Wallace, "Smörgåsbord Circuit."
35 **I was a prima donna:** IB, p. 41.
35 **She is superb!:** *Svenska Dagbladet*, Feb. 23, 1935.
36 **Because in the background:** Steele, p. 20.
37 **As if he was:** IB, p. 42.
37 **You are really:** Ibid.
37 **I found working with:** Ibid., p. 44.
37 **Don't leave, Ingrid!:** Fritiof Billquist, in *Aret runt* (Sweden), no. 10 (1962).
37 **I am insecure:** Bill Davidson, *The Real and the Unreal*, p. 43.
38 **She is not very intelligent:** Ibid., p. 155.
38 **Lindstrom's parents' house:** Ibid.
38 **giving Ingrid good advice:** Ibid.
39 **From the very beginning:** Ibid., p. 154.
39 **What a dreadful hat:** Billquist, in *Aret runt*.
40 **I thought we should:** Ibid.
40 **Ingrid Bergman is blindingly:** *Social-Demokraten*, Feb. 4, 1936.
40 **Ingrid Bergman has:** *Svenska Dagbladet*, Feb. 4, 1936.
40 **rates a Hollywood berth:** *Variety*, Aug. 20, 1936.
40 **natural charm:** *New York Times*, Aug. 27, 1936.
41 **I remember:** To DS, Aug. 6, 1975.
41 **an ardent Nazi:** Petter Lindstrom to DS, Dec. 27, 1995; the same remarks occur many times in Petter Lindstrom's private letters and papers—e.g., to Lennart Groll, March 13, 1987; in handwritten notes in 1988 and 1989; in his typescript "Some Comments Regarding I.B." (undated, probably 1986); and in a letter (undated) to Stig Nahlbom.

Chapter Three

PAGE
43 **Ingrid most certainly:** Petter Lindstrom to DS, Dec. 27, 1995; often elsewhere, as in a 1988 letter to Stig Nahlbom, and in notes prepared many times between 1984 and 1990.
43 **We were all:** Bjorn Sjö, in *Arbetet* (Malmo), Dec. 27, 1987. See also Petter Lindstrom to Kerstin Bernadotte, Nov. 21, 1980.

44   **Everybody around her:** To DS, Dec. 27, 1995.

45   **She always moved:** Quoted in IB, p. 56.

46   **At five o'clock:** Billquist, in *Aret runt*.

47   **I long to:** IB, p. 43.

47   **Ingrid Bergman adds:** *Ny Tid* (Stockholm), Nov. 17, 1936.

47   **I know he is:** IB, pp. 55–56.

49   **Owing to:** *Svenska Dagbladet*, Sept. 6, 1938.

50   **My lover!:** IB to Petter Lindstrom, June 20, 1937, in Barbro Alving (known familiarly in journalism as "Bang"), *Saxons* (Sweden), no. 40 (Sept. 29–Oct. 5, 1980).

51   **My father:** Pia Lindstrom, in the television documentary *Ingrid Bergman Remembered*, a Feldman-Winters/Wombat production for the Arts & Entertainment Network (1995).

51   **Before the wedding:** Steele, p. 22.

51   **When my husband married me:** "An Interview with Ingrid Bergman."

51   **Well, yes:** A. E. Hotchner, "The Enduring Courage of Ingrid Bergman," *McCall's*, May 1982; see also David Lewin, "Love—and Three Husbands," *Daily Mail* (London), May 7, 1974.

52   **a piece of junk:** IB, p. 45.

54   **The sincerity of the acting:** *New York Times*, Dec. 25, 1937.

54   **a talented:** *Variety*, Dec. 22, 1937.

55   **The idea to sign:** *Stockholm-Tidningen*, Dec. 1, 1937.

55   **With this contract:** German text: "Mit der Verpflichtung durch die Ufa steht Ingrid Bergman am Anfang einer neuen künstlerischen Entwicklung," in Nachrichten fürs Ausland (Ufa), Berlin, Dec. 2, 1937.

55   **I know you're always looking:** Quoted by Ingrid Bergman on *The David Frost Show*.

56   **A group of us:** Ronald Haver, *David O. Selznick's Hollywood* (New York: Alfred A. Knopf, 1980), p. 226.

57   **He did something:** IB, p. 45.

60   **an institution likely:** *New York Times*, Jan. 11, 1934.

60   For commentaries on the Swedish-German relationship before and during the war, see Steven Koblik, *The Stones Cry Out: Sweden's Response to the Persecution of the Jews: 1933–1945* (New York: Holocaust Library, 1988), and Irene Scobbie, *Historical Dictionary of Sweden* (Metuchen, N.J.: Scarecrow Press, 1995).

60   **I took the German offer:** John Kobal, *People Will Talk* (New York: Alfred A. Knopf, 1985), p. 461.

60   **If I knew anything:** Francis Sill Wickware, "The 'Palmolive Garbo,'" *Pageant*, September 1946.

60   **You could feel there was something brewing:** Kobal, p. 467.

61   Petter Lindstrom always insisted that he had nothing to do with negotiations for Ingrid's career, but in a letter to her dated March 26, 1980, he wrote: "I contacted Helmer Enwall in Stockholm" (p. 5).

61   **I asked him:** Lindstrom, "Some Comments Regarding I.B.," unpublished and undated notes.

61 **Enwall obtained:** Petter Lindstrom to Irene Mayer Selznick, May [no date] 1984.
61 **we made up the name:** Petter Lindstrom to Pia Lindstrom Daly and Joseph Daly, Nov. 1, 1982.
62 **The Lindstroms were very nice:** Jenia Reissar to DS, June 7, 1996.
63 **and not come home:** Rudy Behlmer, ed., *Memo from David O. Selznick* (New York: Avon, 1973), p. 133.
63 **A cold shudder:** Ibid., p. 162.
64 **I am happy I was born:** Oriana Fallaci, "Ingrid Bergman," *Look*, March 5, 1968.
64 **It was really Petter Lindstrom:** Signe Hasso to DS, July 15, 1996.
64 **trained and organized:** David Lewin, "Ingrid Bergman Looks Back," *McCall's*, October 1974.
64 **if it hadn't been for him:** Essy Key-Rasmussen, "Intelligent . . . and Beautiful!" *WHO*, November 1941.
65 **She was an altogether:** Laurence Evans to DS, Sept. 23, 1995.
65 **Sweden seemed too small:** Kobal, p. 474.
65 **But I was scared to death:** Haver, p. 228; similarly to DS, May 8, 1975.

Chapter Four

66 **I never did:** IB, p. 79.
67 **When I came to America:** Joan Barthel, "Bergman: 'I Am the Way I Am,'" *New York Times*, Aug. 27, 1967.
68 **Her lack of affectation:** Irene Mayer Selznick, *A Private View* (New York: Alfred A. Knopf, 1983), p. 225.
68 **God! Take your shoes:** Ibid., p. 65.
69 **Bergman is a good name:** Donald Culross Peattie, "First Lady of Hollywood," *Reader's Digest*, September 1943.
69 **I think you've made:** Ibid., p. 66.
70 **He said it:** Ingrid Bergman to DS, May 8, 1975; see also Kobal, p. 460.
73 **He was temperamental:** Kobal, p. 470.
74 **There is no single thing:** Behlmer, p. 168–169.
75 **Tears came to her eyes:** Ibid., p. 171.
75 **the most completely:** Ibid.
75 **All of this:** Ibid., pp. 171–172.
76 **I'm a down-to-earth:** *Christian Science Monitor*, March 17, 1977.
76 **always sending notes down:** IB to DS, May 8, 1995.
77 **it's so much easier:** Quoted in *Dagens Nyheter* (Stockholm), June 21, 1939.
77 **There are more people:** Kobal, p. 459.
78 **I have cabled UFA:** Petter Lindstrom to Kay Brown, July 28, 1939, in the Selznick Archives of the Harry Ransom Humanities Research Center, University of Texas at Austin; hereinafter, cited as Selznick Archives.
78 **I suppose:** Kay Brown to Daniel T. O'Shea, Aug. 8, 1939; interoffice communication, Selznick International Pictures, Inc., Selznick Archives.

78   **What a marvelous time:** IB, p. 80.

78   **I prayed:** Steele, p. 27.

79   **Dear Ingrid:** IB, p. 80.

79   On Lindstrom's involvement in the UFA contracts during the summer of 1939, see his letters to Kay Brown, Selznick Archives.

79   **never really recovered:** Kenneth Tynan, "The Abundant Miss Bergman," *Holiday*, August 1958.

80   **My German picture cancelled:** IB to David O. Selznick, cable, Selznick Archives.

80   **Sweden's Ingrid Bergman:** Frank S. Nugent, in *New York Times*, Oct. 7, 1939.

81   **David O. Selznick was exceedingly smart:** Howard Barnes, in *New York Herald Tribune*, Oct. 7, 1939.

81   **Tall, beautiful:** *Film Bulletin*, Oct. 4, 1939.

81   **She is beautiful, talented:** *Variety*, Oct. 8, 1939.

81   **She is the finest thing:** *New York Daily News*, Oct. 7, 1939.

81   **I cried all that day:** Steele, p. 28.

82   **I was never unhappy:** Kobal, pp. 473–474.

85   **Leaving Petter behind:** Ibid.

Chapter Five

PAGE

86   **Although I was shy:** Lillian Ross, *The Player* (New York: Simon & Schuster, 1962), p. 39.

86   **I was going mad:** IB, p. 85.

87   **Oh, you may have hurt him:** Kyle Crichton, "Big Girl," *Collier's*, Sept. 14, 1940.

88   **Picture the sweetheart:** Bosley Crowther, "The Lady from Sweden," *New York Times*, Jan. 21, 1940.

88   **Lunching with her:** Quoted in *Time*, Aug. 2, 1943.

89   **The first time:** Åke Sandler to DS, Nov. 26, 1995.

90   **What are you talking:** Crowther, "The Lady from Sweden."

91   **The part of Julie:** *New York Times*, March 26, 1940.

91   **Ingrid Bergman, who is making:** *New York Times*, March 31, 1940.

92   **Miss Bergman scored:** Ernest Lehman, in *The Hollywood Reporter*, March 26, 1940.

92   **Put it down:** *New York Journal-American*, April 2, 1940.

92   On Anderson's 1940 promise to write a play about Joan of Arc for Ingrid, see Burgess Meredith, *So Far, So Good* (Boston: Little, Brown, 1994).

93   **They were a part:** Laurinda Barrett to DS, April 12, 1996.

93   **Look at this:** IB, p. 90.

93   **not a success:** Ibid.

94   **I always look at:** Key-Rasmussen, "Intelligent . . . and Beautiful!"

94   **Dear God:** IB to Ruth Roberts, Sept. 2, 1940; see IB, p. 90.

95   **I am one of:** Ibid.

95 **She survived:** Kay Brown to DS, March 10, 1981; similarly in IB.

96 **made up:** IB, p. 91.

96 **Ingrid had a quality:** Aljean Harmetz, *Round Up the Usual Suspects: The Making of Casablanca—Bogart, Bergman and World War II* (New York: Hyperion, 1992), p. 90.

96 **completely believable and engaging:** Howard Barnes, in *New York Herald Tribune*, March 29, 1941.

97 **Why don't you stay:** IB, p. 94.

98 **Can you imagine that:** Ibid., p. 97.

98 **I do not care:** Quoted in *New York Herald Tribune*, Aug. 10, 1941; see also IB, p. 91.

98 **Darnedest thing:** Quoted in Sidney Skolsky's column in the *Hollywood Citizen-News*, Aug. 20, 1942.

99 **I feel like a race horse:** Key-Rasmussen, "Intelligent . . . and Beautiful!"

Chapter Six

PAGE

102 **To keep you up to date:** David O. Selznick to Kay Brown, Jan. 31, 1942, in Behlmer, pp. 349–350.

105 **Ingrid is not only:** *Lion's Roar*, no. 1 (the publicity bulletin of Metro-Goldwyn-Mayer Studios), 1941.

105 **It must have been Fleming:** Kobal, p. 479.

108 **I'm a little surprised:** Quoted in *New York World-Telegram*, Aug. 26, 1941.

108 **I would have paid:** IB, pp. 102–103.

109 **but Spence was too:** Larry Swindell, *Spencer Tracy: A Biography* (New York: World Publishing, 1969), p. 172.

109 **The only thing:** Bill Davidson, *Spencer Tracy: Tragic Idol* (London: Sidgwick & Jackson, 1987), p. 80.

109 **By the time:** IB, p. 102.

110 **like a cat:** Aljean Harmetz, *The Making of The Wizard of Oz* (New York: Alfred A. Knopf, 1977), p. 146.

110 **He got things:** Peter Waymark, "Bergman in London to Play Shaw's Ellen Terry Role," *Times* (London), Jan. 13, 1971.

111 **She always looked:** Memo to DOS.

111 **Once, she made me:** Bill Davidson, *The Real and the Unreal*, p. 153.

113 **Here is a report:** Petter Lindstrom to David O. Selznick, April 18, 1941, Selznick Archives.

113 **It is impossible to reconcile** Lindstrom's 1941 letters to Kay Brown and David Selznick with his protests, loudly and constantly voiced after Ingrid's death: "My selection of and admission to the University of Rochester Medical School had nothing to do with David Selznick" (Lindstrom to Irene Selznick, May [no date] 1984); similar statements occurred in his papers and correspondence from 1982 to 1995. In her memoirs, Irene Selznick (p. 238) confirmed the circumstances of Selznick's help with Lindstrom's career.

113 **My mother had to face:** In the television documentary *Ingrid Bergman Remembered*.

114 **handsome after:** Eugene O'Neill, *Selected Plays* (New York: Random House, 1969), p. 47.

114 **Ingrid was a joy:** John Houseman, *Run-Through: A Memoir* (New York: Simon & Schuster, 1972), p. 481.

115 **I see Anna Christie:** *New York Post*, Aug. 26, 1941.

115 **They expected:** IB, p. 105.

116 **She has given O'Neill's:** Key-Rasmussen, "Intelligent . . . and Beautiful!"

116 **He took me to his study:** On *The David Frost Show*; see also Rex Reed, *Conversations in the Raw* (New York: World Publishing, 1969), p. 42.

117 **It was unbearably dull:** Steele, p. 34.

117 **In all our married:** IB to Ruth Roberts, quoted in IB, p. 106.

118 **although it's wonderful:** Pia Lindstrom, in the television documentary *Ingrid Bergman Remembered*.

118 **It's nice:** DOS Archives, Austin.

118 **I think I have tried:** IB, p. 107.

118 **Only my reading:** Ibid., p. 109.

119 **Having a home:** IB to Ruth Roberts, Jan. 12, 1942; see IB, p. 110.

Chapter Seven

PAGE

121 **I'm down now:** IB, p. 112.

121 **Hard work:** Irene Mayer Selznick, p. 237.

122 **because Petter:** David O. Selznick to Dan O'Shea, April 6, 1942, Selznick Archives.

122 **We are going to decide:** Petter Lindstrom to Dan O'Shea, Aug. 18, 1942, Selznick Archives.

122 On the matter of Selznick's paying for Lindstrom's medical license, see E. L. Scanlon to Peter Lindstrom, March 9, 1942, Selznick Archives.

122 **The picture is called:** IB, p. 114.

124 **No one had:** IB to DS, May 8, 1975.

127 **In *Casablanca*, I kissed:** Many times—e.g., "Why Ingrid Bergman Broke Her Long Silence"; IB, p. 116.

128 **Well, it was a very:** IB to DS, May 8, 1975; similarly elsewhere.

128 Regarding Ingrid's conversation with Paul Henreid (and other matters relevant to production), see Frank Miller, *Casablanca: As Time Goes By—50th Anniversary Commemorative* (Atlanta: Turner Publishing, 1992), p. 30.

129 **I don't think:** *Boston Sunday Globe*, Sept. 5, 1982.

130 **ultimatum ruthlessly engineered:** Vera Zorina, *Zorina* (New York: Farrar, Straus & Giroux, 1986), p. 268.

130 **could get her to stop:** Thomas Carlile and Jean Speiser, "Ingrid Bergman," *Life*, July 26, 1943.

131 **I am sorry:** Petter Lindstrom to Dan O'Shea, Aug. 21, 1942, Selznick Archives.

131 **Lindstrom is still doing:** Selznick to Feldman, Aug. 24, 1942, Selznick Archives.

131 **She didn't:** Quoted in Bill Davidson, *The Real and the Unreal,* p. 145.

131 **I personally:** Selznick to Whitney Bolton, Sept. 11, 1942, Selznick Archives.

134 **I hated every moment of it:** IB to Roger Lobb, spring 1982, London; Lobb to DS, June 20, 1996.

135 **It was all very difficult:** IB to DS, May 8, 1975.

135 **but generally a little faint:** James Agee, in *The Nation,* July 20, 1943.

135 **He was one of:** On *The David Frost Show.*

137 **You should see:** IB, p. 125.

137 **I never got to be:** Stuart M. Kaminsky, *Coop: The Life and Legend of Gary Cooper* (New York: St. Martin's Press, 1980), p. 130.

138 On Lindstrom's meeting in New York with Scanlon, see the correspondence in the Selznick Archives between Lindstrom and Selznick, Nov. 4, 1942, and between Selznick and Scanlon, Nov. 11, 1942.

138 **He was the perfect host:** W. H. Dietrich to DS, Oct. 23, 1995.

138 **The Lindstroms were delightful:** Alfred Hitchcock to DS, Aug. 18, 1978.

Chapter Eight

PAGE

140 **If Sweden should:** *New York World-Telegram,* May 23, 1942.

143 **If they thought less:** Wickware, "The 'Palmolive Garbo.'"

144 **Selznick to Steele:** DOS Archives, Austin.

145 **There is a steady:** IB, p. 126.

145 **so good:** Ibid., p. 133.

149 **Miss Bergman is superb:** Frank Leyendecker, in *Film Bulletin,* May 1944.

150 **That maid bears:** Joseph Cotten, *Vanity Will Get You Somewhere* (San Francisco: Mercury House, 1987), p. 58.

151 **not only Ingrid:** "Comments Regarding Film Comments and Negotiations," an undated document by Petter Lindstrom; he also referred to "our heavy preoccupation with our professional work," in a two-page, undated document (probably 1986), which he entitled "Comments for Lisa Winnerlid but never mailed to her since she did not correct the lies in Husmodern as she had told me she would." The reference was to the editor and to a Swedish publication that had published statements to which he had objected.

151 **The simple truth:** Petter Lindstrom to IB, March 26, 1980.

151 **He knew that:** Steele, p. 74.

153 **Like everyone else:** Quoted in "Bergmansucces som fältartist," *Dagens Nyheter* (Stockholm), May 4, 1944.

153 **We danced:** IB, p. 129.

All the Lindstrom–Selznick correspondence is preserved in the Selznick Archives, Austin.

Chapter Nine

PAGE

155 **People tell me:** Barnett, "Ingrid of Lorraine."

155 **He told me:** IB, pp. 140ff.

155 **Petter wanted me:** Ibid., pp. 141–142.

156 **I make mistakes?:** Hotchner, "The Enduring Courage of Ingrid Bergman."

156 **She was always the subservient wife:** Bill Davidson, *The Real and the Unreal*, p. 159; see also Lewin, "Ingrid Bergman Looks Back."

156 **Her husband handled:** Steele, p. 57.

156 **Often, in the interviews:** IB, p. 140.

156 **Some I was:** Ibid., p. 141.

157 **To be truthful:** Hotchner, "The Enduring Courage of Ingrid Bergman."

157 **But when we were together:** Pia Lindstrom, as told to George Christy, "My Mother, Ingrid Bergman," *Good Housekeeping*, October 1964.

157 **Do I have to?:** "A Redbook Dialogue: Ingrid Bergman/Van Cliburn," *Redbook*, January 1962.

157 **My mother was super-devoted:** Hotchner, "The Enduring Courage of Ingrid Bergman."

157 **I felt guilty:** Mira Avrech, "A Profile in Courage, Ingrid Bergman Plays Golda While Battling Cancer," *People*, April 26, 1982.

157 **I was too young:** A. E. Hotchner, *Choice People: The Greats, Near-Greats and Ingrates I Have Known* (New York: William Morrow, 1984), pp. 114–115, 235.

157 **I couldn't understand:** Irene Mayer Selznick, p. 218.

160 **got hold:** PL to DOS, April 13, 1944, Selznick Archives.

161 **You have a tendency:** David O. Selznick to Petter Lindstrom, April 15, 1944, Selznick Archives.

162 **It amounted to complete submission:** *American Weekly*, Sept. 21, 1952.

162 **I'd like to stress:** Selznick memo to Margaret McDonell, July 10, 1943, Selznick Archives.

164 **Constance regarded herself:** Francis Beeding, *The House of Dr. Edwardes* (New York: World Publishing, 1945).

164 **I won't do:** Quoted in Ben Hecht, *A Child of the Century* (New York: Simon & Schuster, 1954), p. 481.

165 **I remember:** IB to DS, May 8, 1975.

166 **There was certainly:** Gregory Peck to DS, April 14, 1981.

167 **Hitchcock was one:** IB to DS.

167 **Selznick believed:** Peck to DS.

168 **crack like a shell:** AH to DS, July 18, 1975.

168 **It was a wonderful:** IB to DS, May 8, 1975.

172 **like a race horse:** Steele, pp. 48, 57.

173 **This is impossible:** IB, p. 137.

173 **That was a great shock:** Ibid., pp. 136–137.

173 **Thank goodness:** Ibid., p. 137.

174 **suddenly subdued:** Steele, p. 73.

174 **No, I don't think:** Ibid., p. 75.

174 **Wait till Ingrid Bergman:** Bill Davidson, *The Real and the Unreal*, p. 154.

175 **If you don't let me:** Steele, p. 73.

175 **I won't argue:** IB, p. 145.

175 **You always do:** Steele, p. 308.

176 **I think I was:** IB, p. 145.

Chapter Ten

PAGE

178 **Your artistry:** Mason Wiley and Damien Bona, *Inside Oscar* (New York: Ballantine Books, 1988), p. 147.

178 **I am still in a daze:** IB to George Cukor, March 18, 1945; in the Cukor Collection at the Academy of Motion Picture Arts and Sciences, Beverly Hills.

179 **Bing Crosby was one:** "Why Ingrid Bergman Broke Her Long Silence."

180 **When she walks:** Bill Davidson, *The Real and the Unreal*, p. 150.

182 **One side of me:** Law, "Life and Ingrid Bergman."

182 **Ah, now you're coming:** IB, p. 151.

183 **Capa is wonderful and crazy:** Steele, p. 66.

183 **It was, it is:** Richard Whelan, *Robert Capa: A Biography* (New York: Alfred A. Knopf, 1985), p. 241.

183 **Outwardly:** Ibid.

184 **the most romantic:** Ibid., p. 238.

184 **so romantic:** IB to DS, May 8, 1975.

185 **I fell in love:** Larry Adler to DS, June 3, 1996.

187 **You have become:** IB, p. 156.

189 The quotations are from Marcia Davenport, *Of Lena Geyer* (New York: Grosset & Dunlap, 1936).

191 **Miss Bergman just can't help:** Frank S. Nugent, "That Phenomenon Named Bergman," *New York Times Magazine*, Dec. 16, 1945.

193 **It has cost us:** Petter Lindstrom to John O'Melveny, Oct. 15, 1945, Selznick Archives.

194 **As to Dr. Lindstrom:** Selznick to John O'Melveny, Oct. 26, 1945, Selznick Archives.

197 **The girl's look:** Ibid.

202 **It was very good:** AH to DS, July 18, 1975.

202 **I really don't know:** IB to DS, May 8, 1975; see also Ross, p. 39, and "A Redbook Dialogue: Ingrid Bergman/Van Cliburn."

202 **I like to portray:** "Ingrid Bergman," *Look*, Feb. 19, 1946.

204 **He was very exclusive:** IB to DS, May 8, 1975.

205 **I was being psychoanalyzed:** Larry Adler to DS, June 3, 1996.

Chapter Eleven

209 **Hollywood was stifling:** John Gruen, "Interview with Ingrid Bergman," *Interview*, vol. 1, no. 8 (1970).

211 **What are we doing:** From an unpublished draft of the obituary of Katharine Brown Barrett, prepared by her daughters Kate Barrett and Laurinda Barrett.

211 **all tied up:** Quoted in Steele, p. 92.

212 **Because:** IB to DS, May 8, 1975.

212 **I fell in love with Roberto:** On *The David Frost Show*.

212 **I fell in love:** Fallaci, "Ingrid Bergman."

214 **He did the damndest:** Bill Davidson, *The Real and the Unreal*, p. 159.

215 **Under Lindstrom's:** Muriel Davidson, "Ingrid Bergman: The New Happiness in Her Life," *Good Housekeeping*, May 1969.

215 **But [Lindstrom] had:** Lawrence J. Quirk, *The Complete Films of Ingrid Bergman* (New York: Citadel/Carol, 1991), p. 29.

216 **At last I was:** "Why Ingrid Bergman Broke Her Long Silence."

216 **She was a simple peasant:** IB to DS, May 8, 1975.

217 **This has been going on:** Quoted in a letter from Petter Lindstrom to Stig Nahlbom, of the Swedish newspaper *Expressen*, n.d. (probably 1987).

217 **Ingrid Bergman said tonight:** United Press wire release, Oct. 27, 1946—in, e.g., *New York Times*, Oct. 28, 1946.

218 **My white rose:** Whelan, p. 247.

218 **London is so quiet:** Ibid.

219 **She is with few peers:** Howard Barnes, in *New York Herald Tribune*, Nov. 19, 1946.

219 **There is no doubt:** Brooks Atkinson, in *New York Times*, Nov. 19, 1946, and Nov. 24, 1946.

219 **a performance that may be:** IB, p. 173.

221 **outstanding acting:** *New York Times*, Jan. 4, 1947.

222 **He knows we are:** IB, p. 191.

224 **Well, it looked good on paper:** A. H. Weiler, "By Way of Report," *New York Times*, March 20, 1949.

225 **Ingrid is changing:** Steele, p. 143.

227 **This is Petter:** PL to DS, Dec. 27, 1995.

227 **Like a lover:** IB, p. 179.

228 **I am very tired:** Ibid., p. 175.

229 ***Under Capricorn* I made:** Charles Thomas Samuels, *Encountering Directors* (New York: G.P. Putnam's Sons, 1972), p. 233. See also François Truffaut, *Hitchcock* (New York: Simon & Schuster, 1967/1985), p. 138.

229 **until 1949 most of our income:** Petter Lindstrom to Pia Lindstrom, in a drafted but unsent letter, n.d.

230 **I had a lovely daughter:** Bill Davidson, *The Real and the Unreal*, p. 160; repeated in Lewin, "Ingrid Bergman Looks Back."

230 **I was bored:** Steele, p. 235.

231 **Those were very beautiful:** Frank Thompson, *Between Action and Cut: Five American Directors* (Metuchen, N.J.: Scarecrow Press, 1985), p. 57.

231 **She is bullet-proof:** Laurence Stallings, "The Real Ingrid Bergman Story," *Esquire*, August 1950.

232 **I must have my hands:** Ibid.

232 **She approached:** Ibid.

232 **But to the surprise:** Petter Lindstrom, unpublished document, "Some Comments Regarding I.B."

232 **A few days later:** Petter Lindstrom to DS, Dec. 27, 1995.

232 **I was never perfect:** Petter Lindstrom to Pia Lindstrom, drafted but unsent letter, n.d.

233 **We decided to rebuild:** *New York Journal-American*, Sept. 25, 1959.

233 **But every time:** Alan Burgess, "Ingrid Bergman: Stories She Left Untold," *Good Housekeeping*, April 1986.

233 **I lived with that:** Lindstrom to DS, Dec. 27, 1995.

Chapter Twelve

PAGE

236 The account of the damaged statue was repeated to DS by IB on May 8, 1975.

239 **Miss Bergman and Mr. Boyer:** *New York Times*, April 21, 1948.

239 IB's letter to Rossellini is in IB, pp. 4–5.

240 Rossellini's letter to IB is reproduced in IB, pp. 7–10.

241 **Rossellini said he was most anxious:** Notes by Jenia Reissar, dated June 30, 1948, drafted into a report for Selznick July 8, 1948, Selznick Archives.

241 **He is a temperamental:** Jenia Reissar to Selznick, Sept. 28, 1948, Selznick Archives. Other letters from Reissar, Le Maitre and Graziadei, cited below, are from the same archival source.

242 **The man lives:** Quoted in IB, p. 9.

243 **I'm going to be:** IB, p. 186.

244 **I didn't like it:** IB to DS, May 8, 1975; see also IB, pp. 187–189; also on *The David Frost Show*.

246 **He got such pleasure:** IB to DS, May 8, 1975.

246 **The one gorgeous scene:** Ibid.

246 **She got into a terrible:** Alfred Hitchcock to DS, July 24, 1975.

247 **My mother sometimes compared herself:** Pia Lindstrom, in the television documentary *Ingrid Bergman Remembered*.

248 **Do we make:** Howard Taubman, "A Live Story," *Look*, Jan. 29, 1952.

248 **I shall be honored:** Omar Garrison, in *Los Angeles Mirror*, Feb. 13, 1950; also in *New York Post*, Feb. 20, 1950.

249 **I expect a cable:** Taubman, "A Live Story."

249 **Certainly:** IB, p. 277.

250 **his parents wished:** Contained in a memorandum prepared by Ercole Graziadei for the Selznick office, dated June 1948, Selznick Archives.

250 **We'll get married:** Burgess, "Ingrid Bergman: Stories She Left Untold."

253 **Swedish women:** Barbara Grizzuti Harrison, "Oh, But They Were Marvelous Parents!" *McCall's*, July 1979.

253 **I met a director:** Cotten, p. 92.

253 **When it finally happened:** Arthur Laurents to DS, Oct. 19, 1981.

254 **I like him:** *Dagens Nyheter* (Stockholm), Oct. 6, 1948.

254 **There is no resisting:** John Mason Brown, in *Saturday Review of Literature*, Dec. 4, 1948.

254 **a masterwork of:** *Los Angeles Daily News*, Dec. 23, 1948.

255 **It's true that people:** Earl Wilson's syndicated column, in, e.g., *Los Angeles Daily News*, Nov. 17, 1948.

256 **Dear Mr. Rossellini:** The letter was published first in Taubman, "A Live Story."

256 **Physical problems:** Petter Lindstrom to Irene Selznick, May 1984.

Chapter Thirteen

PAGE

258 **For a long time:** Robert J. Levin, "The Ordeal of Ingrid Bergman," *Redbook*, July 1956.

259 **I was uncontrollably:** Bill Davidson, *The Real and the Unreal*, p. 162.

259 **I don't need stars:** *Time*, Feb. 9, 1949.

259 **The truth:** Isabella Rossellini, in *People*, Aug. 2, 1982.

259 **It is a great place:** *Time*, Feb. 9, 1949.

259 **He was so warm:** Bill Davidson, *The Real and the Unreal*, p. 162.

259 **What [Roberto] was:** Peter Brunette, *Roberto Rossellini* (New York: Oxford University Press, 1987), p. 110.

260 **We spent months:** Garrison, in *Los Angeles Mirror*.

262 **He needed:** IB, p. 209.

263 **Ingrid, you're falling:** Bill Davidson, *The Real and the Unreal*, p. 163.

264 **Oh, he won't have:** Weiler, "By Way of Report."

265 **I would say:** *Los Angeles Times*, Nov. 2, 1950.

265 **Wholesome as a girl scout:** Pete Martin, "Big Beautiful Swede," *Saturday Evening Post*, Oct. 30, 1948.

265 **I cannot understand:** Ibid.

265 **Nobody could have lived:** IB to DS, May 8, 1975.

265 **I wanted to keep:** DOS to PL, April 15, 1944, Selznick Archives.

266 **It must have been symbolic!:** Irene Mayer Selznick, p. 375.

267 **She had no idea:** Lars Schmidt to DS, June 19, 1996.

267 **She came to:** Darr Smith, "Real Lowdown Given on Ingrid-Rossellini Romance," *Los Angeles Daily News*, Sept. 24, 1949.

267 **The last thing she did:** *Los Angeles Times*, Nov. 2, 1950.

268 **One had the feeling:** Uno Myggan Ericson, Myggans Nöjeslexikon (Höganäs, Sweden: Bra Böckers Publishers, 1989–1993), vol. 2, p. 91.

268 **I knew Roberto:** *Los Angeles Mirror*, Feb. 14, 1950.

269 **IB's letter to PL:** IB, p. 216; Steele, pp. 170–171.

270 **jilted before the:** Åke Sandler to DS, Nov. 27, 1995.

270 **All this talk:** George Weller, "Ingrid's Rossellini," *Collier's*, Nov. 12, 1949.

270 **I wanted to flee:** *Los Angeles Mirror*, Feb. 14, 1950.

271 **You can have:** IB, p. 230.

271 **He doesn't need:** Earl Wilson's syndicated column, in, e.g., *Los Angeles Daily News*, Aug. 13, 1949.

272 **I thought we:** Steele, p. 172.

272 **I do not choose:** *Los Angeles Times*, April 20, 1949.

272 **I have come to Italy:** *Los Angeles Examiner*, May 5, 1949.

273 **lost and wan and bewildered:** IB, p. 244.

273 **There will be no divorce:** *Hollywood Citizen-News*, May 5, 1949.

274 **he didn't love me:** Affidavit sworn by IB in 1952 in support of her request to have her daughter visit her in Italy that summer; *Dallas Morning News*, June 5, 1952.

274 **If Mr. Lindstrom:** Camille M. Cianfarra, "Bergman Nuptials Wait on Divorce," *New York Times*, Dec. 15, 1949.

274 **I have seen nothing:** Steele, p. 173.

275 **I cannot go back:** Steele, pp. 175-176.

275 **We have been trying:** Robert Conway, "Ingrid Confirms Romance with Film Director Rossellini," *Los Angeles Times*, May 3, 1949.

275 **Fantasy on the Black Island:** *Time*, May 16, 1949.

276 **miserable—there is no other term:** Pia Lindstrom to DS, Oct. 22, 1996.

277 **I thought sensible:** Levin, "The Ordeal of Ingrid Bergman."

277 **IB to Pia Lindstrom:** IB, p. 253.

278 **I should have handled:** IB to DS, May 8, 1975; see also Gene Shalit, "What's Happening," *Ladies' Home Journal*, December 1978, and *Time*, Aug. 15, 1949.

278 **In recent days:** Joseph I. Breen to IB, April 22, 1949; in IB, pp. 235–236.

279 **Wanger to IB:** IB, pp. 236-237.

279 **So if I had been:** Earl Wilson, "Ingrid Has Big Artistic Film Dreams," *Los Angeles Daily News*, Aug. 6, 1949.

281 **Ingrid Bergman is the ideal:** *Los Angeles Herald Express*, Sept. 7, 1949; see also United Press wire release, same date.

282 **Don't do anything:** Cholly Knickerbocker, in, e.g., *Los Angeles Examiner*, Sept. 21, 1949.

284 **a poor, miserable way:** Steele, p. 255.

284 **No picture:** Ibid., p. 257.

284 **Roberto is going to make:** Ibid., p. 258.

284 **before anybody:** Ibid. p. 260.

285 **I am not afraid:** Ibid., p. 269.

285 **I think they were tears:** Kobal, p. 472.

285 **Why do they talk:** Steele, p. 270.

285 **Ingrid dearest:** Ibid.

285 **After all:** *The New Yorker*, Oct. 23, 1989.

285 **Having been so loved:** *Expressen* (Stockholm), Jan. 17, 1972.

Chapter Fourteen

PAGE

287 There is no fuller or more lively account of the news surrounding the birth of Ingrid's baby than that filed from Rome by Genêt (Janet Flanner) for *The New Yorker*, April 8, 1950. My treatment of this time depends heavily on her chronology.

291 **the forms of hypocrisy:** *Expressen* (Stockholm), Feb. 4, 1950.

291 **Isn't it funny:** IB to DS, March 12, 1980.

291 **I'll never forget:** "Why Ingrid Bergman Broke Her Long Silence."

292 **The actions:** All quotations in this paragraph: United Press wire story, "Pastors Blast Ingrid, Urge Screen Purge," Feb. 6, 1950.

292 **sex exhibitionism:** *Los Angeles Daily News*, Feb. 15. 1950.

293 **The Devil himself:** *Boston Pilot*, Feb. 20, 1950.

294 **It is our policy:** Quoted in the *Hollywood Citizen-News*, Feb. 3, 1950.

294 **feeble, inarticulate:** *New York Times*, Feb. 16, 1950.

294 **no depth:** *New York Herald Tribune*, Feb. 16, 1950.

294 **vacant:** *New York Times*, Feb. 16, 1950.

294 **How can they:** IB to Steele, p. 281.

297 **The worst part:** Levin, "The Ordeal of Ingrid Bergman."

300 **People saw me:** Often—e.g., IB to DS, May 8, 1975.

300 **Of course, we were:** International News Service wire dispatch, May 31, 1950—e.g., *Los Angeles Examiner*, June 1, 1950.

300 **Roberto lived and worked:** *McCall's*, October 1974.

301 **Save some dust:** Alice Hope, "Playing It for Comfort," *Daily Telegraph* (London), Oct. 16, 1973.

301 **He knew that Fellini:** Ibid.; see also Steele, p. 299.

301 **but Ingrid doesn't want:** *Hollywood Citizen-News*, Sept. 6, 1950 and *Los Angeles Times*, Sept. 7, 1950.

302 The settlement of the divorce case was widely reported—e.g., in *Los Angeles Times*, Nov. 2, 1950.

Chapter Fifteen

PAGE

304 **so the dogs know:** Steele, p. 299.

305 **Why don't we sell:** Melton S. Davis, "The New Heartbreak in Ingrid Bergman's Life," *Good Housekeeping*, January 1967.

305 **Unlike my big empty house:** Bill Davidson, *The Real and the Unreal*, p. 167.

305 **He was so Italian:** *New York Sunday News*, April 18, 1976.

305 **I relax with:** David Lewin, "Joan of Arc? My Life Will Help Me Play It," *Daily Express* (London), Oct. 6, 1954.

306 **that if he left the house:** David Lean to Alan Burgess, in IB, p. 290.

307 **The child was wonderful:** IB, p. 293.

309 **all the troubles:** Ibid., p. 79.

310 **obviously and bitterly vindictive:** David O. Selznick to Judge Mildred L. Lillie, June 7 and 9, 1952. Selznick Archives.

310 **I would say:** *Los Angeles Examiner*, June 10, 1952.

310 **if Pia is asked:** Robert Lumsden, D.D.D., June 1951 Superior Court Proceedings before Judge Mildred Lillie, State of California, County of Los Angeles; see also Steele, p. 302.

311 **I don't love:** Pia Lindstrom to Judge Lillie, June 13, 1952; Superior Court Proceedings before Judge Mildred Lillie, State of California, County of Los Angeles.

311 **My father won:** Pia Lindstrom, in the television documentary *Ingrid Bergman Remembered*.

311 **I could never:** Signe Hasso to DS, July 15, 1996.

312 **No one will:** IB, p. 300.

312 **and bang:** IB, pp. 244–245.

312 **underwent an immediate transformation:** William Safire, "As Time Goes By," *New York Times*, Sept. 6, 1982.

313 **There she was:** IB to DS, May 20, 1975.

313 **without a script:** IB to DS, May 8, 1975.

314 **I could see:** Larry Adler to DS, June 12, 1996.

314 **and the marriage:** IB to DS, May 8, 1975.

314 **they come face to face:** Roberto Rossellini, *My Method: Writings and Interviews* (New York: Marsilio Publishers, 1987), p. 120.

314 **We never knew:** Ibid., p. 159.

315 **You read it:** Quoted by IB to DS, May 8, 1975.

315 **a total failure:** Ibid., p. 120.

315 **The language:** IB to DS, May 8, 1975.

315 **If a good picture:** IB to Steele, Sept. 19, 1954; Steele, p. 315.

316 **I heard that:** Ibid., p. 317.

317 **She travels around:** Stig Ahlgren, "Visa sig För pengar," *Vecko Journalen*, Feb. 20, 1955.

317 **Ingrid Bergman would like:** *Stockholms Tidningen*, Feb. 28, 1955.

318 **They have driven me to:** *Daily Express* (London), March 1, 1955.

319 **She wanted:** Robert Anderson to DS, May 13, 1996.

319 **Ingrid, it is trash:** Steele, p. 320; see also Lewin, "Love—and Three Husbands."

322 **So long as I:** Muller, "Bergman Stars Again—Alone."

322 **But I had decided the time had come:** Hotchner, *Choice People*, p. 113.

323 **has gone on:** IB, p. 329.

326 **Is anybody still:** IB to Robert Anderson, RA to DS, May 13, 1996; similarly: Lewin, "Ingrid Bergman Looks Back"; see also "Ingrid Bergman, in Her Own Words."

326 **He was red:** Bill Davidson, *The Real and the Unreal*, p. 173.

326 **It won't last a week:** Quoted by Robert Anderson to DS.

329 **nothing short of superb:** *New York Times*, Dec. 15, 1956.

Chapter Sixteen

PAGE

330 **Look what I bought:** Quoted by Robert Anderson.

331 **needed to play:** Lars Schmidt, *Mitt Livs Teater* (Stockholm: Bra Böcker, 1995), p. 53 (trans. from the Swedish by Gunvor Dollis).

332 The account of her press conference was filmed by Movietone and reported by Murray Schumach, *New York Times*, Jan. 20, 1957.

333 **No one could be:** Bill Davidson, *The Real and the Unreal*, p. 143.

335 **I got the news:** Nancy Nelson, *Evenings with Cary Grant* (New York: William Morrow, 1991), p. 208.

337 **I found that:** IB, p. 347.

337 **Sometimes I said:** Cathleen Young, *Isabella Rossellini: Quiet Renegade* (New York: St. Martin's Press, 1989), p. 86.

337 **I was, I suppose:** Pia Lindstrom to DS, Oct. 22, 1996.

337 **I want to put:** Stephen M. Silverman, *Dancing on the Ceiling: Stanley Donen and His Movies* (New York: Alfred A. Knopf, 1996), p. 269.

339 **Isn't it strange:** IB, p. 356.

339 **You are still:** Steele, p. 336.

340 **I was not really crushed:** Gruen, "Interview with Ingrid Bergman," p. 11.

340 **She never felt:** Kay Brown, in the television documentary *Ingrid Bergman Remembered*.

341 **She felt:** Phil Gersdorf to Sheilah Graham, Nov. 17, 1957; production memorandum preserved in the Warner Bros. Archives at the University of Southern California, Los Angeles.

341 **I don't relish:** Gruen, "Interview with Ingrid Bergman."

341 **It didn't hurt me:** Isabella Rossellini, in the television documentary *Ingrid Bergman Remembered*.

341 **We had two months:** Joseph Gelmis, "A Child of the Movies Makes Movie," *Los Angeles Times* (Calendar), May 23, 1982.

341 **And when Mamma came:** Harrison, "Oh, But They Were Marvelous Parents!"

341 **The guilt over:** In the television documentary *Ingrid Bergman Remembered*.

342 **One reason:** Bill Davidson, *The Real and the Unreal*, p. 174.

342 **I admire her:** Ibid.

343 **when everything is:** *New York Times*, July 4, 1958.

343 **I want to live with you:** Schmidt, p. 63.

343 **I love you:** Ibid., pp. 63–65.

345 **It isn't fair:** Quoted by the Baron Göran von Essen to DS, June 20, 1996.

345 **I swore:** Tynan, "The Abundant Miss Bergman."

347 **I am from the south:** *Los Angeles Herald & Express*, Nov. 27, 1959.

347 **Try not to make mistakes:** IB, p. 381.

347 **He is a great director:** Sidney Fields, "Ingrid Yearns to Be with Children," *Los Angeles Herald & Express*, Feb. 1, 1961.

347 **For two years:** Barthel, "Bergman: 'I Am the Way I Am.'"

349 **a crazy man:** IB to DS, May 8, 1975.

349 **If you're going to yell:** *Newsweek*, Oct. 19, 1959.

350 **By marrying:** Pia Lindstrom, "My Mother, Ingrid Bergman."

351 **ninety percent:** Stephen Weiss to DS, Aug. 28, 1996.

351 **There she lived:** Lasse Lundberg to DS, June 18, 1996.

351 **We had to:** Jon Whitcomb, "Ingrid: Older, Wiser, and Wrinkleless," *Cosmopolitan*, July 1961.

353 **We never thought:** John P. Shanley, "Ingrid and Lars Schmidt—New TV Combine," *New York Times*, Feb. 12, 1961.

353 **Ingrid had no comment:** Schmidt, p. 162.

354 **I'm at a very:** "A Redbook Dialogue: Ingrid Bergman/Van Cliburn."

354 **It hurts so:** IB, p. 392.

355 **Well, here I am:** IB to Pierre Barillet, quoted to DS, Sept. 18, 1995.

357 **at loose ends:** IB, p. 399.

358 **Ingrid was:** Lars Schmidt to DS, June 19, 1996.

Chapter Seventeen

PAGE

361 **I wasn't ready:** "Ingrid Bergman—A Stable Romantic Ideal in the Midst of Change," *Times* (London), Dec. 6, 1965.

362 **I do not know:** *Evening Standard* (London), Oct. 28, 1965.

362 **She was not:** Michael Redgrave, *In My Mind's Eye: An Autobiography* (London: Weidenfeld & Nicolson, 1983).

362 **Miss Bergman's performance:** *Times* (London), Sept. 24, 1965.

362 **A most skilfully:** *Punch*, Sept. 29, 1965.

362 **It is by her Natalia:** *Daily Telegraph* (London), Sept. 24, 1965.

362 **Ingrid Bergman has softened:** *Evening Standard* (London), Sept. 24, 1965.

364 **I tried to be brave:** There are many contemporaneous accounts of the ordeal of Isabella Rossellini's scoliosis: see, e.g., IB, pp. 407ff.; Barbro Alving, "Mardrömmen är slut," *Vand* (1966); Ingrid Bergman, "Min flicka kan åter gå rak," *Allers* (1966); and Davis, "The New Heartbreak in Ingrid Bergman's Life."

365 **Mama stopped work:** IB, p. 410.

365 **Ingrid, stop this:** Ted Kotcheff to DS, Sept. 25, 1996.

367 **Anything I don't mention:** Stephen Watts, "All Alone by the Telephone," *New York Times*, Jan. 15, 1967.

369 **The unfinished manuscript was about:** Elliot Martin to DS, Aug. 29, 1996.

370 **Everyone in the company:** Arthur Hill to DS July 9, 1996.

370 **My God!:** Rex Reed, ". . . But Colleen Almost Does," *New York Times*, Nov. 12, 1967.

370 **I drove:** IB, p. 423.

373 **Swedes will sit:** *Playbill*, Jan. 1968.

373 **It does O'Neill's memory:** Clive Barnes, in *New York Times*, Nov. 1, 1967.

376 **Our professional lives:** Schmidt, pp. 74–75.

376 **it wasn't really:** IB, p. 426.

376 **I am rather proud:** Sven Rye, "After 20 Years, Ingrid Returns to Hollywood," *Film World* (UK), vol. 5, no. 3 (1969).

377 **I remarked:** *People*, Sept. 19, 1983.

377 **so awfully inhibited:** Muriel Davidson, "Ingrid Bergman: The New Happiness in Her Life."

378 **I think Gene Saks:** IB, p. 429.

378 **a sensational combination:** Ibid.

379 **cooperative, modest:** Guy Green to DS, Jan. 16, 1996.

379 **You are not:** IB, p. 432.

379 **very tiresome:** Ibid., pp. 432–433.

380 **There are no movie scripts:** IB to DS, April 22, 1972; see also *Evening News* (London), Aug. 10, 1973.

Chapter Eighteen

PAGE

383 **The tears:** Jane McLoughlin, "Tears Make You Human—Be Grateful for That," *Daily Telegraph* (London), Jan. 14, 1971.

383 **pretty tiresome:** *Telegram* (London), Jan. 29, 1907.

384 **You can't do that:** Kobal, p. 455.

384 **stumbling around:** IB, p. 436.

385 **You know:** IB to the Baronne Phillipine de Rothschild, thence via Pierre Barillet to DS, Sept. 19, 1995.

385 **I wanted success:** Ronald Bowers, *The Selznick Players* (New York: A.S. Barnes, 1976), p. 88.

386 **I haven't read:** Proceedings of the National Press Association for March 15, 1972; see also *New York Times*, March 18, 1972.

386 **Mr. President:** *Congressional Record*—Senate, April 19, 1972.

387 **Dear Senator Percy:** IB, p. 441.

388 **People keep asking me:** Michael Thornton, "Why Gossip Makes Miss Bergman Smile," *Sunday Express* (London), Oct. 14, 1973.

389 **it's hard:** *Celebrity*, July 1975.

389 **We found him:** Sir John Gielgud to DS, Mar. 18, 1996.

389 **The first night:** *Evening Standard* (London), Nov. 22, 1974.

390 **Oh, I'm so sorry:** Quoted by John Gielgud to DS.

391 **She was really not:** Stephen Weiss to DS, Aug. 28, 1996.

392 **Insured?:** Griffith James to DS, Nov. 9, 1995.

392 **You simply could not push:** Laurence Evans to DS, Sept. 23, 1995.

393 **She gave a very:** Sidney Lumet to DS, Aug. 27, 1996.

393 **Which is more:** IB, p. 449.

394 **I didn't take it:** IB, p. 450.

395 **You've got the:** *Daily Express* (London), Sept. 27, 1982.

396 **Really, it was very nice:** IB to DS, May 8, 1975.

396 **that always came first:** Lars Schmidt to DS, June 19, 1996.

397 **My whole life:** Richard Dyer, "The Constant Stardom of Ingrid Bergman," *New York Times*, April 20, 1975.

397 The writer to whom IB was so generous then and later is DS.

398 **I am still working:** IB to DS, May 8, 1975.

399 **She is just the opposite:** *Time*, Jan. 19, 1976.

399 **She didn't have:** Lars Schmidt to DS, Oct. 5, 1996.

399 **I love all my husbands:** Often—e.g., Lewin, "Ingrid Bergman Looks Back."

Chapter Nineteen

403 **I am worried:** IB to DS, March 6, 1979.

404 **Ingrid, my dear:** IB, p. 461.

406 **Also, we had to get her:** Dame Wendy Hiller to DS, Dec. 6, 1995.

406 **Can you imagine:** IB, p. 461.

408 **There was trouble:** Schmidt, pp. 90–91; also Lars Schmidt to DS, Oct. 5, 1996.

408 **There's a lot of me:** Mason Wiley and Damien Bona, *Inside Oscar* (New York: Ballantine, 1987), p. 556.

409 **I always felt guilty:** Shalit, "What's Happening."

411 **He had originally:** McKeon, "Bergman on Bergman."

412 **She intended to finish:** Ingmar Bergman, *The Magic Lantern*, pp. 184–185.

412 **Her conduct:** Ingmar Bergman (trans. Marianne Routh), *Images: My Life in Film* (New York: Arcade Publishing, 1994), p. 334.

412 **The superficial part:** *Boston Sunday Globe*, Sept. 5, 1982.

413 **a woodland setting:** Burgess, "Ingrid Bergman: Stories She Left Untold."

413 **She really was:** Dame Wendy Hiller to DS, Dec. 6, 1995.

414 **Ingrid Bergman captures:** Milton Shulman, in *Evening Standard* (London), Jan. 27, 1978.

414 **more assured:** Felix Barker, in *Evening News* (London), Jan. 27, 1978.

414 **There's no pin-spot:** Michael Thornton, "Bergman," *Daily Express* (London), Sept. 18, 1982.

414 **Closer:** Hirshhorn, *art. cit.,* and IB, p. 478.

415 **Well, I've had it done:** Margaret Johnstone to DS, Dec. 5, 1996.

416 **Reviews of** *Autumn Sonata:* IB, p. 482.

417 **Hitch struggled:** IB to DS and Teresa Wright on that same night of the gala tribute, March 7, 1979.

419 **What was my reaction:** Petter Lindstrom, "Final Comments," undated typescript, probably c. 1987.

419 **He took both my hands:** IB to DS, April 30, 1980.

420 **Time is shortening:** Ann Todd to DS, Jan. 6, 1984.

Chapter Twenty

421 **Self-pity was not:** Pia Lindstrom, in the television documentary *Ingrid Bergman Remembered*.

421 **I liked Lars:** Larry Adler to DS, June 9, 1996.

422 **Now dear Hitch:** IB to DS, April 30, 1980.

422 **I don't know:** IB to DS, April 30, 1982.

423 **It holds up:** DS attended the event with Anderson.

423 **I must be:** Shirley Flack, "The Woman Who Brought Bergman Back to the Screen," *Woman* (UK), June 2, 1982.

423 **She wanted to do:** Göran Von Essen to DS, June 19, 1996.

423 **Pessimism:** *Observer* (London), Dec. 29, 1974.

424 **I wanted to follow:** Flack, "The Woman Who Brought Bergman Back to the Screen."

425 **loved our children:** Often—e.g., Natalie Gittelson, "Caroline and Robertino: The Fated Romance," *McCall's*, July 1983. See also *New York Sunday News*, Jan. 31, 1982.

425 **I understand:** Jane Friedman, "Ingrid Bergman Plays a Prime Minister," *New York Times*, Oct. 25, 1981.

425 **I was very stubborn:** Joan Borsten, "Bergman as Meir: From the Newspaper to Television," *Los Angeles Times* "Calendar," Oct. 11, 1981.

426 **Work is wonderful:** *People*, Aug. 26, 1982 and Sept. 13, 1982.

427 **We're walking along:** Burgess, "Ingrid Bergman: Stories She Left Untold."

427 **gravel grounded in authority:** I am grateful to my research director, Greg Dietrich, for his singularly perceptive comments on *A Woman Called Golda* and other IB pictures.

428 **It's true:** *Aftonbladet* (Stockholm), Sept. 4, 1982.

428 **Well, my dear:** Ibid.; see also *Newsweek*, Sept. 13, 1982.

429 **See, the camera:** Gene Corman to DS.

429 **It has been a wonderful:** Hotchner, *Choice People*, p. 117.

429 **I came back here:** Ibid.

429 **Good-bye:** *New York Times*, Feb. 24, 1982.

430 **She survived:** Ann Todd to DS, May 8, 1992.

431 **traces of my mother's lips:** Isabella Rossellini, in the television documentary *Ingrid Bergman Remembered*.

432 **I have a three o'clock:** Robert Anderson to DS, May 13, 1996.

436 **I cannot carry:** Antoine de Saint-Exupéry (trans. Katherine Woods), *The Little Prince* (New York: Harcourt Brace/Harvest, 1971), p. 106.

Bibliography

Ackland, Joss. *I Must Be in There Somewhere*. London: Hodder & Stoughton, 1989.

Adler, Larry. *It Ain't Necessarily So*. New York: Grove Press, 1984.

Andersson, Ingvar. *A History of Sweden*. London: Weidenfeld & Nicolson, 1956.

Barrow, Kenneth. *Helen Hayes: First Lady of the American Theatre*. New York: Doubleday, 1985.

Beeding, Francis. *The House of Dr. Edwardes*. New York: World Publishing Co., 1945.

Behlmer, Rudy, ed., *Memo from David O. Selznick*. New York: Avon, 1973.

Bergman, Ingmar (trans. Joan Tate). *The Magic Lantern: An Autobiography*. New York: Viking, 1988.

Bergman, Ingmar (trans. Marianne Routh). *Images: My Life in Film*. New York: Arcade Publishing, 1994.

Bergman, Ingrid and Alan Burgess. *Ingrid Bergman—My Story*. New York: Delacorte Press, 1980.

Bowers, Ronald. *The Selznick Players*. New York: A.S. Barnes, 1976.

Brunette, Peter. *Roberto Rossellini*. New York: Oxford University Press, 1987.

Bruno, Michael. *Venus in Hollywood*. New York: Lyle Stuart, n.d.

Casper, Joseph Andrew. *Stanley Donen*. Metuchen, N.J.: Scarecrow Press, 1983.

Cotten, Joseph. *Vanity Will Get You Somewhere*. San Francisco: Mercury House, 1987.

Davenport, Marcia. *Of Lena Geyer*. New York: Grosset & Dunlap, 1936.

Davidson, Bill. *The Real and the Unreal*. New York: Harper & Bros., 1961.

——. *Spencer Tracy: Tragic Idol*. London: Sidgwick & Jackson, 1987.

Ericson, Uno Myggan. *Myggans Nöjeslexikon*, Vols. 1–14. Höganäs, Sweden: Bra Bökers Publishers, 1989–1993.

Gabler, Neal. *Winchell: Gossip, Power and the Culture of Celebrity*. New York: Alfred A. Knopf, 1994.

Harmetz, Aljean. *The Making of The Wizard of Oz*. New York: Alfred A. Knopf, 1977.

——. *Round Up the Usual Suspects: The Making of Casablanca—Bogart, Bergman and World War II*. New York: Hyperion, 1992.

Haver, Ronald. *David O. Selznick's Hollywood*. New York: Alfred A. Knopf, 1980.

Hecht, Ben. *A Child of the Century*. New York: Simon & Schuster, 1954.

Hotchner, A.E. Choice *People: The Greats, Near-Greats and Ingrates I Have Known*. New York: William Morrow, 1984.

Houseman, John. *Run-Through: A Memoir*. New York: Simon & Schuster, 1972.

Kaminsky, Stuart M. *Coop: The Life and Legend of Gary Cooper*. New York: St. Martin's Press, 1980.

Kobal, John. *People Will Talk*. New York: Alfred A. Knopf, 1985.

Koblik, Steven. *The Stones Cry Out: Sweden's Response to the Persecution of the Jews: 1933–1945*. New York: Holocaust Library, 1988.

Lambert, Gavin. *On Cukor*. New York: G.P. Putnam's Sons, 1971.

Meredith, Burgess. *So Far, So Good*. Boston: Little, Brown, 1994.

Meyer, Donald. *Sex and Power: The Rise of Women in America, Russia, Sweden and Italy*. Middletown, Conn.: Wesleyan University Press, 1987.

Miller, Frank. *Casablanca: As Time Goes By—50th Anniversary Commemorative*. Atlanta: Turner Publishing, 1992.

Nelson, Nancy. *Evenings with Cary Grant*. New York: William Morrow, 1991.

O'Neill, Eugene. *Selected Plays*. New York: Random House, 1969.

Redgrave, Michael. *In My Mind's Eye: An Autobiography*. London: Weidenfeld & Nicolson, 1983.

Reed, Rex. *Conversations in the Raw*. New York: World Publishing, 1969.

Ross, Lillian. *The Player*. New York: Simon & Schuster, 1962.

Rossellini, Roberto. *My Method: Writings and Interviews*. New York: Marsilio Publishers, 1987.

Samuels, Charles Thomas Samuels. *Encountering Directors*. New York: G.P. Putnam's Sons, 1972.

Sanders, George. *Memoirs of a Professional Cad*. New York: G.P. Putnam's Sons, 1960.

Schmidt, Lars. *Mitt Livs Teater*. Stockholm: Bra Böcker, 1995.

Scobbie, Irene. *Historical Dictionary of Sweden*. Metuchen, N.J.: Scarecrow Press, 1995.

Scott, Franklin D. *Sweden: The Nation's History*. Minneapolis: Minnesota Press, 1977.

Selznick, Irene Mayer. *A Private View*. New York: Alfred A. Knopf, 1983.

Shnayerson, Michael. *Irwin Shaw*. New York: G.P. Putnam's Sons, 1989.

Silverman, Stephen M. *Dancing on the Ceiling: Stanley Donen and His Movies*. New York: Alfred A. Knopf, 1996.

Spoto, Donald. *The Art of Alfred Hitchcock* (2nd rev. ed.). New York: Doubleday/Dolphin, 1992.

——. *The Dark Side of Genius: The Life of Alfred Hitchcock*. Boston: Little, Brown, 1983.

Steele, Joseph Henry. *Ingrid Bergman—An Intimate Portrait*. New York: David McKay, 1959.

Swindell, Larry. *Charles Boyer: The Reluctant Lover*. New York: Doubleday, 1983.

Thompson, Frank. *Between Action and Cut: Five American Directors*. Metuchen, N.J.: Scarecrow Press, 1985.

Whelan, Richard. *Robert Capa: A Biography*. New York: Alfred A. Knopf, 1985.

Wiley, Mason and Damien Bona, *Inside Oscar*. New York: Ballantine, 1987.

Young, Cathleen. *Isabella Rossellini: Quiet Renegade* (New York: St. Martin's Press, 1989.

Zorina, Vera. *Zorina*. New York: Farrar, Straus & Giroux, 1986.

Index

462   *INDEX*

Belfrage, Kristina, 381, 382, 388, 404, 407
Bells of Saint Mary's, The, 174–180, 434
Bennett, Joan, 279
Benny, Jack, 182, 184, 190
Bergman, Ellen (aunt), 5, 9, 11, 12, 15, 16, 21, 22–23, 117, 434
Bergman, Frieda Adler (mother), 1, 6
  death of, 8
Bergman, Hjalmar, 17, 36
Bergman, Hulda (aunt), 5, 8, 14, 15, 21, 23–26, 147
Bergman, Ingmar, 11, 354–355, 389, 407, 408, 410–412
Bergman, Ingrid
  acting career of, 24, 43–44. *See also specific movies and plays*
    after leaving Hollywood, 308–309
    choice of career, 24
    classes and training, 24–29, 202
    inactive periods (1940), 86–87, 94, 99
    inactive periods (1941–1942), 118, 121
    primacy of, 38, 47, 71, 113, 155, 361, 396–397, 410
    in Sweden, 24, 29, 33–41, 44–49, 52–55
  acting technique and style, 35–37, 46, 202, 366, 386
    Hitchcock, lessons learned from, 165, 169
    Intermezzo, 76–77
    stage acting, 91, 360–361
    underplaying, 39, 95
  autobiography (memoirs), 422
    "as told to" Burgess, 402–403
  awards, 221, 239, 331
    Emmies, 348, 427–428
    Oscar nominations and awards, 178, 181, 255, 332, 335, 395–396, 413, 433
  bond tour (1944), 171–172
  childhood and adolescence, 7–24
    Aunt Ellen's death, 22–23
    birth, 1
    choice of acting career, 24

    death of mother, 8
    illness and death of father, 19–21
    photographs and home movies, 7–9, 16, 417–418
    recitations and acting, 15–19
    religion, 11–13
    school, 13–18, 22, 25
    theater attendance, 16–17
  contracts with studios, 36, 55, 61–64, 72, 78, 79, 82, 121, 122, 131, 160–162
    1945 negotiations with Selznick, 193–195
  critical and press response, 54, 149
    adulation, 88–89, 149
    Anastasia, 329
    Autumn Sonata, 416
    birth of son, 288–294
    divorce from Petter, 272–278, 282, 283, 287
    Dr. Jekyll and Mr. Hyde, 116
    Hedda Gabler, 356
    Intermezzo, 80–81
    Joan of Arc, 254–255
    Joan of Arc at the Stake, 317
    Joan of Lorraine, 219
    Lilliom, 91–92
    A Month in the Country, 362–363
    More Stately Mansions, 371, 373
    Stromboli, 293–295
    in Sweden, 34, 35–36, 40, 49
    Tea and Sympathy, 326
    Waters of the Moon, 414
    A Woman Called Golda, 431
  custody fight with Rossellini, 323, 343, 347–348
  death of
    attitude toward dying, 428, 429
    last days, 432–436
  diets, 155
  divorce from Petter, 176, 232–233, 273–278, 281–283
    financial aspects, 283
    Ingrid's request for, 175, 216
    MacDonald (Ingrid's lawyer), 281–283
    Mexican divorce, 295

Printed in the United States
91988LV00007BA/43-48/A